EATING

WITH THE

ENEMY

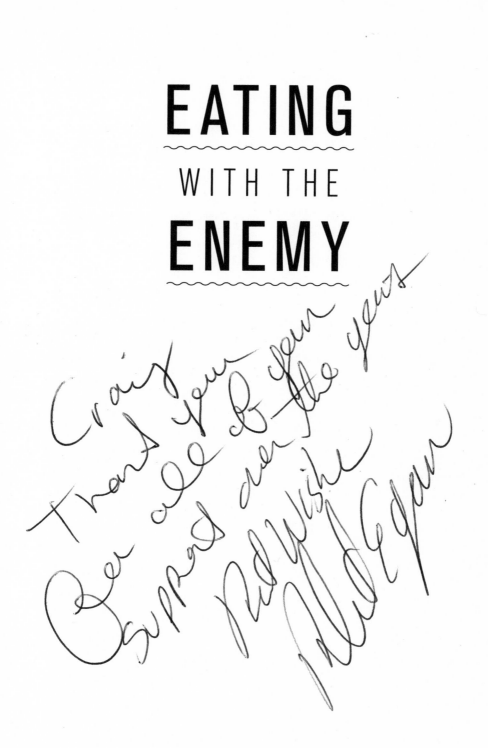

EATING
WITH THE
ENEMY

How I Waged Peace with
North Korea from My
BBQ Shack in Hackensack

ROBERT EGAN AND KURT PITZER

St. Martin's Press
New York

www.stmartins.com

All photographs courtesy of Robert Egan.

"A Rare Public Appearance in Bergen for N. Koreans" by Tom Topousis on page 47 appears courtesy of *The Record*.

Design by Kathryn Parise

LIBRARY OF CONGRESS CATALOGING-IN-PUBLICATION DATA

Egan, Robert, 1958–
    Eating with the enemy : how I waged peace with North Korea from my BBQ shack in Hackensack / Robert Egan and Kurt Pitzer.—1st ed.
      p. cm.
    ISBN 978-0-312-57130-6
    1. Egan, Robert, 1958– 2. Restaurateurs—New Jersey—Hackensack—Biography. 3. Diplomats—New Jersey—Hackensack—Biography. 4. Political participation—United States—Case studies. 5. Friendship—United States—Case studies. 6. Han, Song Ryol. 7. Koreans—New Jersey—Hackensack—Biography. 8. United States—Relations—Korea (North) 9. Korea (North)—Relations—United States. 10. Hackensack (N.J.)—Biography. I. Pitzer, Kurt. II. Title.
CT275.E365A3 2010
974.9'043092—dc22
[B]   2010002172

First Edition: May 2010

10 9 8 7 6 5 4 3 2 1

This book is dedicated to all the people
who never knew their place.

CONTENTS

EATING

WITH THE

ENEMY

1

~~~~~~~~~
~~~~~~~~~

No Son of Mine
(Is Gonna Turn Pinko)

THE SOLES OF MY Italian dress shoes made a nice clacking sound as I crossed the marble floor of the United States Senate's Dirksen Building. I wore my only suit, a black, wool-silk blend from Anore Men's Shop in Paramus, and a plain black necktie out of respect for the seriousness of the occasion. I'd splurged on an eighty-dollar haircut, enhanced with a little gel and a dash of cologne on my neck. I felt good.

It was Monday, November 23, 1992. Washington politicos were trying to clear a path for normalized relations with the government of Vietnam, almost twenty years after the end of the war there. They needed a little help, and I jumped at the chance. How often does a guy from Hackensack have the ear of the U.S. Congress?

I found the small deposition room on the second floor, where I was greeted by John McCreary, the strong-jawed, gray-bearded attorney for the Senate Select Committee on POW/MIA Affairs. McCreary shook my hand with the grip of an old warrior and introduced me to his stenographer, Mary Grace, a rosy-cheeked brunette in her thirties. The three of us took our seats around a wooden table. McCreary asked if I understood I'd be speaking under oath. I said I was relieved to be under oath and not accused of anything for a change, but neither of them laughed. The stenographer began typing.

McCreary: *What do you do for a living?*

Me: *I'm a restaurant owner.*

McCreary: *Have you ever been granted or denied a national security clearance?*

Me: *No, I have not.*

McCreary: *Have you ever been paid by an agency of the U.S. government for information?*

Me: *No, I have not.*

McCreary: *Are you in fear for your life or your livelihood because of your cooperation with this committee?*

Me*: I'm concerned about it, yes. I am concerned.*

McCreary frowned like a chess master pondering his next move. He had been one of the top strategic analysts for the Pentagon for almost forty years during the Cold War and beyond, serving the chairman of the Joint Chiefs of Staff and the Secretary of Defense. He seemed square but cagey, like his idea of fun was going toe-to-toe with some freedom-hating Kremlin negotiator. I fidgeted in the wooden chair and crossed one foot over my knee.

The committee was interested in me because I had stuck my nose where a lot of people would say it didn't belong. During the past twelve years, while flipping burgers for a living, I'd befriended a group of Vietnamese diplomats at the United Nations, and a few weeks earlier I'd convinced a Foreign Ministry official, Le Quang Khai, to defect from his communist regime. We held a news conference at my restaurant, Cubby's BBQ in Hackensack, New Jersey, where he stated that his government had hidden evidence of American prisoners held after the end of the Vietnam War. He suggested that a few of them might still be alive and in captivity somewhere in Southeast Asia. Not everybody in Washington and Hanoi was happy about this. The two governments were trying to put old ghosts to rest.

McCreary: *Why did you do this . . . Was it curiosity?*

Me: *I set out to help. I see no reason why both governments couldn't resolve this issue. I couldn't see any reason they couldn't come together.*

McCreary: *What made you think you could make a difference?*

Me: *I know that if you work hard enough at something and your intentions are good, no matter who you are, you can make a difference.*

McCreary: *So you just took it upon yourself, is that right? To butt into this?*

Me: *Not butt in. To become a part of the solution. I still cannot believe that none of our intelligence agencies have infiltrated the Vietnamese in the manner that I did.*

I couldn't tell whether, as an intel guy at the Pentagon, McCreary was offended or whether he secretly agreed with me. He exchanged a look with the stenographer, Mary Grace. She had nice brown eyes behind her librarian-style glasses. I could smell Chanel perfume, and the scent reminded me of an ex-girlfriend, Nancy, who I stayed with in Colorado when I was fresh out of rehab in my twenties, but that's another story. I peeked under the table and saw that the stenographer wore a tight, knee-length skirt, skin-tone stockings, and low heels.

McCreary: *What schools did you attend?*

Me: *Excuse me?*

McCreary: *What schools did you attend?*

Me: *Adlai E. Stevenson Elementary School, West Essex Junior High School, West Essex High School.*

McCreary: *What is the highest academic or professional level you attained?*

Me: *I graduated from high school.*

McCreary: *Have you had any college courses?*

Me: *No, I have not.*

McCreary: *Are you a veteran?*

Me: *No, I'm not.*

I knew what he was driving at. Why was an undereducated burger chef mixing himself up with big political topics? What did I know about the issues surrounding the plight of the American POWs—the territorial disputes on the South China Sea or the peace agreement with Cambodia? Who did I think I was?

It was a legitimate question. I grew up in the 1960s in Fairfield, New Jersey, which didn't produce a lot of politicians and diplomats. Our dads were cement pourers, drywallers, beat cops, and small-time crooks. Those of us who got out of the rat race were the ones who moved up the ranks in a Mafia family, and that was only if we were full-blooded Italians.

My neighborhood was tough. We survived with street smarts, not by learning to drink tea with our legs crossed and our pinkies in the air. We didn't have playdates and sing-alongs. We fought with our bare fists; that was our main form of recreation. I was two years younger than the next oldest kid on our block, Big Mike, and if he wasn't putting me in a headlock and punching me in the face on any given afternoon, his buddy, Little Mike, was. These were guys who started shaving when they were ten. When they started shaving, I started lifting weights. By the time I was eight, I knew I needed to bulk up.

America's halls of power were not throwing open their doors to the Muscarellis, the Rizzos, or the Egans. We didn't go to college. Nobody was giving us scholarships or trust funds. A lot of us didn't even finish high school. We were on the bottom of society. If we broke the law and the cops caught us, we got the crap kicked out of us. There was no soft-bellied thinking that said, "Let's try to relate to this individual. Let's try to empower him."

My dad, Walter, was the kind of disciplinarian who smacked you first and asked questions later. He was one of the best hot-tar roofers in Fairfield, but he was also a binge drinker who had a hard time keeping steady work. Dad had been in a bomb disposal unit in the Korean War, and I think he'd seen some pretty nasty stuff, but when I asked him about it he'd just clam up. He'd come home plastered after hours of shots and beer with the guys at the bookie's and admit he'd lost his paycheck on the horses. He couldn't stay ahead of the mortgage on our little house, so Mom took a job working in the cafeteria at our elementary school. Mom's people, the Marmos, were originally from Salerno in the middle of Italy, but that didn't help me with the purebred Italian kids. "What's your last name?" the older kids always asked. "You know it," I said. "Say it out loud," they said.

"Egan."

"You're a half-breed, Egan," they said. "You'll never be a made guy."

Fairfield was corrupt to its core, and even us kids knew it. The powerful people were the gangsters and the guys with badges, or the businessmen who paid them both off. Everyone knew the cops were running their own burglary ring, and we also knew nobody would ever get busted for it. Roofers who knew the right people could hire non-union. One contractor built a shopping mall on top of wetlands, while another couldn't get a permit to put a new roof on his house. It wasn't what was right or wrong that mattered, it was your relationships. I learned from an early age that if you didn't have relationships you didn't have anything. On the other hand, if you had nothing and you made certain relationships, that could eventually lead to something.

That made school an afterthought. My buddies Mike Nigro and Earl Swenderman and I ditched classes and spent our free time sucking up to the wise guys who made business deals in low voices at the steakhouses where we bussed tables as teenagers—the "made" guys who wore expensive suits and winked at each other as they reached their gold watches and pinky rings in our direction and slipped us a few extra bills.

All us kids looked up to a guy named Bobby Vesco, who drove around in a six-Cadillac convoy of bodyguards armed with machine guns. Vesco was among the richest men in America at that point, but he was still one of us. His father had worked the assembly line at a Chrysler plant in Detroit, and his mother was a secretary. Vesco dropped out of high school and lied about his age, got involved in a New Jersey machine tools company, and when it went bankrupt he bought it on the cheap. By the time he was thirty, he was a millionaire. A few years later, he had control of a Switzerland-based investment company and upwards of a billion dollars to play with.

All of Vesco's crew had speedboats and flashy cars, but Vesco had something much greater than money. He had power and influence, and pretty soon he was business partners with Donald A. Nixon, Jr., the president's nephew, and buddies with the likes of Billy Carter and Mohammar Qaddafi. He had ventured way beyond his station in life as the son of a factory worker and made it into another world. He may not have had a pedigree, but he owned an airline, several manufacturing plants, an office building in downtown Fairfield, and a custom Boeing 707 equipped with a sauna.

I met him when I was ten. I had an after-school job pulling traps at the

North Jersey skeet shooting range where Vesco came for target practice. It was hot and nasty work, cramped inside a metal, bulletproof bunker, tripping the pigeon shooter every time somebody yelled, "Pull!" At the end of the day I'd come out roasting in my own sweat and covered in creosote tar. The wise guys and the big shots got used to seeing me around. I knew the cardinal rule: see no evil, speak no evil. I pulled trap and didn't run my mouth, and soon they were comfortable around me. One day I came out of the bunker for a drink of water and there was Vesco himself, all alone. So I went up to him and said, "Mr. Vesco, I noticed the lawn at your office needs mowing. How about I cut it for you? I'll give you a good rate."

He looked down at my dirty, sweaty face. Maybe he recognized a little of himself in a scrappy young man who'd do anything to get a leg up, because he said, "All right, kid, come see me at my office. Let's see what you got."

The next day I skipped school and waited outside his office all morning. When he showed up just before lunchtime, I walked over to him casually, so I didn't look desperate. "Most guys would charge you twenty," I said. "But I'll do it for ten." He grinned. "Just don't screw it up," he said.

I would have done it for free. Cutting Vesco's lawn had an immediate bene-fit: I was no longer just Bobby Egan, the half-breed kid. I was Bobby Who-Works-For-Bobby-Vesco Egan, the half-breed kid. Vesco's office was right on Fairfield Road, and I took my time pushing the lawnmower around his grass. I wanted everybody driving by to get a good look at me. I got a whole new level of respect around the neighborhood, even from the older kids.

About a month after I started, an FBI agent approached me as I climbed out of the bunker at the trap-shooting range. It was the end of the day, and the agent followed me to where I'd parked my ten-speed. "It's a crime not to tell us what you hear," he said. I'm sure he figured he could peel me away because I was just ten years old. I should have been intimidated. He showed me a black-and-white picture of Vesco's business associate Ralph Dodd and asked if I'd seen him. I said I'd been in the bunker all day, keeping an eye on the traps, and the agent nodded his head and went away. But he and other agents started dropping by regularly, asking who came and who went at the range. They asked about the contractors Joey Muscles and Sammy Malfitano and other guys who were doing well for themselves, but they were especially interested in Vesco. How often did I see him at his office? When did he come to the range? Who was he with? Did he talk about traveling anywhere in particular? Did I hear anything else he said?

Even at that age I saw the double standard. Senators and mayors and corporate bigwigs could get fat on other people's money because they make the right friends and talk the right language, but anytime a guy with dungarees tries to make a buck he's suspected of being a criminal.

It was pretty exciting stuff, though. I was in the middle of the action, between the cops and the gangsters. For the first time in my life I was getting respect for the position I had put myself into. So I strung them along with useless information. "Have you seen Sammy?" the Feds would ask, and I'd say, "Sammy who? Oh, yeah. Sammy. He was here yesterday. Or maybe it was the day before. He was wearing some nice-smelling cologne. I think it was Old Spice. But it might have been Dante." And I'd watch them write all this stuff down.

Vesco got run out of the country on a $200 million embezzlement rap when the FBI finally caught up with him in the early seventies. The rest of the country vilified my hero as a swindler and a douchebag, but we still revered him. The tragedy was that I lost my lawn-mowing connection and all the credibility that went with it. I took on extra hours at the range, bought a shotgun, and learned to shoot. By the time I started high school, I was hunting birds in the woods behind my parents' house and spending lots of time alone.

West Essex High was a rude awakening, because it served several very different communities of northern New Jersey. Suddenly us working-class kids from Fairfield were thrown together with the kids from the richer towns of North Caldwell and Essex Fells. They drove to school in Camaros and Benzes and didn't have to work so they could buy a pair of jeans. They wore scarves around their necks. I'd never even seen one before. Where I came from, we buttoned up our jackets when it got cold. That first winter of high school I asked one of the rich kids, "What's that thing around your neck?" and he said, "It's a scarf," and looked at me like I'd just fallen out of a tree.

They'd come back suntanned from Florida or the Bahamas or from skiing vacations in the Rocky Mountains and ask, "What did you do over break?" I wouldn't tell them our family had driven three hours each way for an afternoon at the Jersey shore, where we'd eaten soggy baloney sandwiches because we didn't have enough money for a hot dog at the Sandy Hook concession stand. I'd brag about the deer I shot with my twelve-gauge and gutted with my own hunting knife. I loved to see them squirm when I described pulling the ropey intestines out of an animal. They were headed for Princeton and the soft-bellied lives of businessmen, and they couldn't dissect a frog in biology class without turning green.

I learned early on from Dad that I should stick with our own kind. That's where he was comfortable. He sat on the Picnic Committee of the Roofer's Local 4, and the best time of the year for our family was the fall picnic. The union brought in an ice cream truck for the kids, and we played shuffleboard and softball and ate clams on the half shell and sausage and pepper sandwiches until we got sick. A guy with a panoramic camera fit all two or three hundred of us into a frame, and in those old photos you can see Mom standing by Dad and looking proud, because it was his day to shine. At some point in the picnic, Dad always came over and put his arm around my shoulders. "Best damn people in the world," he'd say.

Around the middle of tenth grade, I stopped going to school on a regular basis. I lied about my age and got part-time roofing work. I bought a hunting dog, a German short-haired pointer named Heidi, and she and I spent as many days as I could roaming the woods. When I did go to school I was not a model citizen. I'm not proud of this now, but that's how it was. I was like Tom Sawyer, if Tom Sawyer had been a mixed-breed kid from a mobbed-up town in New Jersey. Once I brought Heidi to English class and told the teacher, Mr. Hilton, "I can read and I can write. I can shoot a gun and I can put a roof on a house. What else am I supposed to learn?" When he threatened to fail me, I got some of my friends together and surprised him in his classroom after school. I put a paper bag over Mr. Hilton's head, and we hung him upside down and made him sing the old Schaefer beer jingle: "The one beer to have when you're having more than one!"

I wanted out of Fairfield, but I didn't know where to go. At that point in our history, young American men of my background had one good option to get out and see the world: the Vietnam War. All the older kids were getting drafted as soon as they turned eighteen. My neighbor Jimmy had just come home and couldn't wait to get back to the Vietnamese jungle, but they wouldn't let him. He was a clean-cut kid growing up, but he'd cracked. He wouldn't wash himself, and he tried to fight everybody in town. His eyes darted around and he didn't make sense when he talked, and whenever we went past his house he'd run out of his front door and chase us down the street. Something in that faraway country had flipped his world upside down. He'd touched the flame. I wondered what that terrible thing was.

McCreary: *Did you participate in any protests at the time?*

Me: *None whatsoever.*

McCreary: *When you were in high school, did you ever go down to the U.N. mission to protest or anything like that?*

Me: *No, never.*

McCreary: *Perhaps I misunderstood. I thought you said during high school you got interested in this.*

Me: *Yes. I was interested, but on my own level of interest. It is an internal interest that doesn't necessarily have to be expressed outwardly.*

I told myself I had to start preparing to be behind enemy lines. I read everything I could about the war: comic books, news reports, pulp novels. Some of my friends talked about killing all the slant-eyes and the gooks, but I had respect for the enemy. I'd read that it's a basic rule of warfare—if you consider your enemy a worthy adversary you are less likely to underestimate him.

Vietnam took over my imagination. On the other side of the Passaic River, not far from the Willowbrook shopping mall, we've got the swamps of Big Piece Meadows. I'd go in there for days at a time with my fishing pole and my hunting rifle, pretending I was the only survivor from my platoon. I taught myself to deal with mosquitoes and heat, boil and ration my water, make tea from birch bark, shoot duck and rabbit and cook them over a fire. I trained my mind for the harsh conditions of the swamps and jungle. I was going to be way ahead of the game by the time they drafted me. I figured if I could track a buck, I could track a human, and I was not afraid of blood. Vietnam was going to be my big ticket. Not just my ticket out of Fairfield: I was trying to find a way *in*—into something beyond what I could imagine.

And then, on January 23, 1973, President Nixon declared the end of the Vietnam War. I couldn't believe it. After more than ten years of sending guys over to battle in the jungle, we were just going to call it quits? It wasn't fair to all the men who had sacrificed, and it wasn't fair to me. I was seventeen years old. I'd fully trained myself for the unknown. And now the unknown was over?

We watched TV the night they announced the Paris Peace Accords and paraded all the guys out of Hanoi. The news anchor said the communists were releasing 591 American prisoners of war. Nixon flashed the peace sign and said all the boys were on their way home.

"There's no way," I said. "That can't be everybody."

"What do you know?" my dad shouted. "That's the president of the United States. You think you know more than him?"

"I know more than you."

Dad stood up from his easy chair and took a step toward me like he was going to crack me over the head. I stood up, too, and faced him. I had grown bigger than he was, and he was sober, so he sat down again. "You don't know what war is like," he grumbled.

McCreary: *Did you meet the Vietnamese officials while you were in high school?*

Me: *No.*

McCreary: *Did you meet with them after high school?*

Me: *Yes.*

McCreary: *Were you still in the roofing industry business?*

Me: *Yes, I was still in the roofing industry when I had my first contacts with the Vietnamese.*

McCreary: *What prompted you to make contact with the Vietnamese?*

I couldn't stop thinking about our men who were left behind. The North Vietnamese were supposed to return all their American prisoners within sixty days of the Paris Peace Accords. Starting in February, the Pentagon ran

Operation Homecoming, in which dozens of C-141 flights brought former U.S. prisoners out of South Vietnam. Some had been held captive as long as eight years. America celebrated the 591 who returned. But more than 2,200 Americans were still missing.

Were they all dead, their bodies decomposing in the jungle or buried somewhere? Or were some of them alive, in the bamboo cages and secret prisons of the smaller Vietcong fighting units, the hill tribes, the Khmer Rouge, the Pathet Lao? With all the factions and groups, it seemed impossible that the enemy was organized enough to just blow a whistle after more than a decade of war and suddenly hand over all the prisoners.

This didn't seem to bother our politicians in Washington. Nixon didn't have any sons or nephews left behind. Neither did presidents who followed— Ford, Carter, Reagan, or Bush—or any of the congressmen or business leaders who could do something about it. The missing weren't their classmates from the Ivy League schools. They were working-class guys, who should have been home doing honest work during the week and getting drunk and chasing tail on weekends—enjoying life, like me, not rotting in a jungle where they'd been sent, many years earlier, by the guys with privileges and fraternity scarves around their necks.

This is the stuff that obsessed me during the long and brutal hours of hot-tar roofing. Why did I spend so much time on it? I didn't have anything else in my life that was as exciting. I missed out on the war, so I was looking for the next best thing. And this is what led me to cocaine. I loved cocaine. It's the quick fix for a dull life. I'd work roofing jobs all week and then on weekends blow my cash on beer and eight-balls of coke. I lived part-time with my girlfriend and her parents in Pelham, New York, but I'd sneak away to get high with a girl in Lodi, New Jersey. One night we were partying with some South Americans in Lodi, and I got so crazy I jumped through her plate-glass window and ran down the middle of Route 46 until somebody called the paramedics, who took me to the hospital and put sixty stitches in my right hand. I missed weeks of work. You'd think that would have been a wake-up call for me, but it wasn't.

I fought guys in bars. I got arrested for stealing firewood. I got caught with unlicensed firearms. On a few occasions, I dumped baggies of coke out the window as the cops pulled me over. I threatened to shoot a neighbor who told my friends and me to stop making so much noise. Sometimes I'd wake up and not know what I had done for the past twelve hours or what kind of junk I had put into my body.

I was addicted to the rush. I could admit that. I went to rehab, but I couldn't stand the sense of dullness afterward. I relapsed as often as I went.

When I was sober, I hung around POW/MIA gatherings, which were full of people still living with the Vietnam War. I was inspired by the friends and relatives of the missing, like Lynn Standerwick, who I met at a rally in the late seventies. She was a tiny lady from Kansas, whose father, Robert L. Standerwick, ejected safely when his plane went down in Laos in 1971. His copilot returned to the United States convinced that Standerwick was still alive. When I met Lynn, she lifted a chain from beneath her collar and showed me her father's dog tag. "Either he's going to be buried with this, or I am," she said. In the mid-eighties, she went with a guy named Bo Gritz on a freelance recon mission to Southeast Asia and ran radio communications for him while he and a few guys sneaked into Laos to search for their fallen brothers. She was fearless.

Other than Lynn, most of them seemed ineffectual, marching in circles with their signs and slogans and selling memorabilia to each other. Some of them were part of a biker movement, Rolling Thunder, and they rode around on Harleys and made a lot of noise, but it wasn't getting us any closer to seeing live Americans coming home. The fate of the men was in the hands of the Vietnamese. Did anybody think they'd listen to a bunch of emotional American citizens who couldn't even get the attention of their own lawmakers?

McCreary: *How did you first meet Vietnamese officials?*

Me: *I just called them up. I believe I called the Russian embassy or the Russian mission. They called the Vietnamese, who said, "It's okay for this young guy to give us a call back." I made a call—made a contact, talked to him on the phone a little bit, got to know him over a few months on the phone, went down, met some of their agents. I said I wanted to form a friendship. I had some concerns, like why I had this hate inside me for them. And they went with that.*

McCreary stared at me over the top of his glasses and then wrote something down on his pad of paper. I glanced at the stenographer, who looked up from the keyboard. I winked at her.

Me: *You have to understand something. At the time here, they didn't have a lot of friends.*

McCreary: *Do you recall the names of any of the early officials that you talked with?*

Me: *Yes, I do, but I would prefer not to say. They're back in Hanoi and I don't want them to get in any trouble.*

McCreary: *Did they encourage your phone calls and visits?*

Me: *Oh, absolutely. Right from the beginning. They had suspected that the FBI was trying to plant a young recruit in with them to monitor their activities here . . . And one of their intentions was to turn me.*

McCreary: *So in a sense, what I understand, and correct me if I'm wrong, is you were something of—they thought you were a pawn in a game between intelligence services?*

What else were they going to think? When I first contacted the Vietnamese embassy in 1979, I'd just stop by and chat with whoever would talk to me. It was just the doormen and the cooks for the first couple of years. But even the lower-rung guys were trained in basic counterintelligence, and they were very curious about me. They'd never experienced a regular American citizen asking if he could get to know them. Also, they had nothing better to do. Because Vietnam had no diplomatic relations with the United States at the time, the only presence their government had in America was their mission to the United Nations. They were isolated, and maybe they responded to me out of boredom.

At first, I didn't tell them I wanted to find out about American POWs. I let my intentions seem mysterious. I grew up around wise guys who always spoke in generalities. Even if they weren't talking about something dangerous and exciting, you thought they were. You only learned the truth after reaching the inner circle, and sometimes you didn't learn it even then. In my neighborhood, if somebody comes up and says, "Hey, Bob, this is Joey, he's a friend of ours. He wants to talk to you," I don't say, "What about?" I say, "Hey, Joey, nice to meet you." And Joey doesn't say, "I want to discuss X, Y, and Z." He says, "Come sit down. Have something to eat." Then we sit and get to know each other. We talk about our families. We talk sports or politics. We talk about broads. And *if* we get comfortable with each other, issues can be brought up. Maybe that's a few hours later. Maybe it takes a few days or weeks. Maybe it never happens. But the relationship comes first, because important issues are too dangerous to be brought up between strangers.

I didn't get close to the Vietnamese right away, either. But in 1981, I opened a roadside hot dog restaurant, Cubby's Texas Wieners, in Hackensack. I started inviting the Vietnamese diplomats there. It wasn't exactly Camp David. Cubby's sits right on River Street, which runs from the center of town to the on-ramp for Highway 80. I'm ten minutes from the George Washington Bridge and half an hour from upper Manhattan, depending on traffic. It was convenient. The Vietnamese could leave the city for a breath of fresh air, have lunch, and be back at their embassy a couple hours later. Cubby's became a place where the Vietnamese diplomats could meet a wide cross section of northern New Jersey. They'd come in, have a hot dog, and see how I ran my business. We'd compare notes between their communist system and our capitalist one.

We served hot dogs, burgers, some chicken. I had booths in an L-shape around a long counter, and behind that a double door led to the kitchen where short-order cooks slipped the plates through a little window. Later I moved into cheese steaks, fish sandwiches, chicken fingers, and roast beef, but starting out the menu was simple. My formula was quality food with quick service, and this was important because I've got Riverside Square Mall and the Garden State Plaza nearby, and many of my customers are people with forty minutes for lunch. I get people on jury duty at the courthouse, factory workers and sheriff's deputies, inmates coming and going from the Bergen County jail, work release guys, housewives out shopping. In 1991, I even got the chaplain for the New York Giants and Howard Cross, the Giants' tight end. They came in and ordered steak sandwiches on their way to their team Bible group meeting. I got to talking to them and invited their Bible group to a free meal. A few weeks later, I went into the Giants' office in East Rutherford and sealed a deal to cook for the team every Friday after their short practice. I thought: only good things can come from being the chef to the Giants.

When I started palling around with the Vietnamese in the early eighties, I was living with my parents and trying to stay clean. One afternoon my dad leapt up from his chair as soon as I walked through the front door. He dragged me into the kitchen, pointed accusingly at the table, and shouted, "You better have a good explanation for this!" Fanned out across the tablecloth like a poker hand were a bunch of pamphlets and press releases the guys from the Vietnamese embassy had given me.

"You went in my room?" I asked. "You can't just go into my room and take whatever you want. You—"

"This is *my* goddamn house and you're going to tell me right now where you got this crap!" He was shaking with rage, and little white dots of spittle appeared at the corners of his mouth. "You think you can bring commie propaganda into my house? You want to be a drug addict? Fine. But no son of mine is gonna turn pinko."

"I'm more of a capitalist than you are—I'm a business owner!" I picked up the sheets of paper, many of which had the red flag with the yellow star of the Socialist Republic of Vietnam stamped on the top.

"You don't know these people like I do," he said. "They'll get inside your head and twist your ideas around. I fought them in Korea, and they're the same—"

"What if I'm the one who twists their thoughts around?"

"Don't be stupid." He balled his hands into fists, and I could tell he wanted to whack me. "They're experts in thought manipulation. They've probably infected you already, you ignorant little prick."

I started to walk out of the kitchen. I didn't give a fuck what he thought.

"You up to something with them?" he asked more hopefully. He unclenched his fists and relaxed a little. "You got a little something going on the side? You earning?"

I shook my head. "I'm not that stupid," I said.

"Then what the hell are you doing? You're not careful, you'll lose your restaurant, too."

"I don't want to do just one thing in life," I said.

"What's that supposed to mean? You're not happy going out and making a living? You could get a job with the union but you're too screwed up to keep it." I knew that was about the worst insult Dad could serve up. Ever since he'd gone sober and semi-retired, he'd developed an annoying habit of glorifying the roofing business.

"It means I don't want to be like you and Mom," I said.

"Get the hell out!" he screamed. He swept his hand across the table and pushed the pamphlets at me. "Get out of my house. You want to be a commie? I never want to see you again! You hear me?"

I didn't find out until years later that Dad turned me in to the FBI after he found those pamphlets. The Feds told him they were already watching me and knew about my involvement with the Vietnamese. They had their eye on me.

McCreary: *Do you believe that the Vietnamese—a faction of the Vietnamese—are using you to convey information to the United States?*

Me: *Yes. I've been told this: there is no chance for any live Americans to come back from Southeast Asia if we normalize ties and the embargo is lifted, because they will not risk losing what they have and losing how they look in the world community.*

McCreary: *And these are your conclusions?*

Me: *No, their conclusions.*

McCreary: *And how were they conveyed to you?*

Me: *By many countless hundreds of meetings with Vietnamese officials.*

During the 1980s, Hanoi allowed U.S. investigators to excavate a few sites where American pilots crashed during the war. The investigators closed dozens of cases and brought remains home for burial. But a lot of people criticized Washington for not demanding information about possible live American servicemen.

Radical POW activists formed the National Alliance of Families to lobby on behalf of prisoners. If any Americans were still being held captive in Southeast Asia, we had a sacred duty to get them out. A few Vietnamese officials wanted the United States to push harder on Hanoi, too. I don't know if they were truly concerned about the fate of Americans, or if they felt it would be easier to normalize relations if all the POW issues were finally cleared up. Or maybe they had political scores to settle at home. Whatever their reasons, some officials told me *they* wanted their government to disclose whether it had any live U.S. prisoners.

McCreary: *Who is Khai?*

Me: *Le Quang Khai.*

McCreary: *Second word?*

Me: *Quang. Q-u-a-n-g.*

McCreary: *Third word?*

Me: *Khai. K-h-a-i.*

McCreary: *And he is whom?*

Me: *He is the Vietnamese official who was on leave studying at Columbia, who has been working with me to help advise his government on the POW/MIA problem, as to a solution to it, and we have become friends.*

Vietnam's Deputy Ambassador to the United Nations, Nguyen Can, introduced me to Khai a few days after he arrived in New York in 1991. He was a young foreign ministry official who seemed eager to spend time with me. I liked being associated with him despite the fact that he was an intellectual. The fingernail of his right-hand pinky was nearly an inch long, which showed that he didn't do any work with his hands.

Khai told me the top officials of the Vietnamese government knew that live U.S. servicemen were kept prisoner in Vietnam after the 1973 Operation Homecoming. Although he didn't know if any were still alive in 1992, Khai believed secret archives in the defense ministry could give a fuller picture, if his government ever opened them. And he hinted that he might go public with the information if he could avoid punishment from his superiors.

One afternoon in August 1992, I drove to the indoor track at Columbia University to go jogging with Khai. I wore gym shorts and a tank top because I'd been lifting, and Khai wore a full sweat suit, and we jogged at an even pace.

I could tell something was up with him. He made strange small talk, and his eyes darted around the track.

"It's good to get out for a run," he said as we passed a guy in the outside lane.

Afternoon light filtered through the high windows of the gym. "Yeah," I said.

When we got out of earshot, he pointed to an Asian man doing stretches in the infield. "You see that Chinaman over there?" he asked. "He defected a few months ago."

"I'll bet they don't let you get near him," I said. We jogged a few more paces. "You like it here in America?" I asked. "You want to stay?"

Khai turned and, as we exchanged a look, I knew. "Let's pick this up to-morrow," I said. "Come down to my restaurant, and we'll talk."

I didn't know much about defection, so that night I made a few calls to guys from the neighborhood. "Call a briefcase," they said. The next day I had Khai meet with a local lawyer about making an asylum request, and before he could have too many second thoughts I convinced him to make a state-ment to the media. I called Tom Topousis, a reporter for Bergen County's *The Record,* and told him I had a major story for him.

"Some Living Men Were Kept" ran the headline of Topousis's story a few days later, quoting Khai and putting his plans to defect on the record, so there was no backing out. My body tingled with excitement when I read the story. I'd done something important. I could change things.

Soon afterward, McCreary called on behalf of the Senate Select Commit-tee and asked to take a deposition from Khai. On October 26, 1992, I brought them together in an interview room of the Hackensack Police Department, just down the road from Cubby's. Khai told McCreary the same thing I said in Washington a month later: before you normalize relations with Hanoi, demand access to the defense ministry's archives. Demand the release of live American POWs, or at least account for where they went. If you don't, the chance will be gone. The leverage will disappear, and so will the urgency.

Despite being led by war veterans John Kerry and Bob Smith and the former POW John McCain, the Senate Select Committee seemed to have other priorities. The Soviet Union was falling apart; the Chinese were flexing their muscle in the South China Sea. And with alliances in the region shifting, it looked like the communist Vietnamese were ready to move closer to Washington. And so the U.S. senators had more important things to think about than a couple thousand blue-collar guys who'd been missing for twenty years.

"It's going to be a whitewash, isn't it?" I asked McCreary as we finished my deposition in Washington. It was after five-thirty in the afternoon, and we'd been at it for six hours, with just a few short breaks. Mary Grace looked at her watch and quickly packed up her equipment and left.

"It's a national disgrace that we left men there," McCreary said as we walked out of the Dirksen Building together. "I'm going to keep doing my best. But there are people on the committee who want to normalize, and that's their priority."

As we shook hands on the sidewalk outside, McCreary told me he appreciated how I'd brought Khai out to defect. I thought to myself: this is the highest ranking guy in Washington I may ever rub shoulders with. I didn't want to let the connection go, even though we probably had almost nothing in common.

"Hey, John," I said, ribbing him. "Other than playing chess and reading big books, what do you do in your free time? You like sports?"

"Are you kidding me?" he said. "I'm a huge Giants fan."

It was like he'd dropped into my lap. "I cook for the Giants!" I shouted. "You want to come up and meet the players?"

The next week I called the Giants' management and told them I'd get them an intelligence briefing from one of the top Pentagon analysts, and soon afterward I invited McCreary to the Meadowlands in East Rutherford, where he sat in on a practice and met the players on the field afterward. It was a perfect two-way street. McCreary gave me extra credibility with the Giants at the same time that being associated with the Giants gave me an inroad to friendship with McCreary. Not long after that, he invited me to his daughter's wedding.

My relationship with Khai took on a life of its own, too. Ever since he'd announced his decision to defect, the FBI had been coming around to his apartment on the Upper West Side. Khai said they wanted him to go back to Hanoi as a double agent, which would have been insane since he'd already switched sides.

I told Khai he could stay at my three-bedroom apartment in Hackensack, to hide from the FBI. I already had roommates—a Canadian guy we called Karate John in one room, and Tony from the Mexican restaurant living in the other—so Khai slept on a roll-up mattress on the floor of my bedroom.

It took the U.S. government almost a year to grant his asylum, during which time the Feds came to my apartment looking for him at least half a dozen times. They'd bang on the door while I was at Cubby's, bothering my super and scaring the bejesus out of Khai. "If you're the only one home, don't answer the door," I told him. "Hide under my bed."

Khai lost his stipend from the Vietnamese Foreign Ministry, and after a while I got tired of paying his rent and groceries. I gave him a plastic apron and had him prepping vegetables and washing dishes in the kitchen at Cubby's. He started complaining right away, and I realized he was a spoiled communist son of a diplomat who didn't know how to survive without his government paycheck.

"You want to be an American? Learn to work," I said. "And cut your fingernail!"

In January, the Senate Select Committee issued its final report which, no surprise to anybody, found "no compelling evidence that proves that any American remains alive in captivity in Southeast Asia." That spring I took Khai to a meeting of the National Alliance of Families, where a few hundred POW/MIA activists spoke out against the committee's findings.

The Texas businessman H. Ross Perot was there. He'd come in third place in the presidential election a few months earlier, but he'd repeatedly brought up the POW issue in his campaign. He testified to the Senate Select Committee that we should never abandon the POWs. Despite being a billionaire, Perot was one of us.

Khai took the microphone near the end of the meeting. In a soft but clear voice, he told the audience that he believed American servicemen "survived in captivity" after the war ended. It was the first time anyone had heard such words from the mouth of a Vietnamese official. The audience rose from their seats and gave Khai a standing ovation.

Afterward, Perot was so moved that he handed me a business card with his home phone number written on the back, "in case you or this fellow ever need help with anything." When we got back to Hackensack, I dialed the number. A woman answered.

"Is this Mr. Perot's house?" I asked.

"Yes," the woman said, sounding slightly amused. "This is Mrs. Perot." I told her I was just checking to make sure Mr. Perot had really given me his home number. "Yes," Mrs. Perot said. "Ross does that."

After my testimony to the Senate Select Committee, I returned my attention to my restaurant. I bought a new soda fountain. I advertised in *The Record*. And I cleaned up my life. With the help of the New York Giants' chaplain, Dave Bratton, I stopped using coke for good. In the winter of 1992, I fell in love with one of my cashiers, Lilia Mani, a beauty from a Mexican immigrant family. I wasn't sure what she saw in a guy fourteen years older who had a Vietnamese diplomat hiding under his bed. But we clicked. When I brought her over, I asked Khai to go out for a walk. He was cramping my style. One afternoon that summer, when I had him washing dishes, he asked me when his next day of vacation would be.

"Christmas Eve," I said. And that was the final straw.

"What's the point of living in a free country?" he shouted. "I'd rather go back home and spend the rest of my life in jail than wash another stupid dish in your stupid restaurant!" He whipped his plastic apron over his head and threw it on the floor and stormed out of Cubby's. I followed him out and watched him walk down River Street toward the expressway.

I shouted after him, "Hey! All we guarantee you is the *pursuit* of happiness. It doesn't guarantee that you're going to be happy. That part's up to you, pal."

Khai and I lost touch. As the United States and Vietnam moved toward normalized relations, public interest in the fate of the missing GIs faded. It looked like my venture into foreign affairs was over. But I felt I made a mark on the history books. I'd helped a Vietnamese official defect and tell what he knew. Maybe it was just a footnote, but it was more of a mark than most kids from my neighborhood were going to leave.

On the front wall at Cubby's I hung pictures of the Vietnamese officials for my customers to see. On another wall I had a local artist paint a mural that's supposed to represent me at the Vietnam Memorial in Washington, D.C., communicating with the spirits of the fallen and missing.

I added ribs, grilled chicken, and steak to my menu, to cater to the shopping mall traffic. I changed the name from Cubby's Texas Wieners to Cubby's BBQ. I moved in with Lilia at her low-rent garden apartment a couple blocks from the restaurant. Lilia had a two-year-old daughter, Andrea, and suddenly I found that I was part of a family unit.

I spent my days running my business and sharing time with Lilia. We threw Andrea a birthday party with balloons and a rented clown. And I settled into the comfortable obscurity of a restaurant owner in a medium-sized New Jersey town.

2

~~~~~~~~~~~

The First Date

W HEN THE PHONE RANG at Cubby's one afternoon in October 1993, I had a
spatula in my hand and I wasn't expecting anything more exciting than
a take-out order. "Some people want to meet you," said a voice with a Vietnamese accent. "Important people." Whoever it was sounded like he was reading a
script for a mobster movie. An anonymous call on behalf of somebody else: this
was how you heard from a Mafia capo either bringing you into the family or
luring you to a quick and bitter end. "Go to the lobby of the U.N. Plaza Hotel,"
he said. "Tomorrow evening, eight o'clock."

I thought I recognized the voice of an old colleague of Khai's, but I couldn't
be sure. It had been more than a year since the Senate Select Committee
hearings, and I had started to put the Vietnamese adventure out of my mind.
I was just a regular guy from Hackensack again. In fact, I already had plans
for the next night. Lilia and I had a date at her favorite lobster restaurant.
Her sister was going to baby-sit.

"Are they friends of yours?" I asked.

"They're from the DPRK."

I repeated the letters to myself. "Doesn't ring a bell," I said.

"North Korea," he said.

North Korea. My dad's old enemy: the world's most mysterious dictatorship, full of America-hating commies and such a threat to world peace that the Pentagon kept almost forty thousand troops stationed next to the border in South Korea. What did they want with me?

"Eight o'clock is perfect," I said.

I told Lilia we had to postpone our date. I promised to make it up to her with three dinners anywhere she wanted, but she still gave me a look. Maybe she already sensed a rival. I ducked into the back office and dialed McCreary. As one of our nation's top intelligence analysts, he was the perfect guy to give me a briefing. "Can I ask you something off the record?" I said.

He chuckled. "Are you working for the press now?" When I told him about the anonymous call, he gasped. "Did you get any names? Are you sure he said 'North Korea?'"

"First he said DPRK, and I didn't know what he was talking about."

"My god, they must be desperate," he said. "No offense."

McCreary said that the Democratic People's Republic of Korea (the DPRK) had a small group of diplomats stationed in New York to represent their country at the United Nations. They'd had no official relations with the United States since the end of the Korean War in 1953, so they were like the Vietnamese in that way. But their situation was far more extreme, McCreary said. They were almost completely isolated from the international community. More importantly, they were trying to build a nuclear bomb.

A few months earlier, the North Koreans had declared that they were pulling out of the Nuclear Non-Proliferation Treaty (NPT), which discourages countries from building nuclear weapons by offering them peaceful nuclear technology instead. If they withdrew from the treaty, weapons inspectors could no longer monitor what was going on in the DPRK.

McCreary said everybody suspected Pyongyang planned to weaponize the plutonium from its nuclear reactor at Yongbyon, which the Soviets gave them ten years earlier as a sweetener for joining the NPT. It sounded like the North Koreans were trying to have it both ways. They wanted nuclear weapons *and* nuclear energy.

President Clinton urged sanctions and called them an unpredictable, paranoid regime. He further angered the North Korean dictator, Kim Il Sung, when he went to South Korea and told a group of reporters that if the DPRK ever used a nuclear weapon it would mean "the end of their country." Now, McCreary said, a couple of high-level American diplomats were trying to negotiate a way out of the crisis.

"Why do you think they want to talk to me?" I asked.

McCreary laughed. He was quiet and thought for a few moments. Then he said he didn't know. "I can tell you the North Koreans are unpredictable," he said. "You have that much in common."

Maybe I was getting suckered into a dangerous situation, but I was curious. The next evening I drove to the Millennium U.N. Plaza, a four-star hotel near the United Nations building in Manhattan. The lobby was full of mirrors, glass chandeliers, and foreigners in transit—busy and anonymous. I stood near the reception desk watching people come and go until a middle-aged Asian man approached and greeted me quietly. Behind him stood two others—a little guy with a soft face who looked like a Boy Scout, and a thin-lipped, reptilian man with leathery, pock-marked skin and dark sunglasses. All three wore suits that looked like they came off the everything-must-go rack at Sears: the kind of suits you could buy if the FBI ever had a garage sale.

They invited me downstairs to the dimly lit Ambassador Lounge, and I thought, *Hey, this is appropriate. They're ambassadors. I'm an ambassador, of sorts.* We sat in big red velour chairs. The middle-aged Korean introduced himself as Ho Jong and the young man as Mr. Han and then asked me if I'd like a drink. He didn't introduce the reptile guy. I ordered a Diet Coke.

"Ah, you are behaving yourself," Ho Jong said. The Vietnamese must have told him I was a former cokehead. Or maybe they told him about the time I got so hammered while visiting their country that I picked a fight with some police officers and woke up in a jail cell with a Russian agent. But if they weren't going to bring it up, I wasn't either.

While we waited for our drinks, the reptile chewed on a toothpick and scanned the lounge from behind his shades. He was a security goon, no doubt about that. He might as well have worn a name tag that read, "Plainclothes

Surveillance." He was probably there to spy on his comrades as much as to protect them.

The Boy Scout–looking kid took a pen and paper out of his coat pocket. I figured he was some kind of clerical assistant—not worth my attention.

Ho Jong said he knew about my work with American POW groups, and that he understood I had been a friend to Vietnamese government officials. He had done his homework. "You must have some good friends inside your government in Washington, too," he suggested.

"Funny you should mention that," I said. "I was just talking to McCreary yesterday about how things between our countries seem to be coming to a head."

"John McCreary?" Ho Jung asked. He glanced at the kid, who scribbled notes.

"Yeah," I said. "John and I talk all the time." I reached into the inner pocket of my coat and, pretending it happened to be there just by coincidence, I pulled out a photo of McCreary, me, and a few of the New York Giants standing at the fifty-yard line of their practice field.

"I'm close with the Giants, too," I said. "Don't think *they* don't have friends in high places." Ho Jong studied the picture for a few moments and handed it to the Boy Scout, who wrote something on his notepad.

"That's at the Meadowlands in New Jersey," I said. I turned to the Boy Scout. "M-e-a-d-o—"

"I can spell," the Boy Scout said. He wrinkled his face like he'd just bit into a lemon.

"Why did Le Quang Khai defect at Cubby's?" Ho Jong asked. I was flattered that he knew the name of my restaurant.

"I make a pretty good plate of ribs," I said.

"They said you like to joke around," Ho Jong said with a smile. "That's good. But if we're going to work together, there will be certain conditions."

If we were going to work together? What was he saying? What kind of work? Before I could ask, Ho Jong leaned in closer. "Any talk of defections is completely off limits. We are not like Vietnam. You do not talk about defections. You don't think about it. No double-crossing."

I didn't know how to respond, so I put my hand to my breast. "All I want is to see our countries come together as friends," I said.

"No illegal activity," Ho Jong said. "You must not do anything that will get us kicked out. Also, you must respect our leader."

"I'm as clean as a bird," I said. "Anything else?"

Ho Jong looked at me intently. "Come when we call. We have to know you are somebody we can rely on."

I got a chill down my backbone. This was the same sort of thing the Italians say when they start working with someone they don't trust. It was the same language Bobby Vesco used when he let me cut his lawn. Vague but forceful: just don't screw up. I had no idea where this was leading, but it appealed to me on every level. It was my way back into the action. I missed it, I had to admit.

Ho Jong and I smiled at each other for a few seconds. "I'm in," I said. I wondered if it was time to shake hands.

"Which intelligence agency do you work for?" the Boy Scout blurted out. His voice was soft and high-pitched. He stopped writing in his notebook and looked right at me. I was surprised by his straightforwardness.

"I'm a restaurant owner; I'm my own boss," I said. Then I pointed my thumb at him and turned to Ho Jong. "Who the fuck is this kid?" I asked.

The Reptile grinned as he stared into the depths of the Ambassador Lounge. The bar lights reflected in his shades.

"Mr. Han just arrived from Pyongyang," Ho Jong said. "He is about the same age as you. Thirty-three, isn't that so?" Once again I was impressed. The Boy Scout and I sized each other up across the table. I could tell he didn't think much of me. I didn't like the looks of him either. He seemed like a spoiled brat, a pudgy-faced kid with an arrogance he didn't deserve yet. "You should become friendly with Mr. Han," Ho Jong said. "He will be your contact."

I wasn't fully awake when I opened my eyes the next morning and saw a strange phone number written on a cocktail napkin sitting on my bedside table. My first thought was, "Oh no, a one-night stand!" I sat up and was relieved to see Lilia's body curled up next to me and Andrea asleep in the crib at the foot of the bed. After a few seconds, the events of the night before came back to me. I put my arm around Lilia. "What did they want?" she murmured.

"I don't know," I whispered. "I'm not even sure they know."

"This isn't going to be another Vietnam, is it?" she said. She rolled over and nestled her head in my neck. "Tell me we're not going to have a North Korean living under the bed."

I stroked her hair. "It's not going to be like that," I said.

I'd given Ho Jong and Han my number, too, and we left it up in the air which of us was supposed to contact the other. Just like when you first start dating somebody, I figured it was better to play a little hard to get than to seem overeager.

Instead of calling the number on the cocktail napkin, I called McCreary. He listened intently as I described the meeting at the Ambassador Lounge. He couldn't imagine how I was going to "work" with the North Koreans either.

"Maybe they think I'm somebody I'm not," I said. I wondered what they saw in me. Ho Jong knew that I'd been friends with the Vietnamese when they buried the hatchet with the U.S. government. "Do you think they have POWs?" I asked. "What are the chances any of our men were left over there?"

"There were plenty of men unaccounted for at the time, but nobody's asked about them for ages," McCreary said. "The war's been over for forty years."

"Why aren't we pushing for information?"

McCreary grunted. "There are bigger issues. Like not letting them get a nuke."

I kept an eye on the phone for the rest of the afternoon and all the next morning. When the North Koreans hadn't called by four o'clock the following day, I went into my back office and dialed the number on the napkin.

"DPRK Mission," said a man with a thick accent. I asked for Ho Jong. After a few minutes, a soft voice I recognized as Han's came on the line.

"Mr. Han?" I said. "It's Bobby. Egan. We met two nights ago."

"How can I help you, Mr. Egan?"

"Call me Bobby." Han didn't say anything. After a few moments, I said, "You guys asked me to meet. I'm just following up."

"What are you following up?" he asked.

Outside my office, a dishwasher noisily stacked plates in a tray. I shut the door with my foot. "Our meeting," I said. "I figured you guys would want to meet again."

"Are you requesting a meeting?"

"I'm not requesting anything. But if you want to meet, we can meet."

"Why do you want to meet?"

I wondered if he was trying to piss me off. "Did I say *I* wanted to meet? I didn't say anything about wanting to meet. I said *if you* wanted to meet, we could meet." This wasn't getting us anywhere. I switched the phone from one ear to the other. "We could continue our conversation," I said.

"What do you want to talk about?"

I thought about bringing up my interest in POWs, but I wanted to form a relationship first. "We can talk about whatever you want."

"I'm busy," Han said.

This must be how a girl feels after a guy takes her on a date and then decides she's too ugly for another one. "Is Ho Jong there?" I asked.

"He's busy, too. We have a delegation coming from Pyongyang." Maybe speaking for Ho Jong was Han's way of showing me that they were on equal footing. I didn't want the call to end like this.

"Did you get them something?"

"Who?" Han asked.

"Your delegation," I said. An idea was starting to take shape in my head. "Have you got them a welcome present?"

"What are you talking about?"

"Like when you go backstage after a concert or to a fancy party, they give you a T-shirt in a doggy bag."

"You think I should give our delegation a T-shirt? Why would I do that?"

"It's customary here," I said.

"Why is it called a doggy bag? Is it for dogs?"

"It's like the doggy bag you take home from a restaurant. You know when you can't eat everything on your plate, and they give you a bag to put your leftovers—" I realized that in Han's country people were starving and they probably never had leftovers. "Call it a goodie bag," I said. "You can call it whatever you want. It's for souvenirs."

"Why do dogs get a souvenir?"

"That's just when it's from the restaurant," I said. "This is different. Call it a gift bag."

"Why do you give a T-shirt?"

"It doesn't have to be a shirt," I said. "Forget the shirt! It could be almost anything. You get a bag, and you fill it with little things your colleagues can't get in Pyongyang. Decorative soaps for the ladies back home. Bottles of bourbon. Panty hose." I was thinking of "swag," which stands for Stuff We All Get. "Give them something to remember their visit in a good light," I said. "Something that says, 'We're happy you're here.' Make them feel like VIPs. You know what a VIP is, right?"

"Yes."

"These guys must be VIPs if your government is sending them to New York. The question is how you're going to make them feel about their visit." I told him I could use my membership at a discount warehouse and put together gift bags for twenty bucks a pop. "Let me do it as a favor," I said.

"I'm not going to give them something for a doggy," he said. And he hung up. But about an hour later Lilia answered the phone and beckoned me over.

"It's your Korean boyfriend," she said, handing me the receiver.

"Not bourbon," Han said. "Scotch. And vodka."

I didn't know at the time that I'd touched on one of Han's responsibilities as the new Minister Counselor to the U.N., which was to make sure the DPRK delegations gave a good report when they got home. We put together a quick list of things a visiting group of North Koreans might enjoy. As I was to learn many times in the years to come, Han was not shy about saying what he wanted. He was very specific: candy bars, especially with nuts; Marlboro and Camel cigarettes (full strength); vodka and scotch; gummy bears; chewable multivitamins; fruit, vegetable, and flower seeds.

"Seeds?"

"For gardening," he said. "Hard to find at home."

I drove to National Wholesale Liquidators in Lodi wondering how it must be to live in a country where growing flowers in your window box was a luxury, even for a high-ranking government official. Lilia covered for me at the restaurant so I took Andrea along, and with her little legs sticking out of the seat, I wheeled the shopping cart around the store until I found gift bags that I could stuff with goodies. In the gardening section I picked up packets of seeds: strawberries, cantaloupe, pumpkins, peas, and carrots. As I moved into the flower section, I thought to myself, what the hell am I doing here? I could barely pay my meat bill at Cubby's. How much was I going to spend? Two hundred bucks? Three? I had a little girl sitting in front of me. The responsible father thing to do would be to spend the money on her and Lilia. But my gut said to go with it, and I realized something: I felt more alive than I had for many months, ever since I was in the thick of it with the Vietnamese. In the scheme of things it was a small act to buy gifts for the North Koreans, but who knew where it would lead? I'd never been someone who planned things out. My M.O. was to get into a situation and then see what came of it. I grabbed more packets of seeds: pansies, snapdragons, morning glories. Yarrow, poppies, and flax. Calendulas and forget-me-nots. I filled Han's requests for candy, booze, and multivitamins. Along with the cigarettes, I threw in some nicotine patches to try to get the North Koreans to quit smoking. At the checkout stand, I picked up a few boxes of beef jerky.

Han asked me to bring the bags to his embassy the following day. The North Koreans worked out of an office on 72nd Street, in a brick and glass building half a block from the East River. The foyer was dark and cavernous, and when I told the old guy at the reception desk where I was going, he glanced at my eight gift bags, gave me a strange look, and asked for ID.

The wooden door of the mission had a gold plaque with a few lines in what I assumed was the Korean alphabet, underneath which it read in English:

PERMANENT MISSION OF THE DEMOCRATIC PEOPLE'S REPUBLIC OF KOREA TO THE UNITED NATIONS. A small surveillance camera eyed me from the ceiling above the door. I knocked. A skinny man let me into a waiting room like you find in a dentist's office.

"I'm here to see Mr. Han or Mr. Ho Jong," I said. The skinny man disappeared behind an inner door, leaving me alone. I sat on an imitation leather chair and flipped through a magazine in Korean. It had pictures of flags, statues, and military leaders visiting schoolchildren. Government propaganda. Beneath it on the table was a six-month-old copy of *Fortune* magazine. The minutes ticked by. Fifteen minutes. Half an hour. Why did they invite me to their mission if they were just going to make me sit around? Maybe they wanted to see how I would react. Were there surveillance cameras inside this room, too? Probably. I sat back and tried to just seem comfortable. I leafed through the pictures of the North Korean magazine with an interested look on my face. Then I picked up *Fortune* and flipped through it with exactly the same amount of interest, so anyone watching would see how evenhanded I was. Would our guys be watching, too? This had to be one of the most spied on offices in America, considering its occupants. Who else knew I was here? I barely contained my urge to wave around the room at wherever the hidden cameras might be, to let anyone who was monitoring me know that *I* knew.

After more than an hour, I was thinking I should pack up and leave when Han came through the door without apologizing for my wait. I made a point of not peering past him into the next room, so he'd know I wasn't trying to snoop. He rifled through the bags. Then he dumped the contents of each onto the coffee table.

"What are you looking for?" I asked, as he separated a few of the beef jerky packs from the others. "Microphones? Poison? Ho Jong said we should trust each other."

"No teriyaki," he said, handing them to me.

"What do you mean? I thought you people loved teriyaki."

Han looked like he was trying to figure out whether I was kidding. "We don't like the Japanese flavor," he said. Later, when Han sent me to Pyongyang and I saw photos of the atrocities committed by Japanese troops there, I understood. I had a lot to learn about my new friends. For one thing, I had to get into the psychology of a people who had been occupied by the Japanese for the first half of the twentieth century. When Han talked about Japan, it was with the resentment of a kid who got bullied in school and wasn't going to get over it. Was that what North Korea was like? The lonely, weak kid? It was surrounded by more powerful neighbors, Russia, Japan, and China, and threatened by the Republic of Korea and the United States from the south.

"Fine, no teriyaki," I said. "How about barbecue next time?"

Two days later at around nine in the morning, I had just put the key in the front door of Cubby's when I heard a hard clack on the pavement behind me. It wasn't the sound of rubber-soled shoes, which is what everybody in the restaurant business wears to work. I turned to see an Asian guy in a dark blue suit coming up the walk. He was alone, and my first thought was that it was one of Han and Ho Jong's guys here to break things off with me.

"Good morning!" He had no accent. He held out his hand, so I gave it a firm, New Jersey hunting shake. He winced, but kept smiling. A big, American smile. "Can I talk to you?" he asked.

"You're a Fed. I don't want to deal with you guys."

"We're not all the same," he said. He glanced around the empty parking lot. "Can you give me a minute or two?"

"I got to set up my restaurant." I let him follow me inside, and when I walked back to the kitchen, he came to the door. I went about my business, getting meat out to thaw, cutting roast beef in the circular slicer, sectioning tomatoes, and generally sous-cheffing for lunch before my kitchen staff arrived.

"Can I give you a hand?" he asked. That was strange. No cop or Fed had ever asked me anything like that before. I didn't say no, so the agent walked around our cooking line and followed me to the fridges. I started pulling out steam table pans that had been prepped the night before, and he helped me load them onto my bus cart.

"You ever work in a restaurant?" I asked.

"My parents had a Korean place in the city," he said. I lit the steam table, and we filled it with pans of sauces and sides: barbecue sauce, brown gravy, white gravy, sauerkraut, melted butter, marinara, and chili—hot and mild. "We know you're talking to the North Koreans," he said.

"That was quick," I said. I wiped my hands on a towel. Had they already ID'd me from surveillance footage? Or had McCreary tipped them off? I didn't think so. I trusted McCreary to have told me if he was going to pass the information along, and I was already learning that our government's intelligence agencies don't like to share information with each other.

"I just want you to know that the door is open," he said.

The agent stopped by a few more times. He was a friendly guy, and once he helped me unload a meat delivery when I was short-handed. Just as I started to warm up to him, though, he told me he was retiring. "I want to refer you to someone from counterintelligence," he said. "Would you be open to that, if he came to visit?"

"Is that what this was about?"

"I was asked to check you out," he said. "You seem reasonable, so I gave you a good report."

I pulled a pan of barbecue sauce out of my fridge. "I'm not interested in being a stooge for the Feds. No offense."

"You never know," he said. "You might need help staying out of trouble." I could have taken that as a threat, of course. The only trouble I could imagine was going to come from the FBI. This is how they operate, just like the mob. They say, "Help us out and we'll protect you." And you think, protect me from what? Oh, I see. Protect me from you. A nice little circle. But this Korean agent had a respectful tone, and I liked him. So I agreed to talk to his guy.

A few days later, Special Agent Ted Kuhlmeier showed up at nine-fifteen, an hour and a half before I opened for business. He was thin with short hair that had receded a couple of inches, leaving behind a polished strip of skin that shone in the morning light as though he'd been leaning his forehead against a shoe buffer. He had a firm handshake and a no-nonsense, military way about him. It turned out he was a former marine who joined the FBI in his twenties and had worked his way up the ladder in counterintelligence. A career guy.

I brought out two cups of coffee and we sat at the front table, where I could clearly see through the window if someone drove into my parking lot. He thanked me for meeting him. Call me Bobby, I said. He said okay, call me Ted. He asked about business; I told him it was fine.

"There's some information gathering we'd like you to do," he said.

"Why would I? You guys have been busting my balls since I was ten years old."

"To be quite frank," Kuhlmeier said, "the government is not going to let you continue a relationship with the North Koreans unless it is monitored by us."

"What relationship?" I said. "I've only met them a couple of times. We haven't even got to first base yet."

He pointed his shiny brow in my direction and looked at me as though he was peering over an imaginary pair of reading glasses. "I don't know whose side you think you're on," he said. "But this isn't Vietnam. And it isn't your mobster buddies, either. We're dealing with a country that is directly threatening our troops and our allies in the Pacific. It is run by some very bad people who hate us. And they are trying to build a nuclear weapon." Kuhlmeier slurped his coffee. "This is a serious matter of national security. Not a game." He sat back. "Why don't you start by telling me how you approached the North Koreans and why."

"They approached me," I said. Kuhlmeier looked skeptical. He took out a small pad of paper and jotted notes as I described the meeting at the U.N. Plaza Hotel's Ambassador Lounge.

"What do they think you'll be doing with them?"

"I've been wondering that myself," I said. "They know I'm interested in POWs."

Kuhlmeier asked me how to spell the names of Ho Jong and Han Song Ryol. "How the fuck should I know?" I said. "They didn't give me their business cards. Aren't you guys supposed to know these things? Don't you tail them wherever they go?"

"They don't really go anywhere," he said. "Let me be straight with you, Bobby. The North Koreans are a black hole in terms of our intelligence."

"How can they be a black hole?" I said. "They're on Seventy-second Street."

"I'm referring to their government," Kuhlmeier said. "*Including* their people here. You're in a unique position to help your country."

Smart move to appeal to my pride, I thought, but what did I care about helping the Feds? Screw them. They'd never once given me credit—through all of my work with the Vietnamese, and even when I was a kid—for any of my insights. They never said thank you. I had half a mind to send Kuhlmeier packing. Let him scrap for tips from some other sucker.

On the other hand, it was an issue of national security. Maybe a regular guy off the street could contribute something to his country's safety. And I liked seeing how the FBI was reduced to coming hat in hand to a restaurant owner in Hackensack.

"What would you want me to do?" I asked.

"Develop some psychological profiles. Explain how they're related to each other. The hierarchy. Their schedules. Everything. What kind of medications are they taking? Which of them is single?" Kuhlmeier glanced out the window at a car passing on River Street. "We may ask you to get some tissue samples."

"What kind of tissue samples?" I said. "I'm not scraping any dirty sheets in any motel rooms for you sickos."

"Hair is fine," he said. "Teeth are ideal."

"How am I supposed to get teeth?"

Kuhlmeier shrugged. "Don't think you're going to make a profit off this," he said. "We'll be watching you."

"I'm not in it for the money," I said. "Don't insult me."

"That's good," Kuhlmeier said. "Because if you try to make a buck, you'll be breaking the law. And if you break the law, we will enforce it. You can be sure about that."

As Kuhlmeier left, I had a sinking feeling. This guy was going to be all over me like a bad smell. All I had done was talk to Han and Ho Jong, and he'd come to my restaurant and threatened me.

I could have stopped right there, just folded up and left the North Koreans and the U.S. government to worry about each other. Things would be nice and peaceful if I kept my nose in my own business and focused on running my restaurant. But that wasn't going to happen. I'm not the kind of guy who can see a cookie jar and walk past it without putting his hand in.

I could see a thousand ways in which it could turn out badly for me, though. The stakes were much higher than with the Vietnamese. Washington had put the North Koreans on the list of countries that supported terrorism after its agents blew up a South Korean airliner in 1987 and killed 115 people. They were accused of all kinds of human rights violations.

If the FBI ever thought I was being uncooperative or didn't like the information I provided, they'd bring the law down hard. The Feds always assumed the worst about people, and they would hunt for evidence that I was up to no good with the enemy. They could probably even have me arrested for buying Han some carrot seeds. If I was going to hang around the North Koreans, I needed a legitimate reason. Only one thing gave me that coverage and played to what I knew: POWs.

Eight thousand American GIs never came home from North Korea when the war ended in 1953—almost four times the number of POW/MIAs from the Vietnam War. Couldn't some of them have survived? North Korea had been the most sealed-off place in the world for all those years, with dozens of prison camps that no outsider had ever seen. A kid who fought in the Korean War would have been in his sixties by then. Who's to say one of those eight thousand guys wasn't still rotting away somewhere, surviving two-thirds of his life in captivity, learning Korean to get by with his captors but never giving up the hope that one day his own countrymen would come for him?

I started to put together a plan that would bring the North Koreans out of their comfort zone and into New Jersey, where they'd be on my turf. As enemies of the United States, they were forbidden from traveling beyond a twenty-mile radius from an imaginary point in the center of Columbus Circle, in the middle of Manhattan. But the restrictions said nothing about crossing state lines.

In early December I called Dave Bratton, the chaplain for the New York

Giants. I'd served barbecue to his Tuesday afternoon Bible study for long enough that I figured it was time to call in a favor. "I need eight or ten VIP tickets to a game," I said. "For some very special guests." It was a tall order, he said. The Giants were still in the hunt for a wildcard spot in the playoffs, and it was impossible to get that many seats together. I knew the Giants had juice with the other sports franchises at the Meadowlands, so I said, "How about a Nets game, and we invite some of the Giants to meet the North Koreans? It's for our POWs."

"Call the front office," he said. "Tell them I think it's a good idea." I dialed the Meadowlands and asked to speak with the Giants' owner, Duke Mara. I'd met him before, and he was a man of excellent character. His grandfather was a bookie, and he was from blue-collar stock like me. He was a patriot, and he had been impressed with my efforts on behalf of the Vietnam POWs. When I got Mara on the phone I explained I was trying to find out what happened to Americans left in North Korea. I wanted their star running back, Rodney Hampton, and another player or two to help us in this goodwill gesture.

"Just keep them out of trouble," he said. "We have the playoffs to think about."

"Don't worry, sir," I said. "I'll have them home by midnight. I've got money on your postseason."

I called Han and asked him to meet me the next day. It was important, I said. Han reluctantly agreed and gave me the name of a coffee shop on Second Avenue. Ho Jong was with him when I arrived.

"Our relationship has got to be out in the open," I said. "It can't be a secret. This is going to be one of my conditions for working with you."

"We're not hiding anything," Han said stiffly. I could tell from his tone of voice that he was going to resist any plan of mine, so I turned my attention to Ho Jong.

"We need to get you out in public," I said, figuring what was good for me could also be good for them. "One of the biggest problems you have is how you are perceived by the American people. Everybody here sees you as a sponsor of terrorism. We need to help demystify your country."

Han looked like he wanted to say something, but I kept my gaze on Ho Jong, who waited for me to continue. "I've arranged a special invitation for you to a basketball game." I said a couple of America's greatest athletes would escort them. "Think of it as your coming out party," I said.

"Who is making the invitation?" Ho Jong asked.

"I invite you as a representative of the U.S. government," I said.

"But whose idea is it?" Ho Jong pressed.

I felt I could legitimately claim to be working on behalf of the FBI, after the visit from Kuhlmeier. The FBI is part of the U.S. Department of Justice, which reports directly to the president. "The executive branch is involved," I said. I let that sink in for a few seconds. "You're aware that our government can't invite you to anything, since we don't officially have relations with each other. So we have to start unofficially, right? That's why the New Jersey Nets and the New York Giants organizations are involved."

I could see him racking his brain. He and Han probably assumed I was a spy, and this wasn't typical spy behavior. Spies operate in secret. The North Koreans were the same: doing anything publicly was not their way. As far as I could tell, their representatives were supposed to attend U.N. meetings, deliver statements written in Pyongyang, and otherwise stay out of sight. On the other hand, their Great Leader, Kim Il Sung, had recently issued a statement that his nation wanted to create a dialogue with the United States.

"You guys need to loosen up and get out of the office," I said.

"Wouldn't we need special permission from the State Department?"

I explained that all we had to do was drive over the Hudson River on the George Washington Bridge and down the Turnpike. "Well within twenty miles," I said.

Ho Jong looked at Han and raised his eyebrows. Then he turned back to me. "Okay," he said.

Okay? I couldn't believe it was that easy. Had nobody ever asked them out before? I told them we'd have a steak dinner at Cubby's before driving down to the game. It would be the first time a North Korean envoy had made this type of public appearance in the United States, and I admit I didn't mind getting a little free publicity for my restaurant.

I needed to get my event on the record, so no one could ever question that it happened. As soon as I left the Koreans, I called Tommy Topousis at *The Record*. "Have I got a story for you," I said. Then I called a few buddies of mine from the Vietnam POW groups, to cover that side of things. I called the Giants again to lock in Hampton, their all-star running back, and defensive end Chad Bratzke. I invited Bratton, to make sure God was represented, and John Ziza, the mayor of Hackensack.

Then I called in a favor from a buddy who manages a limo rental. Since it would be a Wednesday night four days after New Year's, he gave me a good deal for eight hours. Lilia was not happy. "Why can't they pay for it themselves?" she asked. "If they can afford a nuclear program, they can afford a limo."

You could say she had a point. But I was starting to realize how broke the North Koreans were—at least the ones stationed in New York. "You don't understand, baby," I said. "This is about diplomacy."

The day before the game, I went to meet Han in person to go over the itinerary. As I left home I draped a hand towel over the leather headrest of the passenger seat. Then I put another one on the driver's side so it wouldn't appear conspicuous.

Han waited for me on the sidewalk outside his mission. When he climbed into the passenger seat I handed him a manila envelope containing an itinerary and an official letter of invitation, which Bratton had printed on Giants stationery at his office.

"How are the negotiations going, Mr. Counselor?" I asked.

"We made an agreement," he said, opening the envelope. "More talks in Vienna." The North Koreans had said they were open to new inspections of their alleged nuclear sites. The idea unraveled a few weeks later, but that was another story. It was the first time he had shared a piece of information with me. It wasn't secret information, but I liked his willingness to let me in on his news.

Han looked at the printouts as I drove around a few blocks. He had wanted to know every detail. Five o'clock pickup, six o'clock dinner at Cubby's, seven o'clock leave for the Meadowlands, eleven-thirty return to Manhattan. "Where are our tickets?" he asked.

"At will call," I said.

"Will call?" he asked. "Who?"

I made it through a yellow light on First Avenue and got sandwiched between two taxis. "What do you mean who?" I said.

"Will call who? Who will call?"

"It's a place. At the ticket counter."

"What is?"

"Will call."

Han sighed. "It's a place who will call? You call? Have you called?"

"You go in person," I said. "It's where you pick the ticket up. There's a guy there at the gate. He has the tickets waiting."

"You call him?"

"Nobody calls. You just go. The place is called 'will call.'"

"Why?"

"How should I know? It's just called that. It's probably from a long time ago, before there were phones."

Han looked at me like I was the biggest idiot in the world. "How could they call before there were phones?"

"Not 'call,'" I said. "Call *on*. Like to visit."

He leaned back against the headrest. "So it should be called 'will call *on*,'" Han said, seeming pleased with himself. "Who is the guy? Shouldn't you call him first?"

"He's the ticket guy. He probably doesn't even have a phone. Don't worry."

"Nobody calls?"

"Nobody calls."

Han had a lot to learn about America: will call. Doggy bag. I wondered what else he didn't know. Kuhlmeier said they were a black hole of intelligence. Were we just as mysterious to them?

We went over the list of other invitees, and Han was not happy about the idea of a news reporter coming along. I assured him that *The Record* was a small paper and that the writer, Topousis, was a friend of mine.

"This can't be about our relationship with you," he said. He looked at me then. "It could be embarrassing to us. You must not embarrass us."

"I won't," I said. "This is about turning the page. Changing the dialogue."

As soon as I let him out in front of his mission, I checked the headrest. Bingo. Stuck onto the fibers of the towel was a three-inch strand of black hair. I opened the glove box and got a sandwich baggie. I carefully dropped the hair inside and sealed it. I felt a little guilty for betraying a guy I was just getting to know. But Han was the enemy and I was doing my patriotic duty. Besides, it was just a piece of hair, and it wasn't like I ripped it out of his head with a pair of tweezers while he was sleeping. It fell out of his scalp all by itself. He left it on the headrest in my car, and therefore it was technically my property.

I turned my attention to the important business of what to serve for dinner. I had heard that Koreans loved barbecue, and I wanted their first visit to New Jersey to be a memorable one. I called Bert Posess, the best meat man in the tri-state area, and told him I needed the finest porterhouse steaks he could find and two choice slabs of Danish pork ribs. The porterhouse is the king of steaks, cut from the most prized sections of beef, the short loin and the tenderloin. The best steaks are dry aged, where the meat is hung in a low-humidity box, with fans blowing on it, which allows the enzymes to soften the muscle. After thirty days, you trim away the hardened rind and you have the most beautiful piece of meat you can put on the fire. Posess sent ten steaks, from which I selected three. At twenty-five bucks a pop wholesale, they weren't cheap, but I wanted an extra in case Han and Ho Jong both ordered steak and I miscooked one.

The morning of the game I was as nervous as a teenager taking a girl out for the first time. I wore my black wool-silk suit, and my palms were sweaty. The limo showed up at three o'clock, and I set off for Manhattan early. I got to 72nd Street an hour ahead of schedule and had the driver park a block away, so they wouldn't see me if they came in or out of their building. At five-thirty we pulled up outside the mission and the driver and I both hopped out to open the door for Han and Ho Jong. They had on the same FBI-style suits and khaki trench coats they'd worn the first time we met. They seemed unfazed by the limo, and after some small talk we rode in silence. I knew Han and Ho Jong were having a busy start to 1994 and probably had a lot on their minds. An editorial in *The New York Times* that day criticized the Clinton Administration for agreeing to inspections of the North Korean nuclear sites on a one-time basis. A lot of people in Washington were calling for tougher action.

Han clutched the manila envelope with the itinerary I had printed for him and the letter of invitation from Bratton. As we crossed the George Washington Bridge and entered New Jersey, they peered through the windows as dusk settled over the Hudson River. We turned off the ramp onto River Street and into my parking lot. I had customized my roadside sign for the occasion to read: CUBBY'S WELCOMES AMBASSADOR HO JONG AND COUNSELOR HAN TO HACKEN-SACK.

"Why did you do that?" Ho Jong asked.

"You're very important people," I said, "and it's an honor to have you here." I could feel Han tensing up.

My other guests were already at the restaurant. I introduced Han and Ho Jong first to Hampton and Bratzke, because I wanted to impress the North Koreans with the caliber of the people they would meet as long as they were friends of mine. I figured the Giants would be in a good mood and talkative. They had just clinched a wildcard playoff spot with a 16-13 win over the Dallas Cowboys three nights earlier and were relaxing before their upcoming game against the Vikings. None of this group was exactly gifted with the social skills, however. On the field Hampton was a powerful, smashmouth runner who could wear down a defense over four quarters of play, but in person he was modest and shy. The same was true of Bratzke, a 275-pounder who was polite and reserved whenever he wasn't slapping offensive linemen around. The Giants and the North Koreans shook hands and nodded at each other, and for a second there I thought Bratzke would bow. The football players wore much nicer suits than the North Koreans and were about twice as big.

"The DPRK has a great regard for sports," I said. "It's an honor and a privilege to bring together your two esteemed organizations—one country that is very united and one champion football team." I wondered why I sometimes sounded like a different person when I got in these situations. "Big guys, huh?" I said to Han and Ho Jong, pointing my thumb at the Giants.

I brought the Koreans to the table that ran along the south wall, where we would be separated from other customers, and introduced them to the rest of our party. Topousis, the journalist from *The Record*, stood up and shook hands with Han and Ho Jong. He was playing it cool, though I knew he was itching to pull his notebook out of his back pocket, ask the North Koreans a tough question or two, and get his story. Next to Topousis sat John Ziza, the mayor of Hackensack. On the other side of the table sat Bratton and Mike Van Atta, a Vietnam vet and POW activist. I kept an eye on Van Atta. He was into some pretty weird shit, including mind travel, and he claimed it was possible to remote-view aliens aboard their spacecrafts. A few years earlier he said he had left his body and slipped into a prison cell somewhere in Southeast Asia, where he saw an American prisoner of war still being held after almost twenty years. He might not have been the most credible guy in the world, but I wanted a POW activist at the table without having to pay somebody's travel expenses, and Mike lived in Chatham.

I gestured at the guests seated around the table to emphasize how they represented the many sectors of society: politics, religion, sports, the military, and the media. "We are all dedicated to getting American prisoners of war back," I said to the Koreans, by way of introduction. "If you can help us account for the missing, America is ready to help you."

Ho Jong smiled. "Thank you for inviting us to your restaurant," he said. Van Atta sidled in closer. Topousis went for his notebook and pen. The Giants sat back in their chairs. I dipped in and out of the kitchen to personally oversee the grilling of the meat, while Lilia served salads and baked potatoes. I was mainly interested in Han's and Ho Jong's steaks. Each was a pound and a half trimmed, and as I put them on the fire I could hear the marbled fat hissing as it melted, turning the meat soft and buttery. I served the North Koreans first—perfect slabs of beef with a sprig of parsley for garnish—then went back for the others. When I came out again I saw that Han had already hollowed out his potato and he and Ho Jong were waiting to cut into their meat until I sat down. I took the empty chair next to Han.

"No quotes in the newspaper," he said. "We agreed."

"No quotes," I said, looking at Tommy. "No problem." Topousis and I had already hashed out the requirements: he could characterize what happened and paraphrase what the North Koreans said, but he could not quote them directly. I looked around the table. *"Buon appetito!"* I said.

Han sliced off the first piece of steak and inserted it into his mouth, and I tried to pretend I wasn't watching. He chewed slowly and looked at his plate. I know when people are enjoying a meal, and Han and Ho Jong were fully involved in the pleasure of the moment, their minds far away from nuclear negotiations and dealing with the United States as an enemy nation. What was he thinking? Was he thinking that, if he had to be paired up with an American, at least the American knew how to cook meat?

Van Atta leaned toward Han and Ho Jong, looking a little deranged. "I want to get into your military archives," he blurted. Conversation at the table sputtered to a stop. Where I come from, you don't ask somebody a sensitive yes-or-no question before you get to know them. I stared at Van Atta. If he was such a psychic, he should have understood what I was thinking: *That's my angle, pal. Back off.*

Ho Jong looked back and forth between Van Atta and me. "We will try to facilitate any research that you want to do."

"How's your steak?" I asked Ho Jong. "Can you get a piece of meat like that back home?" I instantly regretted the question, because I could tell from the faces of my guests that they couldn't. And if these guys couldn't, what about the rest of their country? What did they eat? Most of their comrades back home had probably never dared to dream of a piece of meat like the one that Ho Jong was sticking his fork into.

"Of course we can," Han said. I wondered whether he was having a good enough time that this date would lead to others. Only his empty plate gave him away. He wore a poker face all the way through dinner and on the drive to the game.

Ho Jong and Han peered through the tinted windows as our limo pulled into the parking lot of the arena. Basketball fans ran past, waving blue-and-red Nets flags. Stereos pumped, vibrating the chassis of their cars. In North

Korea, a sporting event like this is an official gathering where the top-ranking ministers and government functionaries show off their status. "Don't worry," I said, "we're the biggest VIPs here."

We used the Giants' influence to get Han and Ho Jong access to the Nets' locker room. The basketball players towered over the North Koreans and gave them hats and T-shirts. The Nets were at home against the Milwaukee Bucks, and although the arena was only about half full, the fans were loud and pumped up on beer.

We took our seats near the center line, and Han sat with his hands on his knees. If he was nervous, it was probably because he hadn't been out of New York City yet. Crossing the border into a mob of suburban sports nuts, he was deep into enemy territory for the first time. I got him a basket of nachos, which he held in his lap. Rodney Hampton and I pointed out the best players and explained the finer points of the slam dunk and the no-look pass. I tried to see it through his eyes: the baseball caps, the flashbulbs, the different colors and stripes of the fans, white people, black people, yellow people, and everything in between.

At halftime, the Nets' cheerleaders took over the floor. I wanted to surprise Han and Ho Jong with a little extra honor, so I briefly excused myself. The cheerleaders were still on when I got back. They wore plaid schoolgirl outfits and shook their short skirts to a heavy beat. I thought this would impress Han, but he said that in Pyongyang they had the world's largest sports stadium, which can hold more than 150,000 people, where they put on shows that perfectly synchronize tens of thousands of performers.

At the end of the routine, the arena seemed quiet without the cheering or the music. The announcer's voice boomed through the loudspeakers: "We have a couple of very special guests here with us tonight."

I looked back and forth between Han and Ho Jong with a shit-eating grin on my face. Ho Jong didn't flinch, but Han had an expression that said, "Please tell me you're not—" And the announcer boomed: "Let's give a warm New Jersey welcome to our friends from the U.N.—the representatives of the DPRK!"

Han spilled his nachos on the floor and for a second I thought he was going to make a run for an exit. "You go too far," he huffed. A few of the Nets fans sitting nearby turned to look, and I helpfully pointed to Han and Ho Jong so people would know who they were. There was a polite smattering of applause. Somebody took a picture of Rodney Hampton. It was obvious most of the fans in East Rutherford couldn't have told you (or cared) whether DPRK stood for an unpredictable nuclear-armed country or a small-town charity organization.

I nudged Han with my elbow as the crowd's attention turned back to the cheerleaders. "Relax, buddy," I said. "See how welcoming everybody is?"

Two days later, *The Record* ran the following story:

A RARE PUBLIC APPEARANCE IN BERGEN FOR N. KOREANS
TOM TOPOUSIS

North Korean officials seeking to end an impasse over inspections of their country's nuclear facilities took time out from their negotiations this week to eat steak in Hackensack and take in a New Jersey Nets game.

The unusual appearance by Ambassador Ho Jong and Counselor Han Song Ryol on Wednesday came at the invitation of a local activist seeking North Korea's cooperation in the search for 8,100 missing servicemen.

The diplomats assigned to the United Nations are the communist nation's only official presence in the United States, which has not had ties with North Korea since a cease-fire was decleared between the two Koreas 40 years ago.

The story went on to quote me by name. It was exactly what I needed. Nobody could ever deny that I was involved with the North Koreans for good reasons, now that I was on record as befriending them for the sake of missing U.S. servicemen. I decided not to show the story to Han, since he'd been so jumpy over the Nets announcer's welcome. I figured he'd never see a copy of *The Record* on his own.

The Saturday morning after Topousis's story appeared, Kuhlmeier stopped by Cubby's unannounced and pointed his shiny brow at me. "Let's go over what you've learned about Han," he said once we had our coffee and were sitting across the table from each other.

"They don't talk about their personal lives," I said. "What's the big deal with Han?"

Kuhlmeier said there was speculation at the Bureau that Han might be the rising star of the North Korean diplomatic corps. The timing of his arrival in New York was intriguing because it coincided with Kim Il Sung's announcement that he wanted to pursue relations with the United States for the first time since the Korean War. From what I could tell, Ho Jong was grooming Han to be his successor. "The other thing we're still trying to figure out," Kuhlmeier said, "is why they approached you."

I figured three things made me valuable to the North Koreans. First were my ties to U.S. intelligence. They knew from the Vietnamese that I had a relationship with McCreary and the FBI, but they couldn't figure out what the nature of that relationship was. Many years later, Han admitted to me that between him and Ho Jong and the others at the North Korean mission there was no debate at first: they assumed I was a fully employed spy, acting on behalf of at least one U.S. intelligence agency. End of story. Who else would spend so much time with them? Courting them and doing favors. They come from the world's most controlling regime, where anybody who even talks about the government is instantly reported to his higher-ups. To them, it was inconceivable that a private citizen—even in a free country—would be allowed to deal with them without the full knowledge and support of Washington. I probably confused them. I didn't act like an intelligence agent. I ran a restaurant and had a criminal history and had endeavored to get myself and the North Koreans into the newspaper. I was mysterious, and it's possible this led them to believe I was more connected than I was. The North Koreans equate mysteriousness with rank. In North Korea, information flows one way: up, never down. Superiors know everything about their underlings. Underlings know nothing about their superiors. If they tried to find out who I was and couldn't, they probably assumed I was a big-time player. The crazy Americans had a president who was a saxophone player; why not an emissary who was also a barbecue chef? It was an impression I was doing my best to encourage.

The second thing that the Koreans saw in me—and this shouldn't be underestimated—was my barbecue. I knew from that first steak dinner that I had them. They didn't have a budget to be out fine-dining around New York City. I was willing to feed them the biggest, juiciest pieces of meat they could get anywhere. And as my invited guests, they ate for free.

The third thing was that I was willing to do them favors that they wouldn't have dreamed of doing for themselves. The goodie bags, which Han would call "doggy bags" for years to come, were just the beginning.

Even more than the Vietnamese, the North Koreans were isolated in New York. Only ten or twelve were posted here at any one time, including the ambassador to the United Nations and a counselor in charge of American affairs. They lived in an apartment building in Spanish Harlem, twenty blocks uptown from their office, and they had no social life. It boggled my mind that U.S. intelligence agents hadn't taken advantage of their loneliness before. With all the clamor and fear over their nuclear program and the talk about how secretive they were, nobody had thought to invite them out to dinner and a ball game or tried to become their friend.

"What can I tell you?" I said to Kuhlmeier as we finished our coffee. "I have a better personality than you guys." I dug into my coat pocket, pulled out the sandwich baggie, and put it on the table between us.

Kuhlmeier spread it flat against the table. We stared at the fine black strand of hair that had curled itself into the shape of the number six.

"Han's?" Kuhlmeier asked.

I nodded. "A little piece of the enemy," I said.

3

~~~~~~~~~~
~~~~~~~~~~~

Language Lessons

KUHLMEIER HELD THE BAGGIE up to the light and looked at it approvingly. Han's genetic code would soon be digitized and filed in the archives of the FBI. "Are you sure it's his?"

"No doubt," I said. "No doubt at all."

Kuhlmeier stuffed the baggie with Han's hair into his coat pocket and took out a notepad and a ballpoint pen. "How do you plan to proceed?" he asked.

"I proceed by running my restaurant and seeing what happens," I said. "You forget I'm not working for you, Ted."

I'm not a planner. I've never been somebody who looks at a problem, builds a strategy, and then waits until all the pieces come together before I make a move. I go on a hunch. I'm a street guy. An entrepreneur. I find the overlooked angle. When I saw an empty stretch of road between a shopping mall and a busy highway on-ramp, I opened a restaurant that can put a top quality burger in front of a commuter in less than five minutes. When a Vietnamese official with information about American POWs wanted to defect, I got him a lawyer, a dishwashing job, and a hearing at the U.S. Senate.

When I plan, it's in response to an opportunity. The North Koreans hadn't presented me with any real opportunities yet, and I had no idea what I was getting myself into. All I knew was that I was being sucked into a vacuum between two very powerful groups. I had an enemy country on one side and FBI counterintelligence on the other. It had the potential to spin out of control and get me in trouble, and I liked it.

"What do you two talk about when you're together?" Kuhlmeier asked. He drew a chain of little circles on his notebook.

"Guy stuff," I said. "You know."

"What do you mean? Football? Cars?"

"Yeah, sports. Fishing. Broads. We talked about your wife the other day." Kuhlmeier clicked his pen shut. "Lighten up, Ted. I just wanted to see if an old marine had a sense of humor."

"That's not funny," he said.

"I think Ho Jong's leaving next month," I said. "He asked me to help him get seeds."

Kuhlmeier clicked his pen open again and wrote Ho Jong's name. Then he wrote the word "seeds" next to it. "What kind of seeds?" he asked.

"Petunias. Gladiolas. I don't know. I drove him to Costco. He picked them out."

Kuhlmeier sighed. "Tell me about the new American Affairs department."

The way I interpreted it, the Great Leader decided it was time to change relations with the United States because his own neighborhood was changing. The Soviets no longer had the North Koreans' back. Easy money wasn't flowing from Moscow anymore. The Chinese alternately helped and bullied Pyongyang. Only one country could make or break the security of their dictatorship: the United States.

They sent Han to set up the North American Affairs Department to gain insight about their archenemy. The question was, how far would Pyongyang and Washington let him go? It was uncharted territory, and I'm sure that's what had made him so nervous at the Nets game. He'd been in the United States for just a couple of months, and he couldn't afford to screw up. In his country, a guy who screwed up a big assignment could spend the rest of his life in a concentration camp, getting his toenails pulled out and surviving on bugs.

"Let's go over Han again," Kuhlmeier said. "How well do you think you know him?"

What do you ever really know about other people? You learn their names, ages, and jobs, their likes and dislikes. You might know enough about somebody to predict what's going to piss him off or make him laugh. But with most people, you can never be sure what's deep inside them. Sometimes they don't know themselves. The proof of this is that people are always doing surprising things. You can live next door to a guy thinking you know everything about him because you watched him grow up and you know his parents and his brothers and sisters. All the neighbors think he's just an average jerkoff until one day, out of the blue, he discovers the cure for diabetes or sets himself on fire in front of the supermarket. Then everybody tries to figure out how they failed to see it coming, but the answer is simple. They never knew the guy.

On paper, Han was the enemy in a way the Vietnamese were not. His government showed open hostility to my country, and they were trying to get nuclear weapons. Han might have some very bad intentions, and I had no idea what he was capable of doing. But that only made me curious.

He mostly asked for favors. I'd drive him to Costco or Shop-Rite to pick up household stuff for the apartment in Spanish Harlem he shared with the other North Korean envoys. Other times we ran office errands, like Xeroxing a box of papers at a copy shop near the embassy. We'd toss the stationery in the back of my Explorer and drive around as an excuse for him to get out of the office, where everybody was highly suspicious of each other. Pretty soon, Han invited me past the waiting room and into the inner sanctum of the embassy, and I was able to describe its layout to Kuhlmeier, who sketched it in his notebook.

During the first months of 1994, I became the only American regular at the mission. It was a bare-bones operation. Other than the posters of The Great Leader hanging everywhere, it was a generic-looking office with a large conference room and a few smaller rooms, including one with their only computer and a telegraph machine with paper trailing out that I assumed was what they used for some of their communications with Pyongyang.

Soon after the Nets game, Han asked me to cater a lunch at the embassy, which became a regular gig. They had a small kitchenette with a rice steamer, a microwave, and a hot plate. They cooked eel and fish soup, which they ate with kimchee—a spicy, fermented vegetable dish they serve with everything—around the fold-out table in the conference room. The embassy always smelled of stale food because of the poor ventilation.

I didn't want to seem pushy, so whenever I met people at the embassy I asked for their first names only. This frustrated the hell out of Kuhlmeier, but it probably made me seem more trustworthy to the North Koreans. I met Americans of South Korean origin who were trying to get a little extra food slipped to their relatives in North Korea. I also met people who were introduced to me as so-and-so from Syria or our-good-friend-Reza from Iran. They were mostly diplomats posted to the United Nations, and they were always very friendly. If they were trading nuclear secrets and selling missiles to each other, they didn't do it in front of me. I figured these guys had one thing in common: forced to live on enemy turf, they stuck together for protection like the unpopular kids in school.

As Han and I spent more time together he was becoming more mysterious, not less so. I met him almost every day, and still I wasn't learning much about his personal life. He had a wife and two daughters who were a little older than Andrea. His father had been a general and a hero in Kim Il Sung's army, so our fathers had fought on opposite sides of the Korean War. He was stepping in as Minister Counselor which, as far as I could tell, made him the North Koreans' number three man in New York. McCreary suspected he was being groomed for something higher. Who could tell? In ten or twenty years, when North Koreans got their hands on the bomb, he might be the guy with his finger on the button, deciding whether to fire a nuclear missile across the Pacific.

Sometimes I'd drive into Manhattan to meet him in the evening. He'd wait for me on the corner of 95th Street and Third Avenue, a couple blocks from their apartments. He always stood in the shadows of a bagel shop, and when he saw the Explorer he'd cross the sidewalk and quickly climb into the passenger seat. He wasn't hiding the fact that we went out together, but he wasn't advertising it either. We'd get pizza at a place called Il Panini or a sandwich at one of his neighborhood delis or just drive around.

We made a strange-looking pair. He was short, tightly wound, and aggressive. You could see he was thinking about everything he did, whether it was opening a door or picking up a fork. I was practically twice his size and looser—a foot taller, a hundred pounds heavier, and I generally went with the flow of things. "You're bumbling," he liked to say, after he learned what the word meant.

Han liked to be in charge. Anytime we went to a restaurant, Han wanted to be the one who talked to the maitre d'. "We will have a table for two in the corner," he'd say. And if he didn't like the table, he'd ask me, "Do you think we can say we want to change?" And I'd say, "Of course. We're paying."

We weren't paying, though. Han was always broke, and I insisted on picking up the check because I wanted to avoid the awkward moment of him counting out his change to see if he had enough. "You've got alligator arms," I told him once.

"What do you mean?" he asked.

I drew my hands up to my shoulders and flailed them around. "Arms too short," I said. "Can't reach your pockets."

I could see that he felt bad, so I quickly added that, where I came from, not paying was a sign of status. When you go out to eat with a group of wise guys, it's always the low man on the totem pole who picks up the tab. The little guy has got to make the big guy happy. Han liked that idea, and for years to come he assumed I was paying. He never left anything on his plate, either. He'd ask for any scraps to go in a "doggy bag."

In some ways he acted like a proper English gentleman. When he used a toothpick, he'd cover his mouth so you couldn't see him digging around in his gums. When he squeezed a lemon into his iced tea, he'd put a hand over it so the juice wouldn't go flying—things my buddies and I generally did *not* do. But he was also a macho guy, and I figured I could take him fishing without embarrassment. This was important if we were going to be friends. I'd taken Le Quang Khai bass fishing off Sandy Hook, and the spoiled commie spent the whole trip complaining about the rough sea and filing the long fingernail of his right pinky. Standing on the back deck of the charter boat with a nail file, he never even dropped a line in the water. I heard about it from the captain for years afterward.

During his first year in America, Han's English was still pretty shaky. He could get by all right, but he spoke in a monotone and tripped over words. With me, he got to practice without feeling intimidated or inadequate. He'd call me to prepare before meetings at the U.N. where he'd be in the same room with Americans or other English-speaking diplomats. I don't know if learning the North Jersey vernacular would have been his number one choice for going up against the Harvard and Yale crowd, but it's not like anybody else was offering to tutor him. I told him not to worry about it: he sounded fine.

"Our government officials are half jackasses anyway. They're a bunch of drunks and perverts. Look at Ted Kennedy. Guy leaves a girl drowning in a car and he runs away. They're just normal fucking people like you and me. You don't have to be afraid of them."

"That's how you look at your officials?" he asked. He couldn't believe, until he saw how I interacted with some of them, that I had no regard for Camelot.

Sometimes I'd be at the counter at Cubby's and he'd call with a question about a word he read in the newspaper. "What does 'serendipitous' mean?" he'd ask. And I'd say, "Lucky." And he'd say, "But does it mean lucky with skill? Or just lucky?" And I'd say, "How the fuck do I know?" and head back to my office where I kept a dictionary. "Just lucky."

After a couple months of this I brought the dictionary to our meeting spot in Spanish Harlem and presented it to him. "Keep it," I said.

"You're not interested in expanding your vocabulary?"

"Fuck no," I said. "I'm interested in hunting and fishing and eating."

He turned the dictionary around in his hand and thumbed through some pages: his way of saying thank you. We went to a place he liked near his apartment, a Puerto Rican bodega next to a Blockbuster, where you could get a hot buffet or a sandwich and pull a stool up to a little table to eat. As we unwrapped our hoagie sandwiches, he asked why Americans were so obsessed with North Korea.

"They're not," I said.

"You don't know," he said. "Negotiations are very bad. Our countries can start fighting tomorrow."

He was right: the situation was very tense and getting worse. In February 1994, the North Koreans agreed to let foreign inspectors look at their reactors, but they changed their minds after President Clinton went ahead with plans for a huge military exercise with South Korea and Japan. In March, Kim Il Sung ordered his military to "switch to a state of readiness for war."

Clinton called a meeting of every four-star general and admiral in the U.S. military and asked them to draw up new plans for a full-scale attack on North Korea. Around the same time, U.S. senators Sam Nunn and Richard Lugar proposed arming South Korea with short-range nuclear weapons, and Sen. John McCain threatened North Korea with "consequences that will hasten the collapse of that despicable regime." I figured they were bluffing. Clinton was just coming off of two failed military interventions, and even a burger chef from Hackensack could see he didn't have the balls to back up new threats.

"We just got our asses kicked in Somalia and Haiti," I told Han. "If Clinton wanted to go to war with you, he'd have to convince the American people. He'd have to get the Democrats in Congress fired up. You'd hear baying for your blood in the media. And none of that's happening." I could tell that Han hadn't thought of this before. "Remember the basketball game, when the announcer welcomed you?" I asked. "Nobody even knew what the DPRK was. You think that's a drumroll for war?"

"A what?"

"A drumroll. The part that leads up to the war. Like a preamble."

"You want to put your nuclear weapons in Korea," he said, meaning South Korea. "Isn't that a drumroll?"

"It's a response," I said. "You guys are trying to develop nukes."

Han wrapped the unfinished half of his hoagie and stuffed it into a plastic bag. "Who are these senators who want to put nuclear weapons in Seoul?" he asked.

It was the first time we'd gone back and forth like this, so we were treading lightly. "They're hawks," I said. "Hardliners."

"That's obvious," he said. "Can you tell me more about them?"

I said I'd check into it. And that was the beginning of my double role—informing the FBI about the North Koreans and teaching Han about America.

I called McCreary, who told me Nunn and Lugar were behind a U.S. program to dismantle nukes in the former Soviet Union. Then I called Topousis at *The Record* and asked if he could go into the archives and print some stories about the senators' views on nuclear issues. I drove them over to Han the next day, and when I handed him the packet and told him what McCreary said, he looked at me with a new appreciation.

Han was giving me things to read, too. He said he wanted to "educate" me. Every week he'd hand me a pamphlet published by his government in English. Pretty soon a box of them started piling up in my office at Cubby's: *Young People Must Accomplish the Revolutionary Cause of Juche, Upholding the Leadership of the Party*; volumes of Kim Il Sung's speeches; *Forests of Korea*; *Kim Il Sung: The Great Man of the Century*; a pamphlet on the health benefits of ginseng; back issues of *North Korea Today* magazine; and a book called *The U.S. Imperialists Started the Korean War*. Who read this kind of propaganda in English? Maybe that's why I had so much of it sitting in my office—they had nobody else to give it to.

"What do you think?" Han asked one day.

I hesitated. "It's interesting," I said. It was obvious I hadn't read any of them, and I felt bad about that. That night I picked up *The U.S. Imperialists Started the Korean War*. It was a 250-page paperback with the silhouettes of soldiers on the cover, published in Pyongyang in 1977 and updated in 1993.

Reading this book was like one of those *Twilight Zone* episodes where you enter another version of reality. In America, the well-known facts about the Korean War are that on June 25, 1950, the communist North Koreans invaded South Korea, and within hours the U.N. Security Council voted unanimously to support military action. The United States and its allies pushed the commies back almost to China before a seesawing war that lasted three years and ended in a stalemate at the 38th Parallel, more or less right where everybody was before the North Korean invasion.

The book from Han gave a completely different picture. It claimed that "U.S. imperialism" started the conflict in 1947, when its South Korean "puppet army" raided North Korea 270 times, and escalated its attacks over the next few years until, on June 25, 1950, "U.S. imperialism launched a surprise invasion in the hope of breaking through the 38th parallel in a breath and having breakfast in Haeju, lunch in Pyongyang, and supper in Sinuiju."

In the DPRK's version, there was no North Korean invasion. Instead, Kim Il Sung called a meeting of the Party Central Committee and "ordered the Republic's Security Forces and People's Army to go over to counteroffensive immediately. Thus started the Korean People's Just Fatherland Liberation War to repulse the U.S. invasion and defend the freedom and independence of the fatherland."

Their books made a big deal of the fact that "U.S. imperialism" armed its bombers with nuclear weapons and was ready to use them against communist positions near the Chinese border. So what? The point is that Washington acted responsibly and *didn't* use nukes, even though, six years earlier, the Pentagon had seen how quickly a nuke could end a war.

"Did you disagree with it?" Han asked the next time we met.

"I'm not a big reader," I said. I didn't want to tell him I thought his country's version of events was nuts. "Listen," I said, "if you want to talk about these things we should do it man to man. I can't have this relationship and come over every night and meet you on a street corner, where you hide in the shadows so nobody sees you. You treat me like I'm some kind of mistress you're ashamed of. Are you ashamed of me?"

"No," Han said.

"Okay, then. We need to get more personal. We need to get on the golf course together."

"I don't play golf," he said.

"Me either," I said. "I meant it like an expression."

"When you say 'play golf,' it also means to get personal?"

"Sure," I said. "It could."

Han nodded slowly. "You need to be checked out first," he said.

"What do you mean?"

"I take a risk being with you. You don't understand. Something happens, I get in trouble with you, and everybody knows I make a bad choice." I was going to point out that Ho Jong set us up, but then Han dropped a bomb. "You need to be seen in Pyongyang," he said.

"Me?" I asked. But as soon as he'd said it, I understood. Han needed coverage. Just like I'd needed to get it on the record that Han and I were involved with the New York Giants on behalf of American POWs, he needed somebody higher up to sanction what he was doing with me. I imagined flying to North Korea, the Hermit Kingdom, where you could bet nobody from West Essex High School had ever set foot. Any asshole with a fraternity scarf can buy himself a plane ticket to Rome, Tokyo, or Rio. But who gets invited to Pyongyang? That's right: the kid who dropped out of tenth grade.

"Say the word," I said. "I'm ready anytime."

"We'll see," he said. "Be patient."

Patience was my middle name. I hung around the Vietnamese for twelve years before one of them defected to my restaurant. "While we're being patient, what are you doing next weekend?" I asked. "Why don't you come out to my parents' house? I'll get my dad to barbecue." Han shook his head.

"Don't worry, he won't mention the war." I laughed. "You want to be cooped up in New York? It's less than twenty miles away. No special permissions. I've got my parents' pool fixed up. Bring anybody you want from the embassy and your swim trunks. We can race. You too chicken to race?"

He smiled. "No newspapers?"

"No newspapers," I said. "Just family."

I called Dad, who was beside himself. "You're not bringing any of those dirtbags into my house!" he shouted.

"They're my friends," I said.

"Pull your head out. They aren't friends. I know these people; I fought against them. They are enemy cocksuckers who will stick their dick in your ass."

Suddenly I was eleven years old again. Back then, Dad yelled at me for hanging around kids who were mobbed up, flunking out of school, and into drugs. Now it was a political problem. There's no pleasing the guy. I reminded him that the only reason his pool was fixed was that I had paid for it with profits from Cubby's. He owed me. "Try to be polite," I said. "That's all I ask."

I called McCreary and told him the North Koreans were coming over for a Memorial Day barbecue. I could almost hear him shaking his head in disbelief on the phone.

"For some bizarre reason, they're letting Han hang around with you," he said. "Don't get your hopes up. Nobody has ever had a meaningful relationship with a member of the North Korean government."

I appreciated McCreary. He always took my calls, and he freely offered me his expertise and guidance. But I felt like he was jealous, too. He said he couldn't meet Han himself, either officially or unofficially, because of his position with the Pentagon. Although you'd think an intelligence guy should be doing exactly what I was doing, McCreary said it wasn't in his job description. The amazing thing was that it wasn't in the job description of anybody in our government.

I hoped McCreary respected me, but I sensed that deep down he felt that if the dictatorship in Pyongyang wanted to work with an American, they should have chosen more carefully. It didn't seem bizarre to me. The North Koreans needed to change their relationship with the United States, and it didn't take a Harvard-educated genius to figure out that Han didn't know where to start. The only people he knew were the other North Koreans, and the only people *they* knew were Iranians and Syrians and other enemies of the United States. Han was looking for more—a deeper understanding of what America was about. At least that's the way I decided to interpret it.

"So far I'm the only one willing to put the time in," I told McCreary.

"I want you to be very clear that they're not coming forward because they want to be friends," he said. "They can't feed eighty percent of their people, and if they don't do something their regime will collapse."

The sun shone bright and hot and a breeze whipped through the skyscrapers of Manhattan as I picked Han up outside his embassy on 72nd Street. He'd brought along a lower-ranking embassy guy named Shun Hak Ban, who climbed in the backseat and asked if it was okay to smoke. I handed him a piece of beef jerky and told him he should have more respect for his body and my upholstery.

As we crossed the George Washington Bridge the tires of the Explorer whined against the pavement. Han whistled absentmindedly, and after a few notes the words floated through my head: "All around the mulberry bush, the monkey chased the weasel . . ."

"How the fuck do you know that song?" I asked. "You learn that in school?"

Han finished the line in a thick Korean accent: "'The monkey stopped to pull up his sock, pop goes the weasel.' In the Army," he said. "On the DMZ."

"When were you there?" I asked. Han shrugged, and I could tell that, even though they worked closely together, he didn't want to go into details with Shun in the backseat. Later he told me he was stationed on the DMZ for two years in the late seventies, around the time that I was meeting the Vietnamese and using my weekly roofer's paycheck to buy eight-balls of coke. He said that almost every night the soldiers on the other side would blast American songs from loudspeakers to torment the North Koreans. He knew all the words to "Yankee Doodle," "My Country 'Tis of Thee," and "Love Me Tender."

We had an hour to kill before we were expected at my parents' house. I drove by the North Jersey Clay Target Club, where I worked as a kid. A couple of marksmen stood on the gravel shooting pads holding twelve-gauge shotguns. Beyond them, a meadow stretched toward a stand of birch trees. I rolled down the windows and slowed to a crawl so Han could get a good look at the shooters. They called for targets, tracked the targets, and fired: "Pull!" *Crack.* "Pull!" *Crack.*

"You like to shoot?" I asked. Han nodded. "I'll take you hunting one of these days."

I pointed out the bunkers where, during the blazing summer months, I loaded the tar-coated birds onto the mechanical arm of the trap, imagining myself behind enemy lines in Vietnam. I forced myself to keep still and told myself that if I were held prisoner, they'd put me in a hotbox like this. I stayed in the bunker for hours. My legs cramped up. I played mind games with my-self, breathing deep and getting negative thoughts out of my head, until I was ready for a hostile environment.

"Maybe your government doesn't let me have a weapon," Han said. "Don't forget, I'm enemy."

"I know the guys here," I said. "You want to shoot? We'll shoot. No prob-lem. America and the DPRK will shoot together."

I drove a few miles, past my elementary school and the office building where I used to mow Bobby Vesco's lawn. Shun leaned forward until his head was between our seats.

"Why do your leaders want to destroy our government?" he asked. I liked Shun. He was direct, but easygoing. And he obviously had enough status to speak up in front of Han, his superior. He sounded genuinely curious.

"They don't," I said. "Washington doesn't want to see you guys collapse."

Han looked at me like I was a complete moron. "They say they do," he said. "All the time."

"But they don't really want it. Look what happened when East Germany went bust. The wall came down. The economy of West Germany went to shit. Refugees flooded across the border. Nobody wants to see that in Korea. Mc-Creary told me that."

"He did?"

"That's what they say at the Pentagon, behind closed doors. Unofficial version. I talked to him about it the other day."

Han exchanged a look with Shun. "You need to tell me when you get opin-ions from behind closed doors," he said as though I'd been holding out on him.

Maybe an "unofficial version" carried extra weight with him. In his coun-try, the government controlled what people said. An unofficial version was probably hard to come by. I wondered if he would communicate some of what I said back to Pyongyang. He had to file a report every day, and that was a lot of space to fill.

I slipped a cassette into my tape player, and when the first tune started I tapped the steering wheel a couple of times and sang along with the tape: "'Wake up, Maggie, I think I've got something to say to you.'"

"You like this music?" I asked Han.

He listened for a few moments. "Not bad," he said. "But the singer sounds like he has a sore throat."

"He's Scottish. It's supposed to be sexy." And that was how I initiated Han into the wonders of rock and roll. We listened to many hours of music together over the years to come, and my favorites became his favorites: Steely Dan, Celine Dion, the Eagles. He liked soft rock for its relaxing qualities, same as me.

"What are those?" Han asked. We were deep into residential Fairfield now. Small lawns and oil-stained driveways gave way to houses set back fifteen yards or so from the street. I realized this was their first visit to suburbia.

I turned to Shun. "Do *you* know what they are?"

"Are they for birds?" he asked. I shook my head. He thought about it a few more seconds. "Religious offering?"

"It's where the mail gets delivered. They open at the front. See the little metal flag? When you want to send something, you put it up."

"They don't have locks," Han said. He'd been watching cops and murder investigation shows on TV at night, and he was obsessed with the American crime rate. "Doesn't the mail get stolen?"

"Are you kidding me?" I said. "It's a federal offense, like robbing a bank." I explained the differences between state and federal crimes and between misdemeanors and felonies—and that each one had its own level of punishment.

"What's worse," Shun asked, "stealing mail or stealing money?"

"It depends on how it's done," I said. "Armed robbery is more serious than pickpocketing." I pretended to pull a wallet out of my back pocket, to demonstrate pickpocketing. "What happens to a thief in Pyongyang? You cut his hands off?"

Shun sat back in his seat. Han stared out the window at a minimall with a Dunkin' Donuts, a discount nail salon, and a pizza joint. It was obvious I'd asked a sensitive question. "We don't have a crime problem in the DPRK," Han said.

We turned onto my parents' street and I pointed out the yard where Big Mike and Little Mike used to beat me up and the house where Jimmy lived when he came back all messed up from the Vietnam War. Our neighborhood was on the edge of the boonies, so the lots had at least ten feet more grass between them than the ones we'd driven past in the rest of Fairfield. As we pulled in my parents' driveway, I saw a piece of gutter hanging down from the eaves that Dad hadn't fixed like I'd asked him to. I hoped Han wouldn't notice.

We walked through the house to the back patio, where everybody else was. Lilia sat on a lawn chair watching Andrea play patty-cake with Dave Bratton, who I invited so Han would see another familiar face. Dad stood at the barbecue, scowling as the smoke rose from a couple of pieces of chicken. He wore a wife-beater that showed off the contrast between his milky white biceps and the reddish brown of his neck and forearms. I closed the screen door with a bang, but he didn't look up.

Lilia and Bratton stood up and shook hands warmly with Han and Shun. Han squatted down and told Andrea she was very pretty, and that he had two daughters about her age in Korea.

"Dad," I said. "This is Mr. Han Song Ryol and Mr. Shun Hak Ban."

"How ya' doin?" he said, without looking up. He held up a long spatula as a way of greeting us and stared at the grill as though something very fascinating was happening in the embers.

"Don't you want to say hello?" I asked.

"I just did," he said. He held up his other hand, which was gloved with an oven mitt, and pointed furiously at the chicken as an excuse for not shaking hands.

We stood there awkwardly watching him poke at the grill with the spatula for a few moments. Finally, Lilia asked the Koreans if they wanted a beer. "You have Bud?" Han asked.

I went over to the barbecue and kept my back to our guests. "What's wrong with you?" I whispered. "I thought you were going to be polite."

After Lilia had gotten drinks for everybody, Han raised his beer glass. "Thank you for welcoming us to your family," he said. All of us raised our glasses but my dad. Han turned to Lilia. *"Me dice Bobby que usted es de Mexico,"* he said, asking something about Mexico.

"Habla Español!" she beamed at him. He was the first person I ever introduced her to who spoke her language.

"They teach you Spanish in the DPRK?" I asked.

Han sipped his Bud. "Before I came to New York, I was stationed in Cuba."

Dad's eyebrows went up so fast I thought they'd shoot off the top of his head. He gave me a gloating look as if to say, "I told you so." He threw a few wieners and buns on the grill.

I told Han I had a surprise for him. I went to the Explorer and brought back a cassette I'd picked up at a Korean shop near Han's apartment building in Spanish Harlem. I popped it into the tape deck in the living room and opened a window so we could hear it better on the patio. A traditional Korean folk song came warbling out of the speakers.

"No, no!" Han said. "We listen to Korean music in Korea. Put the other one. I need to learn American experience. Understand?"

I put on a tape of the Steve Miller Band. "You want the American experience?" I asked Han. "You guys have come to the right place." I looked around at our little party and thought of the diversity we represented. We had a minister, an immigrant, a roofer, his wife, and an entrepreneur. It wasn't the kind of A-list gathering we had at Cubby's before the Nets game, but already I was introducing the North Koreans to a wide variety of people. "I'll give you the whole smorgasbord," I said.

"What's smorgasbord?" Shun asked.

"You don't know smorgasbord? It's a buffet. Like at a Chinese restaurant."

"How do you say it again?" Han asked. I sounded out the word for him. "Smor-gas-bord," he said. "It's what you call a Chinese buffet?"

"Just a buffet," I said. "It's serve yourself. You take your plate up, put whatever you want on it, and then take it back to your table. Like that place next to Blockbuster in your neighborhood—"

"I know what a buffet is," Han said.

Bratton cleared his throat. "It's a Swedish word," he said. "It means 'sandwich table.'"

"That's right," I said. "But it's also got meatballs and scalloped potatoes."

"Why did you say it was Chinese?" Han asked.

"I didn't," I said. "What the fuck difference does it make? It's a buffet. Chinese buffet, smorgasbord—why do you want to pick apart every word I tell you?"

"Because if I use it, it has to be correct," he said. "I can't afford to make mistakes."

"Come and get it!" Dad cried. He set a tray of chicken, burger patties, wieners, and buns on a glass table.

After lunch, we changed into our swim trunks and sat around the pool enjoying the warm sunshine. Dad stayed in the shade of the patio with a day-old *Record*.

"Who wants to race?" Bratton asked, looking back and forth at me, Han, and Shun. Han stood up and shook his arms and legs. I probably should have told him that Bratton was a former competitive swimmer. They agreed on four laps of the short pool and took their places at one end. Bratton hunched over into launch position. Han put his arms back like a skier. Lilia and I counted off the ready-set-go, and they dove in. A few seconds later when Bratton executed his first flip turn, he was already a body length ahead. Han churned the water without looking up. After two more laps Bratton was a pool length ahead. He glided to the finish line, touched the wall, and bounced up triumphantly. Dad came out from the patio and stood with his arms folded, and we all watched Han complete the last lap of shame. He hoisted himself out of the pool, breathing hard and dripping wet. When Bratton got out he looked at me apologetically, like he realized that the diplomatic thing to do might have been to let Han win the race.

"Horseshoes?" Dad asked. Bratton toweled off and joined him on a little strip of ryegrass behind the pool, where Dad had pounded two stakes into the dirt. Lilia and Shun followed, leaving Han and me alone for the first time that day. I got a can of Bud for him and a Diet Coke for myself and we sat side by side on deck chairs to soak up the sun. I closed my eyes.

The Steve Miller Band's "Fly Like an Eagle" wound down, and in the space between songs a Weedwhacker's motor hummed somewhere in the distance. Horseshoes clinked against each other as they landed in the ryegrass. I heard one thwack into a wooden stake. "Right there, suckers!" Dad yelled. From the edge in his voice I guessed he was throwing against Shun. It was going to be USA-2, DPRK-0. I squeezed some sunscreen out of a tube and spread it on my nose.

"You think I can jump through that?" Han asked. I sat up. Andrea's inflatable life preserver floated in the middle of the pool. A grinning duck's head popped out of one side, and its hole looked only about a foot wide.

"No way," I said. "I know *I* couldn't."

Han leapt up from the chair, took three running steps, and launched himself over the water. His body hung gracefully in midair in the shape of an inverted V for a moment, then he kicked his feet skyward and fell, arms first, through the donut hole of Andrea's floaty toy. He burst out of the water with a big grin on his face for having redeemed himself for losing the race against Bratton. He retook his place on the lounge chair and looked around the yard to see where everybody was. "Let's see you try it, motherfucker."

I laughed. It was the first time Han had ever dropped the F-bomb. He sounded like he was testing it out to see how he liked it. "Your English is improving!" I said.

We leaned back. The afternoon sun warmed my skin. "Good thing about those exercises getting cancelled, right?" I said, referring to Operation Team Spirit, the practice maneuvers between the U.S. and South Korean forces that took place every spring and completely pissed off the North Koreans. Clinton had put them on hold as a conciliatory gesture a few weeks earlier. If I could get a reaction from Han, it could be worth reporting to McCreary and Kuhlmeier.

"They are imperialist provocation," he said. Now he was spouting the official B.S., or at least what I understood of the official B.S., about how Operation Team Spirit got started in the first place. But I had done my own reading, to back up what I'd learned from McCreary.

Operation Team Spirit was a quote-unquote defensive military exercise that President Carter started in 1977, after the DPRK attacked a group of soldiers who were trimming a tree. It's hard to imagine that the world's most militarized nation, the DPRK, almost went to war against the most powerful military in human history over a tree. But it happened.

The tree stood in the demilitarized zone, next to the farthest forward observation post of the United Nations Command. It was a poplar tree, and every spring its branches sprouted with shade-giving leaves that hid the observation post from other friendly posts on the South Korean side, making it more vulnerable to the North Korean enemy. To fix this, thirteen American and South Korean troops entered the DMZ before dawn one morning in 1976, armed only with axes. They set up ladders and hacked branches off the poplar, making as little noise as possible. The North Koreans caught wind of the operation, however, and blared warnings that the tree cutters had violated the terms of the border area. When the American engineers kept chopping, dozens of armed North Korean soldiers rushed in, took away their axes, and beat them with the handles. The North Koreans clubbed two Americans to death. At least that's the official version in our history books. I was sure the North Koreans had a different version that makes them look better.

But what happened next is well documented. Three days later, the United States and allied Republic of Korea troops launched Operation Paul Bunyan, a surprise move to get rid of the tree once and for all and send a message to Pyongyang. At seven A.M., in broad daylight, sixteen military engineers with chain saws entered the DMZ, backed up by two lightly armed, thirty-man platoons, who were backed by sixty-four Korean special forces and a U.S. infantry company. The North Korean soldiers saw them. What they didn't see at first was that twenty-seven attack helicopters lurked just out of sight. Above the helicopters, B-52 bombers and F-4 fighters patrolled the skies above the operation. The aircraft carrier USS *Midway* moved directly offshore.

The North Koreans sent two hundred soldiers armed with machine guns and assault rifles to confront the tree cutters. U.S. commanders gave the signal, and the attack helicopters and F-4 fighter jets rose up on the horizon. As the engineers went to work cutting down the poplar tree, the North Koreans started shooting at the helicopters. The situation escalated to within a trigger pull of a full-scale battle.

The Cobra gunners took aim at the North Korean positions. As their lasers locked on target, the Koreans must have realized they were screwed, because they stopped shooting. The tree came down minutes later, and the forces pulled back to their respective sides of the DMZ. War was averted, at least for the time being. The engineers left a tall stump, as a memorial to the two dead Americans and a reminder to Pyongyang that when America wants to cut down a tree, step aside.

"U-S-A!" Dad shouted. He'd just landed a perfect horseshoe throw. He celebrated his victory over Shun, the evil commie bastard, by high-fiving Bratton.

"Why did your soldiers kill those two guys?" I asked Han. "They were just doing some pruning."

"Were you there?" he asked. "Do you know the whole story? If you weren't there, then you don't know. Just because you read it in your history book doesn't mean your government isn't lying. Did you think of that?"

It was a strange thing to hear from a guy compelled to believe his own country's official version of events. It's not like he was there and had some special knowledge, either. Because he was my age, he was too young to have been stationed at the DMZ during the Paul Bunyan affair. Maybe some of his older buddies or relatives had been there. Out of politeness I didn't push him about it, but I couldn't help thinking that if Han expected me to question my government's version of events, then maybe he was willing to question his. Maybe he was speaking to me in code, trying to tell me that behind the official Han, who was obliged to spout government propaganda, there was a real man with his own opinions.

Han lay back and closed his eyes. "Put some of this on your face," I said, holding out the tube of sunscreen. "You need to protect your skin." Han took the tube and dabbed cream on his face. He already looked older than when he arrived seven months earlier. Little stress lines creased the corners of his mouth and eyes, even when he held his face still. I knew that look. It was the look of a guy in the Mafia who'd gotten jammed up. It was the look of a guy keeping loyal, trying his best not to make the wrong move or offend his bosses. You could say any guy in America with a job has this kind of stress, but the difference with the mob or a regime like North Korea is that if you offend the wrong people, you end up dead.

In a mob family you're judged by what you bring them today, not what you did yesterday or what you promise for tomorrow. You've got to be an earner. It's a constant struggle. I could hardly imagine the pressure Han must have been under as the North Korean in charge of American affairs. He was supposed to bring them closer ties to the United States. I had no idea what restrictions his government in Pyongyang was putting on him. But Washington wasn't exactly ready to cozy up and be friends.

Han twisted the cap back on the tube of sunscreen and handed it to me. "You think the war is over," he said. "But it's not."

4

≈≈≈≈≈≈≈≈≈≈

Pinned in the
Hermit Kingdom

"YOU SURE THIS IS A GOOD IDEA?" Bratton asked. The Russian-made jet bounced and shuddered as it descended into North Korean airspace. Through the pressurized window, we could make out gray rectangles of rice fields that looked like concrete slabs. A few clusters of trees dotted the earth, but we saw no houses, buildings, or any other signs of people in the world's most isolated and mysterious nation. We were about to enter the Black Hole.

Bratton bowed his head and started to pray. I looked up and down the aisle at the other passengers. Besides me and Bratton, there were about thirty Asians in cheap business suits, a couple of tall Africans with colorful hats, and three Middle Eastern–looking guys wearing robes. Nobody talked. Everybody stared straight ahead like they were going to their own funeral. It was the only international flight into Pyongyang that day.

A flight attendant came over with a plastic bag to collect the remains of the sandwiches she'd given us at the beginning of the hour-and-a-half flight from Beijing. She wore a red skirt suit, a pink floppy bow, and a stern expression on her face. Her hair was pulled back in a bun. Over her left breast she wore a small pin with the face of Kim Il Sung on it. I caught a whiff of a light, flowery fragrance and was impressed. Even though she came from a sealed-off, totalitarian regime, she seemed to have a more tasteful perfume than the thick, sweet-smelling stuff a lot of the ladies wear in New Jersey.

"Nice pin," I said. She gave me a little commie pout and pretended she didn't understand. "So tell me," I asked, leaning toward her and lowering my voice, "where are the hotspots in Pyongyang? Is it a party town? The Vegas of the DPRK?"

No response. She didn't try to joke around like American flight attendants do. I picked up the sandwich container and tried to sweep some uneaten hunks of bread off my tray table into the bag she held open, but I used too much force and overshot it. A piece of crust bounced off her skirt and left some crumbs sticking to the thigh area. I wanted to do her a favor and brush off the fabric with my fingers, but another look at her face told me this was not a good idea, so I stopped my hand in midair.

"Is your friend going to be sick?" she asked.

I glanced at Bratton, who leaned forward with his eyes closed, deep in prayer. I put my hand on his shoulder. "You okay, buddy?" I joked. "The stewardess is worried about you."

Bratton folded his hands in his lap but kept his eyes closed. "Can't you take anything seriously?" he said. He brought his hands back up to resume praying. "You may want to join me."

Bratton was nervous because Han had made all the arrangements and told us nothing beforehand. Han said the trip was his way of having me checked out in Pyongyang to see if we could take our relationship to the next level. It was like when you're a kid and you've been on a few dates, you finally have to go to the parents' house and shake hands with the girl's father and say, "Pleased to meet you, Mr. So-and-So. No, I don't drink or do drugs. Yes, I'll take very good care of your daughter." It's also exactly what happens when somebody gets inducted into a Mafia family. Before you can be a made guy, you get brought around to meet the boss. You get vetted. "It's important," Han had said. "You'll have to pay homage to our leaders."

"You mean get down on my hands and knees or something? That's not really me," I said.

"If you're going to get anywhere with us, you will."

The autumn of 1994 was a very delicate time between our nations. A few months earlier, after the Clinton Administration considered arming South Korea with short-range nukes, former President Carter flew to the DPRK and convinced Kim Il Sung to reopen negotiations about his nuclear program. Carter's visit in June went off without any problems, and I thought, great, he's paved the way for me and Bratton. He's tested the waters. How many guys from Jersey get a former president as their crash test dummy?

Things were more complicated now, though. Three weeks after Carter left, the Great Leader died suddenly of a heart attack, throwing the DPRK's political system off balance while everybody wondered when and if his son, Kim Jong Il, would take over. A power vacuum is the most dangerous thing in the world.

"Why are you bringing a religious man with you?" Han had asked.

"Insurance," I'd said. "If anything happens to me, I need somebody to perform my last rites." It was one of the first times I saw Han laugh spontaneously. But I wasn't kidding about insurance. There were rumors that the North Koreans routinely kidnapped foreigners and forced them to work for the regime in Pyongyang: Americans who played bad guys in their movies; Japanese who made sushi; Romanian hookers. What if Kim Jong Il had a secret love for BBQ? What if he'd sent Han to lure me to Pyongyang, where I'd soon find myself chained to a broiler in the kitchen of one of his palaces?

I asked Bratton to come along so that, if something went wrong, it wouldn't just be a one-column obituary in *The Record*. "Restaurant Owner Missing" wasn't going to grab the same headlines as "New York Giants Chaplain Detained in North Korea." If the trip went south, the Giants would come to the rescue of their holy man. Rodney Hampton or one of his teammates would call a press conference, and the media would put pressure on our government. It was like the two American women who were arrested in North Korea in 2009. After five months as Pyongyang's "guests," they were eventually released because they were journalists and they had Al Gore and Bill Clinton behind them. A guy who flips burgers in Hackensack wasn't going to get that kind of attention.

Bratton had his own motives for coming. In a small duffel bag at his feet he carried four English-language Bibles, which he planned to leave with anyone he met in North Korea who showed an interest. The only problem was that owning a Bible was illegal in North Korea, and distributing them could get you put to death by hanging. Han assured me that his government would make an exception for Bratton. But he was nervous, I could tell. He was praying.

My own preparations had been minimal. I didn't have a credit card, so I paid for my ticket by dipping into the cash I needed for sales taxes on Cubby's receipts. Han secured our visas in Beijing, and all I did was pack a bag, reorganize the shifts at the restaurant, and get to the airport.

Lilia was against the trip from the start because it meant leaving her to run Cubby's by herself, with our four-year-old daughter and five grand in un- paid meat bills to worry about. And she read the newspaper. "You don't know what could happen," she said.

"You got to understand," I begged. "This is my chance."

"Your chance for what?"

"To play in the big arena," I said. "To walk in a president's shoes. You know who gets invited to Pyongyang by a North Korean ambassador? A VIP. Big shots like Jimmy Carter and Billy Graham. And now Bobby Egan. I can't *not* go."

Lilia put her head on my shoulder and I planted a big kiss on the top of her head. I told her I'd make it up to her and Andrea as soon as I got home. "Just stay out of trouble," she said, punching me in the ribs.

We touched down on a runway in the middle of a flat, empty field. A couple of MiG fighter jets sat at one end of the airfield but otherwise the place was completely empty. We walked across the tarmac to the terminal, which looked like it was built in the fifties and left untouched. A giant portrait of Kim Il Sung loomed over us as we entered. Inside the terminal there were no other travelers, but lots of workers. Everywhere we looked, somebody was mopping or wiping something. The faded plastic shone with polish. It was so clean you could lick the floor. Outside a window several women knelt in the grass, trim- ming the edge of the lawn with scissors.

Four men in gray suits met us in the arrivals area. Our lead handler was a short, stocky guy who looked like an Asian Danny DeVito on steroids. "You ever see the movie *Get Shorty?*" I whispered to Bratton. Shorty told us to hand over our cell phones and passports and said they'd be returned when we left the country. Digging through our luggage they found Bratton's four Bibles. They walked away a few yards and argued among themselves, pointing back and forth between the Bibles and us. Then they returned the books without another word and escorted us to a minivan waiting in front of the terminal building.

We rode for nearly half an hour through flat fields before we saw the first tall, communist-style apartment buildings of Pyongyang. Willow trees, pines, and sycamores lined city streets as wide as rivers. Gardeners had painted the bottom section of each trunk white to keep insects from damaging the trees, and on every street corner they'd trimmed hedges and shrubs into perfect spheres and cubes. There were no telephone poles, wires, satellite dishes, or any of the other things that clutter the rest of the world's cities and towns. Pyongyang had no billboard advertisements, no neon signs, and even the commercial-looking buildings announced themselves with modest plaques in Korean. Red banners hung from the gray and white buildings. The city looked fresh and clean.

We passed some empty buses and trolleys, but other than that there was almost no traffic. About halfway into the city, a 1950s-era military truck rolled by. Soldiers held onto the wooden slats and oversized fenders for balance. Everything looked like it was lifted from an old movie. Instead of streetlights, the intersections were presided over by traffic women, and I murmured in appreciation as we passed the first one. She stood in a white painted circle in the middle of the street, with a baton in one hand and a whistle in her mouth. She wore a matching blue jacket, necktie, and skirt, white socks, and white gloves. Her bare, muscular calves flexed nicely as she pivoted in her sturdy, high-heeled shoes.

"No wonder the Dear Leader wants to keep foreigners out of your country!" I said to Shorty, who sat in front of us next to a handler with a wide gap between his front teeth. Neither of them smiled.

We stared at the few pedestrians on the sidewalks. Groups of soldiers stood around in olive green military uniforms. Civilians strolled the sidewalks in pairs and alone. The men wore suits and ties, or shirts tucked neatly into their pants. The women wore knee-length skirts and jackets that looked freshly ironed. Everyone looked perfect; I couldn't get over it. I'd been expecting a gloomy, poverty-stricken place, and here were beautifully landscaped hedges and neatly dressed people. No one looked at us. Weren't they curious? Had the Dear Leader forbidden people to look at foreigners?

"The Arc de Triomphe," the gap-toothed handler said as we approached a huge freestanding archway. "Same as the one in Paris, but three meters taller."

The Great Leader and his generals must have ordered those dimensions to show off to the few outsiders they let into the country. They seemed obsessed with being seen as a major player on the world stage. They wanted international recognition. Esteem. And as Bratton and I rolled through Pyongyang that afternoon the only thing standing in Pyongyang's way was the deep mistrust between them and Washington.

Carter's visit had opened the door for a non-binding commitment called the Agreed Framework. Under that agreement, Pyongyang would dismantle its five-megawatt nuclear reactor at Yongbyong and stop building two slightly larger ones, and Washington would help provide two state-of-the-art, thousand-megawatt reactors that ran on "light water" and couldn't be used to produce atomic weapons. The light-water reactors would be built and administered by an international organization funded by the United States and its allies called the Korean Peninsula Energy Development Organization (KEDO).

It seemed like a win-win deal. Under KEDO, the North Koreans would get a huge boost in their energy supplies, including half a million tons of heavy fuel oil a year while the reactors were under construction. The United States and its allies would breathe easier knowing that North Korea remained a party to the Non-Proliferation Treaty and had rid itself of its A-bomb-making potential once and for all. The two sides even agreed in principle to move toward normalized relations. The problem was that the generals in Pyongyang suspected Washington's main goal was to topple their regime.

We stopped at a wide square surrounding a sixty-five-foot bronze statue of Kim Il Sung. As we stepped out of the minivan a woman gave us a wreath of flowers, and our handlers motioned for us to lay it at the foot of the statue. The Great Leader towered over us as we walked forward—one hand on his hip and the other outstretched with his fingers pointing forward like he'd just tossed a bunch of birdseed into the air.

A group of what looked like high school students in blue and white uniforms bowed low in unison at the foot of the statue. When they finished, Bratton and I faced the giant bronze ankles of the Great Leader. It was our turn. Gap Tooth walked to the left of us with a video camera to record our bows. If this was the first test, I wanted to make a good impression. I propped the wreath next to the flowers that others had left and stepped back. "Go as low as you can," I said.

"Do we have to?" Bratton whispered. I looked over my shoulder. Shorty and the other handlers watched from behind.

"Pretend it's Jesus," I said. I bent my waist and lowered my chest toward the ground. I'd never really bowed before, so I tried to copy what I'd seen in old movies. I kept my arms straight at my sides and bent to a ninety-degree angle, like an Olympic swimmer about to jump into a pool. For the sake of the video camera, I held the pose long after Bratton bounced back up. I wondered if Han would ever see it.

On our way back to the van we took a detour through a small park, where we saw something I never would have expected: an ice-cone vendor with a little cart. Three well-dressed children lined up, despite the cool afternoon temperature. As we passed, a girl with her hair in pigtails reached for a paper cone filled with red ice. She looked about ten years old, and as she took the cone her face radiated pure joy. I thought, how can this country be all bad? Look how happy that girl is!

We arrived late in the afternoon at the Koryo Hotel, whose towers rose like two fat missiles aimed at the sky. The lobby was brightly lit with gold-colored ceilings, marble floors, and a painting of a waterfall near the reception area. Shorty and Gap Tooth escorted Bratton and me to our shared room. I didn't ask why they put us together: as far as I could tell, the place was

empty. Shiny silk bedspreads covered our single beds. A rotary phone connected to a receptionist downstairs, but I figured that was where the line
ended. Dave sat on one of the beds and switched on the TV. A news anchor
wearing what looked like a purple karate outfit spoke in Korean against a
plain blue background.

As we unpacked I heard shuffling and bumping noises on the other side
of our wall, so I went out into the hallway and noticed something I'd missed
on the way in. The doors were spaced farther apart than in any hotel I'd ever
seen. If the next room was the same size as ours, there had to be an extra space
between us. I put my ear up to the wall next to where I figured our room
ended. The paneling felt thin and loose under my fingers, and behind it I
heard whispering and more shuffling.

McCreary told me we'd be closely watched in Pyongyang, but I never
imagined they'd have guys peeping through holes in the walls. They weren't
trying very hard to hide. It almost seemed like they wanted us to know. If you
could say one thing about the North Korean security personnel, it's that they
were confident. They didn't flash weapons around like they do in New York
or Mexico. They didn't have to.

The safest, least scary countries in the world are the democracies like
Sweden, where the policemen don't carry weapons because the people are so
well-behaved. Then there are the democracies like the United States, which
puts armed police on the street because the people are less well-behaved.
Then there are the scary dictatorships, where order is kept by heavily armed
police and military, because you never know when the people might rise up in
rebellion. But the most frightening places in the world are the dictatorships
that look like Sweden at first. The police aren't armed because there's no need:
the eyes of the government are everywhere and the people are well-behaved
because the control over them is total. The citizens watch each other.

That night Bratton and I ate alone in the restaurant on the first floor of the
hotel. Outside the windows, Pyongyang had gone almost completely dark, in
the way cities must have looked ages ago, before streetlights took hold. A
waiter brought paper-thin slices of meat on a tray. With a pair of tongs, he

spread them onto a skillet to cook at the table. "Steak," Han had called it the first time I saw him and some of the embassy guys preparing it in their kitchen. "That's not steak!" I'd said. "Don't talk to me about steak unless it's T-bone, porterhouse, or rib-eye. Nothing under twenty-two ounces, baby."

"That's why you're so big," he said.

"You think anybody over one hundred and ten pounds is big." I'd noticed that Han had already put on a few pounds in his first few months in New York. But his countrymen were all thin. On average, kids Andrea's age from North Korea are fifteen pounds lighter and five inches shorter than those from South Korea. Our waiter couldn't have been much over a hundred pounds. When he came back with little trays of vegetables and sides of kimchee, I asked if he wanted to join us. He didn't understand, or at least pretended not to. "Very hot," the waiter warned, pointing at the kimchee.

"You kidding me?" I said. "You ever have a habanero pepper? You don't know hot until you've had a habanero pepper. You get yourself over to Jersey and Lilia and I will take you to Mexican—my treat—and for one thing we'll fatten you up. And for another, you'll be crying into your beans as soon as you even *look* at a habanero pepper. Kimchee is for sissies." The waiter nodded and went off.

"We should have an itinerary," Bratton said. "I don't like this not knowing what we're going to do tomorrow."

I couldn't see what he had to complain about. Everything was going smoothly. The city was clean and full of well-dressed people. He'd gotten his four Bibles into North Korea, which was a remarkable feat and a sign that they had confidence in us. Han said our handlers would test us throughout our trip, and I felt like we'd passed the first test at the Kim Il Sung statue. We showed we were not afraid to bow to their leader.

"Just see what happens," I said. "We'll build some trust."

The next morning, Shorty and Gap Tooth drove us out of the city on a smooth, six-lane highway. It headed directly south toward the DMZ, and it clearly wasn't built for civilian traffic but for military convoys and columns of tanks in case they were needed in a hurry at the border with South Korea.

Only a few cars passed us, and I guessed they were carrying government officials or military brass.

As we left the capital we turned west onto another wide, empty highway toward the coast. We stopped at the mouth of Nampho Bay to see a dam that stretched miles across the inlet and kept salt water from flowing up the Taedong River and flooding the farmland. Shorty and the gang took us to a little green island in the middle of the dam, where we sat in a small auditorium and watched a film about its construction. There was a lot of underwater footage of scuba divers wearing old-style helmets as they prepared to set the foundations on the floor of the river. The North Koreans built the dam in the early eighties, and they were obviously proud of it. The handlers kept an eye on Bratton and me in the semidarkness. I watched the screen and tried not to fall asleep as the silhouetted men floated through streams of illuminated bubbles.

On our way back to Pyongyang we drove through rice paddies with little white pyramids piled here and there. "Salt?" I asked. Shorty nodded and said something to the driver, who pulled to the side of the road. Shorty got out of the van and held the door open for me. Gap Tooth put a hand on Bratton's arm and motioned for him to stay in his seat; then he followed us out of the van. I exchanged a surprised look with Bratton as they closed the van door, separating us.

"Come," Shorty said. He took me by the elbow and led me to the back of the van. My heart leapt into my throat. This was how people get executed. Somebody takes you out of a vehicle, forces you to kneel, and shoots you once in the back of the head. Before I thought about running, we reached the back bumper. Shorty marched a few paces in front of me. I thought he was going to lead me into the salt fields. At the edge of the road, he spun around to face me.

"You're CIA!" he shouted.

I rocked back on my heels in surprise. "I'm a private citizen," I said. I wondered if the term "private citizen" had any meaning in a country where everybody works for the government one way or the other. Gap Tooth stood behind Shorty and crossed his arms.

"We know it already," Gap Tooth said. "Don't lie." He was like a wife who suspects her husband is cheating and brings it up at an unexpected moment to see how he reacts.

"You know it?" I said. "Then why don't you tell me where my paycheck is."

"You're a funny guy," Shorty said. He took a half step back and shifted some of his weight to his left leg. The fighter in me reacted instinctively. There was no other way to interpret his body language.

"I'm a funny guy?" I rocked back into a boxing stance. I didn't know where this was going, but they were testing me. If the episode at the statue had been a test of my humility, to see how low I would bow in front of the Great Leader, maybe this was a test of my spine. Maybe they wanted to see if I would stand up for myself. I had to gamble. From what I knew of Han, the North Koreans were macho guys. They liked typical guy stuff: a good meal, some nice-looking broads, and a show of strength. The absolute worst thing would be to show weakness. "You keep the sarcasm coming and we're going to dance," I said. I let my arms hang loose, ready for action. "You want to dance with me, pal?"

Shorty moved to my right, and I moved with him. I didn't want to get into a position where he was in front of me and Gap Tooth was behind me. Who knew if he carried a weapon in his coat there? Shorty turned half-sideways, setting his feet for some martial arts action. He looked buff and scrappy, with a low center of gravity. If the punching started I figured my best shot was to stay outside where I could use my longer arms and legs to my advantage. We shuffled away from the van, like a couple of crabs facing off. "I don't dance with men," he said.

"I don't mean 'dance,'" I said. "We can have it out, you and me. Right here on the road." He widened his stance and put his fists up, and so did I. "We can go toe-to-toe," I said. "I'll go a few rounds. You want a piece of me?" Through the rear window of the van I could see Bratton's worried face peering over his seat as he tried to see what was happening.

"You want to hit me," Shorty said. It was a statement, not a question. "Go ahead." I wasn't stupid enough to throw the first punch. On the other hand, once we were fighting I didn't have a witness to say that I hadn't started it. It wasn't like we were ever going in front of a judge anyway. If the North Koreans wanted to put me in prison they could do it anytime they wanted.

"First one's on me," I said. I dropped my hands and stuck my chin out. "Take your best shot. I'm all yours."

Shorty looked over his shoulder at Gap Tooth. They said a bunch of stuff to each other in Korean, and both of them burst out laughing. "What?" I asked in confusion. They looked at me, but they didn't say anything as their cackling continued. They turned and walked back to the van. I followed, wondering if they were just messing with me. Or had this been a test? And if it was a test, did I pass?

The next morning I was sitting on the toilet, brushing my teeth and reading a story in the government's English-language *Korea News* about farmers dedicating their crops to the Great Leader, when Bratton barged into the bathroom. "You're using my toothbrush!" he shouted. He looked like a boy who'd discovered another kid eating his candy.

I took the toothbrush out of my mouth and examined it. "They're exactly the same," I said. "How was I supposed to know?"

"They're different colors!" he wailed. "Now I can't use either one."

"Of course you can," I said. I sucked the toothpaste out of the bristles and held it up to him. "We can rinse it off in the sink."

He put up his hand to reject the toothbrush and turned his face away in disgust. "And you're using my toothbrush *while* you're going to the bathroom." He stormed out.

"I'm healthy!" I shouted after him. "What's the big deal?"

I didn't notice that the newspaper had fallen to the floor. Ordinarily I would have picked it up and put it in the wastebasket because Bratton was a stickler for cleanliness and I was trying to be a good roommate. But our little argument distracted me. I finished my business on the toilet, rinsed the toothbrush in the sink, and sat it upright to dry.

"You have no idea what kind of microbes are living inside that brush," Bratton said when I returned to the bedroom.

I put my hand on his shoulder. "You're worried about what happened on the road yesterday, aren't you?"

"I'm worried about everything. These people aren't normal."

"I think they were testing me, to see if I would lose my cool," I said. "We can't lose our cool." I lowered my voice and pointed my elbow at the wall. "Remember they're watching everything we do."

Just then there was a knock on our door. Shorty, Gap Tooth, and the driver stood in the hallway. "You are going to see the War Museum," Shorty said. "Five minutes."

The Victorious Fatherland Liberation War Museum sits on the Pothong River and was built to promote the North Korean version of what we call the Korean War and they call the War of American Aggression. Outside stood a bronze monument of giant, heroic-looking Koreans gazing into the distance with weapons and flags. Inside, a young guide gave us a short speech about the bravery and self-reliance of the workers of the DPRK. Afterward, he led us to a timeline of how the Korean War started when Americans and their "puppet allies" in South Korea launched a surprise attack on defenseless North Korean peasants in June 1950. Nearby, several cabinets contained documents, typewritten in English, shown as evidence that U.S. troops planned to invade North Korea long before the war began. Panoramas displayed how the peasants bravely abandoned their rice paddies and battled the Americans all the way to Seoul.

I was thinking: bullshit, propaganda. This must be another reason they kept their borders sealed, so their people wouldn't find out the truth about history. They could tell themselves a version of events that had them smelling like roses for as long as they controlled all the information.

One room of the War Museum housed a replica of the USS *Pueblo*, a ship the North Koreans captured off their coastline in 1968, at the height of the Vietnam War, while its crew was allegedly on a spying mission for Washington. The government in Pyongyang had never returned the real ship, which was moored to the bank of the Taedong River.

Many of the rooms in the museum displayed American weapons, ammunition, and other trophies captured during the war. In the Hall of American Atrocities, grainy photos showed long rows of corpses said to be North Korean victims of massacre, beheading, torture, germ warfare, and other crimes supposedly committed by U.S. troops. There were a couple of handwritten "confessions" by U.S. pilots who had been taken prisoner. They described their intention to target North Korea, with hand-drawn diagrams of the bombs they meant to drop.

I wondered where they kept items that weren't on display. Was there evidence of what happened to our prisoners somewhere in their archives? McCreary had told me that after the cease-fire in 1953, some American POWs were transferred to China or the Soviet Union, where they either died quickly or rotted in prison for years.

"What about missing Americans?" I asked our guide.

He pointed to a cabinet that held canisters he said were filled with biological weapons and dropped on Pyongyang. "There were four hundred thousand people living in Pyongyang. Do you know how many bombs the American imperialist aggressors dropped on the city during the war? Four hundred thousand. One for every person." The man seemed as upset as if it had happened yesterday.

I remembered Han's words: "You think the war is over. But it's not." For North Korea it wasn't, anyway. In the United States we had other things to think about. We'd gone through a few more wars since then. Even veterans like my dad didn't talk about Korea much. But the DPRK was still fighting it, long after we'd stopped paying attention. It gave them a reason to stay in a constant state of emergency and martial law.

When we returned to our hotel that afternoon we found the door to our room thrown wide open. Inside, two maids and an elderly security guard were huddled next to one of the beds, pointing at something on top of it. I walked in, followed by Bratton. The older of the two maids turned and let out a shriek. She had a pinched expression like she'd eaten something bitter. "What's going on?" I asked. The pinch-faced maid said something in Korean to the younger maid, who bolted past us and ran down the hall toward the elevators. The security guard took a step back as I approached to see what they were looking at, but Pinch Face stood her ground. She spewed syllables at me like a machine gun—"Pa-pa-pa-pa!" She glared at me, trembling with rage. She pointed at the bed.

On the bedspread she had laid out the pages of the newspaper I'd read on the toilet that morning. The front page featured the story of the peasants who dedicated their crops to the late Kim Il Sung. Next to the story was a big portrait of the Great Leader himself. A footprint covered his face. I leaned down to inspect it more closely. The very obvious pattern of an American sneaker zig-zagged across his nose and forehead.

A moment later Shorty and Gap Tooth rushed into the room followed by the younger maid. They saw the newspaper and looked at me in horror as the pinch-faced maid shouted in Korean. Considering the godlike status of their Leader, stepping on his face was probably the most insulting thing I could have done. I'd come halfway around the world to impress Han's bosses and instead I'd committed the ultimate no-no.

Before the handlers could say anything, I turned to Bratton. "How could you do this?" I shouted. He looked completely dumbstruck, and I felt bad for him. But I was the leader of our two-man delegation, and if I was in trouble, we were both in trouble. "This is His Excellency, the almighty *generalissimo*!" I winked at Bratton to get him to play along. "You can't just put your foot on his picture. It's sacred!"

Shorty and the maid looked back and forth between us. Bratton held his palms out and shrugged, and for a second I thought he was going to spill the beans. I had a terrible thought. What if they'd hidden cameras in the bathroom or had somebody peeping through the wall who'd watched me put my foot on the newspaper myself? They would know I was lying, and that would make things much worse. Just like in the Mafia, if you make a mistake you should avoid getting caught, because it can be a very bad thing to get caught making a mistake. But getting caught lying about the mistake is the kind of double offense that can get your body dumped in a river somewhere.

Bratton and I stood quietly like kids about to be punished, while Shorty and Gap Tooth held a miniconference with the maids. Then Shorty carefully folded up the newspaper, shot Dave an icy look, and walked out of the room. The others followed him, and Dave closed the door behind them. "Why did you say that?" he asked.

I put a finger to my lips and gestured at the wall where we'd heard the spies. "Sometimes you've got to take one for the team," I whispered.

Our handlers let the incident go, but from that moment they never liked Dave. I heard about it from Han for years afterward. "What if it had been Jesus Christ?" he'd ask. "Would he have stepped on it then? He showed no remorse!"

The dog and pony show continued for another day and a half. Our handlers drove Bratton and me to the humble hut where Kim Il Sung was born, to the Children's Palace in central Pyongyang, where twelve thousand children study music, dance, and sciences every day, and to the giant Cultural Center for the arts on the bank of the Taedong River. We saw dozens of statues and monuments that I'd heard were paid for with money the United Nations gave Pyongyang in the seventies to feed its people.

Two days before we were scheduled to leave, Shorty and Gap Tooth told us to dress formally. I figured I was about to undergo another type of test. Half an hour later they ushered us downstairs to a black Mercedes and drove us a few blocks to a central square, which was full of men and women in uniform, tightly packed in rows. It was October 10, the anniversary of the founding of the Korean Worker's Party, and the city was as crowded as it had been empty during the previous days. They led us into one of the big government buildings and onto a wide balcony. Below us a sea of military caps filled the plaza. Shorty later claimed there were two hundred thousand people in the square that day. Some wore blue and white. Some wore olive green. Others wore brown. I couldn't make any sense of it.

A voice boomed out over the crowd, shouting something in Korean. All eyes were on the balcony of the adjacent building, about fifty yards away from us, where a bunch of old generals stood. McCreary later told me that was where the Great Leader's son, Kim Jong Il, would have stood, although he wasn't a speechmaker himself.

After we'd been there about twenty minutes, Shorty touched my elbow and told me to follow him for a private meeting, alone. "Very important," he said. I smoothed my hair back and straightened my tie. I was glad I'd brought my suit. I figured I was either going to an audience with a high-ranking official or else a quick and dirty end, and either way it would be good to be well-dressed. I whispered to Bratton that if I wasn't back that night he should find a way to call Han at the embassy in New York. And if that didn't work, he should call the Giants' office at the Meadowlands; get something in the newspapers, or have the Giants wear special armbands during their game on Sunday. Whatever he needed to do to make sure I didn't disappear into the Black Hole.

As I followed Shorty out of the hotel I kept thinking about that scene in *Goodfellas* where Joe Pesci thinks he's going to get initiated into the family, but when he arrives for the ceremony the room is empty. By the time he realizes it was all a setup, it's too late to run. Shorty had been nicer than usual all morning, and where I come from that's a warning flag. When a guy suddenly turns friendly, watch out.

As we entered the square, the crowd started to chant and a wall of noise hit me like a fist. Their voices chopped out syllables in unison. "What are they saying?" I shouted.

"They praise the Great Leader and the achievements of the Worker's Party," he shouted back. Everybody in the square had the same blank expression, the faraway, Jim-Jones look of people deep in a trance. It occurred to me that this wasn't just a form of government. It wasn't about communism or socialism. This was more like a religious cult. I wondered how much these people knew about the outside world. Even a well-traveled North Korean like Han had serious gaps in his knowledge. If he didn't know what a mailbox was, what did these people know?

McCreary told me the North Korean government was determined not to repeat the "mistakes" made by the commies in Russia or Eastern Europe, where messages broadcast by the BBC, Voice of America, and Radio Free Europe got across the border. Realizing they couldn't always jam signals from abroad, the North Koreans made it illegal to own modern radio equipment. The only radio a North Korean citizen could have was a 1960s-era valve set fixed to government frequencies. The state controlled television the same way and set up neighborhood watch committees to make sure nobody found a way to see foreign TV. There were no computers, no Internet, and no way to learn that the Korean War had ended fifty years earlier. Their only source of information about Americans was their government's crazy propaganda. Posters depicted us as two-legged wolves or evil-looking men with long, hairy noses who stabbed babies and threw them into the river. Others showed us cowering like sissies and getting our asses kicked by brave young North Korean men and women in smart uniforms. Schoolbooks asked children to solve math problems like: "Four brave uncles of the People's Army killed eight American wolf-bastards. How many American wolf-bastards did each brave uncle kill?" The whole country was psychologically stuck in a war against us, but did they actually believe all this stuff? When they got under the covers at night, away from their coworkers and neighbors, what were their private fears? Did they fear their own government or did they fear us, the big, hairy American monsters?

The chanting changed and the rows of people thrust their fists in the air. I was pretty sure that this time it was also, "Down with the United States!" or "Kill the American aggressors!" What was I doing here? I thought of Lilia running the restaurant and taking care of Andrea back home in Hackensack. I was stupid for coming. This mob was capable of anything. The dazed expressions and the bloodthirsty shouting—this was probably what crowds looked like in the old days just before they sacrificed virgins or pounded a stake into the heart of an infidel. If they turned my way and recognized me as an American, they might lynch me. Shorty might join them in pulling my limbs off, or he might flash a badge and disperse the mob. It was hard to tell. I wondered if the North Korean leadership had as much control over its people as Washington said it did.

I was relieved when Shorty led me through a narrow aisle in the crowd and into another building. Once we were inside, the chants seemed far away. We entered an empty room on the ground floor that had a couple of chairs and a picture of the Great Leader—nothing else. Shorty sat me in one of the chairs and stood behind me without saying anything. I watched the door and waited. Suddenly I missed the roar of the mob. Bad things happen when it's quiet. I

took a deep breath and exhaled slowly to control my nerves. The most important thing is to never let your adversary sense any fear in you. I learned this
from hunting in the woods. Bears, bobcats, dogs, and all other predatory
animals sense fear, even if you're not moving. I breathed steadily to slow my
heartbeat. Five minutes ticked by, and then the door opened. A man with a
video camera walked in, followed by a couple of officials in suits, including
one whose face I instantly recognized.

"Shun!" I said. I could have hugged him. I stood up and shook his hand
and we smiled at each other. Good memories of him swimming and playing
horseshoes at my parents' house came rushing back.

Shun held a small plastic box in front of him ceremonially, and I realized
he was presenting me with something. The guy with the video camera inched
forward as Shun opened the box slowly. Inside, a red lapel pin sat on the
kind of dark, spongy material you stick an engagement ring into. Except for
the fact that Shun didn't get down on one knee, it felt like he was proposing
marriage. The front of the circular medal was painted with the face of Kim Il
Sung in a heroic pose a lot like the one I had put my foot on a couple of days
before and bowed in front of the day we arrived.

"It's a loyalty pin," he said. "This is a very special occasion."

One of Shun's colleagues said I was only the second foreigner ever presented with a medal like this, after a Romanian guy who must have been a
good friend to the regime. He took it from its box and unhinged its pin. He
slid a couple of fingers behind the lapel of my suit jacket as he looked for
the right place to stick it. He was putting on a show for the cameraman, who
came in for a close-up.

"If it's a pledge of allegiance, I can't take it," I said.

"You don't have to tell anyone," Shun said.

I stood still as Shun's colleague clipped the pin behind my lapel. The video
man kept the camera trained on my face. They were probably curious whether
a U.S. citizen and suspected government agent would allow himself to wear
the pin of the Great Leader. Maybe they thought the video would compromise
me, and they could use it as a blackmailing tool later. The video guy zoomed
in further. Part of me felt queasy about accepting a medal of my country's

enemy, but overall I was flattered. I understood the symbolism of having it presented to me by a North Korean who had been to my father's house in America. They were accepting me. It was more than I'd ever gotten back home in the United States where, after thirty-four years of citizenship, the number of medals I'd received was zero.

Shun and his group stood back and applauded. I bowed—not as deeply as in front of the Great Leader's statue, but respectfully. Suddenly I felt different. The rows of chanting zombies no longer bothered me. I could go back out and walk through that crowd, and nobody was going to fuck with me as long as I had their government's pin on. For the first time, I felt like I was on the inside, not the outside.

"You okay? What happened?" Bratton asked when I returned to the hotel balcony. He said he'd been worried for the past hour and a half because Gap Tooth wouldn't tell him where they'd taken me. I showed him the Kim Il Sung pin.

"Shun gave it to me," I said.

"You saw Shun?" he asked. Bratton looked hurt that Shun hadn't come to see him, too. He held the pin up for a good look at it. "I wouldn't be so proud of having this," Bratton said.

"I think I passed," I said.

The morning of our last day in Pyongyang, Shorty and Gap Tooth announced that Bratton would be traveling south for a tour of the DMZ while I stayed in the capital. Bratton looked concerned, but I didn't ask questions. So far everything had gone smoothly.

Shorty escorted me outside to the black Mercedes. Our chauffeur drove us to the back entrance of a white three-story building with no markings or signs on it. I followed Shorty through a set of double doors, down an empty hall, and into a small room, where two thin men in lab coats stood next to a motherly-looking woman in her fifties. They greeted me in better English than our handlers spoke and asked if I would like to sit.

There was only one chair in the room: a cushy recliner that looked like it had been rescued from a bachelor pad in the seventies. As soon as I'd sat down and leaned back, Shorty left the room and closed the door behind him. These people were obviously high-ranking, but what was this place? I felt like I was in a disco-style dentist's chair, but there was no dental equipment around. Fluorescent tubes on the ceiling hummed with blue light. The room had no windows. The motherly woman leaned over the armrest, exposing a narrow tunnel of cleavage above the top button of her khaki blouse. She smiled and explained in a soothing voice that there were some "procedures" they had to go through.

"It's completely harmless," she said. "We're just going to put you under for a few minutes. Is that all right?"

I glanced at the two men, who also smiled in a friendly way. On the counter next to them sat a syringe and a small brown bottle beside a metal sink.

"You want to knock me out?"

"Not exactly," she said. She moved slightly and I caught a faint whiff of perfume. I could have sworn it was the same scent the young stewardess wore on the flight to Pyongyang. "It's harmless." She smiled.

"Do I have a choice?"

"Of course," she said. "We could take you back to your hotel. All you have to do is ask."

The North Koreans were playing psychological games with me, and it was a strange series of tests. First the bowing and the roadside interrogation, then presenting me with a badge with their dead leader's image to welcome me to their club. Now they were asking to shoot me up with some kind of truth serum or whatever it was. Getting pinned by Shun the day before was a nice boost to my ego, and they probably figured that would soften me up for a chemical interrogation.

I looked at the little bottle sitting next to the syringe. It wasn't poison. If they wanted to do me in, there were much easier ways than this elaborate song and dance. And as long as it didn't kill me or turn me into a vegetable, what was the harm? I thought back to all those nights in my twenties when I'd score eight-balls of coke on a street corner in Newark or East Harlem. I had no idea what I was putting into my body. What the hell, I thought. If you don't take risks, you'll never get past the place where life has put you.

One of the officials told me to stand up and turn around, and I lowered my pants, exposing most of my left butt cheek. The woman came up from behind me, and I felt a sharp prick as she pushed in the needle, pulled back, and rammed the solution into my muscle. Later, when I asked McCreary about it, he said it was almost surely Sodium Pentothal, a fast-acting barbiturate that tends to make people chatty and cooperative, possibly laced with a hallucinogen such as Ecstasy or LSD. It's the classic truth serum still used by covert interrogators.

When the woman finished, I sat down. I was starting to feel good. Very good. The woman leaned over me, and I looked into the face of an angel. Her khaki blouse hovered over me. As I looked deep into her eyes I was filled with love. It wasn't a lustful kind of love, but a pure emotion that I could feel without being unfaithful in my heart to Lilia. I wanted to open my soul to this woman and her nice-seeming friends. I wanted us all to talk openly.

The woman asked me to describe my relationship with the Vietnamese, like Ho Jong did when we first met at the Ambassador Lounge. I explained how I'd become friends with officials from the Vietnamese mission to the United Nations, and become a conduit for messages between them and the POW/MIA activists. She wanted to know if it had been my idea for Khai to defect, and I described the scene at the running track at Columbia University, when Khai raised the issue. She asked whether Khai worked for the U.S. government. I told her it was too bad he didn't work for Washington because, although I'd tried to employ him at Cubby's and found he was no good as a dishwasher, I was sure he had plenty of other good qualities. He was an intellectual, I said. No good with his hands.

"Which agency do you work for? CIA?" asked the other male official.

"I deal with the FBI," I said. "And John McCreary, who has affiliations with the DIA and the CIA. But they don't pay me, and I'm not loyal to either one of them." I felt the urge to laugh, even though nobody had said anything funny. "I operate independently. I'm a lone wolf. And I make burgers for a living. I'm a burger-making lone wolf." Now *that* was funny. I was riding a feeling like the old coke high but without the jitters. I nearly got up out of the chair to give them a group hug. I turned around to smile at Shorty and let him know I had no hard feelings about our incident by the side of the road, but then I remembered that he'd left the room.

I told the three interrogators about my dealings with the FBI stretching back to the Feds' interest in Bobby Vesco and my mobbed-up friends as a kid. I told them I was still unsure about my relationship with Han. We hadn't fully started to trust each other, but already I felt like he was my brother. "You have a good man there," I said. "Han is a good man. I already told him all this stuff."

I must have blacked out for some of it because I lost track of time. At one point I realized I was alone and closed my eyes. When I opened them again, the two men were there, but the woman was gone. The euphoria was also gone. "How long was I out?" I wiped my nose and my hand came away bloody. I suddenly felt so sick and dizzy I thought I'd had a stroke. "What the fuck?"

"You had a little reaction," one of the officials said.

I only later learned that Sodium Pentothal can dilate the blood vessels to a dangerous level. My head throbbed tremendously as they drove me back to the Koryo Hotel. I lay down on my bed and felt worse than I ever had after a weekend coke binge. When Bratton came back from the DMZ I decided not to tell him about my interrogation until we were home safely, because I didn't want to freak him out.

"You should see the guards in South Korea!" he said as he came through the door. "They have much cooler uniforms." He stopped in the middle of the room when he saw how I was sprawled on the bed. "What's wrong with you?"

"I think maybe I have a flu bug." I said I'd met a few government officials but didn't offer any details, and he didn't ask. He had other things on his mind. He spent the evening pacing around the hotel room and wondering what to do about his predicament. After nearly a week in Pyongyang he hadn't met anyone who wasn't a handler or an official guide, and he still had four Bibles to unload.

"Give them to Shorty and Gap Tooth," I moaned from my bed. "Or give them to the guys behind the wall there. Just get rid of them, and let's get the fuck out of here."

We left early the next morning. I was still in a daze with the worst headache of my life. When we reached China the pain worsened, and by the time we landed in New York I had a severe sinus infection. I don't want to complain, though. Others have suffered much worse in enemy hands.

5

~~~~~~~~~~~~

Humanitarians

H OW'S THE BARBECUE IN PYONGYANG?" Kuhlmeier asked.

"Like dental floss," I said. I put two mugs of hot coffee on the back table and slid into the booth opposite him. "I didn't know whether I was supposed to eat it or clean my teeth with it."

Kuhlmeier chuckled. He glanced down at my newspaper. The front page had a picture of a two-year-old boy sitting on a bench at a bus stop in Peterson. Not much going on in North Jersey that December. Weak light filtered through the east window and made my head throb harder.

I went back to my office and got the Kim Il Sung pin out of my safe to show it to Kuhlmeier. "They said I was only the second foreigner to get one of these," I said. I decided to keep the details of my chemical interrogation to myself, for the time being. I didn't want him to think I'd been brainwashed. Kuhlmeier turned the pin around and examined it from all sides. He grunted. It was like the significance of my relationship with Han was dawning on him for the first time.

I told him about all the personal items of American GIs collecting dust in the war museum in Pyongyang. If they let us into their archives, I said, we might be able to find out what happened to our enlisted men who never came home. "What do you think the chances are they're still holding an American prisoner or two?" I asked.

Kuhlmeier sipped his coffee. "Are they making any changes to their embassy?"

That's all he cared about: the local angle. This is how these people think. They're compartmentalized. He wouldn't have cared less if I'd uncovered nuclear secrets or a box of classified war plans in Pyongyang. Counterintelligence was his job, and all he wanted to know was what the North Korean diplomats ate for lunch in New York.

"I think Han's going to be around for a while," I said.

"Did you learn that in Pyongyang? Who told you?"

"I'm just saying, he's putting a lot of time into our relationship."

Kuhlmeier frowned, still trying to puzzle something out. "And now he's friends with the chaplain for the New York Giants, too," he said. "Refresh my memory. Why did you take Mr. Bratton with you?"

"You think I trust the North Koreans? I needed some backup. You can't tell me you guys would have jumped in if something happened to me. I know how it works. You're friendly with me today because you want information, but I'm just a private citizen with my ass on the line."

He balanced the pin on his forefinger and ran his thumb over the face of Kim Il Sung. "We need to talk about your relationship with the U.S. government," he said.

Uh-oh. I was about fifty thousand dollars behind on my taxes. Like any other deadbeat, I was waiting for an immunity period so I could pay it without penalties, but the government hadn't offered one for a while. Maybe Kuhlmeier wanted to leverage my situation with the IRS and ask me to do something I didn't want to.

"This isn't about your taxes," he said. "We need to formalize the way we deal with you." He sat back and waited for my reaction. I must have had a blank look on my face. "We'll afford you a certain amount of protection by working with us."

The clouds parted. Sunshine streamed through the east-facing windows and lit up Kuhlmeier's brow like a Christmas bulb. I couldn't believe it. The FBI was offering me legitimacy. I could stop worrying about my government coming after me for hanging around an enemy country. The Feds would shield me from any inquiries from the Treasury Department or the CIA or Senate committees. If I got jammed up overseas or put behind bars for some reason, they'd have the resources to get me out.

"What would I have to do differently?"

"You're effective the way you are," Kuhlmeier said. "Just see how close you can get to Han."

"What do you want next? A pubic hair?"

Kuhlmeier ignored this. "Do it quietly. There's no reason to go to the press or expose the North Koreans to the press. We don't want you to operate that way. That's the only difference." I was still trying to get a handle on the thing. Up until now, the media was the only source of legitimacy I had. But the media was never going to help me out of a tight spot.

Kuhlmeier slipped a dollar bill under his coffee cup. We walked through the vestibule and out into the chilly December morning. We shook hands. "I want you to meet my supervisor," Kuhlmeier said. "He'll come with me next time. Can you behave yourself?"

"You worried?" I asked.

"Always." He laughed and headed for his car.

As he drove away, I got that good feeling I had as a boy mowing Bobby Vesco's lawn. I was moving up. When McCreary invited me to testify for the Senate Select Committee two years earlier, it was a one-off. It wasn't leading anywhere. But Kuhlmeier proposed a relationship. His boss wanted to meet me. I was gaining juice—power, influence, the ability to walk into a room and have people take me seriously. When you have juice, you're a VIP. You can pick up the phone and get a building permit in five minutes. You always get your table of choice at a restaurant. You get pulled over and the cops take one look at your ID and say, "Have a nice evening, sir. Sorry to bother you."

I picked Han up at our meeting spot on 95th Street that night. He emerged out of the shadows of the bagel shop, got in the passenger side of the Explorer, pulled his seat belt on, and asked, "How's your head?" It was his way of telling me he already knew every detail of my trip to Pyongyang.

"All better," I lied. My sinuses still throbbed, but I wasn't going to complain. We're tough guys. We don't whine. Without going into specifics, I told him I was getting closer to the White House, which was technically true. I said I needed to tell the Feds about my trip to make the information available to the president.

"Don't mention the last day," he said. He must have known that chemical interrogation was covered under the Geneva Convention against torture. But can you torture somebody who willingly submits? I gladly let them inject their truth potion into my ass. I wasn't under duress. I saw it as an initiation ceremony.

"Did I do good?" I asked. He smiled a big, genuine smile. Now that I'd been vetted, I guessed he would have a freer hand to spend time with me. I reached across the console, and we almost hugged, but our seat belts got in the way and instead I ended up patting his shoulder. We sat back, a little embarrassed.

It's one thing to have juice, but the true test of a VIP is how you use it. An opportunity presented itself right away. On December 17, 1994, the North Koreans shot down a U.S. Kiowa helicopter that had strayed almost four miles into their airspace. "Strayed" was the official word from Washington, which claimed the pilots made an innocent navigational mistake. According to the DPRK, they were spying. Like I'd seen at the War Museum in Pyongyang or in the books Han gave me, one event can have two very different interpretations. The DPRK pointed out that four miles was a long way off course for an advanced reconnaissance helicopter in the world's most heavily fortified conflict zone. The Pentagon claimed that the helicopter wasn't equipped with a satellite positioning system.

As soon as the news broke, Han and I were on the phone, gossiping like a couple of old ladies.

"One of the pilots is dead," he told me.

"Are you kidding me?" I said. "That's terrible. What happened? Where's the other one?"

"He died in the crash. The other one's safe."

"You wouldn't lie to me, would you?" I asked. "No foul play?"

"Why would I lie to you?"

After we hung up I called McCreary, who said that was news to him, because Pyongyang still claimed it was holding the two pilots, Chief Warrant Officer David Hilemon and Chief Warrant Officer Bobby Hall. It dominated the news on TV. I overheard my customers talking about it at Cubby's: "Those bastards oughta send our boys back!"

Clinton's guy, Rep. Bill Richardson of New Mexico, tried to intercede. Jimmy Carter got in the mix. After news of Hilemon's death reached the rest of the world, the line from Washington became that if Pyongyang didn't return the live pilot and the remains of the dead one right away, it would jeopardize the Agreed Framework and the gift of a nuclear reactor under KEDO. You could hear the sabers rattling all the way to North Jersey.

"It's a classic he-said/she-said scenario," I told Han a few days later.

"What do you mean?"

"Both our countries want to be right," I said. "You say they were spying. We say they strayed, but—"

"Who is 'he' and who is 'she'?"

It took me a few seconds to realize he was serious. "It's a figure of speech!" I said. "I'm not talking *literally* about he and she."

"The DPRK is 'he.'"

"Okay, fine, you want America to be the 'she'? We'll be the 'she.' Does that make you feel better?" Han said it did, and I laughed to myself. Sometimes there was no telling what was going to set him off. "How are we going to get those pilots home?" I asked. We meditated on this for a few minutes. In a crisis, you bring out your big guns. And I had the biggest guns in the tri-state area eating my baby back ribs every Friday afternoon.

"The New York Giants," I said.

"What about them?" Han asked.

The season-closing home game against the Dallas Cowboys was coming up on Christmas Eve, so the idea of sending the Giants to North Korea was out. "What if their players sign a petition?" I said. "The Giants represent the

National Football League, and the NFL pretty much represents the average American citizen. So this would be like a letter to your leaders from the people of the United States."

"It's a different approach," Han said. "Why not?"

I called Bratton, who thought it was a great idea. He promised to take it upstairs to Giants headquarters, and then we set about putting the right words on paper. I didn't have any stationery for Cubby's, so Bratton and I had it typed up on letterhead from his office as the Giants' chaplain, which seemed more dignified anyway. We came up with this:

The Honorable Minister Counselor Han Song Ryol
Dear Counselor Han,

In our past meeting and correspondence (we) have spoken to you about our desire to help establish goodwill and understanding between the people of your country and ours. At this time, in order to promote such goodwill, we respectfully request your consideration of the release of Chief Warrant Officer Bobby Hall prior to Christmas so that he may be with his family on this most joyous and holy day.

When I took the letter to the Giants' practice that Friday and explained what it was for, I didn't have time to give them a crash course in proper diplomatic letter writing. The players signed it the same way they autograph a football or a team jersey, which is wherever they find some free space, so the end result looked messy with signatures scrawled all over the margins. They may not have understood the finer points of diplomacy, but thirty-three members of the defensive and offensive teams signed it and identified themselves by the number they wore on their uniform.

I told Han I was bringing some top-caliber talent to hand-deliver the letter, so that he would have an impressive story to cable back to Pyongyang. On December 23, Rodney Hampton, Chad Bratzke, Dave Bratton, and I drove to the DPRK mission on 72nd Street. I rang the buzzer. Bratton edged closer into the doorway. Hampton and Bratzke waited eagerly behind us. Han opened the door and stood back a step. Several other North Korean diplomats stood behind him. Bratzke and Hampton must have wanted a better view into the embassy, or else they just pushed forward instinctively, as though a ball had been snapped. Bratton and I got wedged between the doorjambs. The North Koreans looked surprised to see four very large men stuck in their doorway. I held the letter out to Han.

I'd forgotten to prepare my remarks, and the words came out more formally than I intended. "We hereby respectfully present this petition," I said, feeling uncomfortable, like I was trying to be one of those rich kids with a scarf and a big vocabulary. "On behalf of the New York Giants and Cubby's BBQ, we humbly and with a friendly outlook ask that you duly release the American pilot currently in your keeping."

Han accepted the letter and said he would make sure the message from the Giants reached the highest levels of the DPRK.

Bratton invoked the name of God and the birth of Our Savior, Jesus Christ. It was especially poignant for Bratzke to be there. He was going through a lot at the time. Everybody knew the rumor that the Giants had left him unprotected for the expansion draft, so his future was a big question mark. Later, as we were leaving, he kind of choked up as he told me how much it meant to be able to serve a greater cause that day.

A few days later, I was sitting with my coffee, poached egg, and *The Record* when Kuhlmeier's sedan rolled into my empty parking lot at nine-thirty A.M. Kuhlmeier stepped smartly out of the driver's side and stood at attention. A great, blubbery guy with greasy hair and a too-short necktie emerged from the passenger side. I watched him wheeze his way slowly across my parking lot with Kuhlmeier at his side, waiting for his boss every few steps. I tried to imagine the big guy as a younger field agent hustling on the streets. Although, come to think of it, I hadn't seen a lot of agents on the street. They seemed to spend as much time in their cars as cops did. I wondered if all agents of the Bureau got that big after twenty years in a car. I resisted the urge to get up and meet them at the vestibule. Let them come to me.

He finally pushed the glass door open and waddled inside with Kuhlmeier. "John Clochin," he said, as I stood up and shook his pillowy hand. I gestured for him to sit opposite me in my booth by the window. Kuhlmeier shot me a "behave yourself" look and pulled up a chair at the end of the table so he wouldn't crowd his boss. I got three mugs of coffee and sat down. Clochin looked around my restaurant and at the mural of me at the Vietnam War Memorial.

"So you're the self-made spy," he said. He thanked me for the help I had provided the Bureau so far, and said the FBI was ready to make me a full-fledged operative. "You'll be working directly with us on issues of national security that are very important to your country," he said. His fleshy upper lip nibbled the rim of his mug as he sipped his coffee. "You'll be legit."

"You're not going to try to manage me, right?" I asked. "I'll be just as independent as I am now?"

"You'll be independent," Clochin said. "You can't break any laws, obviously. And you'll probably want some legal representation. We need you to sign some agreements."

"What kind of agreements?"

"Secrecy agreements, for the most part," he said.

I turned to Kuhlmeier. "Ted knows I'm not very good at keeping secrets."

"It's important that you don't reveal the nature of your relationship with us," Clochin said. "Especially to the North Koreans."

"You gotta be kidding me," I said. "Han knows I'm meeting with you. Part of what makes me attractive to them is that John McCreary is a friend of mine, and that you're interested in me. That's how the Koreans know I've got the ear of people in Washington. Don't think I don't sell that."

"It's a nonnegotiable," Clochin said. "You keep everything secret about us, and we keep everything secret about you."

That didn't sound like recognition to me. It sounded like a guy trying to hide an affair with a mistress or a screwy business deal. It gave me some serious misgivings, right off the bat. The Feds sounded more restrictive than the North Koreans.

"Ted told me I won't have to change what I'm doing," I said.

Kuhlmeier shook his head. "I didn't say you won't have to change. I said you're effective the way you are. There's a difference."

"You said I couldn't go to the press. That's all."

Clochin and Kuhlmeier exchanged a look. Beads of sweat formed on Kuhlmeier's shiny brow. The meeting wasn't going as he'd planned. "If you're not interested, then we can just leave it alone," he said.

The front door banged open and in walked my sous chef, a kid from the projects who called himself Bulldog. He was early. I waved him toward the kitchen and pantomimed slicing tomatoes and mixing barbecue sauce. Clochin and Kuhlmeier stared straight ahead as Bulldog headed for the kitchen door.

"I'm going to be doing the job of how many of you? How much do you pay the guys who watch the North Koreans from their cars?"

Clochin frowned. "Then there are some legalities and protocols we need to follow. For one thing, we need to start referring to you by a code name."

The whole thing seemed ridiculous. These guys were so bent on secrecy they couldn't do their own jobs and find out about the North Koreans themselves. I thought about it for a few seconds. "I want Double-Oh Seven," I said.

Clochin looked like he couldn't figure out whether I was kidding. "It's taken," he said. "Wrong country, anyway."

Kuhlmeier glanced at the kitchen door to make sure it was closed. "Our guys in the field usually go with something that doesn't attract attention. Something common, like Mike or Bob."

Was he kidding? "How about Bob?" I asked.

"That's fine."

"My name *is* Bob," I said.

Clochin and Kuhlmeier exchanged another look. We raised our coffee mugs to our lips. The problem with the Feds is they have no sense of humor. It's all about the exact color of the law with these guys. "This is why you're not effective," I told Kuhlmeier one time. "You have no warmth. You have no flexibility." They're robots, clones, no better than the Kool-Aid drinkers chanting slogans in the plazas of Pyongyang.

"Double-Oh Seven is the one I want," I said. "What about a budget?"

Clochin gazed into his empty coffee mug. "On a limited scale, we'd set it up so you could work off an expense account."

Now we were talking. Nothing says you mean it like cash up front. It was one thing to tell me I'd be legit, but the offer of a government expense account brought the reality home. I would undeniably be working on behalf of the American people. This kid from the wrong side of town had arrived.

"You'll cover things like travel and meals?" I asked.

"We'll look at it on a case by case basis," Clochin said.

Case by case sounded good to me. I wasn't looking for a salary or health benefits from the Feds. But I wasn't going to complain if they covered a flight to Pyongyang, some of my meals with Han, flower seeds for Ho Jong, or a bottle of vodka for Ambassador Pak. I didn't know how far they'd go on my behalf, but the more I thought about it, the more I liked the idea. Besides the coverage and legitimacy, it was something Andrea would be able to tell her friends someday: Daddy was not just a roofer and a burger chef, he was also a counterintelligence agent with the FBI.

After Kuhlmeier and Clochin left, I turned the agreement over to a friend of mine, JAG attorney Mark Winkler, a paratrooper with the Army who served in Granada. I asked Winkler to drag out his review of the agreement to buy time to feel out my new relationship with the Feds, because I still had my doubts. *Let's see how it goes*, I thought. Case by case. So I never signed it.

Around the same time we presented Han with our petition for the helicopter pilots' return, the general in charge of thirty-seven thousand American troops in South Korea sent a letter to Pyongyang expressing "regret" for violating DPRK airspace, but still claiming a "navigational error." Defense Secretary William Perry said the same thing. Nothing happened for another week.

The day before New Year's Eve, Lilia called me over to the phone at Cubby's with a big smile on her face. "It's Han," she said. "He's got good news."

Han said the pilots would be flown home the next day. He asked me to thank the Giants and Bratton for our letter and said he was sorry he couldn't express publicly that it had an impact. "Privately I can tell you it did," he said.

It's hard to measure what sways somebody's mind one way or the other, especially when they're the leader of North Korea. How much of it was Clinton's people? How much of it was us? Even Han couldn't tell me.

I told him that Bratton would spread the word at the Meadowlands. It was a small consolation for a miserable season in which the Giants failed to make the playoffs. The important thing was that Chief Warrant Officer Bobby Hall spent New Year's Day with his wife and sons in Florida, and the family of Chief Warrant Officer David Hilemon was able to bury his remains at a cemetery in Washington state. I asked Han on behalf of the Giants to send our thanks to Pyongyang.

The letter was a valuable souvenir; not too many people have the signatures of the entire Giants football team. If the Dear Leader was a football fan, maybe he had it framed and hung in his office. I told Han they could probably auction it online for a few G's if his government ever got really hard up for cash.

I soon found out the North Koreans needed my help with more than a few signatures. They needed cash. By early 1995, their economy had gone haywire, and there was no good way of fixing it. Because the central government controlled everything, they were also responsible for putting food on the table of every North Korean. Their system was simple. They gathered all the rice, vegetables, meat, and other produce from collective farms, traded some of it with their big communist neighbors at highly subsidized rates, and then distributed rations throughout the provinces and cities. It had worked for decades. But in the early 1990s, the Russians and the Chinese had switched to hard currencies and stopped giving "friendship" rates to the DPRK. The North Koreans had less cash to buy goods they didn't produce themselves. They couldn't afford to feed all their citizens.

McCreary told me a lot of people in the U.S. intelligence community thought the DPRK government might collapse. He said the regime was still reeling from the sudden death of the Great Leader. It still hadn't officially named his son and the heir apparent, Kim Jong Il, to lead the nation. This suggested a power struggle among the generals who were thought to control things behind the scenes.

It looked like there were delays in making decisions. The Agreed Framework was in place, but the North Koreans weren't moving to dismantle their nuclear program. The United States and its allies weren't rushing to build two nuclear reactors for the DPRK, either. And the economic embargo remained in place, making it harder for other countries to provide humanitarian aid. Nobody was getting what they wanted.

"You could help, Bobby," Han said one afternoon at Cubby's. It was my slow period between lunch and dinner, and we sat in the back booth with a plate of ribs between us.

"Me? I'm not an aid organization," I said. "I'm a restaurant owner. Do you know how many restaurants go out of business? Nine out of ten. Do you have any idea how much I owe Bert Posess for my beef deliveries?"

"You know people."

"Who do I know? I know gangsters. I know drug dealers. I've got lots of friends in North Jersey. None of them are connected with what you need."

He put a clean, fully sucked dry rib bone on his plate and wiped his fingers on a paper napkin. Barbecue sauce dribbled from one side of his mouth. "You have more contacts than you think," he said.

I glanced out the window, where Han's driver waited with the embassy's white minivan. On the other side of the parking lot, two guys sat in a green sedan parked next to a customer's car, making no attempt to hide the fact that they were watching Cubby's.

After Han left, I called Kuhlmeier from the phone by the soda fountain. "Your snoops are taking up valuable parking space," I said. "I thought we were partners now." I told him about my conversation with Han. "Don't expect any help from us," he said. "Just let us know what he asks for."

I called McCreary, who said, "Let Han walk you through it. He probably wants you to help approach churches."

"I don't belong to any churches," I said. And then I started to think. Having juice is about more than your influence and the people you know. It's also about the people *they* know. Everybody is connected to other people who could help you. If there are a maximum of six degrees of separation between everybody in the world, that means you're only five phone calls away from anybody. The real test of juice is how far you can reach.

I called Bratton: two degrees. "I don't think the Giants are in a position to send anything other than a football or two," he said.

"Not the Giants," I said. "The guys who gave you the Bibles. Wouldn't they like to get their toes into Pyongyang?"

I could almost hear a light bulb going on in Bratton's head. "Are they ready to accept Christian aid?" he asked.

"I think that's what Han was telling me, without saying it directly," I said.

The group that employed Bratton, Athletes in Action, fell under the umbrella of a huge global organization called Campus Crusade for Christ. A few days later Bratton asked if I could set up a meeting with Han. Victor Koh, the founding director of the Singapore chapter, which oversaw all of Asia for the group, wanted to fly to New York to meet him in person. Bratton lowered his voice when he said "Victor Koh," so I knew the guy was important.

Korea had almost no history of accepting aid from private charities and Christian groups, and for evangelicals the chance to talk to the North Koreans was a mission handed down straight from God Almighty.

Koh arrived from Singapore about a week later. I finished my lunchtime rush and drove into Manhattan to meet him and Bratton at the embassy on 72nd Street. We rode the elevator together. I could tell from the way he wore his belt that we weren't going to get along. It was cinched tight around his waist, hiking his pants above his hips in that goody-goody way Christians do, as though even their belt loops are straining toward Heaven.

Han brought one of his assistants, and the five of us sat under a portrait of the Great Leader in the embassy's small conference room. After a round of pleasantries and some talk about food shortages in the DPRK, Dr. Koh said the Singapore Campus Crusade for Christ was ready to send hundreds of tons of grain into Pyongyang. He could have the first trainloads of corn shipped from mainland China within a few weeks.

"We want to work directly with you," Dr. Koh said.

"How do you mean that?" Han asked.

Dr. Koh nodded his head so slightly in my direction he probably thought I didn't notice. "You must understand. We're a Christian organization, and we can't be associated with someone of his background," Koh said. Han looked at me, slightly amused. Koh looked at me, too, then back at Han. "The drugs and the crime," Koh said. "It looks bad for us."

"I've never been convicted of a crime," I said. Bratton looked at me apologetically, and I realized he'd told Koh about my encounters with the police and rehab clinics. I didn't mind, because Bratton didn't judge me and his intentions were good. But I knew Koh had an agenda. He wanted to claim the North Koreans for his organization, as though God had singled him out to feed the starving atheists. It was a power grab. And it ticked me off that he had no appreciation for my role. God didn't send the Koreans to him. I did. Maybe God's hand worked through me or something. I don't know; I'm not an expert in these things. But I did know it wasn't fair to go around me and pretend it was all for the glory of God. As I later found out, some Christian charities are worse than gangsters. They'll claw each other's eyes out for a chance to do a good deed.

"Did it bother you, what the doctor said?" Han asked, after the meeting.

"A little," I said. "He's not really a doctor. He's a doctor of religion."

"Like a witch doctor?" Han asked.

"Exactly!"

Han smiled. "If he can talk that way about you, I wonder what he says about us."

Dr. Koh flew back to Singapore, and about a week and a half later Bratton called the restaurant. Koh was frustrated, Bratton said. He wanted to return to New York and meet me at Cubby's. I could tell Bratton felt torn between his friendship with me and his loyalty to his bosses.

"He can come to the restaurant like any other paying customer," I said. "You're always on the house. You know that."

A few days later Bratton walked through the door at Cubby's followed by Dr. Koh, with his pants hiked up around his skinny belly. I let them sit where they wanted and order at the counter like everybody else.

When they were halfway through dinner I joined them. "Dr. Koh says Han won't return his calls," Bratton said.

"I've called fifteen times," Koh whined. "They said I should talk to the embassy in Singapore. But the embassy in Singapore doesn't return my calls."

He narrowed his eyes accusingly. "Does this have anything to do with you?"

"Why would it?" I asked.

"Because the other day Han finally picked up the phone, and do you know what he said? He said, 'I'm in charge of American affairs. I only deal with Americans like Bobby.'"

I had to laugh. Han probably wanted to keep the Christian charities at arm's length. But his loyalty touched me. I felt that by making me his point man for communicating with Campus Crusade he wanted to ensure nobody took advantage of me. I offered Dr. Koh my unconditional help, and over the coming months, we helped Campus Crusade become one of the first groups of its kind to send aid into North Korea.

I was still feeling good about the whole thing when, one Friday in the early summer, Han brought someone with him to Cubby's, and I suddenly felt like he was taking advantage of me himself. I remember that it was a Friday because I'd just received my weekly shipment of fine steaks—my T-bones, porterhouses, and filets mignon—and I was waiting for the beverage guy to deliver the next week's beer and soda canisters.

Han's friend was a Korean woman who lived in Baltimore and spoke English almost without an accent. About my age, she wore a skirt, short heels, and thick makeup. She took off her big fashion sunglasses and revealed a cake of green eye shadow that spread up her eyelids like algae, all the way to her carefully plucked brows. She was a little overdone for my taste.

She excused herself to the bathroom, and Han asked if I could join them for lunch. "I want you to be as generous to her as you are to me," he said. "She's one of us."

I brought out three sixteen-ounce New York strip steaks and three baked potatoes—all equal portions. I sussed her type after he called her "one of us." I'd met people like her at the embassy: Korean-Americans who sucked up to the DPRK envoys, usually because they had a relative somewhere in the North. They did the embassy's dirty work, infiltrating South Korean churches and community organizations in places like Los Angeles, Fort Lee, New Jersey, and Baltimore. They'd have the addresses of Korean-Americans with relatives in North Korea, and go around to their houses, saying threatening things like, "Don't forget about your uncle. Don't forget your grandfather," and shake people down, hoping that getting money for the DPRK government would lead to another bowl of rice for a loved one.

"She's making a trip to California to support the mission," Han said. "She needs a plane ticket."

"Are you American?" I asked her.

"I have a U.S. passport," she said. There was a little defiance to her tone.

I couldn't believe he was squeezing me for this broad. I said very clearly, looking at Han and pointing at the woman, "I don't know her. I don't have any relationship with her. I know *you*. You're my friend." I turned to her and said, "You can buy your own plane ticket."

She stared at her steak and fumed. A few of my customers looked over at us to see what the fuss was about. Han cleared his throat. "Can we talk privately?" he asked.

I took him to the vestibule between my front doors, where the pinball machine is. When the inner door had closed behind us, Han said, "You didn't need to be so rude to her."

"Are you kidding me?" I said. "I can barely feed my family, and you're asking me to shell out for a ticket for some American communist with too much makeup? Her sunglasses probably cost half a flight across the country. Don't tell me she can't afford a ticket."

His driver stood outside smoking. He must have seen me waving my arms around and shouting, because he opened the front door to check on Han. "It's all right," Han said. "We're just talking."

"Don't try to exploit me," I said when his guy closed the door again. "I help you because you're my friend. Don't take me for granted."

A few days later, Han came back alone and apologized. "It wasn't very well thought out," he said.

"No shit," I said.

"I hope I didn't damage our relationship." He looked truly worried.

Lilia brought over our two plates of ribs. "We've got more important things to think about," I said.

I never saw the woman again, and Han never mentioned it again. I was glad I stood up for myself. If he thought I was such a suck-up that I would roll over and do whatever he wanted, then I was ready to end things between us.

In late July 1995, devastating rains hit North Korea and didn't let up for weeks. Most of the country flooded, destroying nearly a million acres of farmland and a million and a half tons of grain, and displacing half a million people. Terraced rice fields collapsed all over the country. Bridges, roads, and whole villages disappeared. They were the first major floods since the breakup of the Soviet Union and, in the months and years that followed, the central government had an even worse time trying to feed its citizens. The newly appointed leader, Kim Jong Il, started a campaign called, "Let's Eat Two Meals a Day!" The official rations dropped from three handfuls of grain a day to two, then dropped below the subsistence level. People in the mountains survived by eating roots and bark. The country flooded again in 1996, and by the late 1990s as many as three million North Koreans died of starvation and disease from the famine.

Han saw it coming, and even before the 1995 floods he asked if I could help find more humanitarian aid. Besides food, they desperately needed medical supplies. I found out that a state senator from Pennsylvania named Stewart Greenleaf wanted to work along the same lines, and I proposed that we team up. Greenleaf was an evangelical Christian whose district included a large population of Korean origin who wanted to help the victims in the DPRK.

Greenleaf knew Bill Henry, who founded America's Heart, a charity that shipped humanitarian supplies to Third World countries. Henry knew how to get supplies, and he had the infrastructure to get them shipped halfway across the world in giant containers. He'd get pharmaceuticals, food, and medicines that were near or past their expiration date, have the stuff tested in labs and relabeled with paperwork extending its shelf life for three or four years, then get it approved by the U.N. for shipment to places like Bangladesh and Haiti.

Greenleaf got me lists of what Henry had in his warehouse, and I took them to Han. He checked them with officials back in Pyongyang and then told me, "More of this, less of that." Aspirin was a big hit, along with antibiotics and stomach stuff like Maalox and Pepto Bismol. One of our first bills of lading included:

Surgical tape, anti-embolism stockings, thigh supports, knee supports, elbow braces, knee braces, compression rib belts, feeding tubes, isotonic liquid nutrition, penicillin G, potassium IV, Lidocaine, propofol, Lorabid, silvadene cream, obstetrical pads, adrenalin chloride, Neosporin, Derma Vite Dietary Supplement, claripel cream, hydroquinone, generators, 12-volt batteries, surgical masks and gowns, acetaminophen, blankets, disposable diapers, papain urea debriding ointment, pediatric stethoscopes, sodium chloride for irrigation, aspirin, calcium, C-section surgical kits, catheters, triple antibiotic ointment, X-ray film developer, silver sulfadiazine.

Henry was dedicated. He'd drive all the way from Florida to Cubby's to discuss how to get Christian powdered milk and generators into North Korea. With his white hair and beard, he looked like a full-sized version of one of Santa's elves. He was eccentric, but that's what you get with somebody who wants to deal with a dictatorship. A normal person wants to have an affiliation with the queen of England, not the mysterious leaders of the Hermit Kingdom. Those of us private citizens who got involved with Pyongyang were unusual. We walked on the edge. We were risk takers.

Within a few months we had a distribution network set up in North Korea that linked Christian aid groups to Han's government. It was a perfect fit. Pyongyang was able to exploit food and medical resources for its needy, and the Christian groups got to feel they had a toehold in one of the last remaining lands of godless communism.

Han made special requests for many items, such as hand lotions, toothpaste, toothbrushes, floss picks, and mouthwash. He wanted any antidepressants we could get our hands on. When Viagra hit the market in 1998, he wanted it.

"That's not a humanitarian item," I said the first time it appeared on one of his "wish lists."

"Sure it is," he said.

"Just because somebody can't get a hard-on doesn't mean it's a medical emergency."

"You'd think it's an emergency if *you* couldn't get a hard-on," he said.

"Never happens, pal," I said.

One of the biggest issues for Han wasn't the items themselves, but how they were packaged. The aid arrived in boxes covered with crosses and doves with olive branches in their beaks and names like Hope Through Service, Inc., Cross International, and Rock of Refuge Church, Inc. Sometimes you'd see the logos stuck one on top of the other in a kind of holy sticker war.

Han wanted the Christian emblems stripped from the aid packages, because admitting the aid came from outside North Korea went against the national idea of *juche,* or self-reliance. (Kim Il Sung came up with the *juche* idea in 1955, saying, "Man is the master of everything and decides everything," and that the citizens of the DPRK were their own bosses and didn't need outside help.) Every package with a cross on it was another hole in the idea of *juche.*

As a hunter and a man of the wilderness, I appreciated *juche.* I liked the notion of self-sufficiency, and I shared with North Korea the urge to go it alone. But I also know the limits. Growing up on the tough streets of Fairfield, I learned the value of connections and knowing how to use them. "You can be self-sufficient *and* accept help from the outside," I told Han. "It's all about how you look at it."

I told Han he needed to compromise. Dr. Koh was especially upset, because the Campus Crusade people liked to slap crosses on anything they touched, and they were threatening to cut off aid if they couldn't take credit for it. So much for the sin of pride. I suggested to Han: let's get them to remove all their logos, and you agree to let a few Christians into the DPRK as a trade-off. Dr. Koh loved this plan, and we eventually got permission for Campus Crusade workers from Sweden and Canada to live part-time in North Korea. Han knew that his government could easily control the movement of a few humanitarians. They were far more concerned about exposing their population to printed materials. Totalitarian regimes hate other peoples' logos. Stalin and Chairman Mao burned all the books they didn't like, and the Nazis did the same thing, because they understood that it's much easier to kill a person than extinguish an idea.

The same issue came up with the negotiations over KEDO. Once the project got going, building a light-water reactor for the North Koreans would eventually require equipment and expertise from other countries. The KEDO site was designed as an autonomous city, with housing for thousands of workers and its own dining and recreation areas. Whenever Han talked about it, he obsessed over making sure every worker was monitored twenty-four-seven; the KEDO site would be so isolated that there wouldn't be any "contamination."

"What do you mean, 'contamination'?" I asked him one evening in late 1995. "From the light-water reactor?"

"No. Contamination from how you people think."

Han was so concerned about protecting the *juche* idea that he was missing the opportunity that was presenting itself right on his doorstep with KEDO and its nine-billion-dollar budget. He was thinking defensively, like a typical commie, instead of like an entrepreneur like me, who thinks in terms of offense.

"Nine billion dollars is a lot of cash," I told Han. "Think of all the details. You're going to need construction materials, heavy equipment, tools, generators, housing for the workers, porta-johns, cafeterias. The list goes on and on. We ought to go after the contracts for those things. Companies from all over the world are going to be bidding for those contracts. There's a lot to be exploited here. Why should you be left out?"

"You think your government would allow that?" Han scoffed.

"We'll demand it! Let me give you an example. Say you've got five thousand workers building your light-water reactor. That's at least ten thousand meals a day, either prepackaged or cooked in a cafeteria. Now you might not have the infrastructure to do the packaged foods, but what about the raw materials? Say you've got workers from all over—Indians who don't eat beef,

Muslims who don't eat pork, etcetera. What's the one thing everybody's going to eat? Chicken. Say you're going to need a thousand chickens a day. Maybe two thousand. And even if you don't have the capacity now, a chicken farm is a relatively easy thing to establish. I've got a meat guy who could hook us up. We build a chicken farm on the expense account of KEDO, and then when all those foreign workers are gone you've got a supply for some of your hungry people. But if it's going to happen you've got to get in early and negotiate. Demand that a certain percentage of the goods have to be produced locally. The question is: are they going to fly chickens in from halfway around the world? Or are they going to be chickens from the DPRK?"

Han liked the idea so much he asked me to float it with my contacts in Washington. I ran it by Kuhlmeier, who couldn't have cared less. "It's an opportunity to get in," I pleaded with him. "When we can finally set up a business in North Korea, we'll have eyes on the ground. Why do you think the place is a Black Hole?" But setting up a farming operation didn't fit into Kuhlmeier's job description.

A couple of years later, I tried to explain it to Clinton's national security chief for Asia, Jack Pritchard, who said I was disrupting delicate negotiations and threatened me with everything short of treason ("The Koreans brought up your chicken farm again!" he yelled at me), which is a story I'll go into another time.

I bent McCreary's ear about it. "Let's make them entrepreneurs," I said. "Let's distract them from the political issues and lure them into business. Right now the guys in Pyongyang see engineers from the United States and South Korea coming into their country, and they're supposed to sit on the sidelines and watch? Of course they're paranoid! But as soon as they're involved in it, taking part, making a buck or two, they won't feel that way. We have to get them into a capitalistic mode of thinking, especially if we want to get them out of their Stalinist, commie mode of governing."

McCreary laughed. "You're forgetting about the embargo," he said.

"We have to prepare for the end of the embargo," I said. "If we can see past it, we'll get past it someday."

And that's how Han and I came up with the idea for the USA/DPRK Trade

Council, with me as its founding president. For the time being, it was an organization in name only, since the embargo kept us from actually trading. I had it incorporated using the address of my lawyer, Mark Winkler, and the back office at Cubby's as its HQ. We set it up in case Washington and its allies ever lifted the sanctions.

The embargo put a damper on the FBI, too. The first time I asked them for money, they balked. It was late 1995, and we'd sent several shipments of humanitarian aid into Pyongyang already. Han took me aside one day when he and some of the other delegates were having dinner at Cubby's.

"I need a return favor," he said. "It's for Shun." Our horseshoes-playing friend in Pyongyang wanted a gift from America for his commanding general, Han said. A big gift could get him a promotion or an extra food ration or whatever it was he needed. Over the years I learned that even Han wasn't so high-ranking that he didn't have to suck up. When he wanted something to send home, I'd help him find it.

I called Kuhlmeier, who came out to the restaurant. "I need about two grand," I said.

"That's a lot of money," he said. "What's the deal?"

"I need some night-vision goggles," I said.

"Jesus, Bob."

"Not for me. It's a gift for one of their generals in Pyongyang."

"I know you're not in this for the money, but I got to have some reason for this," he said.

"To sweeten up my sources," I said. "It's for one of Han's buddies. I want to show them what I can do."

"I don't even know if it's legal," he said. "I can't do it if it's not legal. I'll get back to you."

I figured he probably had to check with Clochin, and I wondered: did Clochin have to check with somebody? How much juice did Kuhlmeier and Clochin have? And how far would they go for me? I called him the next day from the restaurant, and he said, "So far so good. If they're not military grade, it's not technically illegal."

Han's guy was leaving for Pyongyang in a few days, and I couldn't wait any longer. I ordered one of the cheaper, mono-lens, night-vision jobs to the tune of seventeen hundred bucks, rush delivery from Cabala's, one of the finest hunting outfitters in the world. It arrived at Cubby's three days later.

Kuhlmeier called that afternoon. "You what?" he said.

"The guy's leaving tomorrow."

"I didn't authorize the purchase," he said.

Somebody above Kuhlmeier must have put the kibosh on the goggles plan. "But you said if they weren't military grade—"

"I didn't have authorization yet," he said. "It violates the spirit of the embargo. They're an enemy nation, don't forget that. You should be more careful about how much you suck up to them."

This was the first—but by no means the last—time he gave me the Benedict Arnold treatment. "Who's Benedict Arnold?" Han asked when I told him about the call with Kuhlmeier.

"One of the great generals of the American Revolution," I explained. "Maybe greater than George Washington. He defected to the British near the end of the war, making him the most famous traitor in our history. Do you know why he went over to the other side? He was being disrespected by the founding fathers, who were jealous of him."

But that's another story, too. The point is that Kuhlmeier was a stickler. What was the FBI afraid of? That the generals in Pyongyang would reverse-engineer the night vision goggles from Cabala's, mass produce them, and suddenly American troops on the DMZ would be in danger? It wasn't like night-vision goggles were classified. The general could just as easily have gotten them from Russia or China or by ordering them online. Washington decided that giving things to the North Koreans was a bad idea. It's strange how government people think like communists. They'll shut down the free flow of goods for political reasons. I figured giving things to the North Koreans was a great idea. This is the way drug dealers and fishermen think. Get them hooked on our products. Throw some chum in the water. Bring them out in the open. Nothing's going to warm up a commie like an iPod or a pair of night-vision goggles.

"I can't send them back," I said.

"I have a hard time believing that," Kuhlmeier said. "Why don't you just cancel the charge on your credit card?"

"I thought you were an intelligence agent. Haven't you seen my credit rating? I paid with a cashier's check."

I called Han and told him to come over discreetly. That night, the white minivan from the DPRK embassy pulled into the alley behind Cubby's. I'd switched off my security lights, so it was almost pitch-dark. I hid in the bushes and waited until they'd turned off their headlights. I put the goggles on and watched four green figures emerge from the outline of the van; I crept forward using my hunter's walk. I recognized Han's wiry little body and I pounced on him from behind in the darkness.

"Hey!" He jumped about three feet and spun around. "Bobby? You fucker!"

Everybody wanted to try the goggles, so Han, the other North Koreans, and I took turns putting them on and going commando in the dark alleyway. We were like kids on Christmas morning.

A pair of headlights appeared in the parking lot. I grabbed the goggles from Han and aimed them at the intruders. The glowing green chassis of an unmarked car with two figures in the front seat drove slowly past: Kuhlmeier's clones.

I stuffed the goggles into their box and handed it to Han. "Put them in your van," I said. "No more playing around."

Kuhlmeier called the next morning and got straight to the point. "We know the North Koreans were at your restaurant late last night," he said. "Where are the goggles?"

"I don't have them," I said.

"Tell me you didn't give them to the Koreans."

Now, if you think about it, Kuhlmeier asked me specifically to tell him something, so I just followed instructions. "I threw them in the river," I lied.

A few seconds ticked by while Kuhlmeier processed this. "That's too bad," he said sarcastically. "Because now we can't reimburse you for them."

"Yeah?" I was pissed. "Is that the way you want to operate? You want me to go through the same bureaucratic bullshit you use with all your agents? That's a recipe for failure, Ted. You want to cut my balls off and turn me into one of your squares, we're not going to get anywhere with the North Koreans. I have to have some freedom, otherwise I can't be friends with them. That's why they're in my car, leaving hair samples behind; that's why they invite me to their embassy and tell me who's coming from Pyongyang next, and who's going back, and what they eat, drink, smoke, and like to do for fun. That's why you have stuff to put in your reports."

"That's fine, Bobby, but we have to follow some procedures, too. I wish it were different, but—"

"Hey, Ted, I got to go. I need to run my restaurant." I hung up on him.

The honeymoon with the Feds was over before it even got going. After that I said, screw them, I'd be more careful with the information I provided. I'd string them along like I did when I was a kid working at the shooting range. It wasn't like the Feds were going to back off and leave me alone, though. They had counterintelligence to do, and I was between them and their target. So we were stuck with each other.

6

~~~~~~~~~~~~~~

Atlanta Games

BAIT THE CLAM so it sits like this," I said, "so the barb is hidden." I let the hook swing over the side of the boat and showed Han how to grip his fishing pole. "Let the sinker hit the bottom, and then you're going to wait, and when you feel the pull, that's a strike. Keep your thumb on the reel. Let the fish take the line for a few seconds, and when you want to set the hook, lock the spool and pull back."

"I know what I'm doing," Han said.

He turned away from me, unlocked his spool, and let the weight pull the hook into the gray-blue water of the Atlantic Ocean. Monofilament spun out from beneath his thumb. The sun inched up from the water to the east, painting the underside of the clouds orange. Little whitecaps rose and collapsed around us. I closed my eyes and inhaled the smell of salt spray. It was a beautiful morning. I was about to turn away and help some of the other guys when Han jerked his pole back.

"A nibble. I felt it!" He jerked his pole again, to make sure.

"That was the sinker hitting the bottom," I said. After years of catching puny trash fish from the banks of the Taedong River, anything probably felt like a strike to him. "Relax. When you get one, you'll know."

It was the spring after the goggles incident. We were on Raritan Bay, off Sandy Hook, when the striped bass are migrating north, and the waters around the New Jersey tributaries are thick with twenty-pounders and up. It was the first time I ever took Han fishing, so it's a day I remember well. He'd invited Pak Gil-yon, North Korea's ambassador to the U.N. at the time, and a couple of lesser guys from the mission.

We left the dock at dawn on the *Benchmark*, a forty-four-foot charter boat. As we pulled away, two FBI agents ran down to the pier lugging binoculars and a camera with a long telephoto lens. "Say bye-bye to the Feds," I told Han and Pak. We headed out into open water, waving and shouting, "Bye-bye!" as one of the knuckleheads aimed his camera at us.

Kuhlmeier had tried to talk me out of the trip a few days earlier. "That's a no-can-do," he said, until I had showed him on a map that Raritan Bay was at least partly within a twenty-mile radius of Columbus Circle, and therefore within their permitted travel zone. Kuhlmeier just sighed and gave me the Mother Hen routine: "You've got to be careful, taking them offshore. You know what kind of trouble we'll both be in if something happens out there?"

"Then why don't you come out with us, Ted," I inquired with a straight face. "You're the one who wants to know everything about the North Koreans. Come with us, and you can ask Han anything you want."

"It's against regulations," he said.

"Fishing? You can't have a regulation against that. You like to fish, don't you?"

"I can't meet them, Bobby. It's counterintelligence. We do things in secret."

"I won't tell them who you are. I'll say you're just a friend of mine. Of course, you'd need to disguise yourself a little. I never understood why you guys all shop from the same suit and tie racks at Sears and wear the same cologne. People know you're a Fed from a continent away!"

But poor Kuhlmeier wasn't going to break any rules, and the closest he ever got to our fishing trips, or meeting any of the Koreans he was supposed to be spying on, was hearing my reports and seeing pictures taken by guys standing on a pier.

We'd been out less than half an hour when Han caught his first striped bass. I heard his gear whiz and I spun around to see the top of his pole bent and quivering. He let the line run a few seconds, popped the spool, and leaned back hard to set the hook, just like I'd told him. It made me proud to see.

"Take your thumb off the line and start reeling!" I shouted. He jerked the rod up. "Don't jerk the rod!" I shouted. "Bring the pole in. Don't drop it!"

"I got a big one, Bobby." He was having a tough time. He tightened the spool and set his feet as the fish tried to run.

"Move with the fish!" I yelled. "Go easy. Don't break him off! Let him run, and when he stops running, you reel."

Han moved to the stern and let the striper run. "I need heavier line," he huffed. "I better not lose my fish."

"You don't want heavier line. The fish can see it. Just let him go. Wait till he gets tired."

The other guys leaned their poles against the gunwales and came over to watch. Han pulled and strained, and the muscles in his arms and neck bulged. After a few minutes his knuckles were white and shaking. He was getting tired, but he was too tough to say anything about it, and I knew better than to ask if he wanted help. Then he started to get the hang of it. He let the fish go until he felt a slackening off, then pulled up and reeled fast. Then he let the fish run again. His face twisted with exasperation and joy. He looked like a different person than the Han I knew on land. At that moment, he didn't have another care in the world.

In the next ten years that we fished together, I always loved seeing that transformation. Once we got offshore or up into some stream, he would start to relax in a way that was impossible for him in New York. We joked more freely. We weren't from enemy countries anymore, we were two guys on a day off, living their dream. There was nothing either one of us would rather be doing. Nothing. Not many things in life can compare to a couple of fishermen out mugging striped bass. That's utopia for men like us.

I enjoyed fishing with Han more than with anybody else. He was a sportsman at heart—he liked the fight. Most of the other North Koreans were about bringing the fish home to eat. They wanted to use heavier line. Han quickly grasped finesse fishing—the reasoning that the lighter the line you use, the more likely it is that the bigger, older, smarter fish will take your bait. You might lose some here and there, but you're always in play. Han also appreciated the beauty of our oceans and streams, the longer summers than he had back in Pyongyang, and the fact that we could get in the car and head to the Jersey shore with no restrictions. I'll never forget that day when he reeled that first bass up to the boat. He leaned back and his eyes went wide with surprise when a twenty-pound fish popped out of the water and into my net, where it wriggled and beat its tail against the hull. "Look at the size!" he gasped. "Have you ever seen one that big?"

"Might be the biggest one of the day," I said.

In fact we hauled in more than fifty fish that day, some of them more than thirty pounds. Everybody caught some. That afternoon, as we headed to the dock, we could see the FBI men were still on the pier waiting for us with their camera and binoculars. "Everybody hold up your biggest fish!" I shouted. Han, Pak, the other two, and I slipped our fingers under the gills of our best catches and held our trophies overhead, as the federal agent tracked us with his long lens. I'm sure those images are still filed away somewhere in the FBI archives.

We cleaned the fish before leaving the dock, and I was surprised when Han asked the captain to save the heads and guts. "The heads are the best part," he said. And the guts? "Soup!" he said.

We filled three ice chests with fish and fish parts and still had leftovers, so I drove Han to Cubby's to put the rest of the catch on ice. I parked in back of the restaurant, and when I came out with another ice chest I found Han at the tailgate of my car, holding one of the bigger fish. He watched absentmindedly as its red juices trickled from its gills across his hand and down his wrist.

"You like blood," I said. "You've got the killer instinct. You pick that up as an army officer? You learn to kill on the DMZ?"

Han's smile disappeared. He gave me a funny look for a second—an uncertain look, like he'd gotten caught doing something wrong. There are times when the truth is spread out plain to see on someone's face. Sometimes it's just a flicker, but we're all human and we all show our deepest selves from time to time. His expression is imprinted on my memory, because it was the moment I knew that Han had killed another human being. Probably more than one.

"Hey, forget I mentioned it," I said. We started packing the fish on ice in the back of my Explorer, and both of us stayed silent.

"Sometimes we had to do things," he said after a while. "It's probably hard for you to understand."

He was right. I didn't understand the experience. But was I capable of killing a man? In the right circumstances, I think we all are capable of doing terrible things. I'd almost killed a guy in the fall of 1979, over nothing. I was tarring the roof of a diner on Route 46, when I saw a builder pushing the architect, a Greek guy named Taki Langas. Taki had given me the roofing job, and so I shouted down to the guy pushing him, "Hey, asshole!" He came barreling up to the roof to get me. There was no backing down on a construction site. You had only your fists to prove what kind of man you were. As soon as he got up to the roof, I snapped. The next thing I remember I've got this guy's ankles tied to the ladder and I'm pushing it away from the roof. I had my knife out and I was shouting at him that I was going to cut the rope and let him drop on his head. Lucky for him and for me, Langas talked me out of it.

After that I didn't ask any more about Han's past on the DMZ. It's one thing you learn growing up in a mob town. You talk about sensitive issues in generalities. You don't ask for specifics. We put the lid on the ice chest and climbed in so I could drive him back to Manhattan. I changed the subject.

"Who've you got coming for the Olympics?" I asked. The 1996 Atlanta Games were only a couple of months away, and Kuhlmeier had told me there were rumors that the DPRK might not send a team. He also said that with his reelection campaign in full swing, Clinton was desperate to have a complete Olympics. The last time the games were held in the United States, in 1984, the Soviet Union and fourteen Eastern Bloc countries boycotted. Having all countries represented in Atlanta would show the world that the Cold War was finally over, and it was time to move on. Han hadn't said anything about it. "You're bringing your team, right?" I asked.

Han shrugged and said Carter was coming over to Beijing to talk about it. "It's complicated," he said.

"What's complicated? It's a chance for you to showcase your country's athletic skills. And you can put a feather in Clinton's hat at no cost to yourselves. You should do it."

"There is cost," he said. "We would have to move our whole embassy operation to Atlanta, to watch the athletes."

"Can't you watch on TV?" Han looked at me like I was an imbecile.

"I mean watch them when they *aren't* playing. If one of them defects, it will be the last time anybody comes to America. Not worth it."

"Is that what you're worried about? That would keep you from coming?"

"It's a serious issue. Security is the main concern."

"Don't worry about that," I said. "Security can be taken care of. We'll find you a place to stay so you can watch your athletes. I'll take care of it myself."

"You'll take care of it?" Han sounded incredulous.

I had no idea what I was talking about, either. But nobody ever got anywhere by standing around bragging about things they *can't* do. "Consider it done," I said. "I'll take care of security."

"Not FBI," he said.

"Of course not. We'll get somebody who's loyal to me and therefore loyal to you."

I figured that would be the end of it. Just some loose talk between a couple of guys after a fishing trip. But a few days later Han called me at Cubby's and said, "We're going to send a team. Are you happy?"

"Of course I'm happy," I said. "That's great news."

"Good," Han said. "Because you're going to be the host for the embassy."

The Olympics organizing committee would help with housing and expenses for twenty-four athletes and almost as many coaches for the month. My job, according to Han, was to take care of the DPRK government officials, who were going to get a travel exemption from Washington. But where the hell was I going to find housing for more than a dozen diplomats and some of their wives? I didn't know anybody who lived in Atlanta. I'd never even been there.

I was honored, I told Han. It was the opportunity of a lifetime. I was all smiles on the outside, but inside I felt sick. I had way overcommitted. I couldn't afford to go to Atlanta myself. The restaurant desperately needed my attention, because I had a TGI Friday's opening up less than two miles away and I had to do something to keep my customer base. I had my own defectors to worry about. I'd just upgraded the menu to include shrimp and three new sauces, and we were switching from paper plates to heavy china to cater more to the sit-down dinner crowd. For a restaurant like mine that prides itself on quick service, any change is a big deal. It required retraining my staff, more dishwashing capacity, and, most importantly, managerial oversight.

I needed stand-ins. I made an SOS call to Dolores Alfond, the head of the National Alliance of POW/MIA Families, whose network of activists stretched far and wide in the United States. She made a few calls and came back to me with the number of a woman in Atlanta named Jean Fallon. Fallon's husband had gone missing after bailing out of his fighter jet in Laos in 1969, and she was still searching for clues. When I called her, she offered to open her home to Han and his colleagues as a way of reaching out to a country that might have American POWs from another war. The POW community is tight that way, and always ready to jump into action. It's not like our government is giving these long-grieving family members a seat at the negotiating table with foreign governments. Jean was excited. She sent me some photos of her home, a big brick house where she lived alone in the Atlanta suburbs, which I showed to Han for his approval. Then Dolores called and said she would come to Atlanta herself, to cook and do laundry for the group. Things were starting to come together.

I had to reach deeper to find some freelance, private-sector security. When I meet somebody, I keep their phone number in one of several shoeboxes in the office at Cubby's. I dug through them until I found the contact for Joe Jordan, executive director of the National Vietnam POW Strike Force in Houston. I'd met him at a few POW events, where he liked to dress up in surplus military uniforms and sell Vietnam memorabilia. Jordan had some pretty far-out ideas. He claimed that President Clinton had personally ordered the skiing "accident" that killed Sonny Bono, which he said was most likely carried out by an Army ranger who chased Bono down a slope, grabbed him, and skied into a tree using the diminutive Bono as a "shock absorber." He also claimed that once Clinton was impeached over the Monica Lewinsky scandal and Al Gore was "eliminated" by the CIA, Jay Rockefeller would become president and unleash the Antichrist on the world. But it's not easy to find somebody who is willing to take a month off work to chaperone a bunch of communists around free of charge. At the time he was my best available choice. Jordan was in the limousine business, and he had plenty of guns. Where I come from, that's a perfect combination. When the Italians hire a driver they make sure he can shoot, too. Remember when they whacked the Gambino boss, Paul Castellano, outside of Sparks steakhouse? They made sure to get his driver, too, because he was the bodyguard who was packing the heat. "Your driver should always be coming heavy," I told Han, and he appreciated that.

Kuhlmeier was not happy that I'd gotten in the middle of the Olympics trip, but he was even less happy that I planned to house them at the home of a widow who believed her husband was still alive somewhere in Vietnam. "You know what you're doing exposing these people to the North Koreans?"

"I'm exposing the North Koreans to them, Ted. It shows you how open they are to the POW issue. It's our government that doesn't want to talk about it. You understand? Dolores and Jean are extending themselves out of the goodness of their hearts, and because they care about missing Americans. You can't argue with that, can you?"

Kuhlmeier groaned. "And we checked out your security guy. He's got more than a few screws loose. You don't want him around the North Koreans, either."

"I disagree, Ted," I said, since I had no other options anyway. "Generally that's exactly what you want. Somebody who's a little fat on the trigger. Somebody who's alert and ready at all times."

"Nothing better go wrong," he said.

A few days later, an Asian-American stranger walked into Cubby's late in the evening. He waited until the last customers had cleared out, and then approached me at the register and offered me an unspecified amount of cash. "You're going to need help with the team," he said. "We can supply what you need." I guessed he was Korean, and I didn't ask who "we" were or how he knew I was involved. I said I didn't need money for anything, and he left. The next day I told Kuhlmeier, who came out to Cubby's. He thought it was somebody looking to sabotage the DPRK's Olympic dreams. "Watch out you don't get set up," he said.

I didn't know who the visitor was or how he knew so much. There was no way of telling whether his intentions were good or malicious. But I figured plenty of people would've loved to see Han's trip to Atlanta end in disaster: South Korean agents who might want to embarrass Pyongyang, or Americans of Korean origin with old scores to settle, or anti-communist zealots. Han was in enemy territory, after all, and there was no telling what kind of kooks might be running around with a hidden agenda. The travel exemption from the U.S. government didn't mean they were safe. That was the danger of living in a free society.

I decided not to worry about it and just concentrate on getting the North Koreans to Atlanta. Someone needed to escort Han and the delegation from New York in my place. Ideally somebody with a cool head, who I could trust. Since I didn't know anybody who had a cool head, I stopped by my folks' house and asked my dad. "Not a chance!" he said. "They're cheats. They're liars. They'll suck your blood."

"You can help raise awareness," I said. Dad had been sober for years now, too, and he was a neighborhood organizer for the DARE program to help keep kids off drugs. "There'll be hundreds of thousands of people there," I said. "Think how many people you can reach."

"What do you want to help them North Koreans for? You've got a restaurant to run."

"I'm running it. That's why I need you to go."

In the end, Dad couldn't resist a free trip to the Olympics, even with his old enemy. "All right," he said. "But I'm going to hold my nose the entire time, I can tell you that."

In early August 1996, I rented a passenger van from a place in Hackensack. The idea was that Dad would chauffeur all the wives and some of the men on the fourteen-hour drive to Atlanta, and Han would ride shotgun with him. The rest of the delegation would follow with the embassy driver, George, in their van. The morning they left, I drove Dad to the mission on 72nd Street and helped Han pack the rental. I was surprised to see a golf bag in the back, and when I lifted the towel draped over the top I found it was stuffed with four semi-automatic rifles. "Where'd you get these?" I asked Han.

"Don't worry about them," he said. "Double protection."

"Leave them here. You don't need them." I already had Jordan packing heat, and I didn't want more guns around. Han obediently took the golf bag out of the rental, but I'm pretty sure he just packed it in the other van.

I waved good-bye like a nervous parent as they drove away, and made it back to Cubby's in time for the lunchtime rush. It was going to be a nerve-racking few weeks. Ordinarily this was a situation I'd want to handle myself, in person. A lot could happen in three weeks. And just as I'd feared, Dad called in the middle of that first afternoon, practically shouting.

"We almost got arrested by state troopers," he yelled.

I gestured to Lilia to take over for me at the counter. "Where are you? What happened?" I asked.

"They had to pee. All the women at once. I tell Han, they've got to wait till we get to a rest stop. But as soon as they hear this all the women start clamoring in Korean, and so Han says just pull over here. I'm trying to tell him the shoulder isn't wide enough, but he insists. So I pull over, and then George pulls over behind me, and all the Korean women hop out of both vans at once, and do you know what they do? They all squat down in a row, right behind the vans. On the side of the road! Like ducks, Bob. They were squatting there like ducks. And I'm thinking, Jesus Christ, this is quite a show. And then sure enough, flashing lights. A state trooper car pulls right up behind us, and then you know what some of the women do next? They hike up their pants and make a run for the woods. You've never seen anything like it. I don't know what the cops were thinking but they got out of their car in a hurry. So I get out fast, too. I want to head them off before they can chase the women into the woods, because you never know what could happen if they get them in the trees. So I go running up to them—"

"What did you say?"

"I said, 'Sir, you might want to take a look at the license plate of the van behind me. These are North Korean diplomats, and this is a very sensitive international situation.' So they radioed it in. And sure enough, they came back and said, 'Try to get them to a rest stop next time.' And then they left."

"That's good, Dad. Where are you now?"

"I'm at a gas station. There were some of them who didn't pee, and now they've got to go. I pulled into this station, and you know what? The guys running the place didn't want to let them in the bathroom. They wouldn't unlock the door! Three black guys. So I start shouting at them, 'You're discriminating against them because they've got yellow skin. Do you have any idea what—'"

"Dad—"

"I told them, 'You know what they could do? They could squat right here in front of your gas pump and piss all over the place, and nobody could do a thing about it. You know why? Because they're diplomats, and they can piss wherever they want, with immunity.' And that got them. They opened the bathroom door. So now I'm waiting for the Koreans to finish up."

"You're doing a great job, Dad—"

"But that's not why I called you. There's been a change of plans. Han wants to go to Washington, D.C. He pulled out a map about an hour ago—his own map, with all the names of places in Korean. And he shows it to the guys sitting in the back and then he shows it to me and says he wants to go to Baltimore and then to Washington, D.C."

"They're supposed to go straight through to Atlanta. No stops."

"That's what I told him. But he said there's been a change of plans. And you told me he's in charge."

I got Han on the phone and asked him what the hell was going on "Oh, I forgot to tell you," he said sheepishly. His delegation had been invited to spend the night at the home of a rich South Korean in the suburbs of

Baltimore—something he had neglected to tell the State Department, too. I felt like I was dealing with a teenager who'd gotten away from his strict parents and was making the most of his freedom.

I called Kuhlmeier, who was bound to hear about it from his own people anyway.

"That's a no-go, Bob," he said. "You have to be very careful. Tell them the president is grateful they are attending the Games. We want them here, and we want them in one piece. They're on a straight shot from New York to Atlanta. That's what we agreed. Nothing unexpected."

"I'm not in a position to tell Han he can't stop in Baltimore, Ted. Have the State Department tell him."

"You know as well as I do we don't have diplomatic relations, so we can't do that."

"Have your guys pull him over. Give him a ticket."

"Don't be funny, Bobby. You told me you were in charge of their trip. You tell them they are not to make an unscheduled stop."

"You want them to pull out of the Olympics? Because Han will take their delegation and walk. They'll go home and then what will you have? An incomplete Olympics. The president's going to love that. And it'll be because you wouldn't let the North Koreans see the monuments of our great nation's capital. You want to read that headline tomorrow morning? You can start emptying out your desk now. You'll be flipping burgers with me at Cubby's. How's that? I could use the help, by the way."

"You're not following through on what you promised."

"They changed their plans on me. And can you really blame them? How often do they get the chance for a road trip? What would you do, if you were them?"

"It doesn't matter what I'd do. That's not relevant."

"I'm just saying, Ted, put yourself in the other guys' shoes for once."

It must have been nice for Han and his comrades to stay in the home of a big-money South Korean in Baltimore. They don't get out enough. And it must have been done with the blessing of Pyongyang, since Han would never have taken such a politically risky step otherwise. Dad said the place was impressive—a big, brick, colonial mansion with a circular driveway—and that the businessman and his wife hosted a fancy dinner party with hired Korean waiters. Dad didn't understand what was being said, and he went to bed early in a comfortable room in the guest house. He said everybody had been in a good mood, eating barbecue and kimchee and drinking little cups of plum wine.

I passed these details along to Kuhlmeier, who seemed satisfied for the time being, along with my observation that sometimes North Korea can be more flexible than our country. When we declare a country to be our enemy, we go all the way. Look how hard it is for American citizens to go to Cuba. The South Koreans may be the enemy of the DPRK, but Han was happy to accept a sleepover invitation and sit down to dinner with them.

Han never told me why the delegation stopped in Baltimore. Maybe the businessman had relatives in the DPRK, and he hoped to sweeten their situation by doing Han a favor. All I know is that the next day Dad drove them into Washington, D.C., where they all posed for portraits in front of the Washington Monument and the Lincoln Memorial, and then made their way to Atlanta without any further troubles. And they seemed to be settling in just fine at the Fallon widow's house.

Then, a few days later, Han called in the middle of the day, sounding worried. "Have you talked to your father?" he asked.

"Not today. Why? What's wrong? Where are you?"

"I'm at Mrs. Fallon's house. Your father is very angry at me. I made a mistake, Bobby. I wanted to tell you before he does. It's about the tickets." I heard Han cover the mouthpiece of the phone. A rustling sound came through the line. "He wants to talk to you."

"Don't worry, it can't be that bad," I said. "I'm sure we can clear it up, no matter what it is." But Han was gone. Instead, my father's voice came on the line in a lowered voice.

"This is exactly the kind of sneaky commie bullshit I warned you about," he said. "That no-good motherfucker. You want to know what happened? We're driving to the sports center, and we're talking about tickets to the tennis and tickets to the swimming and how fun that's going to be, and he says,

'I have very good ticket for you. Maybe you want to make a contribution.' And I go, 'A contribution? You got to be kidding me!' He's got the tickets in his hand like he's showing me a poker hand, Bob. And he's trying to extort me. I told him, 'Do you know who paid for this van? And all the gas to get down here? And all the tolls? Your friend, Bobby, who you are trying to extort. Not to mention my time, which I'm donating out of the goodness of my own—'"

"It's not exactly extortion, Dad."

"He's getting the tickets for free! Don't you make excuses for him. He might fuck you around, but he's not going to fuck me."

"He called to apologize—"

"Because he knew I was going to nail his balls to the wall. He has no scruples. This is the way these people operate. They take kindness for weakness, and if you are kind to them they shit on you. This is why they have the DMZ in the first place, to keep those two-timing bastards on the other side of it, where us civilized people don't have to deal with them!"

"Dad," I said, "I don't want to keep getting phone calls like this. I want you to call me if there's any issue, but try to keep things under control. Be a gentleman. You two can sort this out between yourselves."

And it turns out they did, to my dad's great satisfaction. He started getting the best tickets you could find, because Jimmy Carter and Ted Turner and some of the other Atlanta liberals were donating tickets to Han in the name of peace, who felt so bad he was donating the best seats to my father. A couple of days later he called with the exciting news that he'd sat in Turner's own seat: "With his name on it. On a plaque!" Dad went to all the swim meets, the tennis and boxing matches, Ping-Pong. He sat along the first baseline for baseball games. He even went to the judo match where the DPRK's sixteen-year-old extra-lightweight, Kye Sun-Hui, beat the reigning Japanese champion to bring home gold. He had his picture taken with Sun-Hui on Mrs. Fallon's front porch, with her medal around his neck. When he wasn't driving Han and the delegates around, he was hanging out in the Olympic Village, getting athletes to autograph plastic DARE cups for his buddies back in Fairfield and trading pins with other tourists. He went through more than twenty disposable cameras posing with athletes from exotic places like Barbados, Estonia, and Belarus.

Then, early in the morning of July 27, I was in a deep slumber, dreaming of grilled shrimp and heavy china plates, when the phone rang. It was pitch-dark outside our bedroom windows. Disoriented, I switched on a bedside lamp and answered. Joe Jordan's tense voice barked me awake.

"We're under attack! Are you watching TV?"

"I'm sleeping, Joe. It's two in the morning. What are you talking about?"

"Terrorists. They've hit us at the Centennial Park. During a rock concert. Right in the middle of the action. Three pipe bombs. This is the real deal, Bob. It's started. We've got—"

"Hang on. Where is everybody? Where's my dad? Where's Han?" I grabbed the remote and clicked on CNN. The screen filled with images of people walking quickly in the darkness. Yellow police tape. Ambulance lights. The anchor said it appeared the bomber left the explosives in a bag in the middle of the Olympic Village during a concert by Jack Mack and the Heart Attack. It appeared to be the work of a lone crazy person. There was speculation about remote detonators.

"Your dad's here. All North Koreans are present and accounted for. I've got the perimeter secured. We're in lockdown."

"What perimeter?" I started hunting for my slippers. Lilia got up and went to the kitchen to make us some coffee.

"The house! Fallon's. There's no telling where they'll strike next. They know where we are. They've had a blimp circling over the house for a few days. They're pointing their cameras and watching us. Did you know the phone went dead today? Too many agencies have their alligator clips on here, so be careful what you say. Everybody wants to know what the Koreans are talking about. I speak Korean, and I am making a point of not listening out of deference to them. It's like when the communist Chinese came to Houston. The city of Houston knows I speak Chinese, but the Chinese didn't—"

"What blimp? Joe, you're in the suburbs. You're not making sense."

"Goodyear. Don't think they're not in on this. And we've found people in the bushes of the neighbors' houses. I flashed my gun at them—"

"They're probably FBI agents," I said. "Take it easy."

"Fuck 'em. This is my assignment. We don't need them."

"Just get the Koreans to the venues on time, okay? And be careful about your weapons. Was everybody in the house when the bomb went off? Where's Han? Let me talk to him."

Han sounded tired when he came on the line. "Your guy is nuts," he said.

"Are you okay? Is everybody okay?"

"Yeah, everything is fine. Most of us were asleep until Joe woke us up. You know, it's funny. Your country is unsafe. You think your system is best. But this would never happen in my country."

He was right. Here in the United States you never know where danger could come from. And Han and I had plenty of debates over whether it's better to have his system, where the only thing people have to be afraid of is their government, or our system, where we have freedom. I'll take freedom any day, because here in America we might have crime and other things to fear, but it's nothing I can't face down with a shotgun, some cash, and a good lawyer.

Not that this was giving me any peace of mind. Between the terrorist bombing in Atlanta and the competition from the TGI Friday's, I was tense from worrying about situations beyond my control. I needed to clear my head, so I took my gun out in the woods and spent a long day shooting. I returned late in the evening, feeling good but exhausted, and went straight to bed. The next morning I got a call from my mother.

"Your father was just on television," she said.

"With the athletes? Are you sure it was him?"

"We've been married forty-four years. You think I don't recognize your father? He was outside of a courthouse, standing behind a news guy, and I don't think he knew he was on TV because he kept picking at his teeth. They were saying something about your North Korean friends getting in trouble for molesting a little boy. Are you sure you should be hanging around with these people?"

The light on my answering machine blinked nonstop: full. I hit the Play button and got sketchy details of what had allegedly happened in Atlanta the day before, August 5. A group of DPRK delegates accepted an invitation to visit the Jimmy Carter Library, without the escort of either my father or Joe Jordan. Somewhere along the line, the fifty-year-old coach and secretary general of the DPRK Gymnastics Association, Gyong Nam Chang, was accused of sexually touching a nine-year-old boy visiting the center with a school group. I called Jordan, who had the local papers. On the front page of its sports section, the *Atlanta Journal* quoted a school official who said the Korean coach "reached over the seat of a child and 'fondled him on the chest and between his legs.'"

A judge set Gyong's bail at fifty thousand dollars, which kept him in jail for the time being, because Han and his group didn't have the cash to spring him.

At first I didn't know what to think. As a father, I wanted to punch the guy's lights out. Whatever he did, if it could even remotely be interpreted as molesting, it was the worst crime I could imagine. It's hard to express how disgusted I was. Then I got Han on the phone, and he said point-blank that the charges had to be false because there were no child molesters in the DPRK. "It doesn't happen," he said. I couldn't believe my ears. I'm pretty sure children are abused all over the world. Was Han just ignorant or was he in denial? Or did he have a different set of moral values than I did? If he was able to kill another human being on behalf of his government, what other kinds of behavior was he prepared to excuse? I'd been around people on the wrong side of the law all my life, but they were hustlers, small-timers making a buck off the system, Robin-Hooders. I didn't want to be an accomplice to guys who were callous about the safety of children. I spent a lot of time helping Han and his crew. They took me away from my family, they cost me hundreds of hours I could have been at Cubby's taking care of business. And for what? To help people who made excuses for a child abuser? I didn't want any part of it.

My mind wandered down some pretty dark pathways that morning. I told Han he should think about these issues, since he was partly responsible for what his regime did. Some serious moral questions needed addressing, as soon as our countries established diplomatic relations and took care of some other priorities, like feeding their people and reassuring the world that they're not going to fling a nuclear bomb into the middle of Tokyo.

Kuhlmeier and I had a few long talks about what to do about the coach. In the days after the arrest, he came down to the restaurant and suggested I help get a local lawyer, so I called Jordan and put him on it. Kuhlmeier said as long as they did it quietly, the Koreans would probably be allowed to take the coach back to Pyongyang, where there was no extradition treaty, rather than creating an embarrassing international incident at this sensitive time. I had very mixed feelings about that, because it didn't take into account any justice for the little boy and his family, and once again the interests of governments were being put ahead of the needs of the ordinary citizen.

Dad was just as disgusted as I was, at first. He'd been at the courthouse for Gyong's hearing, and he was ready to come home. The Olympics were ending anyway. "Too much craziness," he said. "I'm tired." I asked if he was angry at Han for assuming the coach was innocent.

Dad sighed. I could hear him thinking about it. "Maybe you should give him a break," he said. "There could be more to it. We're relying on the story of a young kid and his family, and things can get misunderstood. I know it's not the same, but think about how crowded the trains are in Atlanta right now. It happened to me the other day. I was riding one of the trains when it came to a sudden stop. We were packed in there like cattle, Bob, and it was hard to move, and there was a young woman standing in front of me, a large-breasted woman, and because I wasn't holding onto anything I had my hands out in front of me to break my fall—"

"Jesus, Dad."

"She saw me coming toward her, but we stopped so fast she didn't have time to turn away, and the momentum sort of carried my hands onto the parts that were closest to me, if you know what I mean, and even while it was happening I was saying, 'Excuse me, excuse me,' and when I'd got off her again she said, 'That's okay.' We both smiled. It was no problem at all. She was fine with it."

"Dad—"

"The fact is we weren't there. We don't know what really happened. The coach is a gymnastics guy. Maybe he wanted to show the kid a move. He might have tried to pick the boy up. And you never know if somebody is behind the family, trying to use this to embarrass the North Koreans. We don't know what the motives are. It could be complicated."

I realized there were a couple of lessons we could learn from this story. I told Han he should report this back to his bosses: First, it was important for Pyongyang to have someone they could trust on the ground in the United States, to make sure they avoided situations like this. If they were going to let their people wander around and interact with the American public, they needed to be aware of the cultural differences. I was willing to help with that, and between me and Han we could create a buffer between DPRK delegations and U.S. law enforcement. The second thing I wanted him to relay was the reaction of my father. "Notice how he came around," I told Han. "Before the Olympics, Dad was a commie-hating reactionary who distrusted you. After the Olympics he was still a commie-hating reactionary who distrusted you, but did you hear how he defended your gymnastics coach? I guarantee that his attitude softened during those weeks with your delegation." And I didn't care what kind of hard-line politicians in Washington want to bomb Pyongyang, they didn't compare to my dad in terms of inflexibility. If one trip could turn his opinion around, there was hope for everybody else.

I also wanted Han to relay the story my dad told about a week after he got home from Atlanta. He'd gotten his rolls of film developed, and we were going through the photos when he stopped and held out one picture in particular. It showed him standing next to the judo champion, Kye Sun-Hui.

"This was taken on her birthday," Dad said. "We had a party for all the medal winners at Jean Fallon's house. Did I tell you about that? Right in the middle of the party, Jean brought out a birthday cake with seventeen candles on it. You see that big smile on her face? All of us Americans and even some of the North Koreans had just sung 'Happy Birthday' to her. She said it was the first birthday party she'd ever had. The first birthday party of her life, Bob. I tell you, that got to me.

"We were sitting around the living room. Jean had invited her relatives. Not all of them came. Some of them didn't want anything to do with the North

Koreans. The whole thing's still a touchy subject with some of the POW crowd. You know that. But one of Jean's daughters was there with her baby, and at one point the wife of one of the Korean big shots says, Let me hold the baby, or she reaches for the baby, I can't remember. And Jean's daughter looks around the room, and nobody says it's a bad idea, so she gives her baby to the Korean woman, who takes it in her arms. We're all watching Jean's daughter, whose father was a POW in Vietnam and is still missing. You know that. Then the Korean woman says something in Korean, and us Americans want to know what it was, so we all look at their translator, who says, The lady says this is the first time in history that a member of the DPRK government has sat in a living room holding an American baby. And Jean's daughter sheds a tear. The whole thing was very moving. We were all trying to put our best foot forward. I am not ashamed to say I got a tear in my eye."

He got a tear in his eye. My father.

7

~~~~~~~~~

They Wear Two Faces

I GAVE DAD AN ENVELOPE with two large in twenties, as a stipend for his time in Atlanta. He thumbed the bills, stuffed them in his pocket, and called me a fool. I'd tried to keep the old man in the dark about how much I spent on the Atlanta adventure, because I didn't want to hear it. But he wasn't blind. Between the airfare, travel, and food bills from the Games, and the upgrade to the Cubby's menu, I was more than fifteen grand in the hole by the end of August 1996.

McCreary warned me against going overboard with Han. "The North Koreans are like a stripper in a go-go bar," he said. "You think she likes you, but as soon as you're out of money, she's gone. You'll see."

"Nobody's taking advantage of me," I told him. I was getting what I wanted out of the deal. Other guys spend their money on drugs or gambling or real-life strippers. My weakness was the North Koreans. I didn't see anything wrong with it. As long as I kept my restaurant in business and Lilia and Andrea were comfortable, I wasn't hurting anybody.

Look how many rich people spend fortunes trying to get closer to power. They hire lobbyists. They donate to politicians. Some of them do it hoping for sweetheart deals for their businesses, but a lot of them just want to get their hands on the steering wheel for a moment or two. They sit next to their congressman at a thousand-dollar-a-plate dinner or play a round of golf with a senator. With Han, I was there every day, in the backseat of history in the making, shouting instructions over the shoulder of the driver.

I could have told Han he had to pay my expenses for helping him. But that would have made me a contractor. Winkler told me I should never get paid for services to the North Koreans, because it was dangerous legal territory for a private citizen under the Trading with the Enemy Act. I didn't want to be a supplier to Han anyway. I wasn't his caterer or his travel agent. I was his host. As his host I was his friend, and as his friend I was his confidante.

A few days after he got back from Atlanta, Han asked me to come to the embassy on 72nd Street. We sat in the little conference room with the door ajar, which gave us as much privacy as possible. North Koreans get suspicious when they see a closed door.

"Are we sending me back to Pyongyang?" I asked, rubbing my hands together. "I'm ready. Put me back in the game, coach."

"I want to discuss what happened in Atlanta. Your father and I—"

"Don't worry about that," I said. "He had a great time. You should have seen him showing me all his pictures. He'll remember that trip for the rest of his life."

"He told me you don't have that kind of money to lay out," Han replied. "I thought you were getting expenses from your government. You said your president wanted us to come to Atlanta and you would take care of arrangements, so I thought—"

"Remember what JFK said?" I asked. Han looked at me blankly. "'Ask not what your country can do for you, only what you can do for your country.' It's a one-way street. The Catholic Church is the same way. When that basket gets passed around, it's for you to put in, not take out."

"Don't think I'm like the Catholic Church," he said. "It's just the way we were trained." He stood up and walked out of the room. Han's superiors must have taught him to grab all he could from the evil American imperialists.

I thought of all the goodie bags full of vitamins and beef jerky and little bottles of vodka. I couldn't count the number of meals and deli sandwiches I'd bought for Han, who never offered to pay.

But when he returned less than a minute later, he was smiling and he carried a medium-sized manila envelope with a telltale rectangular bulge. "We can't let Cubby's close down, it's too important to my country," he said.

I looked away. "I'm a businessman. I'll sort it out myself," I said. I was torn, because I was months overdue on my payment to my meat supplier, who threatened to cut me off. I was behind on my state taxes. I was backed up on my mortgage.

Han poked the envelope at my chest. "I don't want you distracted," he said. "Take it."

So I did. I figured if I just "held" the money for Han, it wouldn't violate the Trading with the Enemy Act. I told him I'd pay him back as soon as business picked up in the fall. When I climbed into my Explorer a few minutes later, I opened my envelope and counted: three thousand dollars, all in twenty dollar bills. It was less than half of what I'd spent during the Olympics, but I guessed it was all Han could afford from the embassy budget.

That night as we sat in bed, I gave the envelope to Lilia and asked her to make the deposit. "When you're not borrowing money from the mob, you're borrowing from the North Koreans," she protested, before opening the envelope to count the bills.

"That's about how much we spent on the van," I said. I sat on the edge of the mattress and put my head in my hands. "If we have a good month I can pay it back in a few weeks. Then you'll only have to worry about the mob."

Lilia crawled behind me and massaged my shoulders with her strong hands. She'd watched more of the Games than I did, and she rooted for the North Koreans when their judo champion won. "Think about that girl who made her country proud," she said. "You accomplished something important. Don't forget that."

"It's good to know Han appreciates me," I said.

"Han looks up to you," she said. I kicked my heels against the bed frame.

"Haven't you noticed?" she asked. "He's even started talking like you. The other day I heard him say, 'You gotta be kiddin' me!' He sounded just like you."

Sometimes she was the only other person who understood why I wanted to be involved with the North Koreans. I appreciated that. Lilia believed in what I was doing even when it took time away from the family.

On September 18, right after my dinnertime rush, Han called and asked me to come to the embassy as soon as I could. I hung up the phone, took off my chef's coat, and drove into Manhattan. "You need your money back?" I asked, as soon as we faced each other across the coffee table in the little conference room.

"There's going to be some trouble," he said. "I want to tell you before you hear it on the news." My mind flashed to the coach who molested the little boy in Atlanta.

"If it involves children, I don't want any part of it," I said.

"Listen. One of our submarines has landed in hostile territory. They crashed on the beach. The crew went onshore, and now they're on the run. Twenty-six guys."

"In South Korea?" I whistled. "That's bad."

"Yes. They might retaliate. There's a chance of war, very soon. Washington will get involved."

I could hardly believe what I was hearing. I felt a tinge of pride that he wanted my opinion so urgently. "Why would you jeopardize billions of dollars in KEDO money by sending an antiquated submarine with a bunch of hoodlums to invade—"

"Don't use that word. It was an accident, not an invasion," he said. The smell of fish frying wafted in from the kitchen. The DPRK diplomats were probably in for a long night in the embassy, as their bosses were just waking up in Pyongyang. Han pressed his fingers against his temples. "Don't ask me, I didn't send the sub down there," he added. "They didn't mean to get caught."

"If we go to war with you, I'm going to be like the guy in the Japanese embassy after they bombed Pearl Harbor," I said. "Very popular with my government."

"They're already demanding that we apologize." Han sighed. "We're sending a delegation over."

"Maybe that's a good thing. Say you're sorry you invaded them with—"

"We didn't invade. Stop saying that. How about your helicopter pilots? Did they invade?"

"You shot them down," I said. "Anyway, we apologized for that."

"You expressed regret. That's not the same. You didn't apologize, and we aren't going to apologize either."

"And you want me to pass that along to my contacts, that you won't apologize?"

"Yes. We are sending the same message through the official channels. We won't apologize. This was an accident."

Han saw that he was about to be sucked into a big storm. I wished I could help in some way.

That night I came home from the embassy later than expected. I told Lilia I was sorry I missed tucking Andrea into bed and explained the news as we sat at the kitchen table. If war broke out, it would be bad for our family. I could be called a traitor, I told her.

"You think they'll start a war over a submarine?" she asked.

"Han's worried about it," I said.

"It's bad for the North Koreans, even if there's no war," Lilia said. She had met KEDO delegations many times, and she knew what was at stake. A new fight between Washington and Pyongyang could destroy the Agreed Framework. The deal for the nuclear reactors already looked iffy, because neither side was moving forward. If the deal fell apart, there was no doubt the North Koreans would restart their nuclear program. And that could lead to war, too.

By pure coincidence, I had a pile of papers on the kitchen table from Dolores Alfond, the chairwoman of the National Alliance of POW/MIA Families, including documents submitted that same week to the House of Representatives Subcommittee on Military Personnel. Lilia had asked me to store them in a plastic bin in the basement, out of the way. I wanted to stack them in the bathroom, where I did most of my reading. Between the Olympics, my family, and Cubby's, I hadn't found the time to look at them. I thumbed through the documents. The top paper was a memo from the Pentagon's Defense POW/MIA Office (DPMO) entitled "Accountability of Missing Americans from The Korean War—Live-Sighting Reports." It used surprisingly blunt language:

> There are too many live-sighting reports of Americans in the DPRK, specifically observations of several Caucasians in a collective farm, by Romanians and the North Korean defectors, to just dismiss the possibility that there are American POWs in North Korea.

The memo focused on an interview that took place years earlier with a Romanian named Servan Oprica, who worked in a North Korean factory. Oprica stated that he was on a bus tour of the countryside with other Romanians in 1979, when the bus suddenly turned into a wide field scattered with small houses. A man stepped out of a house, and everyone on the bus gasped because he was tall with light hair and pale skin. Oprica said they saw other workers, farther away, but it was clear that they were tall with light-colored hair. All the men appeared to be in their fifties—the age a Korean War veteran would have been at the time. It sounded like a ghost story, but it seemed highly possible to me. Nobody denied that American servicemen were left behind after the Vietnam and Korean wars. If any of them survived, where else would they be? A collective farm in a remote area, where they could be watched and guarded, seemed as likely as any prison.

The author of the memo, a guy named I.O. Lee, had tracked down another Romanian on that bus, Flarin Tomescii, who corroborated Oprica's story. If the Romanians were right, they saw American POWs twenty-six years after the end of the Korean War. Lee wrote his report in 1996, seventeen years after the sighting. Why had it taken so long for Oprica's story to be officially documented by the Pentagon? And now that it was, why weren't our elected officials chasing the leads? (I later found out that I.O. Lee's superiors transferred him to another department soon after he wrote the report. I wondered if it had gotten him shitcanned.)

As I read on, an old flame rekindled inside me. The memo cited reports

Me, at fourteen, with a string of trout.

Ross Perot gives me and Khai his business card in 1993, with Red McDaniel in the background.

With Han (far right) and Ho Jong (second from left) at Cubby's before the New Jersey Nets basketball game.

Collecting a North Korean hair sample for the FBI, with Mark Sauter standing by.

New York Giants chaplain David Bratton serves sandwiches at Cubby's.

Dad (far left) with North Korean Olympic medalists, Dolores Alfond, and Jean Fallon in 1996.

Pentagon intelligence analyst John McCreary and his wife with Giants quarterback Kent Graham at Cubby's.

Han (left), Minister Counselor Kim Myong Gil (right), and me after a pheasant hunt at Big Piece Meadows.

Colonel Jack Pritchard of the National Security Council pays me a stern visit in 1996.

Our business delegation meets with the Zosonsulbi Group in Pyongyang.

Senator Stewart Greenleaf,
Dave Rovnanik, Red
McDaniel, Bobby "Meats"
McErlean, me, Jay
Gartlan, and Steve "Wall
Street" Miller en route to
Pyongyang.

Pyongyang
pedestrians.

Laying a wreath
at the Kim Il Sung
Mausoleum in
Pyongyang.

Catching striped bass and bluefish off Sandy Hook, New Jersey, with the North Korean KEDO delegation.

Fishing with Han, near the end of his second tour in America.

Han (third from right) and other North Koreans shortly before he returned to Pyongyang in October 2006. Mike O'D is fourth from the right.

Lori, Lilia, and Andrea.

in the Clinton Administration who was likely to listen to a POW proposal from a restaurant owner.

"Does the FBI know about this?" he asked. "You're wading into some pretty tricky territory."

I called Kuhlmeier right away and asked him to stop by Cubby's. "It's about solving the submarine crisis," I told him when he came in the next morning.

"Don't go near it," Kuhlmeier said.

"I have some ideas about getting our POWs back," I said. "Live Americans who may have been held hostage for more—"

"You don't have ideas," Kuhlmeier interrupted. "Not when it comes to a crisis like this. Your role is to get close to the North Koreans in New York and report back to me. That's it."

I should have expected this lack of vision from the Feds. "You keep forgetting," I told Kuhlmeier, "I'm not on your payroll."

As long as I was sinking my own money into this adventure, I was going to do it my way. I needed an ally—somebody with juice. Kuhlmeier and McCreary had no real power. The problem was, I didn't know anybody else with Washington connections. As a state senator, Stewart Greenleaf ranked too low on the totem pole. There had to be somebody out there who was politically connected and yet antiestablishment enough to want to get involved with me and the North Koreans. I needed to find a guy who was shrewd but also had a big heart. Somebody with a sense of adventure. Somebody with imagination.

I fished a number out of my shoebox in the back office of Cubby's and dialed from the phone next to the soda fountain.

"Is this Mrs. Perot?" I asked when a woman's voice answered.

"This is Margot," she said, sounding slightly amused. "Ross is out back. Who's calling?"

I said I was an old friend, and Margot Perot set the phone down while she went to interrupt her husband, the former presidential candidate, from his yard work. I hoped he would at least hear me out. My impression was that H. Ross Perot was a man of the people—the son of a cotton picker, who delivered newspapers on horseback when he was a kid to earn money for his impoverished family. He was the billionaire founder of a computer company, but also a Kmart shopper and a renegade. During the Vietnam War he'd spent a million and a half dollars to get Christmas care packages into the hands of American POWs stuck in the Southeast Asian jungle, and later he single-handedly funded a rescue mission to spring two of his employees from an Iranian prison. He knew what it was like to be on the wrong side of the U.S. government, too. In 1992, he surprised everyone when he pulled out of the presidential race, saying there was a government conspiracy to disrupt his daughter's wedding and force him out of the running. He was on the ballot in 1996, but by October his campaign had more or less petered out.

"How can I help you?" The voice came on the line in his unmistakable, high-pitched Texas twang.

"Mr. Perot, do you remember me? Bobby Egan. I helped Le Quang Khai defect from Vietnam, and you and I met after the—"

"Sure I remember. How are you, Bobby?"

I told him how I'd befriended Han and hosted the DPRK delegation to the Atlanta Olympics with the help of Jane Fallon and Dolores Alfond, whom Perot knew in the early POW/MIA activist days.

"How is Dolores?" he asked. I said she'd sent me some new information about POWs in North Korea and explained my idea of using the submarine crisis as leverage with Pyongyang. Perot had heard the news about the submarine.

"They *should* apologize," he said.

"What's an apology worth?" I asked. "They're feeling the heat, and we could get something much better. If they hadn't done something bad, we wouldn't even be discussing POWs. We've got them by the balls."

"How do you know we've still got men there, Bobby?" he asked. Perot served as an officer in the U.S. Navy during the Korean War, and I could tell I had his full attention.

"The Pentagon memo says there are probably men there. There are the sightings. The North Koreans I'm dealing with are talking about eleven live Americans. Han Song Ryol is their head of American Affairs. He wants to help."

"Who've you talked to in our government?"

"Just the FBI, who, if you'll pardon the expression, sir, are just standing around with their dicks in their hands."

"Huh."

"The North Koreans want to meet you," I said. I hadn't planned out my approach, so I winged it. "Can you come up to New York? I'll have us sitting with Minister Counselor Han the minute you arrive. They may want to release the POWs to someone of your stature. Are you ready to go to Pyongyang? We'll go over there, you and me, and with luck we'll bring back some Americans who haven't seen home in more than forty years. Think about it. The North Koreans are ready. The tomato is ripe. We've got to pick it."

"Okay, let's slow down a sec," Perot said. "We'll go step by step. If you can arrange a meeting, I'll send Harry up to New York. He works with me."

"Thank you, sir," I said. I hung up the phone and stood in amazement by the soda fountain.

I drove into Spanish Harlem to meet Han that evening. "Ross Perot wants to open a back channel to negotiate for the POWs," I said. I was getting a little ahead of myself, but how else do you make progress?

"You know Ross Perot?" Han asked. "And you talked to him about this?"

I pulled out a photo I'd brought along just to prove my credibility. It showed me standing with Perot, Khai, and Perot's good friend and U.S. Navy Capt. Eugene "Red" McDaniel, a former Vietnam POW, a few months after the Senate Select Committee hearings. "He's a friend of mine," I said. "I have his home phone number."

We arranged for a meeting a few days later. Perot's guy, Harry, arrived by private jet into Teterboro Airport in New Jersey, just down the road from Cubby's. He picked me up from the restaurant in a chauffeured car, and we rode together to 72nd Street in Manhattan. He asked what the "protocol" would be. I suggested that he not go into human rights violations or the lack of democracy in the DPRK. "Show reverence for their Dear Leader," I said, which raised an eyebrow.

Harry was an older guy. He seemed blasé about meeting the North Koreans. The meeting lasted only about half an hour. It was pleasant enough, but I wasn't overly impressed by Harry's contribution. He mostly sat quietly, and when he spoke up it was near the end of the meeting.

"Mr. Perot would like to invite you to his ranch in Texas," Harry said to Han. "If y'all can get the authorities to let you travel, we'll fly you down ourselves."

Han asked what kind of plane would take him. "Is it a private jet? Does it go right across, nonstop?" Harry said "yes" and "yes," and Han clearly loved the idea.

I was against the North Koreans going to Texas for a private visit, because it could easily turn into a bunch of polite talk that went nowhere. If it happened behind closed doors, it might as well have never taken place. It needed to be in public. I wanted Perot to come to New York, or Cubby's, where I could make sure his visit put pressure on the Clinton Administration.

When I suggested this to Harry as we were leaving, he said, "I'm not so sure Ross wants to be seen with the North Koreans."

"Listen," I said, "if you're interested in getting our men back, you have to do business with the devil." Harry flew back to Texas right after the meeting, and I wondered what exactly he relayed to Perot.

The crisis on the Korean Peninsula escalated in October. South Korean troops shot and killed eleven members of the submarine crew. They captured one alive. After more hunting in the mountains of South Korea, they found the bodies of eleven more North Korean crewmen apparently shot to death by their own comrades, presumably to keep them from talking. Three of the North Korean crew were still on the run.

The State Department kept demanding that the North Koreans apologize, because the Clinton Administration couldn't afford to appear weak. By the middle of the month, with the presidential election just a few weeks away, Clinton was locked in a fight for his survival in office. Other than demanding an apology, nobody in Washington seemed to care about solving the crisis. It didn't fit into the political campaign, and Clinton's team probably wished the submarine issue would just go away on its own.

The leadership vacuum created a dangerous situation. The North Koreans tried to use the killings of their crew members to paint the South Koreans as aggressors. Pyongyang issued a statement that made newspaper headlines all over the world: "As victims, we have the right to retaliate on the offenders. Our retaliation may be hundredfold or thousandfold."

"What does that mean?" I asked Han. "You're going to attack?" I remembered the story of Operation Paul Bunyan in the seventies, when a tree-trimming operation nearly escalated into full-scale warfare.

"We won't make the first move, but the second move will be all or nothing," he said.

I told Kuhlmeier about this remark and he drove over to Cubby's right away. I unlocked the door and let him in, and we had coffee at the back table as usual. "That's not what their embassy is saying publicly," Kuhlmeier said.

"That's what they're saying privately," I said. "You can tell your higher-ups the North Koreans are not going to strike first, and also that they're willing to negotiate for our POWs. Can you find out if the president is open to that? I need to know."

"I can't ask questions for you," he said. "The information travels one way—up. I'm just a conduit."

It was worth asking, even if I didn't expect Kuhlmeier or Clochin to knock on the door of the White House for me. I leaned back from the table. "Pheasant season opens next week," I said. "Han's been begging me to take him hunting."

Kuhlmeier nearly dropped his coffee mug. "With a weapon?"

"Of course with a weapon!" I said. "Nothing automatic, just a shotgun. We're going out to Big Piece Meadows in Fairfield. My buddy Mike Nigro and I are going to take Han out, maybe with one or two of his guys—"

"Don't you dare put a weapon into that man's hands," Kuhlmeier said. "You can't do that."

"It's good for diplomacy," I said. With all the harsh rhetoric and the stress Han was under, I figured it would be good for him and some of his boys to get some fresh air and pop off a few rounds. "What am I supposed to do—ask them if they want to go birdwatching? I don't have anything against bird-watching, but it's not the kind of thing—"

"They're an enemy nation, and you cannot arm their people with weapons and turn them loose in the woods of New Jersey. It's a no-can-do, Bob. Do you realize what could happen if something goes wrong?"

"I thought you were just a conduit. You said information only travels up."

"You think you're a comedian?"

I didn't think I was a comedian, but I thought Kuhlmeier should lighten up. I'd been hunting in Big Piece Meadows since I was a boy. What could go wrong? I decided to once again ignore the FBI's opinion of how and where I should hang out with the North Koreans.

Han couldn't wait to get into the woods. He'd wanted to go deer hunting, but I knew he lacked the patience to sit quietly in a deer stand for seven or eight hours. I told him a pheasant hunt was more fun, because you get to walk around. Nigro borrowed a golden retriever named Rex from a friend of ours, and I got the guns and the gear together. I picked Han up before five A.M. on a Saturday in mid-November, a few days after the season opener. He stood outside the bagel shop on 95th Street with Kim Myong Gil, a junior minister counselor at the mission.

"You ever hunt over dogs before?" I asked when they got in the Explorer, still looking sleepy.

Han and Kim exchanged a look. "It's a stereotype," Kim said.

"You think we're barbarians," Han said. "You should look to yourselves before you criticize." He glared at me.

"What crawled up you guys' asses this morning?" I asked.

"I thought we were hunting birds," Kim said.

"You said pheasants," Han said.

I turned east on 96th Street and headed for the FDR Drive. "Hunt *over* dogs," I said. "Not hunt dogs. We don't hunt dogs. We use them to flush the birds out. We shoot over their heads. You have to be careful." I laughed. "We *like* dogs. We don't eat them."

"You're an asshole," Han said, rubbing his face.

It was still dark when we got to Nigro's house. Rex the golden retriever jumped into the backseat and lapped at Kim's cheek with his big, sloppy tongue. Kim put his arms up and grunted in disgust. Nigro slid into the empty seat, and we were off. We parked at the entrance to Big Piece Meadows and unloaded the gear as the dark blue morning light brightened to gray. I held up a twelve-gauge shotgun and showed Han and Kim the safety. Han went for the gun, but I raised it out of reach.

"You know how to shoot one of these?" I asked.

"I know guns," Han said, as though I needed reminding that he served on the DMZ. He grabbed the shotgun by the stock and turned it over. "Where's the clip?"

"It's a little different from an AK-47." I showed him how to put a shell in the chamber and click it in, one at a time. "Throw it up the barrel like this," I said. "They're pump guns."

I gave Han a few cartridges of number-eight birdshot and helped him load the first round. Kim watched attentively. Nigro looked at me as if to say, "Are you sure?" Rex ran around our feet, sniffing the damp leaves and grass.

I loaned Han and Kim orange sweatshirts and orange hunting caps, and they wore their pants rolled up over white socks and Chinese-made loafers. We crunched through the grass, feeling the cool air of the November morning stir around our faces. Nigro and Kim paired off about twelve feet in front of me and Han. Rex ran ahead in the meadow, looking for birds to flush.

"Have you had any contact from our government?" I asked with my voice lowered. Clinton won reelection a week earlier over Sen. Bob Dole—I didn't vote because I didn't like either one of those morons—and I wondered if his administration would turn its attention to the trouble in Korea. South Korean forces had killed the rest of the North Korean infiltrators except for one, who remained at large. Both sides still threatened full-scale war.

"I met with one of Clinton's guys," Han whispered.

"When? Why didn't you tell me last night?" I asked. "Who was it? You need to coordinate this with me."

"I'm telling you now." Han said a big cheese at the National Security Council (NSC), Jack Pritchard, came up from Washington to talk about the submarine crisis and push for an apology. "He asked if I knew who you were," Han said.

"He asked about me? By name? What did you say?"

"I said you were a friend of mine. What the fuck else was I going to say?"

Lilia was right: Han sounded like a New Jersey goombah. They say imitation is the sincerest type of flattery. Now I had a North Korean envoy talking like me, and my name was on the lips of important people at the National Security Council.

"What did *he* say? How did he know who I was?"

Thirty feet ahead of us, Rex sniffed a tuft of grass with interest. Nigro and Kim stopped in their tracks. Han and I froze, too. I was about to tell Han to fan out to the side where he could safely get a shot off when Rex lost interest and trotted farther ahead. We walked on. "I brought up POWs, and he asked if I knew you," Han said. "He didn't want to talk about POWs."

No surprises there. A National Security Council guy probably had to spout the official B.S. "Remember," I said, "we're working with Perot. We're going through the back door. Did you say you're willing to put POWs on the table?"

"Yes—" Han said.

A loud flutter broke the morning silence. Rex barked. A pheasant lifted itself from the ground slowly and beat its wings twice directly in front of Nigro and Kim. To the left of me, Han raised his shotgun. I started to put out my hand to stop him, but it was too late. He pulled the trigger as the bird rose over Nigro's head. *Crack!*

Nigro's knees buckled, and he collapsed. Kim dove to the ground and covered his head. "No!" I shouted. I ran toward Nigro's body. He was my childhood buddy, and in our younger days we'd nearly killed each other a few times fooling around with drugs and booze and weapons. I never thought something would happen now that I was sober. A jolt of panic ran through me, as I imagined having to tell Nigro's wife and kids that he'd been shot by a North Korean diplomat. Kuhlmeier's words echoed in my head: "Don't you dare put a weapon in that man's hands." If Han had killed an American citizen, it would have consequences far beyond the lives of a couple of families in North Jersey. With the submarine crisis in full swing, it could tip the balance between peace and war.

I reached Nigro and sighed with relief when he blinked his eyes open. His moustache quivered with rage. "You said these guys knew how to hunt," he spat. He climbed up from the grass, and I put a hand on his shoulder to make sure he didn't run over and deck Han. Kim got up and stood still, with his mouth open in surprise. Amazingly, neither of them had been hit. I looked around to see if we'd been followed by FBI agents. All I needed was for Han's near miss to get back to Kuhlmeier. I wheeled around.

"You can't shoot when somebody is in front of you!" I shouted at Han. "I told you that. Number one rule. Birdshot can take a man's head off, especially at that range!"

Han wasn't listening. Like a typical North Korean who can't admit a mistake, he walked past us and retrieved his pheasant. "I got the bird," he said. "First shot!" He held it up like he expected everybody to ooh and ah and give him a round of applause.

I asked Topousis over at *The Record* to dig up some background on Pritchard. Charles L. "Jack" Pritchard was President Clinton's chief of Asian affairs at the NSC. He spent twenty-eight years in the U.S. Army, during which he served as the Secretary of Defense's country director in Tokyo. He advised President Clinton and his National Security Advisor, Samuel Berger.

"He's the real deal," Topousis said, sounding impressed.

I could smell the juice the same way as when you walk into a restaurant where some *capos* are eating. Even if you don't see them, you know there's juice in the room by the way everybody else talks more quietly than usual and *doesn't* look at the corner table. I was getting closer to decision-making power.

I planned what I'd say to Pritchard when I called him, but he beat me to it. He called Cubby's. When I answered, I pretended I didn't know who he was, to try to level the playing field a little. He said he wanted to talk, so I played it cool and invited him to stop by the restaurant the next time he was up from Washington. He said he'd come the next day at seven P.M.

We had our holiday decorations up. Cubby's looked good. I wore a jacket and tie for the occasion, and I made sure my mom, dad, Lilia, and Andrea were all at the restaurant. I wanted Pritchard to feel a personal connection to me. I also wanted my parents to see how far I'd come. I'd never been in a school play as a kid, but now I had a visitor from the White House.

At five minutes to seven, a black, chauffeur-driven car pulled into the parking lot. The restaurant was about half full, and I'd blocked off the back booth so we'd have a little privacy. Through the front window, I watched Pritchard get out of the car. He wore a suit and tie and the thin, wire-rimmed type of glasses intellectuals wear. He was about my height, with a few extra pounds on him. I met him in the vestibule by the pinball machine and escorted him into Cubby's.

He shook hands with my parents, Lilia, and Andrea, and he and I sat down in the back booth. Lilia came over wearing an apron, and Pritchard ordered ribs and a baked potato. I had a salad with chicken on it. "When you run a barbecue joint, you have to watch your weight," I said. I winked at Lilia.

Pritchard smiled. He asked how business was at Cubby's, and I explained how I recently upgraded my menu with grilled shrimp and chicken to compete with TGI Friday's. He asked me about Le Quang Khai's defection, and I realized he had done some research on me, too. It was flattering to think he'd been boning up on my interest in POWs. "I want to get our men out of Korea," I said. "We have an opportunity that may not come around again. The Koreans are ready."

We talked about the submarine incident, and Pritchard said how important it was that the North Koreans apologize so that both sides could move forward with the Agreed Framework and KEDO. "You should have contacted us first, before you went to Perot," he said.

"What would you have done?" I said it loudly enough for my family to hear. "You would have passed me off to some flunky, and nothing would be happening. Think about it. If I had called your office with this idea first, would you have taken me seriously? Would you be in New Jersey right now enjoying that plate of ribs and discussing this with me?"

There was no point in pussyfooting around somebody in a position of power. Pritchard just looked at me. He knew I was right, and I figured he would respect some straight talk. "I know you're here to try and neutralize anything I might do," I said.

Our conversation turned a little stiff after that. As soon as he'd finished eating, Pritchard said he was tired. He had to get back to New York and catch a flight to Washington the next morning. I walked him out to his car. At the door, he said, "Show me around Hackensack a little bit." So I climbed into the backseat of his limousine with him, and we headed for Main Street. I pointed out the sights—the karate studio, the offices of *The Record*, the unlit alleyways where you could score an eight-ball of coke.

As we headed back toward Cubby's, Pritchard turned to me. He looked straight into my eyes. He held my gaze for a few seconds and then spoke in a low, calm, and unmistakably threatening voice.

"When I tell you to back off, you back off." It was the kind of thing I expected to hear from a tough guy from Pyongyang or somebody from my neighborhood, not from a Washington guy in a suit and wire-rimmed glasses. It was intimidating. But a warning in the back of a limo on a dark autumn night in Jersey is always intimidating. Where I come from it's the kind of message that lets you know you're about to get whacked.

I called Han the next day and put an optimistic spin on things. I said the guys in Washington wanted to talk about POWs, but to get them to forget about the apology for the submarine crisis we should keep working through Perot. That was my angle in. And if that didn't work, Han and his team could walk away from the negotiating table. What was Washington going to do—attack because Pyongyang refused to apologize?

"If they attack, we are ready," Han said. I could hear him puffing out his chest over the phone line.

After Pritchard's visit, I knew that convincing Washington to negotiate for POWs would be an uphill battle. I called McCreary to get his take on it, and he sounded wary. He said a couple of FBI agents had paid him a visit and asked about my conversations with him. "You better be careful," he said. "I know your intentions are good, but you might consider documenting what you're doing."

As soon as we hung up, I went to Radio Shack and bought a cassette tape recorder with phone plugs, and I started recording all of my phone calls. I called Perot.

"Good morning, sir. I spoke last night with the National Security Council, and I also spoke with the Koreans. And what they're doing now is, I'm trying to get them to work out that deal."

"Were they pleased to be invited?" he asked.

"Excuse me?"

"Were they pleased to be invited to Texas?"

"They regard your invitation very highly," I said. "But Minister Counselor Han said we don't know if the Korean-Americans, as he calls the POWs, are going to be on the table for long, because they want to use that issue for a little leverage during the talks. Now the White House is hollering at me because I have some influence on the Koreans. I tell them I want a tiny issue put on the table, and they won't put it on. They said, 'Tell the Koreans to make a public apology for holding the men and to reimburse the families of the men they've held that long. And then we'll talk.'"

"No—"

"And I said, 'Shouldn't you be trying to entice them into talking?' And they said, 'We're not ready to talk now.' They said, 'Politically, it's not the right thing to do now, and we're not doing it.' Can you imagine that?"

"Oh, Lord. That breaks my heart," Perot said. "Are you going to talk to the North Koreans again?"

"I talk to them every day."

"The next step is to go into the country and personally visit with these people. And at that point, we'll have so much hard evidence that there's no place to run, no place to hide, and then we can start to move. This should all be done very gracefully, but this is a critical piece of getting it done."

"I'm glad to hear you say it, Mr. Perot."

"Because the American people will be angry if this is not included in the process. The principle of not leaving men behind is a very strong one with the American people. Maybe not in Washington, but out here in grassroots America, we're talking about their sons."

"That's right."

"What I really, desperately need is to be able to show some people who have been held against their will by the North Koreans," Perot said. "You can tell them it won't be used to embarrass them in any way."

"You know what the NSC told me? They're gonna embarrass the shit out of them. They're going to demand that the Koreans release POWs and publicly apologize and pay back all their families—"

"That's not the way you get it done," he said. "My goal is not to embarrass anybody. My goal is to let everybody be a winner when the guys come out."

"That's not what the attitude of our government is."

"Oh, Lord."

"My friends the North Koreans have their problems, okay. But they want to change. They don't know how to change, but they recognize that they have to. And our government isn't making it easy for them. Mr. Perot, I love our country, and our government has made a lot of good decisions for us. But they don't have to pick on the shortcomings of another country. They need to lend a hand. I mean, when a guy from Hackensack who flips burgers for a living is the only American the Koreans say they can trust, there's a serious problem."

I knew if I could get Perot over to Pyongyang, we'd really have some traction. I was already planning a new trip. Han suggested I could bring a few American businesspeople to talk about funding our chicken farm, and I had some guys lined up. After Thanksgiving, I brought a few hundred spruce saplings onto the west end of the Cubby's parking lot and held a Christmas-tree sale to pay for my plane ticket. I started to fantasize about escorting Perot on a trip to rescue American POWs. It would be good for Han, too, because he'd earn kudos at home for getting Perot into his country.

"What if Washington won't listen to Perot?" Han asked on the phone one night.

"They won't have a choice if we're bringing back POWs," I said. "And if they don't, you guys can bail out. Just walk away from the negotiating table."

I didn't tell Kuhlmeier how much I was advising Han, but he found out anyway. He stopped by Cubby's one morning in late November looking shaken. It turned out Pritchard had paid a visit to the FBI in Washington and told them to have their field agents keep me under control.

"It's a no-can-do, Bob, what the hell are you trying to pull?" Kuhlmeier asked as we sat down. "You can't have influence over foreign governments. You have no right to do that."

"If it's a good idea, why not?"

"You're making the agency look bad," he said. I had to laugh. If he wanted to convince me, it was the dumbest argument in the world. This was around the same time that stories about former FBI Director J. Edgar Hoover's sexual tastes were coming out in the media.

"I'm not the one wearing women's panties under my suit," I said.

"This isn't funny," Kuhlmeier said. "What you're doing is probably illegal. You ever hear of the Logan Act?"

I knew about the Logan Act because Winkler, my attorney, had waved it under my nose as one of the laws the government might hit me with. The text was short but to the point:

> Any citizen of the United States, wherever he may be, who, without authority of the United States, directly or indirectly commences or carries on any correspondence or intercourse with any foreign government or any officer or agent thereof, with intent to influence the measures or conduct of any foreign government or of any officer or agent thereof, in relation to any disputes or controversies with the United States, or to defeat the measures of the United States, shall be fined under this title or imprisoned not more than three years, or both.

The U.S. government had seriously considered using the Logan Act against the Black Panther Stokely Carmichael when he went to Hanoi to protest the Vietnam War in 1967. Senators John Sparkman and George McGovern were accused of violating it when they went to Cuba in 1975. President Reagan said the Reverend Jesse Jackson should be punished under the Logan Act when he went to Cuba and Nicaragua in 1984. And the National Security Council threatened House Speaker Jim Wright when he involved himself in negotiations between the Sandinista government and the Contras in

Cuba. But would the Feds use it against me, their part-time ally? I wondered if they saw me as a double agent, who worked for the other side as much as for them.

"Some of what I've been doing for you is against the law, too, isn't it?" I asked Kuhlmeier. "Isn't it illegal for me to spy on a foreign embassy in the U.S.? I've taken Han outside his twenty-mile travel limit. Many times. You let me do these things because half of spying is illegal. You want me to be effective with the Koreans? I need to be valuable to them."

"I can't protect you on this," he said. "Back down before you get yourself in jail."

Nothing makes me want to do something like somebody telling me *not* to do it. I didn't blame Kuhlmeier for trying to chase me off. He was trying to protect his job, because his boss's boss had gotten a dressing down from a high-ranking NSC colonel. But somebody had to think about missing American servicemen, and it wasn't going to be anybody in government.

I had Perot interested in going to Pyongyang, the North Koreans willing to talk about POWs for the first time ever, and Washington asking them for a concession. I got the feeling a deer hunter has when, after tracking a ten-point buck for days, he finally catches sight of his animal. But it kept moving behind the trees, and I couldn't get a clear shot.

I called Perot's buddy, the former POW Eugene "Red" McDaniel, and asked him to put pressure on his pal from Texas. I called *Newsweek*, *The New York Times*, and the Associated Press, but nobody wanted to run a story. I called Topousis at *The Record*. I called Bratton and tried to think up a way to involve the New York Giants. I worked the phones so hard that Cubby's became like New Jersey's answer to Camp David.

The crisis played out just like Lilia said it might. President Clinton and the South Koreans had called for a "pause in the pace" of building safe nuclear reactors under KEDO until North Korea apologized for infiltrating with its submarine. Twice that November, the North Koreans threatened to quit the Agreed Framework and pull more fuel out of their old reactors, which could be used to produce A-bombs.

One Wednesday afternoon, Han told me proudly that he and Ri Gun met Pritchard in New York the day before and threatened to walk away from all talks about the submarine. The next day, Lilia picked up the phone behind the counter and mouthed, "Pritchard." I went in the back office, clicked on my tape recorder, and picked up the line.

"The meeting on Tuesday was not satisfactory at all," Pritchard said.

I still hoped Pritchard would be our ally, so I offered to help. "Han's coming down tonight," I said, "and you know I'm trying to get them to stay, number one, and number two, I'm trying to get them to make some type of agreement with our government. I'm telling them the thing to do is let's hash it out. I said, 'We'll get the POWs on the table and you'll be able to negotiate for them,' but you know my government's not open to it yet."

"Certainly not after what they pulled on Tuesday," Pritchard said, referring to Han's and Ri's threat to quit talks. "They very well can go home and the whole thing—"

"I won't tell Han that," I said. "It's both your responsibilities not to tell each other to go home. It's your responsibility to compromise with each other. Is it their fault they want to bring this up through Mr. Perot?"

"They brought it up through you," Pritchard said. "You brought it up."

"But Mr. Perot—"

"You brought Mr. Perot into the picture."

"What does it matter how we got here?"

"If they want to bring this up as a bilateral issue, they've got the channels and the mechanisms to do it."

"Maybe they don't trust you guys, Jack. If they want an outside conduit, what difference does it make?"

"We're not dealing with them through outside channels on the negotiations between two countries."

"Why not? I mean—"

"I'm not going to undermine our government's position and our relationship with the South Koreans and the ability to move forward on critical issues like the Agreed Framework—"

"Even if it means we might compromise the POWs?" I asked. I couldn't believe it. Pritchard was an Army guy. The idea of "no man left behind" was supposed to be sacred to guys like him. At least that's what the U.S. politicians and military leaders liked to claim. I didn't understand why he had to see it as an either-or question. Negotiating over the POWs could *help* move the Agreed Framework forward.

"We're not willing to do it under threat of blackmail," Pritchard said.

"Well you've got to give them something. You've got—Hold on, Jack." I put my hand over the mouthpiece because I felt an irresistible tickle in the top of my mouth. I let out an explosive sneeze, followed by four more sneezes. "I'm sorry, I'm selling these Christmas trees," I told Pritchard when I came back on the line. "You've got to pay for these men, or else we're not going to get them back."

"Do you want to go public and say the North Koreans are holding live Americans against their will, and we have to buy them back?" Pritchard asked.

"Wouldn't that be appropriate?"

"Absolutely not."

"See, I disagree with that," I said.

"Well, Bobby, I don't want somebody buying *my* return if I am illegally held by some other government."

"I'd buy you back. I'd put a second mortgage on my restaurant for you."

"You don't want to be—"

"Insanity is trying the same thing time and again and expecting different results," I said. "Jack, you and I know we had men in Laos in the seventies and early eighties, and we missed the chance to get them, okay? And now we're doing the same thing again. So why don't we try a different tactic? Why don't we bring different people in? It seems the FBI welcomes the private sector's help. Why don't you guys want to? I just wish that you and the president would feel a little differently—"

"Bobby—"

"We can help you, Jack."

"Bobby, up to now we've been very straight with each other. Please do not accuse me or the president of not thinking that this is—"

"I'm not accusing. I'm just telling you how I feel."

"The fact that we didn't jump to the tune of the North Koreans based on your offer to provide Mr. Perot, that this makes us not caring—"

"I think another month of these men being there is too long, okay? Another month is too long."

"And, bottom line, who's responsible for that?"

"The Koreans," I said.

"Fine, we've established that. So when I see Han today, I'll give him an ultimatum—turn 'em loose or there's to be no forward movement on the relationship at all. How's that? If you want to talk about commercial contracts, if you want to talk about anything positive at all, turn 'em loose."

"I don't think hardball—"

"We're not going to buy 'em."

"You wouldn't want me to buy you back if you were a POW for fifty years or forty years?"

"Not at all."

"I said I would. I'd mortgage my restaurant for you—"

"I don't want you to."

"But I'd do it without your knowing. You might yell at me when you got back. You'd say, 'How much did you spend for me, Egan?' I wouldn't tell you. I'd say, 'Jack, you're not worth a hamburger.' But I would have done it."

After my conversation with Pritchard, I knew I needed to get Perot moving soon or the whole plan would fall apart. I called him from the phone by the soda fountain during the lull between lunch and dinner.

"We have an old-fashioned political standoff," I said. "The Koreans are ready to go home. We discussed your involvement. The Koreans want to put the POWs on the table now, or they want some type of confirmation from you that you'll meet them."

There was a pause from the other end of the line. "I cannot do anything until Berger calls me back and says go ahead," Perot said.

My heart sank. Perot was referring to Sandy Berger, the deputy national security advisor who was about to take over as national security advisor for Clinton's second term. Perot said, "Until Berger calls me back," meaning they'd *already* talked to each other. Pritchard had obviously brought in his boss to squash my idea.

"What did Berger say to you?" I asked.

"He said he was gonna call me if, you know . . ."

"If you could meet with the Koreans?"

"Yes."

"So there's no way you'll make any type of initial contact?"

"Not until I hear from him."

"As you know, Mr. Perot, there is interest on the part of the Koreans to put on the table live Americans, okay? And he's asked you not to do anything?"

"Mm-hmm."

I knew this was code for "Give it up, pal." I imagined him on the other end of the phone line—the big-eared rebel with a deep Texas twang; the only presidential candidate I'd ever voted for. My hero had turned into a regular sap who took orders from above.

"All right, Mr. Perot, I agree to disagree with you." I laughed, trying to change the tone of the conversation. "I'm asking you to do something, and I understand that—"

"In order to do that, you'd have to understand my situation."

"Yeah, and I don't. But I will do my job to keep this on the table as long as I can."

"If we can get those guys to give me a green light, I'll move immediately," he said. "Lord, I wish I could help you."

"I'm going to talk to the National Security Council again, and so I'll keep pushing them—"

"I said I wouldn't do anything until they said go ahead. Anything they want me to do to help, I'll be glad to. I just need Berger to call me and tell me what to do."

Unless I could work a miracle, I'd hit a dead end with Perot. I didn't have access to anybody higher ranking than Pritchard. "All right," I said, hopelessly. "I'll have Berger call you."

Han called the next day for a status report. We were deep into preparations for my next trip to Pyongyang, and I had several businessmen already buying their tickets to Beijing. All that was missing was the big fish. "Perot's on board!" I said. I felt bad about deceiving Han, but I figured if I could get the Clinton Administration to lighten up, he *would be* on board.

I called Pritchard's number at the National Security Council, and a woman picked up.

"Happy Holidays, Asian Affairs," she said.

"Is Mr. Pritchard available?" I asked.

"Oh, he just left for the State Department," the woman said.

"Good, tell him my Korean friends are anxious for an agreement."

"No!" she exclaimed. "Who's your Korean friend?"

"This is Bobby Egan," I said. "Minister Counselor Han. You know, they're anxious."

"Well, they don't think they're making any progress with Ross Perot, so they think they'll just have to deal with us."

I checked the light on the tape recorder. Who was this woman who obviously knew who I was? "What's your name?" I asked.

"Roseanne," she said.

"Roseanne, you must know a little bit about me, right?"

"Yeah," she said. "I mean, no!"

"Not at all?"

"Who are you, Bob?" she asked sarcastically.

"I'm just a guy floating out there, you know."

Roseanne laughed. It was not a kind laugh. "Whose side are you on?" she asked. "Whose side do you represent, anyway?"

"I represent both sides," I said. "Of course, I'm an American. I'm a capitalist and a businessman, and the communist philosophy doesn't sit well with me. That's what I tell the generals in Pyongyang, that they have more to fear from us businessmen than from my government."

"I wouldn't tell them too much," she said. "You never know what hotel room you might be found in."

Was she threatening me? In my neighborhood, when somebody says something like that, you know exactly what it means.

"I'll go to any length to get back an American who's been in jail in North Korea," I said. "And you must know that the Koreans want to put this on the table now."

"I hope so," Roseanne said in a strange, sing-song voice.

"But we won't do anything with it, and that's what is confusing me a little bit. Let them have a little negotiating chip, and it'll maybe bring our boys back."

"Now, most of them have been gone for fifty years, right?" she asked.

"We don't have enough people in government now who are willing to take the chance to promote change, so what do we do? We sit back and we—"

"No, you don't know that," she said.

"Oh yeah—"

"No, you do not know that."

"Wanna bet?" I said. "I probably know—"

"I bet you do not—"

"Because the Koreans talk to me more openly than to you—"

"Oh, *excuse* me?" she said.

"All the Koreans you guys negotiate with are very good friends of mine."

"We're talking about North Korea, right?"

"I don't usually say 'North Korea.' I say 'Korea,' which is what they say."

"Can I put you on hold for one minute?"

I sat back in my chair and waited. On the other side of the kitchen door, one of the cooks dropped a heavy metal pan and cursed. I wondered what Roseanne's position was, and how she knew so much about me.

"I'm sorry," Roseanne said when she came back on the line. "I'm trying to clear the Chinese. They're coming in to meet the president."

"Oh, are they—"

"Now you can be as friendly as you want with these people, but what I know about them—and the Chinese—is that they wear two faces. And if their good friend's life was on the line, they would not be standing next to him for five minutes."

I watched the little cassette spools roll counterclockwise. I wondered if she would have said this kind of thing if she knew I was recording her. "You'd be surprised," I said. "If you take Jack aside, and you say, 'Hey, Jack, this Egan guy's for real, and we've got to get our boys home—'"

"I would never do that. There's no need to do that. The government, Colonel Pritchard, and the president all want that."

"Then why did it take me—"

"It didn't take you anything!"

"It didn't take—"

"No, no, no, no! Guys on the outside have to understand that the government has to work in a certain way. There is a due process—legally, politically, and every other way—to be met. You can't just go out there and start pushing buttons and moving things—"

"But isn't it worth it to get our boys home?"

"No! No! Because if you make one mistake in the process, you're going to eat it for the rest of your life."

I wasn't going to eat anything. Pritchard might eat it. Sandy Berger might eat it. These were guys with political careers to think about, and they weren't willing to stick their necks out. And that's why nothing ever changes with guys like them running the show.

"But our government has said we don't even want to put it on the table now."

"They have their reasons," Roseanne said. "And you won't know the reasons, because there's national security involved. You guys have to learn to be patient and wait for it to unfold—"

"Ugh. These men have been there for so long that—"

"Well, that's too bad, they're going to have to wait for it to unfold. You can't decide one day to—"

"Could you imagine having to wait fifty years?"

"They didn't want to negotiate for fifty years—"

"I don't mean the Koreans. I mean our men who are still there and had nothing to do with all this."

"Well, the political thing has to happen and we have to just be patient. It has to be done through the due process of politics and international law, and it's just going to have to wait."

What right did she have to decide POWs could wait? She and Pritchard and the rest of them weren't using any "due process" to solve the POW situation. There wasn't any point waiting for it "to unfold." Things don't unfold by themselves. You unfold them. You get in there with your hands, and you open the thing up, and you get to work. Nothing had unfolded for our POWs for forty-three years, and without me, the NSC and the North Koreans wouldn't even be talking about them.

"Now the Koreans are ready," I told Roseanne.

"Are we to trust these people? How about our negotiations? While we're negotiating, they send submarines into South Korea."

"And that's an issue. But why can't we separately take up the—"

"Because we have to slap their hands," she said. "We have to slap their hands and tell them this is not the way to negotiate."

"Is that more important than our POWs?"

"I didn't say that. I'm saying you cannot go in the back door. Even if you're a husband and wife and you're negotiating your marriage, you cannot. If one of you goes out and has an affair, what's that going to do to your negotiation? What's that going to do to your marriage? Come on, wake up!"

"But we're talking about something—"

"They're being their usual sneaky, cagey—"

"Let's say we compromise ourselves a little bit—"

"You're not thinking clearly. You're too excitable about this."

"Isn't it worth a concession—"

"The North Koreans shouldn't be tweaking around with our government. Who the hell are they?"

"Why has Mr. Perot been ordered not to come up?"

"That was the right decision. You're seeing it from your eyes, and you're not seeing it from your government's eyes."

"That's why I call you guys and I talk to you," I said.

"The president speaks for this country, and Ross Perot respects that, even though they were campaigning against each other, he respects his government. He's an American citizen—"

"But don't you think I—"

"We're talking about Ross Perot. He's an American citizen first, and he will do what's best for his country. And he will stand aside and let his government do their work."

"I see it differently—"

"This is a wake-up call to you," she said.

A wake-up call. After the conversation with Roseanne, I became as depressed as on any Sunday morning in my twenties, when I'd wake up on the wrong end of a lost weekend, with a dry mouth, a fuzzy head, and empty coke baggies all over the floor. I finally had to deliver the bad news that Perot wasn't coming to Pyongyang, which was going to make Han look bad at home. I didn't know how many of his higher-ups knew he was trying to get Perot to come. I'm sure they were hoping to gain prestige and credibility from his visit. I called Han and started to tell him, but he cut me off.

"Ask for another meeting with me," he said.

Two days later, I was back in the conference room on 72nd Street, explaining myself in front of Han and the three junior diplomats who furiously took notes.

"The good news is that Perot wants me to bring Capt. Red McDaniel to Pyongyang," I said. "We're going to be Perot's eyes and ears. We'll do some research and come back to Texas with more evidence, and after that—"

Han held up his hand to stop me. "You couldn't deliver," he said. He stood up from his chair and pointed at me. "Your POWs are not an issue with your government, so I don't want you to bring them up with us again."

He was grandstanding for the benefit of the other Koreans, but it hurt my feelings anyway. I never guaranteed the plan was going to work. All I'd said was it was worth trying. And I tried, which is more than you could say for most of the jerkoffs whose job it was supposed to be.

I'd had a wake-up call, all right. The Clinton Administration didn't want me to be part of the conversation about North Korea. I was supposed to provide information to the FBI, but not have opinions. And if I had opinions, I wasn't supposed to share them. They didn't want Perot to be part of the conversation, either, especially if his way in was talking about POWs. It seemed like they were more afraid of looking bad than of missing a chance to rescue American servicemen.

Our leaders say they represent all Americans. But if it was a congressman's son caught behind enemy lines, we'd have him out of there the minute the bullets stopped flying. I can tell you who got left behind. They were the drywallers' sons, the roofers' boys, the kids who would have come home from the war and gotten jobs collecting Pritchard's garbage, building Clinton's roads, and putting a muffler on Berger's car. If there was a tall Caucasian in his sixties still hoeing rice fields in North Korea, it wasn't a kid who grew up with a scarf around his neck. It was one of my people.

8

~~~~~~~~~~~~~~~

Trading with the Enemy

"YOU NEED TO CONTROL THE SITUATION," investigative journalist Mark Sauter said. "Keep everybody together." He stood anxiously by my side, with a video camera in one hand and the handle of his suitcase in the other. Travelers swirled around us in the post-Thanksgiving chaos of New York's John F. Kennedy Airport. The rest of our party was spread throughout the check-in line—a war hero, a senator, a missionary, and four businessmen, all making their first and possibly only trip to North Korea, with me as their guide and chaperone.

"Don't tense up on me," I said. "We're just getting started."

Sauter looked at me suspiciously. "You *do* have this trip organized."

The fact was, I didn't. And I was nervous. I had no idea how I was supposed to lead a group of respectable Americans into a Stalinist dictatorship. I assumed Han set things up on the other end, but just like the first time he sent me to North Korea, he never gave me an itinerary.

Our idea for this trip had been to take some entrepreneurs to Pyongyang to discuss our chicken farm and other business ideas, and also to invite Ross Perot along to negotiate the release of American POWs. After Perot bailed out and Han washed his hands of the POW issue, he softened a little and said I could still get VIP access to the War Museum, to look for evidence of missing American servicemen.

Sauter was the son of the former CBS News President Van Gordon Sauter and the stepson of California State Treasurer Kathleen Brown—he was a Harvard graduate who'd written about POWs and done his own archival research in Russia. I'd met him though Dolores Alfond and the POW activist gang. Sauter would know what to look for if I got him into the War Museum archives, and he brought his video camera to gather evidence for Pritchard, Perot, Berger, or anybody else who could make things happen in Washington. He was also secretly working for the TV news program *Inside Edition*.

I figured people would listen to Sauter. He had the pedigree that I lacked. You could tell our differences from our luggage. Sauter's preppy-looking canvas suitcase matched his khaki pants and blue button-down shirt. I carried a suit bag with a broken zipper that I borrowed from my parents, who bought it years earlier at Target for fifteen bucks.

Behind us in the check-in line, Capt. Red McDaniel wheeled a battleship gray, hard-shelled suitcase. McDaniel was Perot's friend, a Navy pilot imprisoned for six years during the Vietnam War and tortured in the notorious prison camp known as the Hanoi Hilton. He knew what it was like to survive with no contact with the outside world. When he finally returned from Vietnam in 1973, the U.S. Navy gave him enough medals to sink a ship and made him the captain of an aircraft carrier. He spoke with a deep Virginia drawl, and he gave us all a sense of purpose.

Han objected to the idea of taking an American war hero to his country. But I convinced him that if McDaniel came back to the United States with a good report, it might pave the way for a visit by Perot or some other American dignitary, and this would reflect well on Han at home. So he said he'd "indulge" me on this one.

Farther behind us in line stood the four businessmen I'd recruited as the delegation of the USA-DPRK Trade Council, which was the organization I founded with Han's input. Our mission was to make connections in Pyongyang that would give us a head start in international commerce if North Korea ever opened up for business. There were risks. A few weeks before leaving on this trip, I'd gotten a legal memo from Winkler, advising me that:

Under the Trading with the Enemy Act, North Korea is now subject to very stifling restrictions. A lengthy prison term and fines are possible for violating this act.

Violations included selling goods to North Korea or buying from them, financial dealings with anyone acting on their behalf, or "holding assets" for them. Basically, all transactions were out. I put together the business delegation carefully. Every member had two qualifications—enough money to pay his own way to the DPRK and a willingness to negotiate deals that, for the time being, couldn't be put into practice.

Robert McErlean ran exports for the New Jersey meat company D. B. Brown, which supplied Cubby's. He could move beef, chicken, pork, and other animal products anywhere in the world, so he was key to our dream of setting up a chicken farm in Pyongyang. I called him "Bobby Meats."

Our numbers man was Dave Rovnanik, an accountant and a wheeler-dealer who I met through a chiropractor friend with mob ties. Rovnanik had brought along Jay Gartlan, a tax attorney who knew how to draw up letters of agreement.

A few feet behind them, lawyer and international businessman Steven J. Miller stood beside expensive-looking, saddle-leather luggage. A tall, self-assured Jewish guy with round glasses, he wore an Italian suit and a pressed shirt with initials monogrammed on his cuffs. "Wall Street Steve," I called him. He'd spent years working in China, finding third-party companies for American investors who wanted to get in early and avoid trade restrictions. A few weeks earlier, he'd walked into Cubby's like he owned the place, shook my hand warmly, and asked, "You the guy taking me to North Korea?" I liked him right away. He seemed like a guy with the business savvy to make big deals happen.

Some people might have called them fringe businessmen, but they were the guys I could find in New Jersey who were willing to drop everything and take a risk on North Korea. Would I have rather taken Bill Gates and Donald Trump? Sure. But you have to start somewhere.

A few passengers farther back, as though they were deliberately putting distance between us, stood the tall, evangelical Christian state senator from Pennsylvania, Stewart Greenleaf, and his assistant, a heavyset missionary named Rose. They were goodie-goodies who said "shoot" and "darn," so I was trying to watch my language. The senator's wife already disapproved of me. A few days before we left, she came with Greenleaf to Cubby's. When I tried to hug her, she shrank away and claimed to have "tennis shoulder." She was against my inviting her husband to Pyongyang. But after a couple of years organizing humanitarian aid for North Korea, he wanted to see the fruits of his labor firsthand, so he could report back to the donors in his district. He brought boxes of candy and teddy bears to hand out at an orphanage and a few Bibles. "Don't worry," I told her. "Your husband's in good hands."

But now, as we presented our passports at the check-in desk, I wasn't so sure. They all had different expectations for their trip, and they depended on me. These people looked to me for cues about how to behave. It was different from going into North Korea with Bratton. I felt a heavy responsibility.

After an uneventful flight to China, we spent three days in Beijing taking camel rides, photocopying our passports, and getting visas from the North Korean embassy. Han had prearranged all the paperwork, and so far the trip went smoothly. As we climbed the stairs to board our flight to Pyongyang at the Beijing airport, everybody stopped to stare at the tires of the Air Koryo jet. They were so worn they showed more metal radial bands than rubber. The cabin smelled strongly of jet fuel. I sat next to Sauter and Wall Street Steve, and the rest of our group sat behind us. The other passengers seemed to be Chinese and returning North Korean officials. In front of us sat two Germans, who spoke just enough English to tell me they were trying to sell mining equipment.

We flew through a snowstorm over the Changbai Mountains between China and the DPRK. As the plane broke through the clouds over Pyongyang, everybody leaned toward the windows. The land was desolate and white. We couldn't see the runway because nobody had bothered to plow it. "There's nothing there," Bobby Meats said. I thought about those worn tires.

The pilot put the Russian plane down softly in the snow, but as he braked the plane fishtailed. Everybody gripped their seats. Wall Street Steve and I looked at each other with clenched teeth. The plane swerved back and forth on the icy surface. Finally the pilot gained control. As we turned off the runway we saw our woven tracks in the snow. A military-type transport plane stood in the distance. Everything else was white.

In the big, empty terminal building, guards surrounded us, and handlers took our passports and stamped our visas. Sauter had his video camera out and was trying to film something for *Inside Edition* when a guard came up to him and yelled in English, "No filming!" I tried to distract the guard by complimenting him on the cleanliness of the airport, while Sauter shot a few extra seconds of footage.

Customs agents rummaged through our luggage. When they found the Bibles the senator and Rose had brought they paid extra attention to his blue suitcase and her flowered bag. They opened the boxes of teddy bears and American candy. Greenleaf and Rose looked at me, worried. "You hid all your copies of *Playgirl*, right?" I asked Rose, who blushed and gave me a disapproving frown.

I warned our group they'd be watched twenty-four-seven. We heard the spies moving around between the walls at night. I told everybody the mirrors were probably two-way. Wall Street Steve said he waved at them every morning while he was shaving. Rose said she felt uncomfortable going to the bathroom.

Once we were "in country" I had no contact with Han or anyone else back home. I split my time between escorting my business, POW, and religious delegations. Every morning in the hotel lobby, the entrepreneurs and I met four or five North Koreans who took us to a conference room on the ground floor. Their leader, an older guy with silver hair who introduced himself as Vice Chairman Ku Song Bok, said they represented the Zosonsulbi Group. Han had told me this was the organization his government set up to deal with foreign businesses. I wondered if they were also meeting with the Germans who were on our flight.

After an elaborate series of introductions, Chairman Ku and the Koreans sat on one side of the white-topped conference table; Wall Street Steve, Gartlan the attorney, Rovnanik the CPA, Bobby Meats, and I took the other. Chairman Ku's men spent the first half hour pouring tea for everybody.

Wall Street Steve was a straight-to-the-point kind of guy, so after a few sips of tea he leaned forward and cleared his throat. "The first challenge is you have no foreign currency reserves," he said, looking at each of the North Koreans in turn. "Basically, you have no money. Stop me if I'm wrong. You have lots of natural resources. You have coal and iron. But you don't have a way of getting them out of the ground. It's basically axes and picks and human labor, right? You also don't have a reliable way of getting them to the coast or the right international shipping partners." Wall Street leaned back in his chair. "We're here to help."

As the translator spoke, the Koreans shifted uneasily in their chairs and ordered another round of tea. Chairman Ku made a speech about the greatness of the DPRK's economic system. One of the other Zosonsulbi guys brought out books in English and spread them on the table in front of us. They were the same books Han gave me a couple of years earlier, about the beauty of the mountains and the high quality of the red ginseng that grows there.

"We could bring your ginseng to Western markets, too," Wall Street said.

Chairman Ku shook his head. "We export all to China."

By the time we finished talking about ginseng, more than half the day was gone. Wall Street was getting impatient. "Ask them if they want to drink tea all day," he said to the translator, "or if they want to get down to business."

Chairman Ku pressed his lips together as the translator spoke in Korean. He explained the DPRK's plans for a tax-free zone for foreign investment on the northeastern tip of their country, next to the Chinese and Russian borders. They spread a map across the conference table, and we all stood up to see the spot where trains cross into the DPRK. Would we want to invest in the airfield there? If we put in the first twenty million dollars, Chairman Ku said, we could own a quarter of the airport.

Wall Street Steve adjusted his necktie. "What if we wanted to own the whole airport—a hundred percent?" he asked. The Koreans talked among themselves for a couple of minutes. Chairman Ku argued with one of the other delegates. "Eighty million," Ku finally said.

Everyone around the table nodded as though it was a done deal, even though both sides knew sanctions made moving forward with it impossible. We were practicing, greasing the wheels. The North Koreans and Americans smiled at each other as though we'd just made a major breakthrough. We stood up and stretched our legs.

After lunch, we talked about the KEDO site and the thousands of employees who would build and run the nuclear reactors. I proposed opening a branch of Cubby's inside the reactor complex to feed all these people. Chairman Ku especially liked this idea. I said he and I would be partners. "You like ribs?" I asked. "We'll bring the fattest, juiciest ribs you've ever seen for the ribbon-cutting ceremony."

I introduced Bobby Meats and told the Koreans that I could personally vouch for the quality of D. B. Brown's poultry, pork, and beef. We outlined our proposal for a chicken farm. "We know that some of your citizens are eating grass and bark to stay alive," I said, adding that some of the chickens could be used to feed the Korean people, and some could be exported to China or Russia for cash. "It's a flexible business model."

Chairman Ku liked this idea, too, but he quickly got caught up in little details: How many chickens would be needed? Ten thousand or five thousand? Are they for meat or for eggs? How many eggs do chickens lay in a day? How many in a week? He got his map out again. Where should we put it? How many hectares would it be?

"At this stage we need to work out a framework," Wall Street said.

We agreed that our business would be duty-free, but that didn't get us very far. The DPRK was the only country in the world that claimed a zero-percent tax rate. When everything is run by the state, you don't need taxes.

"How do we track and repatriate our profits?" Wall Street asked. Chairman Ku and the others looked at us blankly. "If our company sells X number of chickens to your government and Y number of chickens to the Chinese or the Russians, we need to know how to calculate the profits from X plus Y," Wall Street explained. "And once we have cash in hand in the DPRK, how do we take our percentage out of the country?"

Chairman Ku suggested the Zosonsulbi Group would pay us up front for the chickens through an account at the Bank of China in Hong Kong, which the North Korean government uses for international purchases. Wall Street shook his head. "We're not selling you something," he said. "We're not a supplier. We're starting a business with you, which means we take some of the profits from the business."

This was followed by a ten-minute discussion in Korean, during which Wall Street, Gartlan, Rovnanik, Bobby Meats, and I sat there and realized they hadn't thought this through, either. "It may be against our laws," Chairman Ku finally said.

"Then you'll have to change your laws," Wall Street said. "We're not going to set up a business for you just so we can sell you some birds."

Chairman Ku thought about this for a moment. "You want to make money for yourself," he said as though he had just solved a riddle. "You want to be a rich man with Korean money."

Wall Street rolled his eyes. "No, I'm here on vacation. Of course I want to make money! I'm a businessman. But I want to help your country develop, too. The trick of a joint venture is it has to be win-win. You win and we win."

The Koreans waited for the translation, then had another heated discussion among themselves. Chairman Ku spoke.

"He says, 'We like win-win,'" the translator said. "He says, 'Draw up the documents.'"

We drafted our first memo of agreement between the USA-DPRK Trade Council and the Zosonsulbi Group on the hotel's computer. Gartlan made sure it didn't sound like an actual business contract, which was forbidden by U.S. law. We wrote that "once trade sanctions" were lifted, and "subject to the approval from the U.S. Treasury Department," we intended to develop a chicken farm in the Pyongyang region.

All great things begin with small steps like our memo. I went to bed that night dreaming of a day when Han and I could run a business together. We had all kinds of ideas: real estate; construction; potato and goat farms; tourism. If I could get the chicken farm going, I'd put Han in charge. He'd be one of the first North Koreans in the private sector, and I'd be one of the first American entrepreneurs in the Hermit Kingdom. We'd call our business Egan & Han International Trading Co. Or just Egan and Han International. Egan should come first, because I'd be the one finding the capital. Or we could put it under the umbrella of Cubby's.

"What is this?" Chairman Ku asked when we showed him the agreement the next morning. He pointed to the place where we mentioned the U.S. Treasury Department; we explained that we had to put that language in to avoid any trouble with our government. "You see?" he said, looking at his comrades. "Your government is more restrictive than ours!"

Chairman Ku and his group insisted on finalizing agreements for us to sign, and I realized they had to justify the time they spent with us. We changed the memo every day, with one guiding principle: we planned to develop business together whenever our governments gave us permission.

It was stupid that we didn't have permission. We *should* invest in North Korea. The only reason a destitute country like theirs spends billions trying to build nuclear weapons is that they feel insecure. If they were better off, they wouldn't be so paranoid; and if they weren't so paranoid, they wouldn't want a nuke so badly. Other countries have given up nuclear weapons programs. The South Africans abandoned theirs in the early 1990s when the Apartheid government learned to fear its internal enemies more than foreign ones. Argentina and Brazil swore off nukes when they made peace with each other. Taiwan and South Korea gave up their programs in the 1970s after getting security guarantees from the United States. Libya handed over its nuclear material after normalizing ties with the West in 2003. Nobody frightened them into giving up their nukes. They were coaxed. They were assured. Countries that gave up nuclear weapons had two things in common: they felt safe, and they were tied into the world market.

When you trade with somebody, you have leverage over them. If I told the guy who delivers my vegetables that I wanted him to wear a funny hat on Thursdays, he'd do it. Why? Because he values my business. The problem was that we expected the North Koreans to change *before* we'd do business with them.

We sell ourselves short if we put up conditions beforehand. Why can't we make an investment and then expect that something good will come back? Maybe we'd get a much higher return. Businessmen like me understand this: moving forward always involves risk. Politicians have a lot to learn from us.

I used to buttonhole Kuhlmeier, Pritchard, McCreary, and anyone else who would listen: give North Korea diplomatic relations with the United States, and let's see what happens. Integrate them into the world economy, so they have something to lose. We're the superpower in the equation. We can always take it back.

"I'm the North Korean expert, not you," Pritchard once told me.

"Oh yeah?" I said. "How many times have you been to North Korea?"

"Never," he admitted.

"Have you invited the North Koreans over for a barbecue and a swim?" He hadn't. "Have you helped them bait a fishing hook? Taken them out to a ball game?"

He sighed and took the tone of a parent lecturing a naughty child. "You don't have relationships with your enemies," he said.

We wonder why our diplomats don't get anywhere. There's no personal relationship. No warmth. Here's what happens when our diplomats go to another country to negotiate something: They show up with a list of talking points. They drink cups of tea. They have a photo op. They sit in high-backed chairs. They discuss their talking points, hold a press conference, and go home. And later they try to figure out why their agreements fell apart and their treaties got broken.

Where I come from, we prefer a handshake deal. My people get to know each other over a bowl of pasta or a good plate of meat. Then see how things go. We might negotiate something, but only if we have a good feeling for each other. And if we make the right agreement, the only reason to write it down is for other people to carry it out. We trust the other guy will follow through, not because we think he's a good person but because we took the time to understand his motivations.

We've lost that trust in our society. We've lost it in business. Even in marriages. Everything's about the contract, the prenuptial agreement, the fine print. It's sterile. We run big risks having a sterile foreign policy, because weapons of mass destruction are involved.

Here's an idea: Let's turn our foreign policy over to the Mafia, because they understand this basic rule. Pritchard needed to watch *The Godfather: Part II* and pay special attention to that famous scene where Michael Corleone says his father taught him only one thing: "Keep your friends close, but keep your enemies closer."

Our leaders should be keeping people like the North Koreans very close. They should invite the Dear Leader for sleepovers at the White House, picnics at Camp David, mountain bike rides on Martha's Vineyard. Instead, the North Koreans had *me* for company.

Han made sure his countrymen rolled out the red carpet for Senator Greenleaf, because if he had a positive experience it could lead to more humanitarian aid, and that would reflect well on Han and therefore on his superiors. It made Han a good earner.

The second day after we arrived, one of the handlers asked if the senator and Rose wanted to go to church. "You have churches here?" Rose asked, surprised. "Of course," the handler said. Han once told me his government set up replicas of Western churches outfitted with pews and altars and hymnals, where they did experiments on "congregations" of their people to study the psychological effects of organized religion. They also used them to convince foreign visitors that the DPRK was a tolerant society. Rose and the senator went with the handlers, and afterward the senator said it was "just like a church back home."

The next day, I tagged along as the senator and Rose visited an orphanage in central Pyongyang. I prepared myself for the worst. Orphans in a nation hit by famine had to be some of the unluckiest children in the world. I imagined skin and bones and ragged clothes. We packed the minivan with the boxes of candy and teddy bears and drove to an unmarked building, where a director gave us a tour. It was a bedroom with little cots and a large playroom with a chalkboard in the front and games piled on tables. The place was spotless. A door opened and two dozen children between the ages of three and ten filed in and lined up in front of us. The director opened the boxes, and the children came one by one to collect a teddy bear and a piece of candy each. Each one bowed to the senator, Rose, and me. They looked thin, but healthy. It warmed my heart to see.

At lunchtime, I took a short walk to get some fresh air. A handler followed me as I crossed the park in front of the hotel. About halfway across I slowed my pace, feeling that something wasn't right. Up ahead three children stood at a shaved ice vendor's cart. A cool breeze rustled the bare branches of the birch trees. Clumps of snow gathered at their trunks. Not ice cream weather, but that wasn't what bothered me. The vendor reached into his cooler and pulled out a red ice cone. The first child in line, a little girl in pigtails, reached her gloved hand up. She smiled radiantly. It was the same scene I had witnessed on my first trip to Pyongyang. The girl looked exactly the same as the girl two years earlier. Was it a different child? The vendor saw that I had stopped to stare. He turned and posed, as though waiting for me to pull out a camera.

"Where are their parents?" I asked the handler.

"You like ice cream, Mr. Bobby?"

"Shouldn't those kids be in school?"

"We are very fortunate, thanks to the Dear Leader, for all he gives us," he said, ignoring my question. "We have the best ice cream in the world."

We walked on, but the image stayed with me. Was it just a coincidence? Three children buying ice cream on a late morning in winter had to be unusual, but not impossible to see twice. What haunted me was the *way* the little girl reached for the ice cone. It looked set up. Rehearsed. I felt disoriented, like my mind was playing tricks. I started to notice other things, like how the shops we saw always had a couple of customers browsing, looking interested in the merchandise, but never buying anything. Everybody was well-dressed. Even more disturbing, I saw almost no old people, no mentally ill or physically disabled people. I wondered again how so few people walked the streets of Pyongyang. In other countries that suffer from famine, hunger drives people into the big cities. It seemed wrong that Pyongyang was so empty. The kids at the orphanage didn't look hungry, either. I started to wonder whether it was a real orphanage at all.

As though reading my mind, the next day our handlers brought Greenleaf, Rose, and me to a hospital that had received shipments of medicines and other supplies from Bill Henry, Campus Crusade for Christ, and the senator's constituents. A guide ushered us around, claiming it was the "best hospital in Pyongyang." The air hung damp and cold in the bare rooms, and the place smelled like a dungeon. We saw almost no equipment within the dreary, gray walls. The guide took us to the surgery ward. It was so cold everyone wore heavy coats, including the only patient, whose eyes gazed dully at the ceiling. Grime crusted the edges of the floor tiles. It was the kind of place you come to die—not to get treated. I couldn't tell what they were trying to show us. If this was the best hospital, it was hard to imagine the poorer ones. They either had no idea how bad their hospital was or they wanted us to see their need, with no playacting.

One afternoon, I found Bobby Meats in the hotel lobby, shadowboxing in a white martial arts outfit. "Want to come to the Sports Center?" he asked. He pointed to a couple of handlers sitting nearby and said they were taking him to spar in an exhibition match against one of their top fighters.

Bobby Meats had fear in his eyes. He practiced tae kwon do at a gym in New Jersey, and I didn't like his odds against a professional North Korean fighter trained since childhood to hate Americans. I imagined having to call corporate headquarters at D. B. Brown and explain that I was bringing their export director home in a wheelchair or a body bag. "Take that costume off," I said. He protested, but looked relieved. The handlers watched us with shit-eating grins. "You see this guy?" I said to them. "He couldn't fight my sister. No fight. Understand?"

I felt bad, like I was putting America at a disadvantage. But it's one thing to promote diplomacy through sports, and another to knowingly walk into your own slaughter. The handlers gave Bobby Meats a tour of the Sports Center instead.

That night after dinner, as Rovnanik, Bobby Meats, and I walked down the hallway to our rooms, I pointed out how the doors were spaced much farther apart than in hotels back home. I imagined a couple of North Korean spies sitting in a passageway between the rooms, surrounded by sensitive recording equipment. I was pretty sure they'd be keeping the closest watch on the war hero and the journalist, so about fifteen feet past the room McDaniel and Sauter shared, I stopped and motioned for the other two to be quiet. The panel halfway between the rooms looked like the rest of the wall from a distance, but up close I noticed two indentations where the material was slightly discolored and shiny. I put my thumbs into the thumb-holds and glanced at the other two, who shook their heads no. I ignored them, and in one motion I lifted the panel up and pulled it back and away. Light from the hallway flooded into a four-foot passageway. We stepped back in surprise.

A skinny Korean guy lay facedown on top of a narrow mattress with his pants around his ankles and his ass exposed. I don't know why anybody says Asians have yellow skin. This guy had the whitest tush I've ever seen. He was wedged up between two unmistakably female knees and shins, and we had caught him in mid-thrust. The man's face twisted around at us in an expression of surprise and fear.

"You dirty bastard!" Rovnanik whispered.

The guy looked like he couldn't decide whether to jump up and fight us or ignore us and keep on humping. A woman's voice said something urgently in Korean. Beyond them, a bare bulb shone dimly.

"Whoa!" I said. "Sorry, sorry!"

I slid the panel back in its place as quickly as I could. Even a couple of commie spies deserve to get their rocks off in peace. And nobody likes to be disturbed while doing it. We're all alike in that way. I wondered whether, behind the iron curtain and all the propaganda, the DPRK was really a sex free-for-all where everybody screwed each other between the walls anytime they could. It was the most inexpensive form of entertainment in the world.

Finally, on our fourth day in Pyongyang, the handlers loaded me, Sauter, Red McDaniel, and Senator Greenleaf into a minivan for the short trip to the War

Museum. One of the biggest Koreans I'd ever seen climbed into the van behind us. He was about my height, a hundred-ninety-pounder with broad shoulders. He wore his hair parted on the side, Western style. His hands hung big and heavy like a boxer's, and his mouth puckered like he'd just eaten something sour. I nicknamed him Cranky.

He took a seat behind me. "Where's Mr. Perot?" he asked in almost perfect English.

"You work for the Foreign Ministry?" I asked. He grinned and didn't answer. Who the fuck was this guy? I didn't need his mockery. I spent weeks of my free time trying to get Perot to come and help Cranky's country. He should have been bowing down and thanking me.

Back in the States, I considered Han, Ambassador Pak, Minister Counselor Kim, and the other guys as friends, and we treated each other with respect. But almost everyone I met in the DPRK was suspicious of me. Some were slightly hostile, like Shorty and Gap Tooth, who I hadn't seen since my first trip. Cranky wanted to bust my balls from the second we met.

We parked in front of the War Museum, and our handlers left us standing next to the van while they conferred with a couple military guys at the museum entrance. After a few minutes, I walked over to check on the plan. Han knew that, to make our trip worthwhile, we needed to see more than the propaganda they showed Bratton and me two years earlier. I asked Han whether his government kept pieces of American servicemen's bodies in jars of formaldehyde, as some of the POW activists contended. Even if we didn't film any pickled heads or limbs, I wanted to get Sauter and McDaniel access to the archives. The deep stuff.

"You can see what's in the museum," Cranky said. He seemed to have taken over from our handlers.

I was afraid that once inside, it would be too late to ask to see more. I realized this was my last chance to keep POWs on the negotiating table. If we went home empty-handed, people would stop listening to me about the issue.

"These guys came halfway across the world," I said, gesturing toward the van. "We need to do something special for them."

Cranky said something to the museum guards and turned to me. "Go in the back. No special entrance."

I don't know why it suddenly made a difference to me, but it did. I pointed at McDaniel. "That man's a war hero," I said. "He goes in the front entrance."

"Is he too weak to walk? How long was he tortured in Vietnam?" Cranky smirked. Nothing gets under my skin more than a smirk. It reminds me of those scarf-wearing kids in high school who thought they were better than you because they never had dirt under their fingernails. Cranky turned to the other guys and said something sarcastic in Korean. Sarcasm is clear in any language.

I'm aware that I have a temper. I've been to meetings about it. I've been lectured by judges in New Jersey and spent a few nights in the county jail because of it. Before I remembered I was in a Stalinist dictatorship and maybe it wasn't a good idea, I got into Cranky's personal space and pointed my finger at his chest.

I poked him hard in the ribs. "You think this is a joke?"

Cranky stepped back in amazement. I know two good ways to get to know another guy—eating with him and fighting him. Cranky stood his ground, and I could feel he was one of those North Koreans with a deep hatred for Americans. He inched forward and started mouthing off in Korean. We stood a knuckle's width from each other's noses and shouted at full volume in our own languages. A droplet of his spittle landed on my cheek and I smelled his fermented breath. "Show some respect, you no-good commie motherfucker," I screamed, "or I'll take your head off and wipe your ass with it!"

One of the uniformed guys grabbed Cranky by the arm and held him back. A handler jumped between us and faced me.

"No fighting here!" he shouted.

No fighting at the War Museum? These guys had to be fucking kidding. I didn't care where we were. You insult Red McDaniel at the Lincoln Memorial and I'll pop you in the jaw. I'm not saying it's the right thing to do, but that's how I was raised. I lock my doors at night. I keep a gun in my office. If somebody comes into my territory, I'm going to defend my position. And the Koreans had to respect that my delegates should be treated with dignity.

"You want some of this?" I shouted over the handler's head. "Stop hiding behind your friends, you punk!" I thought Cranky was going to fly at me. Over by the van, Sauter, McDaniel, and Senator Greenleaf watched in horror. "We go in the front door!" I shouted.

Two of the handlers went over to my delegation and escorted them to the front door of the museum. "Not you," Cranky said. "Back door for you." Then he spewed out a stream of words in Korean that didn't need translating.

"Doesn't matter to me," I said. I pointed at Cranky again. "Understand?" The guards followed as I walked around the building. I joined my group inside the museum and didn't see Cranky for the rest of our tour. "What was that about?" the senator whispered, as the guide led us through the Hall of American Atrocities.

"Just a little 'getting to know you,'" I said. As I feared, our guys were getting a tour of the same stuff I'd seen with Bratton. Pictures of Korean corpses and American planes. Captions blaming the "imperialist aggressor."

"What about the archives?" I asked the guide. He ignored me.

We moved into another room. I noticed Sauter had put his video camera, lens-down, on the top of a glass case, discreetly filming its contents. Sauter gave me a look, and I shielded him from the view of the guide. The case contained items Bratton and I hadn't seen—dog tags, ID cards, officers' club and rationing cards. There were dozens of pictures of American GIs, and Sauter filmed these, too. As we moved through displays of captured American weapons and airplane parts, Sauter filmed all the registration numbers he could, so he could do more research once we got home.

By the time we left the museum, Cranky had disappeared. We returned to the hotel, where I sat with Sauter and McDaniel in the meeting room as they tried to match what they saw at the museum with what they knew of the events of the Korean War. I lost focus on what they were saying, because at that moment Cranky walked into the lobby with his fists clenched at his sides. He spotted me through the meeting room window and stared. In this situation, men don't need words to communicate. I knew what he'd come for. I stood and walked toward him.

Cranky headed for a meeting room at the far corner of the lobby. His body seethed with anger. Maybe his uncles, aunts, or grandparents died in the war. Or maybe he just took his government's propaganda to heart. I'll never know, and it didn't matter. I had some pent-up stuff in me, too. After my treatment by Cranky, Gap Tooth, and Shorty, I was tired of getting disrespected by my handlers in Pyongyang, and I was still hurting from the smackdown from Pritchard and Sandy Berger. My legitimacy was on the line. I had to defend the trust Han placed in me when he sent me back to Pyongyang. Anyone who picked a fight with me was challenging Han and the wisdom of our friendship.

I followed Cranky into the meeting room. There was no waiting. No words. As soon as I stepped inside, he lunged at me. I stepped right, grabbed him by his shirt, and threw him against the wall. I swung my right fist but he slipped away to my left. He was a nimble bastard. I turned and rolled my head back as his right arm swung at me. His knuckles glanced off my shoulder and grazed my jaw.

I jumped backward. "Is that all you got?" I yelled. I leaped at him and caught his shirt between my fingers and dragged him down. He grasped at my neck, and we fell on top of the coffee table. Amazingly, it held our weight. We rolled across the table, swinging at each other and trying to get a clean shot. "You are a bitch!" he shouted. I wondered where he learned his English. He kicked me and a burning pain shot up from my ankle. I shouted, "I got my pin, you fuck! You're fucking with the wrong motherfucker!" When I'm riled up, I'm loud, and I'm sure everybody on the ground floor of the hotel heard us.

We rolled onto the floor and I got to my feet first. I picked up the coffee table and threw it at him. He deflected it with his arm and rolled out from beneath it. I was about to leap onto him, because I had him defenseless for a moment, but suddenly the room filled with North Koreans getting involved and pulling at both of us. Cranky shouted in Korean, no doubt accusing me of all kinds of things.

I put my hands on my knees and caught my breath. I had a deep scratch on my neck from his fingernails. Adrenaline coursed through my body, but I was still in control. I hadn't gone as far as the time on the roof when I stood up for Taki Langas.

"Fuck him," I said to all the Koreans at once. "Nobody disrespects the captain. What would happen to me if I insulted one of your war heroes?"

The worried faces of Sauter, McDaniel, and Senator Greenleaf appeared in the doorway. I walked over to them. "What happened?" McDaniel asked.

"The guy said some pretty derogatory things about you," I said. "I had to defend your honor."

McDaniel lowered his voice. "I appreciate that, Bobby, but all I want to do is get home safely."

The next day I played pool with Rovnanik in the hotel game room before our farewell dinner with the Zosonsulbi Group. I didn't say anything to the businessmen about the fight because I didn't want to freak them out. "Slipped in the shower," I said when Rovnanik saw that I was limping. We'd just finished our third rack of eight ball when a Korean handler walked into the game room. Cranky followed him in. I kept my eyes averted. The handler positioned himself with his back to the wall. Cranky pointed to the table and said, "Play."

"Dave's the winner," I said. "Play him."

Cranky took a pool cue from the wall and turned it slowly, feeling its weight. Out of the corner of my eye, I measured about five feet between my left hand and the cue ball on the table. If Cranky made a move, I could smash it across the bridge of his nose. Dave picked up the triangular rack and started filling it with pool balls, oblivious to the tension in the room. I side-walked my way around the table, putting it between myself and Cranky until I reached Dave's side. I leaned toward his ear.

"If he swings his cue at me, crack him over the head," I said in a lowered voice.

"What are you talking about?" Rovnanik hissed.

"Keep your stick handy, and take out the other guy if you need to."

Rovnanik flubbed the break and left a wide-open table. Without looking at me, Cranky set his cue between his fingers and slammed one of the solids into a corner pocket. He grunted with satisfaction. But he was hitting too hard, and his next few shots bounced wildly around the green. Dave couldn't sink a ball to save his life, either. I stood a few paces back, where I'd left my cue leaning against a wall. Cranky and Rovnanik circled the table like cats.

After ten minutes or so, Cranky was down to two balls on the table. He'd ignored me and remained completely focused on the game.

Maybe the North Koreans were testing me, to see if I would apologize or start another fight. I wasn't going to do either one. Maybe they were testing Cranky, too. I'll never know, because nobody ever learns who "they" are or what they want. After three years with the North Koreans, I still had more questions than answers.

That night, I concentrated on not limping as we met the Zosonsulbi Group for our farewell banquet at the hotel. They asked us to donate eighty-five U.S. dollars each to pay for it—a cheapskate move. It's a basic rule of etiquette that when you invite somebody for a meal, you don't ask them to pay. I decided to leave that lesson for another day.

It looked like they had copied an American Thanksgiving menu, because the table was laid out with roast turkey, ham, potatoes, and pickles, with plenty of plum wine served in fancy little cups. We couldn't help watching the lower-ranking Koreans in the group. They couldn't take their eyes off the food. And I realized that a big banquet was probably the meal of a lifetime, even for these privileged members of the government who worked in Pyongyang and had it better than almost anyone else in their country. After the meal, we conducted a small ceremony to sign our non-binding letter of agreement, which stated that both parties intended to "mutually pursue" the following projects:

a) American/Western food restaurant;
b) 2,000 tons-per-year (tpy) chicken factory and 1,500-egg factory;
c) 3,200 tpy pig factory;
d) 500-cow farm;
e) 1,200 tpy duck farm;
f) 700-ton vegetable greenhouse; and
g) cold storage facilities.

The document also expressed our "desire" to: set up synthetic resin and battery factories in the Free Economic Trade Zone; trade coal and cement to the Philippines through one of Wall Street Steve's contacts; and market clothing from the DPRK's Kaeson Garment Factory, including sports tracksuits and children's anoraks.

Chairman Ku signed the document and I countersigned, as though there were no sanctions in place, and we shook hands as business partners.

After we got back to the States, I asked Winkler to request business licenses for the chicken farm in the DPRK and the other ideas we'd talked about with the Zosonsulbi Group. It was all pie in the sky, but nobody gets what they want by *not* asking for it. That's the nature of pioneering. You see an opening and then you move ahead, as if there's no obstacle too great.

The humanitarian mission was more successful. Greenleaf and Rose went home fired up to help the North Korean people. Over the next few years, the senator helped collect hundreds of thousands of dollars worth of aid to be shipped to Pyongyang.

Back in Washington, Sauter checked the names from the dog tags and ID cards he'd filmed against the records of men still listed as missing in action. He found several matches and called the family members he could find, to let them know their relatives' personal items were on display at the War Museum in Pyongyang.

Our findings failed to move anybody in Washington. Pritchard and Berger and President Clinton kept demanding that North Korea apologize for the submarine incident, without using the issue to pressure Pyongyang about American POWs. On Sunday, December 29, North Korea expressed "deep regret" over the submarine incident. South Korea returned the bodies of the two dozen crew members. A few days later, as if to make up for having to apologize, the Foreign Ministry issued a statement that there were "no Americans living in North Korea" from the Korean War, meaning POWs. We lost the chance, maybe for good, to ask about them.

In late January, the U.S. Treasury Department sent its reply to Winkler's office. Unsurprisingly, it read:

Dear Mr. Egan,

This responds to your numerous applications which you recently submitted under single cover to the Office of Foreign Assets Control

("OFAC") . . . your request for a specific license from OFAC is hereby denied in each instance.

The Treasury Department's letter left open the idea of exporting grain on a one-time basis, which fell under the authority of the Commerce Department. Han and I followed that up with the Minnesota-based company Cargill, Inc., but negotiations broke down over a lack of trust between the DPRK and the company's executives.

Han was incensed. On January 31, 1997, he said the DPRK would walk away from peace talks unless the U.S. government helped make the wheat deal happen. *North Korea Links Talks to Grain Deal* ran the February 1 headline in *The New York Times*.

That got me another call from Pritchard. "What the hell are you doing?" he demanded.

"What do you expect?" I asked. "You won't talk about POWs or lift sanctions. All you do is demand things."

"That's none of your business," Pritchard said. "We were back at the negotiating table, and then the North Koreans brought up your chicken farm again."

Han was glad we'd established a plan for the chicken farm with the Zosonsulbi Group. But he wasn't so happy with the incident at the War Museum. He must have heard about it from his superiors. "What happens if you hit somebody in the Mafia?" he asked a few days after we got back.

"You can't lay a finger on a made man," I said. "It's a rule."

"The guy you fought is still talking about you," he said. "It's causing some problems. He has connections."

"I barely touched him."

"You embarrassed him, and you have to apologize."

"*He* should apologize. He showed disrespect."

"It's more important than you think. Will you cook for him?"

"He's coming all the way here?" I asked. "To see me?"

Han nodded.

A few weeks later, he walked into Cubby's with Cranky in tow. He wore a jacket and collared shirt and the same scowl as the last time I'd seen him, around the pool table. Han and Cranky sat at a booth along the south wall. I stayed behind the counter and tended the register.

My manager, Bobby Rella, put a burger tray down for a paying customer and asked, "Who's that guy with Han? He keeps looking over here."

Han came to the register and ordered a New York steak, medium rare, for himself, and an order of ribs, no sauce, for Cranky. "Just serve him," he said.

"Would he serve me?"

Han rolled his eyes. "Can we get past this?"

"I'll spit on his food first," I said.

"I don't care if you piss on it first. Just serve him."

I punched the register to make his order on the house. "Only because you're asking me to, pal," I said.

When their order came up, I carried the tray over to their booth and set Cranky's plate in front of him. He bowed his head a fraction of an inch.

"Get you a beer?" I asked.

Cranky looked at me with a noncommittal expression on his ugly mug. Then he nodded. I brought him and Han each a beer. Ten minutes later I came back to collect their empties. Han excused himself, saying he had to take a leak.

Cranky stared at his empty plate. "Your ribs are good," he said.

9

~~~~~~~~~~~~~~~~~~

The Iraqi Playdate

Y OU NEVER KNOW how one part of your life might affect another. When our daughter, Andrea, turned seven, I wanted her to learn to fight, in case she ever ran into trouble on the street or at school. So in the summer of 1997, I called a friend of mine, Karate Tom, who taught Shotokan-style martial arts in downtown Hackensack, and enrolled Andrea for classes on Tuesday and Thursday evenings. I did it because it's important for a young woman to feel she can protect herself. I never anticipated getting my daughter's karate mixed up with international affairs.

Late that summer, just by coincidence, Sauter and I were talking about a Navy pilot shot down over Iraq six years earlier, during the 1991 Gulf War. His name was Lt. Col. Michael Scott Speicher, and the Navy hadn't recovered his remains after he crashed in the middle of the desert, in a Bedouin area. Some people speculated that he survived and was locked away in an Iraqi prison. Getting information about him from Saddam Hussein's regime was almost impossible, Sauter said. Just like the North Koreans, the Iraqis had no diplomatic relations with Washington. The issue sounded right up my alley, so I told Sauter I'd look into it.

"You guys have Iraqi contacts?" I asked Han the next time he came to Cubby's. "They've got too much oil for you not to be chatty with them."

Han looked at me suspiciously. "Did somebody say something to you?"

"No," I said. "Why?"

"Never mind." Han picked through the remains of a basket of onion rings. It was nearly closing time, and we were planning a fishing trip with a KEDO delegation arriving for negotiations the next week. "We don't get oil from them."

"You help bring Speicher out, it'll push your relations forward with Washington."

"Why would the Iraqis give him to us?"

The way I looked at it, the Iraqis had to be desperate. They were in a worse situation than the North Koreans, in terms of their relations with Washington. Saddam screwed himself for good when he lobbed missiles at Israel during the 1991 war. The United States would never accept him now. "I haven't thought it through yet," I said. "Give me time."

Behind the counter, Lilia glanced at the clock and took the day's receipts to the back office. I went to the fountain to refill my Diet Coke and get Han another beer. I brought our drinks to the table and sat down again. "You help get the pilot back, and we'll work out a deal that involves getting you some Iraqi oil," I said.

"Who says?" Han asked. I shrugged. He sipped his beer. "How much oil?"

"What do I look like, Chevron? How do I know how much oil? The important thing is to get the conversation going. What's their ambassador's name?"

"Hamdoun," Han said. "Nizar Hamdoun."

"I *knew* you'd know it." I felt that little shock of adrenaline you get when a fish tugs your line. "Find out if he's open to meeting me. Put me in touch, and I'll do the rest."

I didn't think Han was going to bite, but the next day he called with the name of a junior Iraqi diplomat. "Talk to him first. Maybe Hamdoun will meet you. Maybe not."

"He'll meet me," I said.

One thing we learn in the private sector is that if something worked once, it'll probably work again. People who went to college are always trying to reinvent things, which is why you get such mixed signals from Washington. Down here in the gutter, we use the lessons of boxing. We adapt to our opponent and we move our feet, but the basic rule is: if your jab works, stay with it.

I still had juice with the New York Giants front office, and that November, I invited the ambassador of Iraq to a home game against the Arizona Cardinals on behalf of Cubby's, Athletes in Action, and the Giants team, which provided complimentary tickets. I guessed that, with relations between Baghdad and Washington in the toilet, Hamdoun had plenty of free space on his social calendar. When I found out he had two daughters about the same age as Andrea, I encouraged him to bring his whole family.

"Is it necessary to take him to a football game?" Han asked.

I knew that tone. It was the kind of thing Lilia asked when I spent too much time with the North Koreans. It was the tone of a guy who asks his girlfriend if she's cheating on him. Han was jealous.

"I'm doing it for us," I said. "You want me to get on his good side, right?"

"You said you were going to talk to him."

"I *am* going to talk to him. But you know how I work. I need to feel him out. I'll tell you everything he says."

"Maybe you want to work with him and not with us," Han pouted.

"No chance, pal. We'll go out this weekend, you and me, okay? You want to go fishing?" Han accepted, and I felt relieved.

When the chauffeured car pulled into the Cubby's parking lot on a Saturday afternoon in November, I came out from the restaurant to greet my guests. Hamdoun wore a dark wool coat over a finely tailored suit and a Giants-blue necktie. I appreciated the touch. His daughters wore dresses and his wife, Sahar, had on a coat with fur sleeves. I gave them all Giants caps to make them feel more at home with the casually dressed crowd at the stadium.

We sat near the fifty-yard line in the nosebleed section. Hamdoun and his family were good sports from the beginning. When freezing rain hit us in the second quarter, they put on the parkas I'd brought and squinted through the weather to catch every play. They rose from their seats and cheered with the rest of us every time the Giants made a first down.

I took a shine to Hamdoun. He was quiet and dignified like the Mafia *capos* from the old country. Back in the 1980s, when President Reagan allied himself with Saddam's Iraq against Iran, Hamdoun was the ambassador to the United States and a popular guy in Washington. Saddam moved him to the U.N. posting in 1991, after our countries broke off diplomatic ties. With that kind of staying power, Hamdoun had to be close to the dictator.

I wasn't going to bring up business at the football game. Hamdoun knew from his people, who knew from Han, that I was interested in POWs. It's possible Han told him I had connections in the intelligence community, too. But these were delicate matters that required trust. We needed to form a relationship. Hamdoun seemed to sense this. He didn't ask why I invited him, and I didn't ask why he accepted.

I held a post-game reception for Hamdoun at Cubby's with the new team chaplain and a couple of players from the Giants' bench, who came by in sweat suits. The Iraqis are like Italians: warm, late-night people who love to eat. We sat around big plates of ribs and chicken and a pot of tea, because I knew that's what Iraqis drank. I watched Hamdoun's expression when he brought the first rib to his teeth. It crunched and popped like sweet corn as he bit down, releasing the juices and barbecue sauce into his mouth. He smiled as he dabbed sauce from his moustache with a paper napkin. In the booth next to us, Andrea played a clapping game with Hamdoun's daughters, Uma and Sama. "Thank you," Hamdoun said later, as I walked his family out to the parking lot. "It was the best night out we've had in some time."

A good fisherman knows when to let his line soak in the water and when to pull back. Fish strike when the bait moves away. I didn't call Hamdoun, even after I received a thank you card from the embassy a few days after the game. If he came to me, I'd have more juice. He wouldn't feel like I was sucking up or trying to win him over.

I guessed Hamdoun was lonely. I learned from Han and the Vietnamese that when you represent a country that is not on friendly terms with the United

States, your phone doesn't ring after hours. You don't get invited to the swanky dinner parties. Nobody wants to be seen with you in public. You're like a girl who's on the rebound after getting her heart broken. So when I come along with dinner plans and tickets to the game, it's tempting.

A few weeks after the Giants game, Hamdoun called Cubby's and invited Andrea to his younger daughter's birthday party. Even though I was dying to go to the Iraqi embassy, I wanted to give him the impression that I was too busy to come. I asked Lilia to take her.

"They're from a bad regime," she protested. "I don't know how much we should expose Andrea to them. She's only seven."

"You get along with Han," I told her. "He comes from a dictatorship."

"That's what I'm saying. Why do all of our friends have to be America's enemies?"

She finally gave in, though. I dropped her off at the Iraqi embassy on Park Avenue, drove a few blocks to have lunch with Han, and picked the girls up a few hours later. All the way home she raved: "Ambassador Hamdoun is such a good father. He played games with the kids the whole time. They are really nice people."

It was time to make my move. After the birthday party, I called Hamdoun to thank him and see if he was ready to raise our relationship to the next level. I mentioned that Andrea took evening lessons at Shotokan Karate Academy in Hackensack.

"A friend of mine runs it," I said. "The kids get a workout, and it builds their self-esteem. In this day and age, girls need to be able to defend themselves." Hamdoun wasn't a physical guy, and I could tell this resonated with him. "Why don't you bring your girls out?" I asked. "We can sit and watch them the whole time."

On a Tuesday evening in early January 1998, Hamdoun brought his daughters to Cubby's, and we carpooled to the academy. Karate Tom gave each of Hamdoun's girls a white *gi* with a white belt and showed them how to put their palms together and bow to their teacher. "I'm trying to get Andrea to do that at home," I said. Hamdoun laughed.

For the next few weeks, he brought his daughters to Karate Tom's every

Tuesday. We stood at the edge of the mat, watching them stretch, kick, punch, and bow. "Do they teach this to girls in Iraq?" I asked one evening.

"Not usually." Hamdoun sighed. "My daughters feel more American than Iraqi anyway."

I looked at him sympathetically. "It must be hard," I said. "Living so long in a foreign society."

He nodded. Our daughters bent their knees, stepped forward in unison, and sliced their arms toward the floor. "I'm surprised you didn't choose tae kwon do," he said, "since you have so many Korean friends."

It was the first time Hamdoun had mentioned my connection to Han and the DPRK. I took it as a sign. I edged away from the other parents standing nearby, and Hamdoun followed me as naturally as if we were strolling down the lane. "I want to ask your opinion of something, Mr. Ambassador," I said, when we'd reached the corner of the mat. "But I'm not sure we know each other well enough."

"Bobby," he said, "consider me your friend. You can ask whatever you want."

"I want to help you guys out of a predicament," I said. He raised his eyebrows and gave me a look that said he wanted to hear more. "I'm not going to beat around the bush," I continued. "As long as Saddam's in power, you're going to be an enemy of the United States. Unless you can pull something very surprising out of your hat, you're in the crosshairs."

When I used the dictator's name, Hamdoun glanced over at the other parents. "You have something in mind," he said.

When I said I was interested in the case of the Navy pilot, Speicher, he didn't seem surprised. "It could change the tone with the Clinton folks if you gave him back," I said. "Especially if you do it as a goodwill gesture."

He shook his head. "Even supposing he were alive, do you think I'd have the ability to get him released?"

"You're the only Iraqi diplomat I know." I smiled, and he smiled back. He promised to look into it.

A couple weeks later, as we stood at the corner of Karate Tom's mat again, he said he thought the Speicher case was a lost cause. "We don't believe he survived," he said. "Of course, it's very hard to prove a negative." I said I appreciated his looking into it.

"I still wish there was a way I could help you," I said. We watched in silence as Karate Tom showed our daughters the right way to position their feet for a kick. Three girls with shiny, dark hair, all about the same height; I wondered what the three of them would grow up to be. "What if you accepted somebody else's prisoners?" I asked. "You could act as a broker."

"I'm not sure I understand."

"I happen to know that North Korea has some American prisoners they might be willing to part with. You could turn them over to us."

"The North Koreans told you they have prisoners?"

"You know Minister Counselor Han? He's a friend of mine. He doesn't dispute it," I said, which was technically true, despite what the North Koreans were now saying publicly.

"Why would the North Koreans give these men to us?"

"They don't want the prisoners. They've had them for forty years."

A new configuration took shape in my head. "All you'd have to do is give 'em a little oil, which they desperately need." It struck me that this could be my best idea yet—an oil-for-prisoners plan.

"Think about the impact if you brought those men to safety," I said, as our daughters spun and chopped. "We'll have news cameras lined up in Baghdad and New York. Imagine the ceremony! The family members reunited after half a lifetime. The tears. The talk shows. That's a game-changing play, Mr. Ambassador. You'll be on the White House guest list and drinking tea with the queen of England."

"You are aware we have limits on what we do with our oil, from the U.N. sanctions."

I lowered my voice in case one of our daughters wandered into hearing range. "If we pull this off, Mr. Ambassador, the U.N. can kiss your ass. The only people pushing these sanctions are in Washington, and when you're on *Oprah* with a bunch of POW families crying and hugging their long-lost loved ones, Clinton's going to have to lick your balls. If you'll pardon the expression."

Hamdoun dug his thumb and finger into his eyes and asked, "Do the North Koreans know you're talking to me about this?"

"It's Han's idea," I said. "His and mine."

The next night, I went to see Han and told him the new plan. "Oil for prisoners," I said. "Elegant, right?"

"We officially don't have prisoners," Han said.

"But you said—"

"I don't even know who knows for sure," Han said, exasperated. "How much oil are they offering?"

"We'll get to that. There are lots of details to work out."

If the North Koreans weren't ready to talk about POWs anymore, I had to make a leap of faith and assume they'd warm up to the idea once the offer was attractive enough. I wanted to get as many pieces in place as I could, so if we got the green light from both parties we could move. My next step was to organize how the handoff would be done. I knew from experience that working with my government was no good, because they'd just screw it up. Perot would have been my first choice, but I couldn't venture down that road again. I knew I could count on Bratton or Wall Street Steve or Bill Henry, but I needed bigger backing.

I called the Giants office and asked to speak to John Mara, the executive vice president and chief operating officer of the team and the oldest son of the legendary Duke Mara. I gave him the bare-bones version, and asked if we could get some of his players over to Iraq for a few days.

"I know your intentions are good, Bobby," he said. "My concern is to keep the image of the Giants clean."

"It's for the POWs, sir," I said. "It's a worthy cause."

"You think you can talk some of the players into going to Baghdad?" he asked.

"I'm sure of it, sir," I said. "The Bible guys. Michael Strahan. Rodney Hampton. Howard Cross. They'll see it as a higher calling."

Mara chuckled. "I'm not going to stop them. Have our lawyer look at it to make sure it doesn't break their contract."

"Thank you, sir."

"And make sure it happens in the off season."

A few days later, Hamdoun and I were back at Karate Tom's, watching our daughters punch the air. "The football team?" he asked.

"They're ready to get on a plane tomorrow," I said.

He shook his head and laughed, like he was trying to remember if he'd ever heard a crazier idea. "Send me a letter," he said.

On March 26, 1998, Bratton and I wrote, on Athletes in Action letterhead, on behalf of the New York Giants:

Mr. Ambassador:

. . . The players believe it to be very important to meet with your President Saddam Hussein for two reasons. First, it would demonstrate to your people the sincerity of the players' visit. Second, as you know, these men have a very close relationship with His Excellency, Comrade Kim Jong Il of the Democratic People's Republic of Korea.

The players have been made aware by the government of the DPRK that Kim Jong Il has inherited a situation from his father's regime in which live Americans from the Korean War are still being held captive by the Korean People's Army. We believe that, with the help of President Saddam Hussein, these seven POWs' release can be obtained through the exchange of Iraqi oil for them. Mr. Egan has finalized an approval from the government of the DPRK for representatives of Iraq's Foreign Ministry and the New York Giants to travel to the DPRK to negotiate such an exchange.

Mr. Ambassador, we believe at this time that your president is the only person who can secure the release of these POWs. The Giants players will let the world know that President Saddam Hussein and his government secured the release of these men.

I followed up the letter with a football signed by most of the Giants' starting lineup, which Hamdoun promised to send to President Saddam himself.

I told Han I thought we were getting somewhere. Once we got the go-ahead from the Iraqis, Han could run with the idea in Pyongyang. They say two wrongs don't make a right, but maybe two enemy countries could get together and do a favor for the United States.

Things got more complicated on the world stage, however. In April 1998, Washington tightened sanctions against North Korea for selling missile components and technology to the Khan Research Laboratory in Pakistan. The North Koreans had a liquid-fueled missile called the Rodong, and with all the international sanctions, exporting it was one of their best sources of cash. They sold it to Iran, Syria, and Egypt, too. Pakistan used it to develop a version called the Ghauri, and when the Pakistanis conducted their first nuclear test in May 1998, leaders in Washington worried that the Ghauri could carry a warhead to any city in India.

Just after noon on a Tuesday in May, I got a call at Cubby's from a North Korean I'd never met. He said a group visiting from Pyongyang planned to stop by the restaurant later in the afternoon. It seemed strange, because Han always organized delegations that came to my restaurant. But Cubby's is open to anybody, and I don't take reservations. I was slammed with lunchtime orders, so I didn't think twice about it.

Six of them piled out of one of the mission's white minivans at around five-thirty. I recognized a few of them from previous delegations. They held the door open for an older guy I'd never seen before. I could tell he was a big cheese by the way the rest of them bowed and made sure not to get in his way as he walked into the restaurant. He wore his thin gray hair combed to the side and an olive green tunic favored by North Korean military types.

I sat his group at the back, in Han's customary booth, and asked Lilia to take orders while I socialized. Outside, an FBI sedan had parked in its usual spot. Through the windshield I could see the outlines of two guys sitting in the front seats, not moving.

The big cheese spoke to me using a translator. He said the group was returning to New York from Washington, and had detoured fifteen miles from the Holland Tunnel just to taste my ribs, which were famous at the mission. I told him I was very flattered. It surprised me that Han wasn't with them, as the head of American Affairs. I wondered whether he orchestrated his own absence or if he'd gotten left out by his higher-ups. It seemed impolite to ask for details, but I guessed the military group had held some quiet negotiations over missile sales.

They ordered plates of ribs and a porterhouse steak for the big guy. I went to the back office and brought out a bottle of Johnnie Walker whisky and a bottle of vodka, which I saved for special guests. The translator poured a round of whisky, and after the first shot, the big cheese asked if I served spicy food.

"You mean kimchee spicy?" I asked. "Or real-man spicy?" I wondered what the translator would do with that one.

"He likes spicy," the translator said.

I went to the freezer in the kitchen where I keep my habaneros in a Ziploc bag. I washed my hands and diced them myself, and brought them out on a little plate. "When your steak comes, sprinkle some of these on it," I said, miming the action so he'd understand. "Not too much. These are for macho guys."

The translator spoke in Korean, but the big cheese had stopped listening because he was looking at the front door. I followed his gaze. It was Han, standing just inside, watching us. He had three of his boys with him, and he looked upset that the military guys were in his booth. His eyes took it all in: me leaning across the table and gabbing with the military chief; the cups of whisky; the little plate of habaneros.

"Hey, look, everybody, Han's here!" I said, for lack of anything better.

Han turned and walked to the register. I realized with horror that I didn't have any good tables left. I asked a young couple sitting at my other back table to move to the front of the restaurant. Then I ran up to greet Han.

"Stay with your new friends," he sulked. "Lilia can serve us." We stepped away from the cash register to the relative privacy of the soda fountain. Han's junior diplomats studied the big menu on the wall. "They're leaving on Thursday," Han said. "See what good they are to you then."

"They came to my restaurant. What am I supposed to do?"

"Don't raise your voice." Han glanced at the military table. "You're supposed to cook for them. Then call me and stay in the kitchen."

Like I was his wife? "What's wrong with talking to my customers?" I asked.

Han leaned in closer. "You go over there and try to be funny, but you don't even know who they are. They don't understand English. They're translating. What if you say something stupid? You offend them, it's a problem."

I asked Han who they were. "Military," he grunted, which I'd figured out on my own. I wondered if they'd come to Cubby's as part of a territorial pissing match with Han. If so, he wasn't saying.

Later, when I talked about the incident with McCreary, I realized how much the North Koreans are split into factions. Each group takes care of its own, like in the Mafia. Han saw me as his asset. But I could also be a liability, because if a negative word got back to Pyongyang about Han's man in New Jersey, it reflected badly on him.

I walked Han and his group to the other back table, which Lilia had cleared and wiped clean. The young couple watched with curiosity as we walked past them. Before sitting down, Han stopped and said something short and polite-sounding to the military chief. The chief didn't stand up. His face had turned red, and his eyes watered. He wiped his nose with a paper napkin and nodded. Han bowed about two inches, quickly, and then sat at the other table with his crew.

"Did you tell him to eat those peppers?" he whispered.

"I warned him," I said. "He didn't have to eat them."

Han looked at me like I had a horn growing out of my head. "Of course he ate them," he said. "He would eat them even if it killed him. Out of pride. But he'll want to get you back."

"You mean he'll want to get *you* back," I said, trying to make a joke.

Han didn't smile. His expression was cold and serious. "That's right," he said.

~~~~~

A few weeks after the habanero incident, I finally got a call from Hamdoun, inviting me to his office. I drove over to the Iraqi mission at the United Nations on East 79th Street, excited about moving forward with our oil-for-prisoners scheme. Hamdoun occupied a townhouse worlds apart from the North Korean mission, with polished mahogany furniture and rich carpets—a sign of how much more money Iraq had and a throwback to the days when Saddam was in favor and the Iraqis threw lavish parties in New York City.

We exchanged greetings from our families, and Hamdoun sat me in a cushioned chair across a wide desk from him. He stubbed out a cigarette and immediately lit another. It was turning into a tough year for the Iraqis. Weapons inspectors accused Saddam of blocking their efforts to find evidence of WMD production, and Saddam's guys claimed the inspectors were spying for U.S. intelligence. Clinton threatened to launch cruise missiles to destroy any site where the Iraqis might have restarted their WMD programs.

"It's not a good time for us to be dealing with the North Koreans," Hamdoun said.

The news hit me like a dead weight. All that work for nothing. "Maybe it's the *best* time," I said. "You guys need to do something unexpected. You need to change your image."

Hamdoun sighed. "I'd like to help you," he said. "You are fighting for a good cause." He rested his cigarette on a heavy glass ashtray. "Maybe your government should listen to you."

I wondered if somebody in Washington had gotten wind of our plan and chased Hamdoun off it. He was surprisingly cold.

"This sounds like good-bye," I said.

We shook hands, and he walked me to the front door of his mission. He looked sad, and even though we'd known each other less than a year, I felt like I was losing a good friend.

Han tried to comfort me a few days later, as we browsed fishing tackle at the sporting goods department at Sears. "You can't trust the Iraqis," he said. "You were spending too much time with him anyway."

For a moment I wondered if Han somehow had sabotaged my relationship with Hamdoun. "And I can trust you?" I asked.

Han looked hurt. "You can't be close with them like you are with us," he said. "Your government won't let you have relations with the Iraqis. Too much oil in their country."

I picked up a fly rod, tested its weight and the spring of its graphite, and handed it to Han to try. "I'm more comfortable with you guys anyway," I said. "You're a bunch of rejects, just like me."

10

~~~~~~~~~~~~~~

Rations

I SAT IN MY UNDERWEAR among the North Korean soldiers on the train north to Kumho. Sweat from my bare legs soaked into the thin mattress. The air in the cabin baked us the way a brick oven bakes a pizza. My skin felt heavy like cheese, about to slide off my body. North Korean trains don't have air-conditioning.

Sitting across from me, Ambassador Kim had also stripped to his underwear—a loose, unbleached pair that looked like old diapers compared to my tighty whities.

Kim was a relaxed guy with a full head of hair. Han introduced him as Ambassador Kim, but I knew so many Kims from North Korea by now that I was getting them confused, so I nicknamed him "Slim Kim." He was so skinny his belly curved inward and his pectoral muscles looked like they were made of string.

"You look like you need a good meal," I said.

"You look like you ate my meal," he joked. He kept staring at my hairy chest and thick legs as though he'd never seen anything like them.

I looked around the train at the soldiers, who'd stripped to their underwear, too. What the hell was I doing here? My barbecue was to blame. Around the time I was befriending Hamdoun, I'd cooked ribs at my parents' house for Han, Slim Kim, and one of the North Korean directors of the KEDO project. They couldn't stop talking about how delicious the meat was, so naturally I proposed putting a Cubby's franchise at the KEDO site. The director loved the idea: two light-water reactors and one barbecue restaurant. I said I had asked the suppliers to bring containers of frozen Danish ribs to the North Korean coastline, as long as we could get an exemption from the sanctions and some startup money. Before Slim Kim and the KEDO director went back to North Korea, I gave them each a copy of the blueprints for Cubby's Hackensack.

When an international team officially broke ground on the KEDO site in August 1997, Han said some people in the DPRK were taken aback that I wasn't there. My feelings were hurt, too, and I told Han so. "After everything I've done for you guys, I don't get invited to the opening ceremony?" I complained. The next thing I knew I was meeting Slim Kim in Pyongyang for the train ride to Kumho.

He and I were the only civilians aboard. More soldiers in uniform got on outside Pyongyang, heading home on leave. A couple soldiers walked down the aisle of our car, stared at me, and slung their bags onto the empty bunks above us.

I stuck out my right hand. "Bob Egan from New Jersey," I said to the first one. "How you doin'?" The soldier looked at his buddy and then shook my hand. I turned to soldier number two. "Bob Egan from New Jersey. How's it goin'?" When he didn't respond, I grabbed his wrist and put his hand in mine and shook it. "Friends," I said. "Good."

"Don't talk," Kim said. "It could make trouble for them."

"They looked like they wanted to say hi."

"They're curious," he said. "Nobody rides a military train. Even I don't. Only soldiers."

Maybe I should have been offended that, while other international visitors were flown to the KEDO site, I rode second-class. But everything depends on how you look at it. Putting me on a train with their soldiers was a sign of confidence, and I considered it a privilege.

The train stalled two or three times an hour, and we'd stare out the window at the electrical line that ran alongside the tracks, wondering when it would bring power to the engine again. Some hours we sat in place more than we moved. Slim Kim told me to prepare for a day and a half of travel. I leaned back against my gym bag, which contained my T-shirts, pants, toothbrush, sneakers, running shorts, one sweater, a package of cookies, three Cubby's baseball caps, and a Cubby's apron I'd brought as a gift for the KEDO site director.

A few bunks away, a soldier squatted in the middle of the aisle, pulled his undershorts around his shins, and stuck a plastic jar under his butt crack. I couldn't believe it. The train didn't have a bathroom? I bent down and saw that almost every bunk had a plastic jar tucked beneath it. The air grew thick and smelly. I said I was ready to climb through the window to see if there was a breeze.

"Don't jump out!" Slim Kim shouted.

When the train stopped farther from the city, soldiers poured out of every car and scattered through some scrawny trees and squatted to relieve themselves. I ran out with them, and for the rest of the journey I restricted my intake of food and water. At night we kept the windows open, but in the morning two uniformed guards came into our cabin, exchanged a few words with Slim Kim, and pulled a thick shutter down. Kim looked at me apologetically. "If you don't see, you don't have to forget," he said in the semidarkness. White light glowed through cracks in the shutter. What could be so bad outside that they didn't want me to see? Starving people gathered by the side of the tracks, begging for food? I was prepared for that. The whole world knew most of North Korea was starving.

I wondered if they shuttered the windows only for my benefit, or whether they didn't want their *own* people to see how their worse-off countrymen lived. Han told me his government worried about foreign ideas "contaminating" its people because they needed to control their message at home.

I put my head on my lumpy gym bag and tried to doze off. A sulfurous stench rose from the plastic jars tucked under the seats. All around me the soldiers snored. The train plodded forward; its iron wheels clacked slowly against the rails.

Han put a foot on a seat at Cubby's and hiked his pant leg up. "Like my boots?" he asked. They were brown leather cowboy boots, the standard Tony Lama style, with simple, machine-sewn stitching and a pointy toe. Nothing exotic. They probably cost him forty bucks at a discount shoe outlet in the city, and he was very pleased with them.

"You look like John Wayne," I said.

"I won't wear them out of the house. Not good for anyone to see."

"You live in New York City," I said. "You can take a few fashion risks."

Han pulled his pant leg down, brushed off some imaginary prairie dust, and slid back into the booth. "I mean, not wear them at *home*," he said, without looking at me. "They're bringing me back to Pyongyang."

He pushed a rib bone across his plate with his finger.

"For a meeting?" I asked. "They want you to make a report or something?"

"I'm being reassigned," he said.

I felt lightheaded all of a sudden. He might as well have revealed he had a deadly disease and a month to live.

"Why would they do that?" I asked. "Look at everything you've accomplished."

I realized Han had been posted to New York for more than four years straight, which was longer than his colleagues. The time had gone by so fast. It's funny how somebody can become your friend and then, before you know it, they occupy your life. I'd spent every day either with Han, talking to him, or thinking about him since the day we met. What was I going to do after he left? He was my line into the deep water. Without him, I was just an ordinary mook from New Jersey with no juice. No angle. Nobody to discuss nuclear intrigue with while bass fishing off Sandy Hook. I had other friends, guys from the neighborhood, to hunt and fish with. But they weren't giving me a front-row seat to history. They couldn't joke around with me the same way Han could. He was irreplaceable.

"Maybe they'll send me back," he said, staring at his boots under the table. "In a couple of years."

A couple of years.

I worried about how they'd treat him when he got back to Pyongyang. Even if he didn't wear his new cowboy boots in public, they'd see how Americanized he'd gotten, and they'd eat him alive. He gained thirty-five pounds in his four years with me, and for a little guy like him that was a lot. He was accustomed to big dinners of steak and ribs with baked potatoes and a couple of Budweisers. How would he deal with rationed rice and sugar?

Slim Kim and I put our clothes on as we neared Kumho. Soldiers began hopping off the train at various stops. We disembarked onto a concrete platform, surrounded by low hills. The air was fresher and drier than in Pyongyang, and after more than thirty hours it felt good to get out of the train car. Two soldiers collected me and the ambassador in a military jeep and drove us north through the mountains. We passed a group of armed guards at a thick wire gate and entered the KEDO compound. A few brick buildings stood among the scrub pines and sandy terrain.

I met the director, who shook my hand warmly and asked after my family in New Jersey. He was a short man with a balding head and unusually hairy arms for a Korean. He escorted me to the room where I would sleep, in a two-story building that still smelled of wet concrete and fresh paint. Seven or eight more housing rows stood on either side. It was a dormitory-type setup with a single bunk and a small desk, a closet with a toilet, and a sink. Slim Kim disappeared to other quarters, and I didn't see him for the rest of my visit. North Koreans like to keep things compartmentalized like that.

The director took me to the excavation site where workers prepared to carve away millions of cubic yards of the mountain to level bedrock for the foundation of the light-water reactors. Giant earthmovers graded a swath of land into a wide plain. Eventually, if the agreements held and the project got fully funded, the KEDO site would be a small city, with banking offices, a church/temple, a golf driving range, tennis and basketball courts, cable TV, and four telephone lines piped in from South Korea—all for the international workers who would provide the expertise to build and run the reactors. The first facilities to be built were housing for construction crews and plants to manufacture special building materials, like the quadri-pod concrete supports for the giant project.

We crossed a graded area of bare earth with a few concrete foundations poured. The director pointed out a bare patch of land where the restaurants would be. He took me to a temporary mess hall, where we ate rice, fish, and vegetables served with kimchee at a long, empty table. After dinner, the director rolled out the Cubby's blueprints I'd given him in Hackensack. A couple of his North Korean project managers stood behind us, and I walked them through the layout of my kitchen, order counter, and the L-shaped dining area.

"Make room for a generator," the director said.

"We're going to have better power than the train does, right?" I asked. "We're building a couple of nuclear reactors here."

The director pouted his lips disapprovingly. "Don't speak about the train," he said. "Just bring a generator." The North Koreans rolled up the blueprints and took me to an empty room with a few chairs and a sofa. "We want you to relax," the director said. "How about a drink?"

"I don't drink," I said.

He nodded as though remembering it. One of his colleagues pulled a tiny envelope out of his pocket, turned it over, and shook a pill into the palm of his hand. "Take this," he said.

Stacks of unpacked boxes lined one wall. Plastic bubble wrap covered what looked like an X-ray machine. I guessed I was in their temporary medical area. "I've already been through this," I said. "On my first visit."

"We just want to be sure. We need to know your intentions are clear," he said.

I took the pill from him and weighed it in my hand. It was a horse pill, chalk white and unmarked. It looked like a vitamin. What the hell, I thought.

It wouldn't kill me. A pill in a brightly lit room was not the way you off some-body. The last time they shot me up with drugs, I got a nasty sinus infection but it felt pretty good at first. Submitting to it let them know that I trusted them, and that they could trust me.

The director handed me a bottle of water, and I gulped the pill down. "I don't mind relaxing," I said with a wink. I believe that we talked for a while after that, but I can't remember a single word either of us said. It's possible I just fell asleep.

The next thing I remember I was walking back to my barracks. I felt happy, like I was in the middle of a pleasant dream. The evening air wrapped around me like a warm hand. Stars winked through the clouds. In the dis-tance a generator purred. I was humming a little tune, probably one of the classics, like "Sultans of Swing" or "Afternoon Delight," and when I reached my door I heard a click of a latch. A door opened two rooms down. Yellow light spilled into the darkness, and out stepped a large-framed man wearing a blue button-down shirt, cycling shorts, and a pair of plastic sandals. "You speak English?" he asked.

"Do I look Korean?" I asked in a jovial tone.

"American?" he gasped. He looked left and right into the darkness to see if anyone was with me. He opened his door wider. "Come in, have a drink!" He turned back into his room and I followed. He already had a little refrige-rator open and was scooping ice cubes into a plastic cup. "Gin? Whisky?"

His room was identical to mine, but some clothes and books were strewn around; it had obviously been lived in for more than a few days. On a table a few bottles of booze stood at various levels of emptiness. The room reeked of solitary late-night drinking sessions. "Do you have a Diet Coke?" I asked. When he looked at me like he doubted my nationality, I assured him: "I abused my drinking privileges a long time ago."

I accepted a glass of ice water, and watched as my fellow American picked up a cup with some melting ice in the bottom and half filled it with gin. "You don't mind if I pour myself one," he said, screwing the cap back on the bottle.

He sat down heavily in a cheap-looking wooden armchair and stared past me at the half-open door. "There's nobody else here," he said. He spoke in a deep Southern drawl. I figured he was one of Clinton's guys, probably a mid-ranking political appointee at the State Department here to oversee the early stages of construction. Maybe he'd pissed off somebody higher up the food chain. This had to be one of the loneliest postings in the world. "I'm a little surprised," he said. "They didn't tell me you were coming."

"Don't worry about it," I said. "They didn't tell me you were here, either."

He grunted and lifted his cup of gin to his lips thoughtfully. "What exactly are you doing here?" he asked.

"I'm putting in a Cubby's."

"What's a Cubby's?" he asked.

I briefly explained my restaurant. "It's where the *real* negotiations happen," I said.

The State Department guy looked unsteadily at my shorts, T-shirt, and sneakers. "They don't have ribs in New Jersey," he said, slurring his words a little. I didn't know who he was, and I didn't care about finding out. We were on different highs, and I needed to get out of there. I was sleepy.

The next morning, I still felt surprisingly good. This was different than the headache and sinus infection I got after my first chemical interrogation. Whatever they put in my horse pill left me with a contented feeling, even if I couldn't remember things very clearly. I put my running shorts on and went jogging along the graded terrain. As I passed the entrance to the KEDO site, workers were arriving from a nearby village. They wore loose cotton pants and gray, collarless shirts and stared straight ahead of them, like zombies.

"Hey guys!" I shouted and waved. But none of them even raised his eyes to me. I jogged away from the complex toward the flat, sandy area, where I felt the breeze coming from. I came around a short rise in the land and stopped at a beautiful sight: dunes stretched down to the sparkling sea below, about a mile away. The salty air brushed my skin. I wanted to run down to the sea and jump into the cool water.

Up ahead, a concrete shack stood in the way. As I got nearer, a guard with an automatic rifle emerged and shooed me away with his hand.

"Don't try to get to the water," the director warned when we met up later. "Landmines."

"Nobody walks on the shore?" I asked. He said the entire beach was mined to protect against invasion by the South Koreans, the Japanese, or the Americans. I felt the sadness of a country where people couldn't get close enough to the sea to enjoy its breezes or feel the beach sand between their toes. They were locked like inmates in a giant prison colony. Except for a few guys like Han, the North Koreans would go through their whole lives without knowing what was beyond, or even seeing their country's borders.

The idea depressed me so much that when they gave me another happy pill that night, I took it without a second thought.

"I'm in for some long-term rehabilitation because of you," Han said. We faced each other over a plate of pork ribs at Cubby's about a month and a half before he was scheduled to return to Pyongyang.

"Shock treatment?" I asked, trying to make light of it.

"Funny to you," he said. He was worried about what lay ahead for him: solitary confinement; reindoctrination classes; chemical interrogations to make sure he still revered his leader. McCreary told me any official from the DPRK who spent time abroad had to go through the process. Still, it was hard to imagine it was necessary for Han. He was a tough guy and a loyal North Korean. He'd have bitten his own tongue off and bled to death for his regime.

"You've got nothing to hide," I said. "You want a letter of recommendation? I'll tell your leaders, 'He's no dove. He's no lollipop.' I'll get the New York Giants to write to them."

"It's more complicated than that," he said.

I thought about the military chief who Han wouldn't sit with at Cubby's and the cliques and alliances that he'd have to navigate once he was back. If the North Korean regime was anything like the mob, there'd be five jealous guys waiting to take his place if he made a misstep.

I whisked the plate of ribs away from him. "Hey!" he protested.

"From now on, you're eating salads," I said, heading for the kitchen to get him something with fewer calories. I wasn't going to let him look like he'd enjoyed his time in America.

I took him to my gym, the Health Spa II in Paramus. I told the owner, Lenny, that I was bringing in a North Korean who needed to get in shape so he didn't get whacked for getting chubby in America. Lenny said, "Just don't let him have a heart attack. I don't want the Feds crawling all over this place." I didn't tell Lenny the FBI would sit in his parking lot the whole time.

We did some pushups and jumping jacks, which is what Han knew from his military days. I stretched him on the mat. I created a regimen for him: twenty minutes on the treadmill, then a short circuit of bicep curls, reverse curls, military presses, and lat pull-downs. Han had no experience with a bench press, so I started him off with just two five-pound weights. I stood behind his head to spot him.

"You need to stop drinking alcohol," I said as I helped him lower the barbell to his chest. "No beer. No vodka. Total abstinence. And not just for your health. You can't afford to take risks."

"I don't have a problem," he said, pushing the bar up. "You're the one who can't drink."

"Don't wait until you do something stupid," I said. "It's one thing if I fall off the wagon and get in trouble—they send me to jail for a couple of nights and then to rehab. You make one bad decision, and they'll send you to a concentration camp with your whole family."

I stopped Han after eight reps and added two more five-pound weights. "Who's the person you most admire in America?" I already knew the answer. Driving around New York City, we talked about him all the time.

"Donald Trump," Han said. He huffed the weight bar off his chest. His elbows wobbled, and I helped him lift.

"Did you know that Donald Trump has never tasted alcohol in his life? Look how much *he* gets accomplished every day. You've got major issues to work on. Feeding your people. Getting thirty thousand American troops off your border. You need to stay focused."

Han got off the bench, and I started adding weights to the barbell until it had 240 pounds on it. I beckoned one of Lenny's guys over to spot me. Han had never seen anybody bench press before. I pushed hard and my veins bulged as I extended my arms and lifted the barbell. The trainer helped guide it back to its holder, where it clanked heavily. I was showing off for Han. I wanted him to see that if you train hard enough, you can shape your body, which is the first step toward shaping your place in the world. In the back of my mind I had the mixed-up idea that if I could lift enough weight, he'd be able to stay. My adrenaline pumped. I pushed the bar again and my heart swelled, as I tried to bench press Han to freedom.

"Superman!" Han said. He poked at one of my pectoral muscles. "You have bigger boobs than my wife!"

I still felt buzzed as Slim Kim and I took our seats with the soldiers returning from Kumho to Pyongyang. As the train got underway, I came up with an idea for the Cubby's DPRK logo: a missile tucked into a kaiser roll, dripping with barbecue sauce. I imagined a big Cubby's sign in the KEDO complex, with the domes of the nuclear reactors behind it. It would make a great picture.

We had fewer power outages on the return trip. But after about seven hours, we grabbed our bunk frames when the train stopped abruptly. This time, the lights in the cabin stayed on. Nobody had bothered to shutter the windows, and I peered out the window at a bare, flat field. The horizon shimmered in the late summer heat. A dozen peasants approached the train wearing rags sewn together over their bony frames. Everybody I'd seen in North Korea was skinny, but I had never witnessed starvation before. A couple of the soldiers reached into their food satchels and held handfuls of rice out the window. The peasants snatched at them. A woman who looked eighty but might have been much younger approached my window. I'll never forget her face. Her muscles were so depleted that her skin looked like it had been dried onto her skull. Her mouth hung slack. Her cheekbones jutted out below dull eyes. I put three or four cookies aside for the rest of my trip and held the rest of the package out the window. The woman grabbed it and turned away.

A few moments later I heard shouting, so I stuck my head out the window. A group of soldiers knelt on their hands and knees and peered under the train a few cars ahead of us. Others stood around and shook their heads and lit cigarettes. After a few minutes, one of the soldiers brought an old blanket off one of the cars. They pulled a body from under the train by its legs and dragged it into the open. I caught a glimpse of gray hair.

"Better not to look," Slim Kim said from the bunk behind me.

McCreary had told me there were reports of elderly people in the countryside so desperate they threw themselves under passing trains or walked into the fields to die, to keep their families from having to feed them. The soldiers draped the blanket over the body. A couple of the peasants watched from a distance, but most kept walking down the rail cars, begging soldiers for a share of their rations. I tried to imagine the state of mind of these people who had no time for the death of one of their own. All they could think of was something to eat.

I tried to get Han set up the best I could. I helped him buy a St. Croix graphite casting rod, with light action and lots of play, so he could outfish his neighbors in the Taedong. I organized a large care package sent via one of Bill Henry's humanitarian shipments, including vitamins, antibiotics, pain medicine, Viagra, and candy.

The night before he left, I went to the mission to say good-bye. Han let me in, and I followed him to the small conference room. Once we were alone, I handed him an envelope. He opened it, mentally counted the five hundred dollars inside, and glanced at the door. "Thanks," he said, stuffing it into his pocket.

Han and I aren't the type to get all weepy. We're macho guys. When we want to express our deepest feelings, we do it with an envelope of cash.

"Want to go out for something to eat?" I asked.

Han bit his lip. "Better if I stay in here," he said. It was the first time he'd ever turned down a chance to get out of the embassy for a free meal. He was being very careful now. It was like a part of him had already returned to Pyongyang.

He walked me to the elevators. "So this is good-bye," I said.

I put my arms out and tried to give him a hug, which he returned stiffly while keeping an eye on his embassy door.

"They could send you back early," I said. The look of uncertainty on his face kicked me in the gut. I wished he'd been able to explain to me why his bosses were recalling him. I knew he didn't want to leave, but I had no idea how to help.

"Maybe things will get better," I said. "We'll start our chicken farm."

"You have to cooperate with the mission," he said. "Stay involved, but not too involved." He thrust his arm toward me and we shook hands, which was silly because we'd already hugged. We didn't know what else to do.

"You're my guy," I said.

He nodded. "If things get bad, ask them to send me back. You'll know how to do it."

The elevator arrived with a *ding*, and I got in and pushed "L" for lobby. Han and I faced each other across the threshold as we waited for the door to close. He wasn't the same Boy Scout–looking kid I'd met four years earlier, but his face still had a certain softness. It was the last time I saw him look young.

11

Missing Han

IN THE FALL OF 1998, a couple months after Han left, Kuhlmeier called and said he had news he wanted to deliver in person. He came to the restaurant earlier than usual the next day. I put two mugs of coffee on the back table, and we sat facing each other.

"You're not going to be my operative any longer," he said, as I stirred milk into my cup. "I'm being put out to pasture."

Suddenly everybody was abandoning me. "Because Han went home?" I asked. Kuhlmeier shook his head. Maybe it was just a coincidence. People get reassigned all the time.

"I hope being associated with me didn't get you in trouble," I joked.

Kuhlmeier sipped his coffee. "It didn't help," he said.

Jesus, I thought. Maybe I'd ruined this guy's career. He told me many times over the years that his superiors had wanted him to control me better. When I took the North Koreans onto the open ocean or put guns in their hands, it made him look bad at the Bureau. And he took a lot of heat for my meddling in the Ross Perot affair.

Kuhlmeier said he was being sent to a desk job in New Haven working white-collar crime. He wasn't happy about it.

"I'm going to report you, Ted," I said, trying to cheer him up.

"For what?" He looked concerned.

"Unfair employment practices; for illegally firing me," I said. "Who's going to tell me, 'That's a no-can-do, Bob,' when you're not around?"

Kuhlmeier half laughed. I thought of all the times he'd forbidden me from doing something. Like buying night-vision goggles. Or helping the North Koreans go to Atlanta. Or the time when Kuhlmeier and his boss, Clochin, told me I needed a code name and got pissed off when I said I wanted "007." Without Kuhlmeier around, I'd be unsupervised. *Bye-bye, chaperone*, I thought.

I tore off the corner of a sugar packet and dumped half of it into my coffee. "So who do I report to now?" I asked.

He slid his coffee mug across the table absentmindedly. "I don't know," he said. "Whoever's around. They'll be watching you."

"Oh, good," I said. "That makes me feel much better. I wouldn't feel safe without those guys sitting in my lot with their binoculars, you know. You guys are saving me thousands of dollars in private security." Outside, the parking space where the agents normally sat was empty. A van pulled up to my front door, and the bread delivery guy unloaded a plastic crate of Kaiser rolls, hot dog buns, and sliced bread onto the walkway.

I wondered if Kuhlmeier would miss me. I'd gotten him closer to the North Koreans than any other source the Bureau had. As I walked him to his car after our coffee and we shook hands for the last time, I decided I was going to miss him. He might have been a tight-ass, but he respected the role I cut out for myself. He gave me credit for developing a relationship with the North Koreans, and he acknowledged that I could be useful.

Without Han, though, my usefulness faded.

I still hosted North Koreans at my restaurant and took them fishing, even after Han left and Kuhlmeier moved on. But it wasn't the same. In September 1999, when the bluefish were running in the waters off New Jersey and Long Island, I organized a trip for eight members of a KEDO delegation, along with Deputy Ambassador Ri Gun and Minister Counselor Kim, who I'd taken pheasant hunting with Han and Mike Nigro a couple of years earlier. I chartered a fifteen-person boat for us on a cool Saturday night. As the highest ranking guy on the boat, Ri Gun took the prime spot off the stern. The rest of us fanned out around the back deck. Within minutes, everybody was catching except Ri Gun, who accused me of giving him a bad position. "You picked the spot yourself!" I said.

A short while later, Kim ran up to me and pointed at one of the KEDO delegates, a middle-aged guy with big ears. "He's bit!" Kim shouted. "The fish bit him!" I reeled in my line and set my pole down. The big-eared guy held his pinky, which gushed with blood from the tip.

"The finger's still there, it'll be all right," I said. I got some antiseptic and cleaned his wound at the galley table. Kim looked helplessly toward the stern, where Ri Gun complained loudly, "They're like pirhanas. They eat fingers. Why don't they take my bait?" and kept fishing with a big pout on his face. I felt like a camp counselor trying to keep a bunch of children happy. Suddenly it hit me how much I was going to miss Han.

In Han's absence, Kim became my main contact at the embassy. But he couldn't replace my friend. Kim would never have stuck his nose out for American POWs the way Han had. He probably wouldn't have taken on the Atlanta Olympics, either. Without Han, the DPRK might have stayed home in 1996. Han took calculated risks, while being careful not to piss off his superiors. He brought ideas to Pyongyang. Maybe he could afford to because he was more connected than Kim, or maybe it was in his character. I never knew.

When I asked how Han was doing in Pyongyang, Kim said it was better for everybody if I didn't make too many inquiries. I imagined my buddy was going through some harsh reeducation after more than four years in New York City. I lay awake at night, wondering what he was doing and if he had enough to eat. I hoped nothing I had done would make his life harder. I feared that somebody with a bone to pick, like Cranky or the military chief who ate my habanero peppers, would take revenge on Han because they couldn't get to me.

As the months passed, I came to grips with the idea that my story with the North Koreans had come to a close. My time on the world stage was over.

There weren't a lot of other countries running around with nobody else to talk to. Even the Iraqis had better contacts than me. Hamdoun may have been a great guy, but he was a different breed. He had pedigree. Only a pariah country like North Korea would ally itself with Bobby Egan.

The DPRK might be the only country in the world that doesn't send its future diplomats to study at the top universities in Boston, Paris, or London. Even the poorest, most backwater countries educate their leaders abroad. When these guys get to the United Nations, they all know each other. They talk the same lingo. They tell the same jokes. The North Koreans are the exception. They've been so closed to the outside world they don't have the same kind of diplomatic corps that other countries have. They were educated in their military system. They learned how to shoot and fight, not how to file their nails or make a perfect knot in a necktie. They were more like those of us in North Jersey who like to hunt and fish and haven't spent our lives with our noses in a book. I told Pritchard one time: "What you guys don't understand is that North Korea isn't run by people like you. It's run by people like me."

I figured I'd see Han sooner if our countries normalized relations. We came close toward the end of Clinton's presidency. The year Han left, South Korea's new president introduced a "sunshine policy" aimed at making peace with North Korea. It seemed like Pyongyang was softening, too. In May of 1999, the North Koreans allowed international experts into a suspected underground nuclear site at Kumchang-ri—the first of two inspections that found Pyongyang was in compliance with the Agreed Framework. As a conciliatory gesture, President Clinton sent former Secretary of Defense William Perry to Pyongyang, offering to improve relations if Kim Jong Il addressed remaining "security concerns." The president agreed to partially lift sanctions that September.

Washington remained wary of North Korea, though. That same month, a U.S. National Intelligence Estimate stated that by 2015 North Korea would "most likely" have a missile capable of carrying a nuclear warhead to the U.S. mainland. But Clinton didn't let these concerns stop him from seeking peace and a foreign-policy feather to put in his cap before leaving office. He was finally following my advice (even if he didn't know it was my advice) by separating the missile crisis from economics.

On October 23, 2000, in the waning days of his presidency, Clinton sent Secretary of State Madeline Albright to meet Kim Jong Il. Albright was the highest-level U.S. official ever to visit North Korea. She took Pritchard with her, so he finally got to visit the country about which he was an expert. Albright came back impressed enough that Washington buzzed with the prospect that President Clinton himself might go to Pyongyang to seal a deal.

The clock ran out on the Clinton presidency before anyone could arrange the trip, though. And when George W. Bush took office in January 2001, he abandoned the progress made in the last days of the Clinton era.

I told everybody who'd listen that we should keep pushing for peace with North Korea. But suddenly I was just a guy with a restaurant who ran his mouth, like any other jackass with opinions and no juice. The FBI stopped coming around so often. They showed up when the North Koreans came to Cubby's for a meal, but they never sent an agent inside to ask me what was said. It was time to face the truth: nobody wanted to hear my ideas.

But I still wondered: why can't an ordinary guy have a solution to an extraordinary problem? We're supposed to believe in a free market in America. As an entrepreneur, if I have a good idea and the right resources, my idea will succeed.

Our leaders don't want government to work this way. There's no competition of ideas. We've got two parties who look very similar from where I'm standing. They raise their money from the same sources. They protect the same interests. And if an ordinary citizen approaches them with an idea they say, "Why don't you write a letter to your congressman?" It's the same kind of disconnect when you call the phone company, and what you hear is, "Press one for a list of our prerecorded services; press two if you want to listen to elevator music with your thumb in your ass; press three to hear this menu again."

We live in a democracy where citizens are supposed to control what's done in their name. The great lie we tell ourselves in America is that we're all created equal. That's a story the privileged invented so they can feel better about themselves. Let's be honest. We have a caste system. My family was lower caste, full of nobodies. And guys like me without a bloodline get excluded from politics.

The big shots don't want the rank and file coming up with ideas. It challenges the power structure. If a guy who flips burgers for a living can work out a deal with the North Koreans, our leaders don't look so good. They don't want a roofer's son in their think tank or on a State Department delegation. How would they explain that? "Sir, the guy with the tool belt just solved the Middle East crisis." Ain't going to happen.

Look around the floor of the Senate. Do you see anybody who knows how to drive a forklift? How many of them have lived out of their cars because they couldn't pay their rent? What would they do if you put them in a room full of gangsters? I don't know how we trust our country to these people. Our government seems designed to exclude anybody who has any street smarts. I'd love to see a congressman put in a room with any coke dealer or restaurant owner in New Jersey. Let them wheel and deal against each other. The congressman'll get fleeced.

But policy isn't for the working man, they tell us. We're supposed to go to the ballot box every couple years and pull a lever, and otherwise leave the governing to the guys with the blue neckties and the red neckties. And maybe that's the way it should be. Most of us are too busy to pay attention. Who has more than a few minutes for world affairs after working a ten-hour day to support a family? Not an entrepreneur in Hackensack with a new baby girl on his hands. I was done.

After my adventures with the North Koreans drew to a close, and I no longer spent my free time with Han, I got my act together. I paid my bills on schedule. I spent evenings with Lilia and the girls at home. I went hunting with Nigro in Wyoming. I sold my Explorer and bought a black Hummer. Lilia and I moved our family into an eleventh-floor apartment of the Ivanhoe building in Hackensack, with a view east, all the way to Manhattan.

The first years of Lori's life engulfed me, and I no longer went to sleep thinking about North Korea. My days became routine. I woke up every morning, hopped in the shower, and fed Lori with a bottle or flipped through a cloth book full of mushy pop-up houses and plastic mirrors. I drove Andrea to school or went to the shooting range. I hit the restaurant by ten. After lunch, I picked Andrea up from school and helped her with her multiplication tables. She started figure skating when she turned eight, and I took her to the rink almost every afternoon.

I focused on my business. I retrained my staff. There's no magic to running a restaurant. It's all about margins. If you get better at your core business, you succeed. I worked on my pickups and deliveries. We got regular to-go orders from offices and work sites in Hackensack, and before Han left we'd put group orders together in a big box. If we delivered a dozen lunches, everybody grabbed their ribs and fries in a free-for-all. I made a new rule: put initials on each order so they were easy to divvy up on arrival. With this one small change, I tripled my take-out business in one year.

Hackensack was changing. Blacks, Mexicans, Koreans, and everything in between were moving to the area, and it wasn't good enough to only serve the plate of meat and potatoes that keeps a half-Irish, half-Italian guy happy. I expanded my side dishes. Lilia and my Spanish-speaking staff told me to add *platanos* to my menu, and that was a big hit. I discovered that side dishes were good for profit margins. I trained my staff to offer every single side to every customer. Instead of, "Would you like a baked potato with that?" it was, "Would you like a baked potato? Barbecued beans? Sweet mashed potatoes? Macaroni and cheese? *Platanos*?" People don't think of ordering something unfamiliar unless you suggest it to them. You have to give them the idea, just like I did with the North Koreans. In two years' time, I brought my business up 25 percent in side dishes alone.

I hired Terry Hughey, a black guy from the South with twenty years of restaurant experience. He suggested that we put more combo platters on the menu because African-Americans like to eat family style—where you get more than one or two things on the plate. So we added steak-and-ribs, chicken-and-pork, shrimp-and-ribs, and fish-and-shrimp combos, and sure enough I started getting more customers of color. I also made a discovery about Koreans. They're crazy for potatoes. With gravy or without. Baked or mashed. I don't think I've ever had a Korean customer who didn't order a potato. So I changed the menu, offering a potato side with any steak or ribs platter for no extra charge.

I also tailored the menu for customers who wanted *no* potatoes. At the time, a lot of customers were following the Atkins Diet. I added an entree that combined steak and a tossed salad with no croutons and no starch. Carb-free.

I got better at buying. I developed a relationship with a local bank, and when the price of ribs went down from $3.25 to $2.90 a pound, I took out a loan and locked in six months' worth of meat at the lower price, like the big chain restaurants do. I enjoyed all these things I'd neglected. I negotiated with vendors for shrimp, steak, and vegetables. I reupholstered my booths. I resurfaced my parking lot. I commissioned a giant street sign that featured a cartoon pig wearing a black Stetson hat and an apron that said "Killer Baby Back Ribs." Lilia and I framed some photos of distinguished former visitors to Cubby's, including Han and the other North Koreans, the New York Giants, Le Quang Khai, and the Rolling Thunder biker gang. We hung them over the booths.

Even though nothing gave me the same adrenaline rush as working with Han, by the time he had been gone for three years, I was content with my memories. There's nothing wrong with being an average Joe. I found happiness in the little things: watching Andrea figure skate and trying to get Lori to draw the Cubby's pig with a crayon. I convinced myself that being a businessman and a father was all I needed out of life.

12

~~~~~~~~~~~~~~~~~~

Above the Fold

I WAS PAWING through the hamper looking for a clean chef's shirt one morning in September 2001, when Lilia shouted, "The Trade Center's on fire!" I rushed into the living room of our eleventh-floor apartment at the Ivanhoe where our front window had a perfect view of lower Manhattan ten miles away. I got out a pair of binoculars. From the top of the North Tower, a plume of smoke streamed westward like a windsock. Lilia turned the TV on. We watched in horror as an airliner quietly glided into the South Tower and exploded in a fiery ball. Lilia and I looked at each other in confusion. How are you supposed to respond to such a sight? Andrea and Lori stood dressed for school, but I decided to keep them home. It was hard to tell what was happening, or whether schools were going to be safe. At 9:56 A.M., the South Tower tilted and collapsed. I thought of all the different types of people in there: janitors and secretaries; financial whiz kids dying with their neckties on; firefighters running up the stairs to save people. At 10:28, the North Tower fell.

I paced around the apartment, like I was supposed to be doing something but couldn't remember what. Like any other red-blooded American, I wanted to personally hunt down whoever was responsible and twist their heads off their necks. Around noon, I drove Lilia and the girls to Cubby's. What else were we going to do? Some of my kitchen staff was already there. "Let's open the fuck up!" I shouted. We prepped vegetables and marinated meat. We didn't have a lot of customers, so I pulled my soda machine off the counter and wiped underneath it for the first time in months. I cleaned behind the freezer, as though I could scrub away what happened that morning. That's what us ordinary, powerless guys do. We respond in our own spheres of influence.

The next morning, the girls returned to school and my regular customers started coming back. My delivery guy showed up in the early afternoon with ribs, steaks, ground beef, and chicken straight from the meat-packing district of lower Manhattan. I felt proud to be a fellow citizen of this man, who hadn't hesitated to drive into the disaster area, and of the workers who kept the meat flowing. Our greatness shines through in the relentless delivery of food to our people. The terrorists may have temporarily knocked out our financial market. But the next day, just a few blocks north of Ground Zero, they were defiantly grinding hamburger at four-thirty in the morning.

That same afternoon, I got a call from a guy who said he was a friend of Kuhlmeier's from FBI counterintelligence. He asked if a field agent from New Jersey could come out to see me.

"Anything I can do," I said.

A Chevy Malibu with lightly tinted windows pulled into the parking lot the next morning and drove slowly to the farthest-back parking spot. Through my front window, I watched a blond, Midwestern-looking kid in his thirties stride toward the door. *Choir boy*, I thought.

I showed Agent Tom Marakovits around the restaurant, pointing out the pictures of Han, Pak, Minister Counselor Kim, and the others; my dad in Atlanta; Vietnamese diplomats. Marakovits clasped his hands behind his back and studied each one like it was a museum exhibit. Unlike Kuhlmeier, he ordered something from the menu. Lilia set him up with a chicken sandwich and a Coke and rang him up $9.25, and he and I sat down to talk.

"You got experience in counterintelligence, Tom?" I asked.

"Actually, my background is accounting," he said. When I looked alarmed, he added, "I'm not here to go through your books. I'm a legitimate field agent. We're all looking for the bad guys now."

"Which brings you to me?"

"We're casting a wide net. I've been asked to see if you've had contact with any North Koreans."

"You think they're involved in the attack?"

"Undesirable types hang around together. They might hear something."

A couple of construction guys I knew came in carrying hard hats. They started to walk over to say hi, but I pointed to Marakovits and waved them off. I put my hands behind my head and leaned back.

"I'm friends with Iraq's U.N. guy, too," I said. "But I haven't talked to him for a while."

"Name?"

"Nizar Hamdoun. He's been their ambassador to the U.N. since the eighties." Marakovits nodded as though he should have known this. "Great guy," I continued. "Very close to Saddam. Good father, with a couple of girls. Lovely wife. I turned him into a Giants fan."

Marakovits looked unsure whether to believe me. He took out a flip-top notebook and a ballpoint pen, just like Kuhlmeier had on our first meeting. "Let's stick with the North Koreans for a minute—"

"You know what we should do? I'll get the North Koreans to introduce you to a Pakistani guy, a former senator. He's from the Taliban area near Afghanistan. Senator Khan. Lives right here in Fort Lee."

"Wait a minute," Marakovits said. "You know a Pakistani who's involved with the North Koreans here?"

"Of course," I said. "They're allies. They sell missile technology back and forth."

Marakovits glanced at the customers lining up to order burgers and barbecue. He looked like Alice stepping into Wonderland, unable to believe he was talking spy stuff in a barbecue joint. "Where did you get that?" he asked in a lowered voice.

"They don't hide it," I said. "Anytime the Koreans have a get-together at their mission you'll meet people from all the usual suspect countries. Pakistanis. Syrians."

"Have you reported this before?"

"I used to tell Kuhlmeier all the time."

"Oh, good," he said, looking relieved. "This is a little out of my league."

"You want to meet the North Koreans?" I asked. "I'll see if I can get you into their embassy."

"I'm not sure I'm supposed to do that."

"That's what Kuhlmeier used to say. You can meet Pakistanis, though, right? We have relations with them. I'll get Senator Khan over to the restaurant. He knows terrorist country."

Marakovits looked like everything was moving too fast for him. "Who is he again?" he asked.

I explained that Senator Khan was a pro-democracy guy who fled the coup by Pervez Musharraf a couple years earlier. "He's a sharp dresser," I said. "He drives a black Mercedes and polishes his fingernails. He lives in New Jersey, so it's your jurisdiction, right?"

I felt the old rush coming back. I was in the center of the action, at a time of national crisis. The Feds had come because they needed me. Marakovits seemed inexperienced, but maybe he'd be more open-minded than Kuhlmeier. Some of my brain's rusty gears came to life. I was a few clicks away from a good idea.

I put my elbows on the table and leaned toward Marakovits. "Why don't we bring in the North Koreans to help hunt for the terrorists?" I suggested.

Marakovits dabbed a French fry into a puddle of chicken juice on his plate. "How would they get visas?"

"Not here in New York," I said. "In Pakistan. You know that's where we'll be looking sooner or later. It's perfect. The Pakistanis trust the North Koreans more than they trust us. They're experts at tracking people down. They come from a totalitarian regime. It's one thing they're very good at."

Marakovits saw me peeking as he wrote "N.K.-Pakistan," and he closed his notebook. He looked at his watch. The lunchtime crowd filled the restaurant. He stood, shook hands, and said he'd be in touch soon.

The next day, I drove into Manhattan to visit Minister Counselor Kim at the DPRK mission. "Harbor any terrorists you can find," I said, when we sat down in the small conference room. He gave me a funny look. "If any guys with long beards approach you, let them into your embassy," I explained. "Let them into your apartments. Then call me."

"Who told you to say this?"

"It's an unofficial request from the U.S. government," I said, which was accurate enough, since Marakovits had asked for any info about terrorists that the North Koreans could provide.

I could tell Kim was worried about getting set up. Harboring a terrorist could be a criminal act, even if the intention was to turn the bad guy over to U.S. authorities. Kim didn't trust me the way Han did. "We already condemned the attack," he said.

"You said you opposed terrorism. It's not good enough. My government needs to know if you're willing to help. Countries are going to be put in the 'friend' column or the 'enemy' column. This is your chance to join the group of friends."

Kim got back to me a few days later. He said he checked with Ambassador Pak, who agreed that I could verbally offer the DPRK's help in catching terrorists.

I told Marakovits to get word to President Bush that the North Koreans were ready to hunt for the suspected masterminds of the World Trade Center attacks, Osama bin Laden, and his al Qaeda organization.

"The United States can handle the situation just fine," Marakovits said defensively. I wondered if he'd already floated the idea and been laughed at.

I asked Kim to put an offer in writing that the commandoes from the DPRK would help U.S. Special Forces move against the terrorists. If they put it on paper, the offer would be undeniable. I promised Kim I'd take it to the FBI and get it to the Bush Administration.

On September 24, Pyongyang issued a carefully worded statement through its news agency:

> It may be a right option taken in line with the policy of each country opposed to all forms of terrorism to make a due contribution to the efforts of the international community to eliminate the root cause of this terrorism.

"Too wishy-washy," I told Kim. "You need to be clearer."

But it was already too late. My plan to get the North Koreans involved in President Bush's War on Terrorism died before I could build the momentum. Washington gathered its allies to support the Northern Alliance against the Taliban in Afghanistan, brushing aside the North Korean offer of help. Then the old hostilities rose to the surface. When the United States launched bombing raids against Taliban positions, Pyongyang criticized the use of force. The Bush Administration responded by demanding new international inspections of North Korea's suspected WMD sites. Pyongyang threatened unspecified "countermeasures."

As the Taliban fled Kabul in late 2001, the FBI, the CIA, the Pentagon, and everybody in between felt the pressure to bring the terrorists to justice. I invited Senator Khan to Cubby's to meet Marakovits, since the leaders of the Taliban and al Qaeda were now in hiding in the mountains of Pakistan. Marakovits was so impressed with the Pakistani's background that he recruited him as an informant. "Not a bad start for a field agent," I said. "See how useful I can be?"

On January 29, 2002, Lilia and I put Lori to bed, started Andrea on her homework, and sat down to watch President Bush's State of the Union address. He told the nation that "Our military has put the terror training camps of Afghanistan out of business" and that it was time to widen the "war on terror."

"Our second goal is to prevent regimes that sponsor terror from threatening America or our friends and allies with weapons of mass destruction.

"Some of these regimes have been pretty quiet since September 11, but we know their true nature. North Korea is arming with missiles and weapons of mass destruction, while starving its citizens."

The president said the United States must also confront Iran and Iraq. "States like these, and their terrorist allies, constitute an axis of evil, arming to threaten the peace of the world."

I couldn't believe that Bush had basically declared war on three countries at the same time. I almost had North Korea ready to join his cause. He could kiss that good-bye. Calling them "evil" made him look ridiculous. Evil is something that infects people, like child molesters or serial killers. Nations aren't evil. They might have different interests than we do. They might do things we don't like. But any Joe Blow off the street in Hackensack could tell you that throwing the word "evil" around wouldn't get us anywhere. I could only imagine what the North Koreans thought.

The week after Bush's speech, I invited Counselor Kim, Ambassador Pak, and Ri Gun to Cubby's to assure them that they were still welcome in one small corner of America, at least. They brought a six-man delegation. Before I served them steak and ribs on the house, they wandered the restaurant to look at the photos I'd put up. Pak stopped in front of one with him, me, and a few other guys on a Sandy Hook charter, showing off our thirty-pound striped bass. "Do you admit to people that's us?" Pak asked. "Won't they put you out of business?"

A few weeks later, with hardliners in the Bush Administration getting more aggressive, the Pentagon recommended developing a series of smaller nuclear weapons to strike targets in North Korea, as well as Iran, Iraq, Syria, and Libya. Pyongyang issued a statement accusing the Bush Administration of "working in real earnest to prepare a dangerous nuclear war to bring nuclear disasters to our planet and humankind."

It got worse. In May 2002, President Bush stood before a group of Republican supporters and called Kim Jong Il a "pygmy" who was like "a spoiled child at a dinner table."

Around the same time, the Bush Administration accused Saddam Hussein of restarting his nuclear program and preparing to give WMDs to terrorists. The president said Saddam posed a "grave threat" to the world, and he threatened military action against the Iraqis unless they surrendered all their weapons-making capabilities. Saddam's regime reluctantly allowed weapons inspectors back into the country, but Bush was unsatisfied when they failed to find WMDs. While the Pentagon sent hundreds of thousands of U.S. troops to prepare for the invasion of Iraq, Bush hinted that North Korea could be next in line. In August 2002, he told a reporter that he "loathed" the North Korean leader.

Kim called me soon after that. "Very important," he said. "Can you come into the city?" The DPRK's Vice Foreign Minister, Kim Kye Gwan, was in New York for consultations at the U.N., and he wanted to meet me.

Han had never told me the exact hierarchy of the Foreign Ministry, but odds were that Vice Minister Kim was his boss. He was the highest-ranking guy ever to reach out to me. At this point, maybe I was the only American willing to talk to the North Koreans. They'd always been unpopular, but this was a new low.

We met in the lounge of a hotel on the Upper East Side of Manhattan. It was a fancy place with a piano player and carved wooden furniture. Vice Minister Kim wore one of those sweaters that buttons up the front like a professor wears, and he carried himself in a regal way that told me he had a higher status than any of the diplomats. I later learned he had a direct line to the Dear Leader, Kim Jong Il.

The vice minister ushered me through the lounge to a restaurant with white tablecloths and two forks and two glasses at every place setting. He ordered a glass of wine and I ordered a Diet Coke. He asked about Cubby's, which was well known to the Foreign Ministry. I invited him to come to Hackensack for ribs and said I was sorry that such harsh words were being used between our countries.

After the waitress took our orders—a sea bass filet for me and a porter-house, medium rare, for him—Vice Minister Kim sat back in his chair.

"How are things at the mission?" he asked, smiling mischievously. "It seems like you talk to them as much as we do."

"I doubt that, sir," I said. "But since you asked, in my opinion we missed a chance after 9/11. I don't want to point fingers or anything."

He shook his head. I took a sip of my Diet Coke and said, "You know the old Chinese saying: whenever there's a crisis, you also have an opportunity. That's how us entrepreneurs and businessmen think."

Vice Minister Kim raised his eyebrows.

"A crisis forces us to adapt and evolve," I continued. "Let me give you an example. At Cubby's, I might have never switched to heavy plates or put grilled chicken or salads on the menu, if TGI Friday's hadn't opened up down the street."

Our entrees arrived, and we tucked in. My filet was flaky and nicely pan-roasted, with a lemon-ginger sauce, but the potatoes were undercooked. "We could have worked together to fight terrorism," I said. "It would have completely changed our relationship. It's like a couple that has great sex after an argument, you know what I'm saying?"

Vice Minister Kim smiled. "You do?" I asked. "Good. Because that's like us. Or it could be. Your country and my country, we always fight, but we never get around to the great sex."

"That's an interesting way of putting it," the vice minister said.

I leaned forward so he could hear me better. "If you ask me, you should send Han back. He had the right personality for the job."

"How is that?"

I hesitated. "I don't want to get him in any trouble." Vice Minister Kim shook his head. "Han had imagination," I said. "He was open-minded. There were times when I wished he had more authority, but . . . he and I were on the same page."

"He follows orders like everyone else," Vice Minister Kim said. He sipped his wine and held it up to the light, admiring its color. "But he has more discretion than you might think. Sometimes he chooses not to use it."

The piano player started in on "New York, New York." The Vice Minister carefully sawed off a bite of steak and lifted his fork to his mouth with his left hand, prongs down, like the English do. I bet he had spent some time abroad. "If I may ask you another question," he said, "why do they hate us so much?"

This took me by surprise. I was honored to be asked. I slurped an ice cube out of my glass, crunched it between my teeth, and carefully considered my answer. I'm a patriot at heart, and I wasn't going to tell the DPRK's vice for-eign minister that my president was acting like a jerkoff. "Don't take it too personally," I said. "Put yourself in Bush's shoes. You want to come out against Iran and Iraq, and also Syria and Libya, but you don't want to seem anti-Muslim. What do you do? You find a non-Muslim country to throw into the mix. China's too big. Venezuela's not dangerous enough. You're the perfect fit. You have a nuclear program. You're selling missile parts to the Pakistanis."

After coffee I reached for my wallet, but Kim held up his hand. "Don't insult me," he said. "You're a good friend."

A month and a half later, in September 2002, I was in the back of Cubby's checking in a delivery of vegetables when Lilia shouted through the door that Kim was on the line. "Which Kim?" I yelled. "The Vice Minister?" I hurried to the phone and found Minister Counselor Kim on the line.

"Thanks a lot," he said sarcastically. "I'm going back to Pyongyang. Your friend Han is here."

"He's back in New York?" I gasped. "Can I talk to him?"

"He'll come to the restaurant tomorrow," Kim muttered. He hung up.

My old pal was back. But why hadn't he come on the phone himself? Maybe he wanted to defer to Kim, who'd been my contact in his absence. I realized I'd forgotten to tell Kim I was sorry he'd been reassigned. He wasn't happy. He must have known that I asked for Han's return when I met the vice minister, and that by doing so I was complaining about the status quo. The timing was too perfect to be just a coincidence.

The next morning, I spent extra time shaving so I looked fresh for my buddy. I could barely contain my excitement. It had been more than three and a half years, with no contact. I wore my best chef's shirt, and tried to keep it clean throughout the lunchtime rush as I kept an eye on the parking lot.

The white minivan pulled into the lot at four o'clock. I wiped my hands, straightened my shirt, and went outside into the bright autumn afternoon. The side door of the van slid open, and a gaunt, middle-aged man stepped out. I barely recognized him. He'd lost so much weight that his cheekbones stuck out, and he no longer looked like a Boy Scout. He walked toward me slowly, without the same energy I remembered. His eyes seemed tired and dull. It looked like they'd sucked out the Han I knew and replaced him with a phantom. I was afraid their reeducation techniques scrambled his brain.

I ran over and gave him a hug, but he didn't move. I felt his rib bones through the back of his light sweater. The driver waited inside the minivan. A security goon stepped out onto the blacktop.

"What did they do to you?" I whispered.

Han pushed back from my embrace. "What did they do to me?" he asked. He squinted at me. "What did they do to *you*? Motherfucker. You're fatter than before."

I burst out laughing, and I tried to hug him again. He might have lost weight, but he hadn't lost his sense of humor. I slapped him on the back a little too hard.

"I never forgot about you," I said.

"You're as sentimental as always," he said as we walked in the front door. He stopped me for a moment in the privacy of the vestibule. "Thank you for asking for me," he said.

Lilia came and shook Han's hand, and they talked in Spanish for a few minutes. I set him up with a plate of ribs. It was time to put some meat back on his bones. Besides the world-changing events, a lot had happened in almost four years. We'd both turned forty, for one thing. Han's daughters in Pyongyang were almost teenagers, and so was Andrea. Lori had turned four.

Han slowly filled me in on the years we'd been out of touch. Despite getting thinner, he hadn't wasted time back in Pyongyang. He established himself as the man who knew his nation's enemy, becoming Deputy Director of American Affairs at the Foreign Ministry. Now back in New York, he had been promoted to the position of Ambassador and Deputy Permanent Representative of the DPRK U.N. Mission.

"So there was an upside to our friendship," I said.

"It was harsh at times. But not too bad." I knew he was sugarcoating it. He hinted at what six months of reeducation was like, with daily interrogations. They kept him in quarantine for weeks at a stretch to rehabilitate him from the lifestyle and freedoms he had enjoyed during our friendship. I wondered what he *wasn't* telling me.

"I came through it as a better person," he said, surprised at my look of disbelief. "You think your system is so good, but you have problems. You talk about freedom, but you don't have an identity. We are different. We belong to something. We are like bees. Each of us has a role in the beehive. We know our purpose in life. You are the lone goose. No purpose."

This was how he had interpreted America for his superiors back home? We were lone geese? Maybe he was right. But he'd changed. The doctrine was back. He was more like the Han I'd first met eight years earlier, who gave me books on *juche* and other propaganda. He also had more responsibility now, so we had our work cut out for us. I couldn't wait to get something cooking. The world was becoming a more dangerous place, and it needed our help.

In early October, the Bush Administration tightened the screws on North Korea as it continued to build a case for war against Iraq. Bush had sent James Kelly, the assistant secretary of state for East Asian and Pacific Affairs, to Pyongyang, armed with evidence of a secret program to enrich uranium for nuclear weapons. Kelly had satellite pictures and other clues that the North Koreans planned to use centrifuges, the same technology used by the Pakistanis and the Iraqis, in violation of the 1994 Agreed Framework. The Bush Administration threatened to scratch the entire KEDO plan to provide nuclear reactors to the DPRK. That left very few options for peace.

If there's one thing a guy from my background knows, it's how to get out of a tight spot. In the mob, if you screw up, your only chance of saving yourself is going to the head of the family, owning up to whatever you did wrong, and asking for forgiveness. In politics, there are other ways.

"You need to get in front of the story," I told Han, who chewed on the end of a rib bone. "We'll go to the media. We'll clearly say what you are willing—"

"We don't talk to your press," he said. "Everything is manipulated against us."

I signaled for Lilia to bring Han another plate of ribs. "My president is ready to invade you," I said. "You have to stand up to him and define your position. Otherwise he's going to define it for you. And when he finishes with Iraq—"

"Let him come," Han said. "We'll turn the peninsula into a sea of red—"

"Don't give me that bullshit!" I shouted. "Things have changed here. Look around! Americans are preparing for battle. It's not just the president and his guys in Washington. Here in New Jersey my customers are buying extra cans of food and taping up their windows. They're ready for war, and they're looking for enemies—and you're on the list of evil countries. It's not just propaganda anymore!"

Some of my customers watched us curiously. Han seemed to be paying attention now, so I lowered my voice. "Look what's happening in Iraq," I said. "Saddam seems suspicious, so he's going to get invaded. If you want to keep that from happening in Korea, you need to declare what you have and say you're willing to compromise. No more of this 'There will be blood all over the Korean Peninsula' stuff. That's fine for your audience at home, but not for here. Not now."

"How do you know? You're just a restaurant owner. You put barbecue sauce on meat. You have no credibility." Han took the paper napkin off his lap, balled it up, and threw it on his empty plate.

I felt like I was starting from scratch with Han. "You're my friend," I said. "And that makes me a friend of your government. So let me tell you something from one friend to another: you guys have too many secrets. There's too much room for misunderstanding. Now you have to minimize that. You say the word, and I'll set up an exclusive interview with any media we want."

"Who told you to suggest this? John McCreary? The FBI? Or is this one of your ideas?"

I could tell I was getting to him. "Let's just say it's a good idea," I said. I leaned back in my seat as Lilia brought out his second plate of ribs.

"Are we going to fish or cut bait?" I asked.

Han brightened. "At the lake?"

"It's an expression. I mean, are you ready to move forward?"

He wasn't. For the next couple of weeks, we fell into our old routines. I took him pheasant hunting. He came to the restaurant a couple times a week. We shopped for supplies for the mission as an excuse to drive around, even though it was far beneath his new title. He loved my new Hummer. We went for sandwiches at the deli. He came a few times to watch Andrea ice skate.

And then, on October 21, 2002, fearing that Saddam Hussein was developing weapons of mass destruction, the U.S. Congress authorized President Bush to take military action against Iraq.

Han called the next morning. "*New York Times.* Page one, Sunday's edition," he said. "Above the fold. Otherwise no deal."

"No problem," I said, wondering how I was going to get a *Times* reporter to promise where a story would go.

"You said no problem about Perot coming to Pyongyang," Han said.

That was a low blow. "I got close," I reminded him. "I had him interested. I have his home phone number. Do *you* have his home phone number?"

"Yes," he said. "You gave it to me."

We both laughed. I told him to hold the line and went to the back office at Cubby's and dug through my shoebox of business cards until I found the number for Phil Shenon, the *Times*' diplomatic correspondent in Washington. Back in 1997, Shenon had wanted to come to Baghdad, if I had gotten the New York Giants over there to accept American POWs from North Korea. I'd asked Ambassador Hamdoun to give him a visa.

"I've got the guy," I said.

"Have him write an official request, and bring it to me," Han said.

I got Shenon on the line before my lunchtime rush started. He had the slow, deliberate voice of a veteran newsman. "North Korea's not really my beat right now," he said.

"I'll get you into their embassy," I said. "Alone. Ambassador Han will talk to you for as long as you want. They've never opened themselves to a journalist like this."

A couple of seconds of silence from the other end of the line told me the significance was sinking in. "They're not going to give a prepared statement?" Shenon asked.

"No holds barred." I promised he'd have the story exclusively. It had to be the kind of scoop a reporter dreams about—and he didn't even have to work for it. It fell into his lap.

"Sounds like they're desperate," he said.

"They're headed for a showdown with Bush, and they see what's happening in Iraq." I said the North Koreans wanted to be on the front page of a Sunday edition, above the fold. "It's their only condition."

"Everybody wants that," he said. "I want it. But it's not up to me."

I liked Shenon, but it was time to play hardball. I could go to *The Washington Post* or any other media. "Tell your editors if they're ready to meet the Koreans' demand, Han's waiting for a written request. He'll give you first right of refusal for two days."

Shenon came back to me the next afternoon. "We can't make any promises on paper," he said.

We set up the interview for the following Wednesday, October 30. I started imagining how it should go. On Tuesday, I took Han out to a deli to prep him. "Tell Shenon that, yeah, you're building nukes, you have a centrifuge program, but everything is negotiable," I said, as we unwrapped a couple of hoagies. "Everything except your sovereignty. Repeat it over and over. Once that's in the newspaper, it's on the record. Nobody can ever go back and say you weren't willing to compromise. It'll put pressure on Bush."

"They're nervous about this back home." Han flicked away a piece of lettuce hanging from his sandwich.

"Trust me, if you make the first move, he can't accuse you of hiding stuff. He can't accuse you of stonewalling. It puts you in the driver's seat." I opened our cans of Diet Coke. "You trust me?"

Han took a big gulp. His eyes watered from the fizz. "What else am I going to do?" he asked.

I met Shenon in a coffee shop on Second Avenue early the next afternoon, an hour before the scheduled interview. "If you want to bring up human rights, save it for the end," I said. "And remember not to insult the Dear Leader."

Shenon gave me an amused look. "I've covered dictatorships in lots of countries," he said. "I'll be all right."

We crossed the street to the DPRK Mission to the U.N. It had moved from the building on 72nd Street to an equally anonymous office tower on Second Avenue and 44th Street, directly above a Hallmark store, deep in the heart of enemy territory. I pointed out to Shenon that you could buy ribbons, balloons, and cheery greeting cards directly below the world's weirdest and most repressive dictatorship. The lobby foyer was paneled in the kind of green marble you find in the bathroom of a high-class hotel. I winked at the receptionist, who recognized me but looked Shenon up and down.

"Can you show us who else you got in here?" I asked as she copied the information from our driver's licenses. She handed us a typewritten list of the occupants, which included the diplomatic missions of Syria, Angola, Nicaragua, and Madagascar. The place was like a roll call of the insignificant and the undesirable. "This is where they put the bad kids," I told Shenon. "Guess what floor they're on."

We rode the elevator to the thirteenth floor, and one of Han's junior diplomats let us into the mission. Shenon scribbled a few notes as I led him past the big photos of the Great Leader Kim Il Sung and the Dear Leader Kim Jong Il and into the embassy proper. "This is where they do their daily chanting," I whispered to Shenon as we passed a conference room with twenty folding chairs facing a blank white board.

"You kidding me?" he asked. We came to a smaller, more informal meeting room with a sofa and easy chairs around a coffee table. Han stood and shook hands with Shenon, who took a seat facing Han and me across the coffee table. Two of Han's underlings sat on a love seat to our side.

Shenon flipped through the pages of his notebook. He seemed hesitant, and Han didn't break the ice, either. Were they both nervous? The stakes were high, but especially for Han. Sitting down with an American newspaper reporter was uncharted territory for the North Koreans. Pyongyang would buzz with the result as soon as the story ran, and Han's reputation depended on a good performance.

Shenon cleared his throat and said that, although his editors wanted him to focus on the nuclear issue, he knew Pyongyang had other concerns. He talked about the food crisis, the flooding, and the hard times for the people of the DPRK. A deputy rolled in a cart with tea, instant coffee for me, and Korean sugar cakes on small white china plates. Han said he appreciated Shenon's sentiments.

We all stirred our drinks.

"Let's make this easy," I said to Han. "Just tell him how many nukes you have and what you're planning to do with them."

The deputies glanced at Han in surprise. He laughed. "I wish I knew," he said.

Shenon laughed, too. He edged forward in his chair. "The administration has accused you of violating the 1994 Agreed Framework," he said. "How do you respond?"

"The interpretation is that the U.S. is preparing for a war," Han replied. He spoke slower than usual, and I could tell he was choosing his words carefully. "There must be a continuing dialogue. If both sides sit together, the matter can be resolved peacefully and quickly."

Shenon wrote in his notebook for a few moments. Then he asked if Pyongyang was willing to give up its nuclear program.

"Our government will resolve all U.S. security concerns through the talks, if your government has a will to end its hostile policy."

"Good answer," I said. Shenon shot me an annoyed look.

For the next half hour, the conversation flowed more easily. They talked about Bush's "axis of evil" speech. Han blamed Washington for backing away from the Agreed Framework first. He listed KEDO's delays on the construction of the two nuclear reactors at Kumho. He said Pyongyang was surprised at the hostile tone coming from the Bush Administration after the two sides nearly reached an agreement at the end of Clinton's second term.

"Your government has made hostile-sounding statements, too," Shenon said.

"The U.S. has put the DPRK on a list of preemptive strikes. So we would like to ask the American people: What is the alternative? What is the choice for the DPRK?"

Shenon's pen raced across his notebook. "Let me ask you, yes or no," he pressed, "are you willing to consider letting international inspectors into your uranium enrichment sites?"

"Yes," Han said.

After forty-five minutes, Han looked at his watch. We all stood up and shook hands, ending the historic interview. Shenon was on a high as we rode the elevator to the ground floor. "That was good," he said.

For the next couple of afternoons I called him to offer help with follow-up questions. On Sunday, I got up early and drove to the newsstand on Main Street in Hackensack. The *Times* was stacked on the bottom shelf. On the front page, above the fold, right under the date and next to a photo of U.S. fighter planes in Iraq, ran the headline: NORTH KOREA SAYS NUCLEAR PRO-GRAM CAN BE NEGOTIATED.

Shenon had been true to his word, without any agreements put on paper. If only our governments could work this way, finding mutual interests and trusting the value of a handshake.

I took a copy to the Hummer and read the story sitting in the parking lot. It quoted Han that the DPRK wanted a new "means of communication with the United States government and its people." It mentioned that "the North Korean Mission contacted the *Times* through a New Jersey restaurateur, Robert Egan, who is the chairman of a trade group that has worked to improve ties between the United States and North Korea."

I liked that. Restaurateur. It sounded French. I called Han. "Have you seen it?"

"Big problem. He got my words wrong."

I said I'd be right there. I drove into the city, and we went to our favorite deli. Han unfolded the paper on the table where we could look at it together. He pointed at the middle of a paragraph which quoted him saying his government was "stunned" when the United States cut off talks on the nuclear issue.

"I never said this."

"You probably did."

"Not 'stunned.' I said we were surprised. 'Stunned' shows weakness."

"No, it doesn't," I said. "It means 'very surprised.'"

Han reached into his coat and pulled out the pocket dictionary I'd given him eight years earlier. He opened it to a page bookmarked with a piece of tissue paper and triumphantly pointed to the word "stun": "to shock (someone) so they are temporarily unable to react."

"So what?" I said. "It's one word."

"We are not unable to react," he sniffed. "Nothing stuns us."

"Relax, let's eat," I said. "It's a good story for you."

I told Han that this one story on the front page of the *Times* would make it a thousand times harder for Washington to launch a preemptive strike. He should be proud to be a peacemaker. I was proud. A guy like me doesn't get a lot of chances to alter the course of world affairs. Even fewer of those chances come to anything. But in November 2002, Han and I pulled off something important. We may have single-handedly prevented war between our countries. It hurt my feelings that he wasn't more excited about it.

I ordered an Italian club sandwich and Han had pea soup, which was unusual. He ate less than half of it and then poked at his gums with a toothpick as I finished eating.

"You okay?" I asked.

"Of course!" He put the lid on his soup and stood up.

Ever since his return, he'd get irritable at little things like traffic delays, rude waiters, and loud music, which had never bothered him before. At first I chalked it up to stress. But then I noticed that whenever we'd sit down to eat anything solid, he would chew on one side. He didn't complain, so I didn't ask any further. Acknowledging pain was a sign of weakness to him.

Besides, we had other things to talk about. The second week of November, a delegation arrived to try to keep the KEDO project alive. I took them fishing. We had a couple of big meals at my restaurant. I filled their social calendar to help make up for the fact that their negotiations were going nowhere. There were too many angles all at once: U.S. threats of air strikes and an oil embargo; Pyongyang's stalling inspections of its uranium enrichment sites; rumors that it would test more long-range missiles. The North Koreans wanted security assurances before dismantling their nukes. And President Bush kept hinting that the DPRK was next, as he prepared for all-out war against Iraq. It was a deadly game of chicken.

In the middle of all this, Han disappeared for a couple of days. When he came back, he said he'd gone to northern Virginia to see a doctor in a Korean neighborhood.

"Infected gums," he said. He winced as he pulled his lip up and his cheek out. His front teeth looked like an old graveyard. I looked deeper. The flesh around his molars was violet-colored and swollen. "Nothing they can do," he said. "Too much money."

It was bad for world peace to have the DPRK's top American expert in terrible pain. And I couldn't stand to see my buddy suffer.

"We'll fix it," I said. "I've got just the guy."

13

~~~~~~~~~~~~~~~
~~~~~~~~~~~~~~~

The Mouth Is the Gateway

JOHN "THE GREEK" KALLIS was the best oral surgeon in northern New Jersey. He once pulled a wisdom tooth for Tom Cruise, and the photos in his office showed the other famous mouths he'd worked on: Kevin Bacon, Jennifer Lopez, Patrick Ewing of the Knicks, Doug Gilmore of the New Jersey Devils, ice skaters Silvia Fontana and John Zimmerman, and cast members from *The Sopranos.*

More importantly, The Greek was a friend of mine. He was a street guy like me—born to a couple of immigrants in Hell's Kitchen and raised in a tough neighborhood of Fort Lee, New Jersey, which was important because I needed somebody willing to take a few risks who wouldn't ask too many questions.

I told The Greek that the North Korean in charge of handling the nuclear crisis had a bad toothache, and that easing his pain was crucial to the stability of the world. He agreed right away to help. And he took it on faith when I said we'd try to get funds from a charity group to pay his bill.

I told him the FBI knew I was organizing dental work for Han, which was true, although Marakovits had tried to chase me off the idea. "Dentistry can be dangerous," he'd said as we discussed the idea at Cubby's. "What if something bad happens, God forbid. Or what if he alleges malpractice? We're at war with these guys."

"What if his infection gets worse, and he dies, because we don't give him access to health care?"

"Don't say that!"

"You're right. God forbid."

Marakovits shifted in his seat. "I checked into it, anyway. We're not responsible for him."

"You mean legally," I said.

"If he is ill, he needs to return to his place of origin."

I gave Marakovits a look. "You've never seen a medical facility in North Korea. If you had, you wouldn't say that."

"I'm looking out for your best interests," he said. "You don't have to take unnecessary risks."

I took a long pull of my coffee. "Sure I do."

"What do you mean, you do?"

"If we only took *necessary* risks, we wouldn't get very far," I said.

"You realize that if you get in trouble, I get in trouble."

"Then I guess that makes us partners." I smiled.

"Think about your family." Marakovits glanced at the kitchen door. "If something happens to you, it will be bad for them, too."

"Now you sound like a North Korean."

He waggled his head back and forth. "If something goes haywire, bigger feet are going to step in from the Bureau," he said. "I won't be able to help you."

I liked Marakovits. I did. Deep inside, part of him probably wanted to be doing what I was doing, mixing it up with the enemy. But he was timid. He had a badge and a cheap suit and a pension to protect. "We're just going to knock him out, pull out a tooth or two," I said. "When you see somebody in pain, don't you want to help them?"

Marakovits sat upright. "Tell me you're not going to put the ambassador from North Korea under general anesthesia." He clasped his hands on the table and fiddled with his thumb. "Who's the dentist? Does he have a license?"

"It's better if you don't know," I said.

I walked Marakovits to his car and lied to him. I said I'd call before we did any dental work on Han.

The Greek cleared his calendar for the second Saturday in November, when his practice normally would have been closed. I arranged for Han to meet me at eight A.M. on a side street nearby, where we could make sure neither of us had been followed by anybody from the Bureau. The less the FBI knew about it, the better. Han came with two guys—a security goon and one of his assistants—in a Chrysler sedan they used when they wanted to travel incognito. I came with Mike "O'D" O'Donovan, an old hunting buddy, who was ex–Special Forces and had just come back from showing coffee *finca* owners in El Salvador how to protect their land. With crew-cut gray hair, crazy-looking blue eyes, and questionable table manners—he liked to gross out my daughters by eating live worms—O'D was not exactly what you'd call refined company. But he was one of the best private security men in the business, and it seemed like a good idea to have somebody who was loosely associated with the law in case anything went wrong.

The dentist's office was on the ground floor of a beautiful residential tower next to the George Washington Bridge, with a view of Manhattan on the other side of the Hudson. We parked in the alleyway beside the building to avoid the surveillance cameras in the garage and left Han's junior colleague with the cars.

An assistant took X-rays of Han's mouth, and while we waited for the results, Han checked out a framed photo of James Gandolfini sitting at a dinner table with a napkin, a bowl of pasta, and a glass of wine in front of him. "The Greek worked on Tony Soprano?" Han asked.

I could tell he was nervous, so I went over and put my hand on his shoulder. "He's the best of the best."

The North Korean security goon sat in a lounge chair in the waiting room, where he stayed for the rest of the day. O'D positioned himself against the opposite wall. They put on sunglasses and pretended to ignore each other.

The Greek called Han and me back into his office. "This is the Panorex," he said as a technician pinned an X-ray of Han's jaw onto a light box. We leaned in for a better look. "The immediate situation is the infection around this lower left premolar, which has to come out right away," he said. "The larger issue is you've got problems brewing in all four quadrants. There is some really primitive dentistry. These could flare up at any point."

Later, when Han was under general anesthesia, The Greek told me he'd never seen anything like it. "Did you get a look at those bridges?" he said. "They're aluminum. Hollow. Crimped on. They used to be called ash-can bridges. You hear about these things in school, but nobody's done this kind of work since the nineteen-forties."

We agreed to remove six teeth and replace them with implants. "I'll do this in stages," he told Han. "It's safer. We can do some today, and then in the next month or so—"

"No," Han said. "All at once." He worried that if war broke out, he could be recalled to Pyongyang with his mouth only partly fixed.

The Greek warned that putting him under anesthesia for hours on end would increase the risk of cardiac or respiratory problems. But Han insisted, and a technician hooked him to an IV drip and a machine to monitor his vital signs.

"I want Bobby to be in the room the whole time," Han said.

Two dental assistants came in and prepped. Mike O'D followed them in, to observe. As The Greek sedated him, Han gripped my hand and then relaxed as he slipped into unconsciousness. O'D watched with a mixture of curiosity and disgust.

"You guys want to be heroes?" he said with a cynical grin. "Don't knock him out. Knock him *off*."

The dental assistants exchanged a look. O'D seemed too excited about the idea of blood and bone being chiseled out of an enemy ambassador. But he was just expressing how a lot of Americans felt after 9/11—looking for black and white, good and bad. Anybody from an enemy country was an enemy. Everything was simpler that way.

The Greek and his assistants went in hard with the drill, and soon the room filled with the sound of metal chipping against bone and the acrid smell of tooth enamel vaporizing into dust and smoke. Other times it sounded like they were sawing through wood. One of the assistants pumped steroids and antibiotics into Han's veins to ward off swelling and infection. The Greek's gloves were spattered red. The second assistant siphoned off the blood and spit pooling in Han's mouth. Another served up a series of tools that looked like torture instruments. I've gutted plenty of animals with my own knife and seen some gruesome stuff in my time, but nothing quite like what they did to Han's jaw that afternoon. I was proud of him for what he endured. I don't care if he was unconscious—it was brave.

They flapped back his gums, yanked out the teeth, and set them in a metal tray. The Greek cut a window in the upper jawbone, lifted the membrane that covered Han's sinuses, and then packed in pieces of bone so that new bone could take root.

The hours of surgery wore on. Outside the window the autumn sky was a clear slate. I thought of my first trip to Manhattan as a kid, and all the flags. They hung from tall poles, high out of reach, rustled by the wind here and there but mostly just limp pieces of green, blue, red, and yellow. Behind them, the mirrored windows of the U.N. building reflected the bright sky and the dark city below. Our chaperones led us off the school bus into the General Assembly hall. We stood on an observation deck and stared at the strange-looking people: Africans wearing full-length robes, the Asian guys in business suits. I had some exposure to blacks and Hispanics. I'd seen a few in Fairfield and on TV. Dad warned me to stay away from them if they were in groups. But the U.N. was like landing on another planet. A caramel-colored man with a face like a wedge shook hands with a round-headed guy with gold-rimmed glasses and a little goatee. Flat faces and long faces huddled together. One wore a white headdress with a black ring around his forehead. What were these people called?

Our teachers made us eighth graders take turns listening to the General Assembly with a pair of headphones. Most kids listened for a few seconds and passed them on. I went last, and when I put the headphones on my ears, I couldn't understand a word. One of the kids before me had switched the dial. I sat at the little desk, turned the knob, and heard translations in French, Russian, Spanish, Chinese, and Arabic. I didn't know what the sounds were supposed to be. Where I came from, there was English, the northern New Jersey variety, and that was it. To us, kids from fifteen miles south in Hoboken talked funny. I couldn't stop turning the knob back and forth. One voice sounded like bubbles. Another sounded like knives. The world was full of people who understood what these noises meant. But I'd never know, and it made me feel small. I tried to imagine all these people, who were loyal to their own flags and their own languages, far beyond Fairfield and Roseland and Hackensack.

"Bolus!" The Greek shouted at one of his assistants. He was starting to sweat. He glanced up at the monitor, barking at his assistants in code words. "Titrate!" he yelled.

"What's wrong?" I moved in closer.

"Arrhythmia. We gave him atropine to dry out his mouth, but it's making his heart beat differently."

"Is that dangerous?" I tried to make sense of the lines blipping around on the monitor, as the anesthesiologist dumped more drugs into the IV. Han's mouth gaped open. He looked like a vulnerable child. Across the room, O'D waved at me, put two fingers up to his lips, and then mouthed the words, "Going out for a smoke."

The Greek and his team kept picking away inside Han's mouth. I took that as a good sign. Then all of a sudden, they shuffled around. "He's stopped breathing," one of the assistants whispered.

"What's happening, doc?" I could hear the alarm in my voice. "Kallis?" The Greek ignored me and swiveled around so he was standing behind Han's head. "Turn down the gas," he said to his assistants. He put his hands over Han's ears and repositioned his head and neck. "Is the oxygen ready? Turn it up." I was sure he knew what he was doing, but Han wasn't a typical patient. His body wasn't used to American pharmaceuticals. Besides the anesthetic, they'd jacked him up on a cocktail of steroids, Demerol, ketamine, Valium, and propofol. If he stopped breathing for too long, he could suffer brain damage, or worse. The second hand ticked around the bottom numbers of the clock on the wall. I thought I was going to have to drag Han's body out to the security goon and the driver and say, "Sorry, here's what's left of him." In which case, I'd be dead meat. Some night, an agent from Pyongyang, somebody like Cranky, would knock on my front door and rub out my whole family. And then he'd come after The Greek's.

Han's family might be targeted. If the regime found it embarrassing that their ambassador passed away in a dentist's chair, his wife, daughters, parents, and who knows how many other relatives could be thrown into a prison camp. I vowed that if I weren't dead or rotting away in Leavenworth, I would find a way to help them. I'd travel to Pyongyang and grieve with them and let them know that Han's last moments were peaceful, and that his friend was holding his hand.

A worse scenario occurred to me. What if Han died, and it led to war? In Pyongyang, the circumstances would look suspicious: the American president is threatening a preemptive strike and the ambassador dies mysteriously in a dental office in New Jersey. That's how the First World War started. An Austrian nobleman gets popped while driving around and minding his own business in Sarajevo and suddenly sixteen million people are dead. The Greek and I would be mentioned in the encyclopedias of the future, as the guys who started a war by trying to fix a toothache. They'd call it The Molar War.

"Come on, buddy," I said. "Breathe for me."

O'D poked his head into the operating room. "Are we on *Headline News* yet?" he asked. And before I could say, "Fuck off, Mike," Han snorted—a drawn-out sound like kids make when they imitate pigs.

"The medication gets them too relaxed," The Greek said. "Like apnea."

"Could it have damaged his brain?"

"I don't think so. Most people can go thirty seconds or more."

Finally, after four hours, it was time to bring Han out of the anesthesia. One of the assistants fed some wake-up juice into the IV, and Han's eyes fluttered open. He recognized me, and looked straight into my eyes. He had a dreamy, spaced-out expression.

"I love you," he said.

The Greek grinned at me. "He's feeling no pain," he said. "Not yet, anyway."

Han turned and held his finger up to quiet everybody in the room. "I love my brother, Bobby," he announced.

O'D shifted uncomfortably by the door. "Looks like you two need some quiet time together," he said. "Get a room!"

The Greek and his assistants left us alone. O'D raised his eyebrows at me and followed them. Han sat on the edge of the dentist's chair and shook his head back and forth, until he got his bearings. "Was anybody else here when I said I liked you?"

"You didn't say you liked me. You said, 'I love you.'"

"No, I didn't."

"You were petting my arm. I thought you said there were no homosexuals in North Korea."

"Don't even talk like that!" he said. "You are a jackass."

I tried to help him up, but he pushed me away and stood on his own. "You gave us a good scare there, pal," I said.

As we were leaving, The Greek slipped me a small manila envelope, which I pocketed. He tried to write a prescription for pain medicine, but Han refused it on the grounds that he needed to keep his mind sharp for the nuclear negotiations ahead.

He rolled his tongue around in his mouth. "I'm hungry."

"You've been knocked out for hours," I said. "You've earned a plate of ribs."

"Take it easy," The Greek said, handing me the prescription. "He's all juiced up on steroids. Give him a milkshake, and get him the meds."

But once Han had heard "plate of ribs," there was no convincing him otherwise. An hour later at Cubby's, he was pulling meat off the bone with his fingers and putting it into his mouth as gingerly as he could. If he was in pain, he didn't show it. He was all smiles. It was too bad the new teeth were hidden by the gravestone-looking things in the front of his mouth.

"We could do something about these, too," I said, rubbing my finger under my top lip. "I know a guy who does veneers." Blank stare. "They're caps," I said. "Like gloves for your teeth. They'd make you look younger."

Han chewed carefully on some rib meat. "I'm a bee in the beehive, remember?" he said. "I don't need to look younger. It's not good for me."

"We'll make you the Eric Estrada of North Korea!" I said. No response.

"You don't know Eric Estrada? Like a movie star. Like Tom Cruise. Think about Tom Cruise's smile. It's powerful."

Han put a bare rib on his plate and wiped barbecue sauce off his fingers with a paper napkin. "Maybe it would make me a better negotiator?"

"Of course it would!" I said.

Han said he'd think about it.

Marakovits was sitting in the parking lot of Cubby's when I arrived the next morning. It was Sunday, his day off. He knew. Lilia told me his agents had made twenty-one calls to Cubby's while we were at The Greek's.

"He's feeling fine," I said as we sat at the back table. "Everything went off without a hitch. No trouble at all."

"I was worried, you know." Marakovits looked like he couldn't decide whether or not to scold me. We were still feeling out our relationship.

I pulled the little manila envelope out of my pocket and put it on the table in front of him. "If we hadn't put him in that chair, I wouldn't have *this* for you."

He gave it a little squeeze between his thumb and forefinger and shook his head in amazement. "Is this what I think it is?" He turned it upside down and a fully intact molar rattled across the Formica. His hand shot out and saved it from flying off the table. "Does he know you took this?"

I didn't tell Han. Even though we were like family by now, he knew we had to do our part for our own sides. Loyalties get mixed up when you reach across borders. My mom's uncle Tony drove a tank in World War II in parts of Italy where relatives sided with Mussolini's fascists. When Uncle Tony's crew fired tank rounds on the enemy, he never knew if he was hitting a cousin or an uncle.

Marakovits dropped the tooth back in the envelope, looking pleased with the trophy. It was more personal than the strands of hair I brought Kuhlmeier years earlier, and they couldn't ask for a better body part for the purpose of identification. The tooth had been in Han's head for four decades, chewing an unknown number of meals for him. A life of meals could probably be detected, if anybody looked closely enough. FBI experts would examine it in some lab, I guessed. But other than Han's diet, what would they learn from it? I wanted to tell them: get inside the North Koreans' heads, not their teeth and hair. Our intelligence guys seemed more interested in Han's chemical structure than his psyche.

They could have learned something from Han's self-image, too. Everybody likes to look good. Han wasn't more vain than anybody else. But he wasn't any less vain, either. A few weeks later, when his jaw had healed, I took him to Jorge Cervantes-Grundy, a cosmetic dentist in Fort Lee, who's also a friend and a regular customer of mine at the restaurant. Grundy agreed to work on Han with zero down. Han was still leery of the idea of veneers. He asked for the yellowest ones possible. He was afraid that if his teeth looked too perfect and too white, some jealous superior back home would rip them out with a pair of pliers and send them back to America in an envelope.

Grundy installed veneers in Han's mouth over the course of two visits in January 2003. Han looked years younger. "I'm going to Hollywood," he boasted. "You think I can be an actor?"

"What do you want to play—the good guy or the bad guy?"

He flashed his new killer smile. "Bad guy," he said.

After he got his veneers, Han became a poster boy for oral hygiene. He'd grin at himself in the mirror when he thought nobody was watching. He started asking me how often I flossed and telling me I needed to get my bottom teeth straightened.

Despite the communist system that says they have to live for the glory of their nation and all that B.S., I'll bet most North Koreans would jump at the chance to get their teeth fixed, if they could. I imagined a dental diplomacy effort, starting with the Dear Leader and his top brass and working our way down the chain of command. I talked to The Greek about it, and he offered to make a humanitarian trip to Pyongyang anytime I asked. I had conversations with Bill Henry and Han about getting dental lab equipment shipped over there, with the idea of opening up a clinic.

They say the little details of your appearance can have a psychological effect on how others see you. Especially the teeth. I've heard that looking at someone's teeth is how we unconsciously measure their vitality. The mouth is the gateway to health, they say. Han was always talking about *juche* and self-reliance. To me, self-reliance starts with self-improvement. Or to put it in terms of politics, if you can't change your adversary, change yourself. I wasn't saying dental work alone would do the trick. But most of the North Koreans I met had plenty of room for improvement in the oral cavity department. A few fixes in that area could help their self-esteem. Imagine what could happen if a group from Pyongyang showed up to a negotiating session and flashed their new and more pleasing smiles—winning smiles—at their American counterparts. The Americans would smile back. It's instinctual. Things like that work on an unconscious level. Maybe the negotiations would take on a better tone. You never know. Sometimes it's the intangibles that make all the difference.

Nobody was smiling in January 2003, when relations between the United States and the DPRK hit a new low as American troops massed in Kuwait. The North Koreans were desperate to avoid becoming the next Iraq. Pyongyang kicked out international weapons inspectors and said it planned to reopen a facility capable of producing weapons-grade plutonium. Spy satellites tracked suspicious movement at the Yongbyon nuclear plant. On January 10, the DPRK government announced its withdrawal from the Nuclear Non-Proliferation Treaty. In his second State of the Union address, President Bush called the DPRK "an oppressive regime" whose people "live in fear and starvation." Pyongyang responded in a statement, calling Bush a "shameless charlatan."

"Why do you have to use such fancy words?" I asked Han. "Say things that everybody can understand. When you call him a 'charlatan,' it sounds wimpy. And 'shameless charlatan' is hard to pronounce."

"It's hard for *you* to pronounce," Han said. "You dropped out of high school."

"Short words have more power," I said. "Look at Bush. He called your leader a 'pygmy.' It wasn't nice, but you remember it."

Despite the nasty tone between our countries, I wondered if the interview

Han gave to *The New York Times* had hit home with some of our leaders in Washington. Around the time the North Koreans pulled out of the NPT, Han received an unexpected invitation to visit the home of New Mexico Governor Bill Richardson. I encouraged him to accept, because nobody else was spending time with the North Koreans. Richardson had been one of Clinton's ambassadors to the U.N. during Han's first tour of duty, and it looked like he was the closest to Washington they were going to get.

Before Han left for New Mexico, he asked me for a couple bucks. I gave him three hundred in twenties and told him to keep it in his pocket. "Don't be picking up any checks," I said. "The governor is inviting you, and he has plenty of money. How long will you be gone?"

"Until Friday."

"Three days? That's a while." It was the longest stretch Han had been away from me since he'd returned from Pyongyang, and I was going to have separation anxiety. I was turning into a regular mother hen. "Call me when you get there?" I asked.

He promised he would and told me not to worry. Han had met with Americans before. Nuclear experts. Intellectuals. National security people like Pritchard. Mostly they were short meetings, not for days at a time. Han always told me these weren't the kind of people he wanted to spend time with. He said he sometimes felt intimidated by their high level of education. But I always pushed him to meet them. I didn't want him to think I was trying to keep him all to myself.

That night I checked my cell phone every ten minutes. At eleven o'clock I got a call from a roofing contractor from the neighborhood asking if I'd seen a guy who owed him money. It was only nine o'clock in New Mexico. Han was probably still at dinner. Around midnight, I switched my phone to vibrate and got under the covers with Lilia. I was just starting to fall asleep when it buzzed. I jumped out of bed as quietly as I could and tiptoed out of the room.

"It's me," he said.

I sat in the darkness of my living room. "How was dinner? What did you have?"

"Green chili. Very spicy. Not as spicy as Korean food."

"And not as good as Cubby's chili, right? How's the governor?"

"He's very nice. He is just moving into his new house."

Richardson seemed like a knock-around guy, not like your typical egg-headed intellectual. I walked through the kitchen in the darkness, opened the fridge, and let out a stream of light and cold air. "It's good for you to align yourself with people like him," I said. "He can do more for you than I can."

"Tomorrow he's going to give us a tour of the mansion. It's on a hill in the desert. Just like a Western movie."

"The governor likes movies, just like your leader." I felt like I did in high school when my family couldn't afford a vacation and afterwards I had to listen to the rich kids talk about how powdery the snow was in Aspen. "How about your new teeth. How do they feel?"

"I think he noticed," Han said. "He told me, 'You look well.' Did he mean I look 'healthy' or 'handsome'?"

"He didn't know you before, so he wouldn't have noticed anything different." I took some milk out of the fridge and drank it straight from the carton. "Don't smile too much, just because you've got a pretty mouth now. Remember who did that for you."

"You, Bobby." Han sighed.

"Do I sound jealous?"

"Yes, you do."

"If the governor was a real friend, he'd take us elk hunting," I said. "They have the best elk hunting in the world in New Mexico."

"They do?"

"Ask him for a couple of elk tags. He runs the state. Tell him you've got a buddy who wants to come out hunting with you. See if he's *that* good a friend."

Han laughed. "I didn't say he was my friend. I said he was nice."

I padded into the darkness of the living room. Outside the window, snow breezed through the orange streetlights of Hackensack. "You going to talk nukes tomorrow?"

"That's the idea."

"Just repeat what you told *The New York Times*. Everything is negotiable."

We knew the phone line was probably tapped, but we didn't care. We mostly kept it to trivial stuff, anyway—my staffing issues at Cubby's; the best way to shoot an elk. We chatted for nearly another hour. Han was lonely, and I guess I was glad that he was. It was nice to be needed.

On March 20, the United States invaded Iraq. Han invited me to the DPRK mission on Second Avenue to watch the news that evening. I don't have a TV at Cubby's, and Han had been busy all day, so we were seeing the images for the first time. I brought two racks of ribs and two baked potatoes to what we called our "shock-and-awe" viewing party. The other North Koreans had gone back to their apartments, and Han and I had the place to ourselves. It was like movie night.

Han had been back for four months, and we were spending almost every day together. Our friendship had matured during our four years apart. It was like they tell alcoholics: if you stop drinking and relapse, you don't start at the point where you left off. Your addiction moves forward without you. I've always had an addictive personality. I needed the hook. The blood. The bang. Han and the North Koreans replaced drugs and the Vietnamese as my substance of choice. Was that necessarily a bad thing? It was healthier for me and better for the world that I wasn't speeding around the suburbs at three A.M. trying to score an eight-ball of coke and, instead, got into politics.

I spent so much time with Han that it was putting a strain on my marriage. At night, when I got home from Cubby's or the DPRK embassy, I'd walk past the sofa where Lilia watched TV and get myself something to eat from the kitchen. We'd stay in different parts of the apartment until it was time to go to sleep. During the day, if I wasn't at the restaurant or driving our daughters to skating practice and preschool, I was with the North Koreans. Lilia resented the fact that I never had time. I didn't blame her, but I reminded her it was what she signed up for. "When you met me I had a Vietnamese guy living under my bed," I said. "This is my life."

I didn't tell Han, but he sensed it. "Don't let what you do with us affect your family," he said. "It's not worth it. One day I'll be gone, and they're all you'll have left."

"What about you?" I said. "At least I get to go home every night. You're the one making the sacrifice."

I put the Styrofoam containers with the ribs on a folding chair in front of us and opened them. The conference room filled with the smell of barbecue.

Explosions rattled the little speakers of the TV set, and the picture blinked from dark to light. "Holy shit!" Han said. Mushrooms of smoke appeared between the flashes. The orange glow of fireballs illuminated the dark Tigris River. Han bit off a piece of rib meat without taking his eyes off the screen.

"That could be Pyongyang," I said. We sat in silence for a few moments and watched the fireworks in Baghdad. The set cracked and boomed in the empty conference room. Even the TV announcers had nothing to say. I was rattled, too. I don't care how accurate our missiles are, there must have been innocent people around those explosions. I know Han was thinking the same thing. We were probably watching children being killed right in front of us. There was nothing to clap at, no matter whose side you were on.

"Maybe Saddam should have gone to Mauritania," he said. There were rumors that France was still trying to work out an exile deal for the Iraqi leadership. "I don't understand why this couldn't be avoided."

"Would your leadership have done any different?" I asked. Han looked at me. We were getting into dangerous territory, especially sitting in a room that was probably bugged by multiple intelligence services, including Han's.

"Why do you have to instill your political beliefs on other people's societies?" he asked. "You confirm the negative things people say about U.S. government. You are expansionist. You are hostile and aggressive with your army."

"Depends on who you ask, and when you ask them. You guys were on our side in World War II. Back then, everybody criticized us for not going in earlier. Same with Bosnia. And Rwanda. Have we made mistakes along the way? Yes. But our responsibility is much greater than yours. You have a hard time feeding your army. You couldn't deploy anywhere. People come to us because we can deploy. We can help."

The TV set boomed with another round of explosions. I tried to pull a rib free without taking my eyes off the set, but half its meat fell on the floor. I picked it up from the carpet and wiped it with a napkin.

"You've been led blindly before," he said. "Invading Vietnam and Cambodia. Laos." He paused and I could tell he was about to launch into a speech about how the Americans started the Korean War but then decided not to. He waved a pork rib at the TV. "This is a mistake."

14

≈≈≈≈≈≈
≈≈≈≈≈≈

Sports Drinks Are
Bad for You

HAN WAITED FOR ME outside his new apartment building on Roosevelt Island, a short strip of land in the middle of the East River that used to house psychiatric patients and now is home to people who work in midtown Manhattan but can't afford to live there. To save money on rent, the North Koreans had moved to the most communistic-looking building of the gray, concrete neighborhood. "You found the part of New York that looks most like Pyongyang!" I used to tell him, and he'd give me that rueful look of his.

He stood in front of the parking structure wearing a plastic raincoat, khaki pants, and cheap running shoes, looking annoyed. Trout season was in full swing, we hadn't been out fishing for weeks, and now we were going to be saddled with a bunch of guys just arrived from North Korea on a stonewalling mission to the U.N. Security Council. I picked him up alone, on the pretense of showing him some new spinning rods. He heaved himself onto the passenger seat of my Hummer and folded his arms across his chest.

"Put your seat belt on," I said.

"You're late," he said, not moving.

"Five minutes," I said. "There was traffic on the bridge."

"Late is late." Han waited until I'd driven a few blocks before he pulled his seat belt on, as if to make a point.

We'd been bickering like a couple whose honeymoon period is over. By April 2003, relations between our countries had deteriorated to the point that when Han went with Ri Gun to meet U.S. negotiators in Beijing, the tone was so unconstructive that everyone went home early and Pyongyang said it would push ahead with its nuclear weapons program. There were other snubs, too. In May, the SARS outbreak forced soccer officials to relocate the women's World Cup tournament, scheduled for September in China, to several U.S. cities. The North Koreans threatened to withdraw in protest. Han felt the heat in his new position as ambassador—you could read the stress on his face. His soft, boyish features had creased and hardened like meat left in the oven too long.

"You didn't forget the snippers, like last time?" he asked.

"That wasn't last time," I said. "Last time you didn't catch because you couldn't cast for shit."

"I caught more than you!"

"But I had the biggest trout. Remember that four-pounder?"

Han sighed. "Some of these guys aren't serious about fishing," he said.

"They're serious about negotiating, right?" I said, trolling for a piece of information I could feed to Marakovits. "Any sign of a breakthrough?"

Han gazed out his window as we crossed the George Washington Bridge. Below us, in the muddy waters of the Hudson, striped bass chased herring upriver to the Adirondacks. "Don't count on it," he said. That was a headline Marakovits could pass up to his superiors: PEACE UNLIKELY THIS WEEK. No surprises there.

After coffee at Cubby's, we set off due west toward Blairsville and Cedar Lake with the rest of the North Koreans following in their white minivan. We picked up the usual FBI tail as we pulled out of the parking lot—a late-model sedan carrying a couple of squares who looked like Lego men in bad sunglasses. They made no attempt to hide themselves a few car lengths behind us, and as we passed the twenty-mile travel boundary, Han kept checking the

side-view mirror. Despite coming from the world's most repressive police state—or maybe because of it—Han never got used to being followed by the Feds.

I got the North Koreans set up along the edge of the lake, and Han and I trekked through the underbrush to our secret fishing hole—a spot secluded by a stand of cedar trees where the stream feeds into the lake from the northwest. We swung our spinning rods and dropped lures into the little eddies a few feet from the fast water, where the trout like to ambush the bait coming downstream.

"What about the women's soccer team?" I asked, as I slowly reeled my lure back towards the bank.

"Not coming." Han lobbed his lure into an eddy at the far end of the stream, and I followed suit.

"Just because it's in America? You can't do that."

"Why not?"

"Because it's a slap in the face, that's why." I realized this sounded ridiculous after my president had called Han's boss a "pygmy." I set my reel and tugged the line softly. "What about the players?" I asked. "They've been practicing all their lives for this."

Han looked at me as though he couldn't understand how a tough guy who loved to hunt and fish could be sentimental about something as useless as women's soccer. "Look at it this way," I continued. "If you're going to make a statement, do it over something that matters."

"You mean like the nuclear program?" he asked, reeling in for another cast.

"Look at the Pakistanis. Did you see them withdrawing from any women's soccer tournaments?"

"The Pakistanis—" I knew what Han was about to say: the Pakistanis couldn't even put a long-range missile together until the North Koreans gave them the technology. But just then his rod bent double and his reel screamed as a fish struck his bait and took off downstream.

Han angled his pole toward the water, let the trout run, and set his feet.

"Too much trouble," he said, keeping an eye on his line. "Security would be a problem." Then he jerked his pole back and—*bang!*—he had the hook good and set.

"Remember Atlanta? We pulled that off without any incidents."

"No incidents?" Han gasped. His face reddened as he reeled in hard. His mind must have flashed to the terrorist attack, Joe Jordan's lockdown over the blimp, the arrest of their coach who touched the schoolboy, and the fact that I'd delegated the job of chaperone to my father, a retired roofer and unpredictable alcoholic.

I pointed out that after the 1996 Games, Kim Jong Il had put the judo champion, Kye Sun-Hui, on a postage stamp and honored her with banquets. "They were happy in Pyongyang," I said.

Two days later, Han called to say that Pyongyang was open to sending its women's soccer team to the United States.

"*If* we can make all the arrangements," he said.

"I'll do it myself!" I shouted. I could barely contain my excitement. I was back in action. "No delegating this time."

Our first job was to find some funding, because the rulers in Pyongyang announced they weren't paying the team's expenses inside the United States. They could afford the world's fourth-largest army, but they couldn't feed their citizens or even send a soccer team halfway around the world.

I called Senator Greenleaf, who arranged visits to two large South Korean churches in his district. We convinced the church leaders that they should support their poorer sisters from the North, and soon we got a van donated and some cash for their lodging.

Han suggested that we look for commercial sponsorships for the team. Now he was thinking like a real capitalist. I offered to do the outreach. In the early summer of 2003, I made dozens of calls from the phone behind the soda fountain at Cubby's. I called Pepsi. No dice. I called Ford and got the runaround. I called oil companies, sportswear brands, beer makers, and restaurant chains. No takers. It seemed that no American company wanted to get behind the North Koreans, which was understandable considering we were technically at war with them, but also pretty closed-minded, if you ask me.

A few days before the team arrived, I got through to a public relations rep at Gatorade and explained that I was helping to promote North Korean women's soccer; would they be interested in a co-promotion? The rep said they'd call us if they were interested. I figured it was a lost cause. But twenty minutes later, as I was going over receipts for meat orders in the back office, a marketing executive named Maria called back. She offered to send some cases of Gatorade to our training camp. I explained that I was thinking about something bigger in scope—cash, to be specific. It cost $1,000 each time we wanted to cook them a meal, I told Maria, not to mention all the security costs, as she could probably imagine.

"These women come from the most secretive place in the world," I said. "Everybody in America will be wondering what makes them tick. And I'm offering you exclusive access."

"Would they drink Gatorade on camera?" she asked.

"They'll drink whatever we tell them to drink!" I said, feeling like now, finally, we were getting somewhere. "They don't have Gatorade in North Korea."

"I see. Yes, I guess we knew that."

I'm not an advertising guy, but what I thought was a brilliant idea popped into my head, and so I laid it out for her: "What if you did a TV ad where you got one of the North Korean players drinking Gatorade for the first time? You show her getting a bottle out of an ice chest and looking at it like she's never seen such a drink. She's curious about what it would do. Of course, it's going to give her extra power because it's Gatorade, right? So she takes a swig and the next thing you know she turns around and kicks the ball like she's never kicked before. And because these are North Koreans you can have a little fun with it and cut away to a nuclear explosion. Which would be your metaphor. Imagine that," I said.

"They'd be willing to do that?" Maria asked.

"Why not?" I said, warming to the idea. "You're paying, so you call the shots. Think about it. Gatorade. Nuclear explosion. People would remember that."

"I don't know." Maria said she would get back to me. I nearly called Han to tell him we had a fish on the line but thought better of it, which was the right decision because the next day when I followed up with Maria, one of her assistants told me that Gatorade wasn't interested after all.

I mentioned the Gatorade idea to Jere Longman, a sportswriter for *The New York Times,* who got in touch with me because he wanted to profile the North Korean team. I told Longman I'd help him with his story. It seemed like a great way to build a bridge between the newspaper's readers and the enemy. I never dreamed that talking to him would jeopardize my relationship with Han. I didn't even think twice about it.

I prebooked the team into the Warrington Lodge in Horsham, Pennsylvania, a drive-up motel where rooms cost twenty-eight dollars a night. It was a few minutes' drive down a secluded country lane from their practice fields at the Ukrainian Sports Center, which Senator Greenleaf was able to secure, and half an hour from their first two games, which would be played in Philadelphia. This kept the travel circle tight, which Han liked because it limited the chances something could go wrong. His nightmare was a defection by one of the players. When the South Koreans invited the team to a church dinner, Han declined it outright. He was also concerned that the media might gain access to the team, and an unauthorized comment would be turned into a piece of propaganda in an American newspaper.

I put O'D in charge of security. What he lacked in social skills, he made up for in efficiency. As soon as I booked the Warrington Lodge he did a complete security analysis, including a vulnerability assessment, emergency management, and worst-case-scenario planning. His first concern was preventing access to the team by overachieving reporters or others who might be interested in them. He did background checks on all motel employees and ran the license plates of every car that entered the parking lot. He checked each room for monitoring devices, and he had two or three freelance security guys patrol the motel periphery day and night. O'D even promised to personally sanitize all the North Koreans' garbage by fire, so that it could not be dug through. He said it was standard operating procedure.

I decided to stay at the Warrington to keep an eye on the team, and I hired a temporary manager to help Lilia run Cubby's. Han and I brought passenger vans to Philadelphia International Airport to meet the team, which arrived just before midnight on a Thursday in late August. The players wore matching red sweat suits and their hair cut in a bowl shape or parted down the middle, making them look more like boys than women. Three coaches and four security goons in cheap suits and sunglasses escorted them. Han and I took the entire group to The Red Lion diner for omelets and home fries and a welcome speech, which Han made in Korean to let them know that I was in charge of their daily routine while in the United States. I'd fastened my pin with Kim Il Sung's face on it to the left breast of my sweatshirt, to show the women that my heart was with them.

They ate quietly. Han pointed out the captain, a large-jawed woman named Ri Song Hui, the goalkeeper. At twenty-eight, Ri was the oldest player on the team and, as the leader, she had learned some basic English before the trip. If I could get her to crack a smile, it would set a good tone for the rest of the players.

"Don't eat that whole thing," I said, pointing at her three-egg omelet. "You don't want to get big like me." I patted my belly and puffed my cheeks out.

Ri looked at me coldly. These young women were all business. When we got to the motel, despite it being nearly three in the morning, the first thing Ri did was go room to room, confiscating the TV cables so none of the players could watch American programming, which was forbidden.

I tried to imagine the women's first impressions. Back home, their only source of information about Americans was their government's propaganda, which depicted us as two-legged wolves. I wondered if I confirmed their stereotypes. I'm big, loud, aggressive, and hairy.

I wanted to be a good host, because it might be the only chance in these women's lives to see my country. My first idea was to take them to the Liberty Bell, to see our nation's great symbol of freedom, but O'D nixed the idea because of security concerns. "Twenty North Koreans in a crowded tourist attraction in a major metropolitan area," he said. "Are you kidding me?"

A few days after the team arrived, Senator Greenleaf handed me a check for fourteen thousand dollars and said his South Korean constituents wanted to send their poorer cousins shopping for things they couldn't get at home. What better way to show them the abundance of America? Divided evenly, fourteen large came to about eight hundred dollars per player—more than the average yearly salary in North Korea. The only question was where to spend it.

The nearest Walmart was only a few miles from the Warrington Lodge, and I proposed that we take the whole team there on a weeknight. Han rolled his eyes but didn't object. The security goons from Pyongyang said they'd do the shopping and distribute gifts to the players themselves, but I smelled corruption in the works as sure as you can smell a burger on a grill. We compromised that two guards, five players, O'D, and I would go to Walmart the following night.

In the morning, we watched their strict routine: calisthenics and jumping rope in the motel parking lot at five-thirty A.M., followed by breakfast. We drove to the Ukrainian Sports Center for practice, lunch, and more practice. When we returned to the motel in the late afternoon, the team gathered in Ri's room to watch videotaped speeches by their leaders, so they could be reminded of who they were. At the end of the video session the players and coaches pumped their fists in the air and shouted patriotic slogans. Then we set off for Walmart.

O'D drove the van, and I positioned myself next to Ri so I could point out the highlights of suburban Pennsylvania. "Those are single-family homes," I said. "We have crowded buildings and poor people, just like you. Mostly in the cities."

Ri stared straight ahead as though she hadn't heard me. How much did she understand? And what was going through her mind as she stared out the window? We drove through the small commercial district of Horsham. A billboard urged us to "Support Our Troops." A church marquee read, "Jesus Is the End of the Trail of Tears." How different were these things from the slogans Ri and her teammates chanted? We passed a restaurant with a giant chicken on the roof. A long stretch of lawn followed, interspersed with oak trees and patches of sand.

"That's a golf course," I said. "It's a game for people who want to chase a ball around, but who don't want to run. They walk or drive a little cart after the ball, which is only about *this* big. You use a stick, called a club, and you hit it as far as you can. Then you look for a hole with a flag in it, and when you see the flag—"

"I know golf," Ri said, scowling.

Of course! I'd forgotten that the DPRK opened a golf "resort" a few years earlier. According to the official reports heard in every North Korean home, Kim Jong Il was such a natural that, the first time he picked up a club, he shot a miraculous 34 on the par-72 course, including eleven holes in one.

"Maybe the Dear Leader will play here someday," I joked. Ri glanced nervously back at the two security guys and then shot me a look as though I'd clearly gone insane.

We pulled into the Walmart Supercenter as darkness fell over Horsham. The parking lot was lit as bright as a sports stadium. As we stepped out of the van, Ri gathered the other four players for a stern pep talk. I guessed she was reminding them not to lose their cool in this capitalistic wonderland and to behave as proper representatives.

I told the North Korean security guys to stay in the parking lot with O'D, because I wanted the players to have an intimidation-free experience. The two goons pretended they didn't understand me and moved toward the entrance. I knew I'd have Han's backing if I needed it, so I stood between them and the storefront. Before I remembered that they were cold-blooded killers, I almost felt sorry for them. Authority figures without authority in America, they weren't used to taking orders from a barbecue chef. When the more senior of the two tried to walk past me, I grabbed his arm. Sometimes you have to raise your voice. What else am I gonna do? I'm from Jersey.

"I'm afraid I'm going to have to pull rank on you, buddy," I said. I pointed to the Kim Il Sung badge pinned above my heart and then to the one he wore. His looked like it was made from cheaper metal, and mine was slightly bigger.

"Do you know who gave this to me?" I asked. "One of your top guys, that's who." He seemed to get the gist of what I was saying this time. I let go of the security man's arm. He and his henchman walked off a few paces and turned their backs on the store as though they wouldn't set foot inside even if you begged them.

The five soccer players and I strolled past a greeter in a blue apron and a one-hour photo counter into the magical shopping world filled with bright colors and the smell of new merchandise. I tried to imagine it from their perspective. The aisles stretched back as far as the eye could see, and it struck me that we put the same kind of grandiose efforts into our shopping centers that the North Koreans put into their monuments. The scale was so big you couldn't really gauge the size of the store, which suggested limitlessness, and maybe even immortality. Other shoppers floated dreamily by, as invisible loudspeakers pumped out a jazz version of the Rolling Stones' "Satisfaction."

Ri seemed unsure of herself as she led the younger women through the racks of clothing. She and the other four players fingered the straps of dresses and looked at purses and belts, but didn't put anything into their carts.

"Anything you want," I urged them. "Everything, if you want it! We have fourteen thousand dollars. I want to see shopping carts full of stuff. Don't let your coaches dress you like boys anymore. Let's get moving. Shop, shop!"

I clapped my hands. Ri gave me that look again, like she was still trying to figure out whether I was for real. The other players waited for her signal. She turned around, surveying the store's unfamiliar territory. Then she took a short, deep breath. With a slight nod to her teammates, she turned her cart back the way she had come, through the racks of blouses and sweaters, dresses and jeans, and began harvesting items off of shelves and hangers as though an old instinct had kicked in.

The shopping carts filled up with eighteen pairs of high-heeled shoes, sheer stockings, flip-flops, sneakers, and cotton socks. Jin Pyol Hui, the right forward, made a beeline for the cosmetics department and filled a cart with bottles of lotion, jars of cream, and pencils to color the eyes, lips, and brows. Saleswomen looked on in amazement as Jin grabbed dozens of hair sprays, neck sprays, and underarm sprays; nail files, nail polish, and nail polish removers. Over in the lingerie department, Ri's quick goalie arms scooped up silk nighties, push-up bras, and pajamas with frilly waistbands. Two of her teammates raided the stationery and gift sections for pens, clipboards, calendars with pictures of kittens and koala bears. No aisle was left unexplored. A couple hours later, we arrived at the registers with four carts each. The

security guys watched through the window with their noses pressed against the glass.

As the cashier rang up our items, Ri disappeared back into the clothing section. She returned—looking just as determined as she had while yanking out TV cables at the motel—wheeling an entire rack of yellow raincoats, in sizes ranging from extra large to a child's small.

"For family," she said.

I bought them all disposable cameras, so they could take home proof of the richness of America and the kindness with which they'd been treated, even though there was a good chance they'd be confiscated when the team landed in Pyongyang.

"Why do you waste money like that?" Han said a few days later. "All that stuff is made in China anyway."

Han was afraid the security guys were so pissed off there was no money left to skim that they'd complain about me. You never knew how far a bad word spoken in Pyongyang could spread.

"What if they were your daughters?" I asked Han. "Would you want somebody skimming off their gifts?" Han waved his hand in the air like he was brushing away my words, which meant that, on some level, he agreed with me.

I called Marakovits at his office in New Jersey and gave him a list of the North Koreans' purchases. I wanted to keep everything aboveboard. "You want to send a spy into the DPRK?" I asked proudly. "There's your shopping list for things that'll seduce a lady in Pyongyang."

"You're going to cross the line sometime, you know," he said. "A couple of months ago, you told me you were just going to find out whether or not their team was coming. Now you're their chaperone. Are you trying to hand them a propaganda coup?"

"I'm trying to help prevent a war," I said. "Isn't that an American thing to do?"

Marakovits didn't answer for a few moments. "Have you got anything else for me?"

"I have a new idea," I said. I'd been mulling something over ever since I started looking for sponsors for the women's soccer team. "What if we bought their nuclear program? We want to make it so they can't build a bomb. Why don't we give them cash?"

"Sounds like bribery. Where do you come up with this stuff?"

"It's their idea," I lied. "Isn't it basically what we're doing with KEDO?"

"I guess so."

"Why don't you come down to Horsham, Tom? I'll introduce you around."

"We've got Pennsylvania guys on it. It's their territory."

"I know," I said. "I see them parked behind the bushes. But *you're* the North Korea expert."

"I'm just a field agent in New Jersey," Marakovits groaned.

"You are what you think you are," I said. "Don't forget it."

On September 14, a couple of weeks into my stay in Pennsylvania, my father called while I was eating breakfast. He asked if I'd seen the newspaper, which I hadn't.

"You'd better take a look at the *Times*," he said.

I found a copy and called him back as I flipped through the pages. In an editorial, the newspaper criticized the Bush Administration for overextending U.S. troops in Iraq.

"They say they need twelve combat brigades for 'standby duty' in Korea," I said.

"Sports section," Dad said.

On the front page of Sports, a story by Longman began with a pep talk I'd given to the North Korean players, about how they should think of themselves as the Rocky Balboa of the women's World Cup—the underdog with a lot of heart. I thought it would inspire them, until I realized they'd never seen any of the *Rocky* movies.

"Keep reading," Dad said. He had that tone of voice he'd used when I was a kid and he caught me at something, but I didn't know what it was yet.

I scanned down the story until I got to the part about the team's economic problems and my role in organizing their stay in Pennsylvania. Longman described my Gatorade proposal in detail. He called it an "outlandish" idea because of "a nuclear explosion that would occur as a player struck the ball."

"Are you out of your mind?" Dad shouted.

"What?" I said. "Doesn't anybody have a sense of humor?"

"About a nuclear bomb? When we're ready to go to war with them? You're the one always telling me those cocksuckers are like the Mafia. You run your big mouth and they're gonna see you as a problem."

Dad was right. A paranoid hierarchy like the mob, or the DPRK government, didn't want anybody making unauthorized statements on its behalf. Pyongyang used its own state-run media to communicate to the West. To them, nothing was printed by accident. Han's bosses were obsessed with what American newspapers said about them. They required that Han send clippings of any story in the major U.S. dailies that mentioned North Korea, so they could analyze each word. But for some reason it never occurred to me that the regime might see my Gatorade proposal.

Later that morning, I walked down to the practice field where O'D kept an eye on the women warming up.

"I think I screwed the pooch, Mike," I said. "We've got to do something."

It was still early. Han was coming to the field around eleven. It usually took him two hours to drive down from New York. If I knew his routine, he wouldn't read the newspaper before he left. He'd come straight from home, so he or one of his assistants would probably pick up the *Times* once they arrived in Horsham.

"Get your guys," I said to O'D. "I want them all. Every *Times* within a five-mile radius."

"That's a lot of newspapers," O'D said, shaking his head. "You're talking a hundred, at least, at a dollar a pop—"

"I don't care how many!" I shouted. "Do you have any idea what kind of fire we're playing with?"

O'D covered the streets north and west of the Sports Center; I took the streets south and east. We hit every mini market, liquor store, sidewalk dispenser, and coffee shop within five miles and then some. When our cars were full, we drove back to the motel and stacked the papers until they were waist-high across the floor of my room. We drew the curtains tight and locked the door until they could be safely disposed of, late at night, after everyone else was asleep.

It was raining lightly by the time Han met me at the practice field wearing a cap and an overcoat. We scrunched our hands in our pockets and watched in silence as the women booted the ball around the soggy grass. Han wasn't the type of guy who held things back, and after a few minutes I guessed he hadn't seen the story.

"How are things in New York?" I ventured.

"Your government is putting more missiles near our border, so John Bolton is happy," Han said, referring to Bush's ambassador to the U.N. "That guy is a hard-ass."

"You called him a scumbag."

"I called him scum."

"'Scumbag' is better," I said. "It has more of a ring to it."

"Okay. He's a scumbag."

We watched one of the forwards slip the ball past Comrade Ri and into the goal. I wanted to keep him occupied for as long as I could, so I decided to test out my new idea, which wasn't fully formed yet.

"I talked to one of my contacts in the administration," I said, which was technically true since I was referring to Marakovits and the FBI. "There might be some interest in a new approach to the nuclear thing."

"What do you mean, 'a new approach'?"

"Cash," I said. "A one-time sale of your whole nuclear program. Everything verifiable. No strings. What do you think of that?"

"Who is suggesting this?" Han asked.

"It's just an idea that's floating around."

"You mean it's floating around between you and me?"

It started raining more heavily, so I opened my umbrella and held it over our heads, tilting it to cover him and leaving my right shoulder exposed. "There have been discussions with the administration, like I said."

Han took his cap off and shook the water off it. He seemed ready to listen now. "Why didn't you tell me earlier?"

"You haven't been around! You should spend more time here in Pennsylvania, where I can keep an eye on you. It's time for some new ideas. People in Washington recognize that."

"What do you mean, 'no strings'?" This was one of the biggest stumbling blocks for the North Koreans. Every time Washington offered anything, there was a catch they couldn't accept.

"I mean some kind of very flexible aid package," I said. "The details aren't important at this stage." I hadn't gotten any further with the idea yet, but I tried to think of it in common economic terms. If you were selling a restaurant, you'd expect about two and a half times your net earnings. KEDO had a budget of seven billion dollars to build the light-water nuclear reactors, which could be thought of as North Korea's net earnings for giving up their bomb program.

"Somewhere in the neighborhood of fifteen billion dollars," I said. "Maybe seventeen billion. But that's not the place to start. What's important is to give it some momentum."

"It would have to be at least twenty billion," Han said.

Out on the grass, Ri and the other women sprinted in formation from the penalty box to the midfield line.

"How about something more realistic," he said. "Are we going to get sponsorships for the team? It's not too late."

I cleared my throat. "It's hard to get companies excited about supporting you," I said. "No offense."

"What about Gatorade? You said they were interested."

I shifted my umbrella to my other hand and turned around to face the parking lot. "That didn't, uh, pan out," I said.

"What's wrong?" Han was looking at me now.

"What do you mean?"

"You seem nervous."

"I do?" I needed to be more careful. Han and I knew each other's moods too well. "It's nothing," I said. "It must be Lilia. It's not helping my marriage that I'm down here all month."

"How is she?" he asked.

"She's good. You know. She's running the restaurant while I'm here."

"You should stay with her."

"You said that before."

The rain beat down harder, and Han and I stepped under the eaves of an equipment shed. "Not being able to hold your marriage together makes you unreliable," he said. "Other people are talking about you. I have to defend you."

"Other people who?" I asked. "In New York or Pyongyang? What do they say?"

"You shouldn't talk about your marriage in public. Too much talking. If you keep your mouth closed, everybody sees you are more reliable."

"If I kept my mouth closed, you wouldn't trust me for other reasons," I said. "You'd think I was a spy."

I kept Han at the Sports Center until the middle of the afternoon, and after he left I spent the rest of the day dreading the moment he'd read the paper and my cell phone would ring. I nearly called him several times to distract him, but thought better of it. When he hadn't called by seven-thirty, I figured I was in the clear. Han would be where he was every night at this time: sitting in his grim little apartment on Roosevelt Island, drinking brandy and watching crime shows. When he wasn't out with me, he had nothing else to do with his evenings, and soon he would be asleep. Tomorrow morning there would be a new paper on the newsstands.

After the close call, I couldn't afford any more screw-ups. I had to keep it cool. I spent the next afternoon preparing the first big barbecue meal for the team and learning to make kimchee. The North Koreans had brought their own cook, a frail little lady named Jung, from somewhere near the Chinese border, who had cracked fingernails and her own way of doing things. We took her to the Asian supermarket in Horsham and bought her squid and whitefish. She hung a clothesline across her room and tied the up fish to dry, as they did in her country. Unfortunately, it rained every day and the fish stayed damp. They hung in midair, getting riper, until you could smell them from across the parking lot and the motel's maids refused to come near the room. The manager threatened to kick us out until I told him it was a cultural custom that had to be respected and slipped him a hundred-dollar bill.

Jung and I sat in her smelly room beneath the half-dried fish and shucked pieces of cabbage into a little vat at our feet. We couldn't speak each other's language, but we got along using hand signals and pantomime. She looked like a slightly healthier version of the peasants I saw outside the train on the trip from Kumho to Pyongyang—one of the half-starved citizens the regime didn't want the outside world to know about. How did she become the cook for the women's soccer team? And with all the food around, why was she so frail? I examined her dry, cracked fingernails, the sickly coloring of her skin, and the brittleness of her hair.

"You need more vitamins," I said, miming the act of popping pills. She scooped her fingers toward her mouth like she was eating invisible rice from a bowl.

"No," I said. "Not just rice." I flexed my arm and compared my bicep to hers. She giggled and grabbed my muscle with her bony fingers. I felt bad for the poor lady. I went to my room and got a mega-vitamin sports drink for her. With thousands of times the recommended daily allowance of the B and C vitamins and other healthy ingredients, it would give her a boost.

"Make you strong!" I shouted, and flexed my arm again. Then I handed it to her, and pantomimed guzzling it down until she understood and drank the whole thing like a champion.

My barbecue was a big success. I laid out some prime cuts of meat I slow-cooked the Cubby's way—for twelve to sixteen hours, so they were popping with juice; then, just before serving, I put each piece on the open flame for a minute or two to give that charcoal taste.

When I stepped into the dining room carrying platters heaped with filets mignon, whole racks of ribs, and seven-pound chickens in a tangy ketchup sauce, a few of the players and even one of the coaches gasped. More platters followed, with fresh fruit, baked potatoes, corn on the cob, and steaming loaves of garlic bread. I thought their eyes would jump out of their heads. With this one meal, I felt I had poked a small hole in their regime's anti-American propaganda. What could be wrong with a country where you could eat such things?

After dinner I went looking for my buddy O'D, who had assigned himself responsibility for washing the team's clothes. He considered the laundry an important matter of security, for some reason. He rotated the laundromats he used, to avoid detection. I knew this because I had seen the hand-written to-do list he carried folded up in his breast pocket, which read: "laundry—change locales—avoid observation by interested parties."

I spotted him through the plate-glass window of the Carousel Launderette on Swindon Road, not far from the motel. He was the only customer working the machines. He stood in the bright light, transferring the women's practice uniforms, underwear, and socks from cloth bags, as though in a trance. He held each handful of laundry to his face for a few moments before putting it into the machine. He closed his eyes and inhaled deeply. When I walked through the door he had his nose buried deep in a wad of sweaty, grass-stained shorts.

"What are you doing, Mike?"

He blinked his eyes open and lowered the clothing. "I was just checking."

"Checking what?"

He shrugged. "There's nothing like the smell of a hard-working woman," he mumbled.

"Put those in the machine!" I shouted. "What if someone sees you?"

O'D was about to toss the clothes into the machine when a car skidded into the parking lot and screeched to a stop in front of the laundromat. It was one of O'D's hired hands, who was supposed to be back at the motel, making rounds of the perimeter. He leapt out of his car and ran to the door.

"All the North Koreans are in the cook's room," he said "There's some kind of ruckus."

"Chanting?" I asked.

"I didn't hear anything like that. I think somebody's hurt."

O'D waved a fistful of ladies' underwear at his hire. "You didn't assess the situation?" he sniffed.

"Put those clothes down," I said. "Let's go!"

Back at the Warrington, I sped down the hall toward a crowd spilling out of the cook's room. O'D followed with his hand on his holster. At first, we couldn't get into the room because the twenty-two members of the national team, coaches, and security goons blocked the way, with everybody yelling in Korean. The place was a wreck. Towels were strewn everywhere, the tail-fins of fish flaked onto people's hair and shoulders like snowfall, and the place smelled like a cannery. Someone had pulled the shades off the lamps. O'D and I pushed our way into the middle of the pack until we could see the cook. She lay on the floor with her arms wrapped around her shoulders, shaking with mini-convulsions.

"Epileptic?" I asked. The team's medic had a wet towel pressed against her forehead, which was having no effect. What if she ended up in critical condition, or worse? I looked outside into the darkness where an FBI car would be parked with a couple of agents inside. I dialed 911 on my cell phone, knowing that an ambulance would make a scene that would be hard to cover up.

The paramedics arrived minutes later and knelt by Jung's shivering body. "Has she eaten anything funny?" one of the paramedics asked. "Poison? Pills?"

She never ate with the team, so it couldn't be my barbecue. "Doc," I said, "can I tell you something confidential—under doctor-patient privilege?"

"You're not my patient," he said. "And I'm an EMT."

"Okay, this woman, who *is* your patient, told me to say that she swallowed some of my vitamin drink."

When I showed him the empty box of mega-formula, he agreed that the vitamins must have been a complete shock to her system. O'D unhelpfully chimed in that it was like those victims of Nazi concentration camps who died after American GIs gave them a can of tuna.

"That's enough!" I stood and got in O'D's face. "You want me to tell everybody what was going on at the laundromat?" O'D didn't back down. He kept one hand on his holster.

"What was going on at the laundromat?" the other paramedic asked.

O'D and I looked at him. "Nothing," I said.

The first paramedic calmed me down. Jung would be fine, he said. She just needed lots of drinking water and some rest. I needed some rest, too.

The next morning the sky was dark and heavy. Hurricane Isabella worked its way up the Atlantic coast, threatening to hit land and ruin the opening of the World Cup. Everybody was talking about the calm before the storm. We were down at the Ukrainian Sports Center watching practice when a white minivan pulled into the parking lot. Han stepped out from the passenger door. An unannounced visit.

He sped across the grass toward me like he was on wheels, with a newspaper tucked under his arm. The look on his face made my blood go cold. He came straight up to me and then stood there, suddenly unsure of what to say.

"You lied to me," he finally said. "I asked you how the Gatorade was going."

"I told you the truth."

"You omitted."

I avoided Han's gaze by looking at the group of North Korean trainers and security goons gathered around the benches. The guy whose arm I grabbed in the Walmart parking lot was smirking at me. "I did not authorize you to speak to the newspaper," he said. "Even I need permission. Do you understand?"

"I was trying to get a sponsor."

"It is a bad time in the negotiations, and you add wood to the fire." Han seemed to speak with another person's voice. A voice from the regime.

"That's old news. Nobody has to see it." I reached for the newspaper, thinking I'd throw it in the trash. But Han held it away from me.

"I have to send this to Pyongyang," he said. "I can't keep protecting you."

"You don't have to send it," I pleaded. "How was I supposed to know what they were going to print in the newspaper?"

Han turned abruptly on his heel in a military way I'd never seen him use before. I tried to read him as he walked away. I knew his beef with me was the result of outside pressure. He was probably afraid someone else would show the story to his bosses. He had plenty of enemies who envied his position and

disapproved of his relationship with me. There was no way to predict the reaction from Pyongyang. It was one thing to get in a fight at the War Museum or feed a habanero pepper to a military bigwig. Making statements to the *Times* on their behalf was another. All I knew was that one word from Pyongyang would be enough to end my friendship with Han.

The cold reality was that Han and I were bound by political forces. The odds were stacked against a friendship like ours. People in Pyongyang and Washington didn't want warm relations. They didn't want a sense of humor. They had no interest in the good intentions of a diplomat and a cook.

I couldn't stand the thought of losing my buddy. Now that he was back, I almost didn't know who I was without him. Knowing Han gave me a sense of purpose, and it was hard to imagine that coming to an end again. There was no telling how long it would take Pyongyang to respond to Han's cable. Until then, I was hanging from a thread.

Han stayed away from the practice field, and I knew better than to call. Even the always supportive Senator Greenleaf kept his distance. He stopped by the field a few times, but when I approached him he said his wife had read the *Times* piece and didn't want him to have anything to do with me, which was no surprise because she had never liked me to begin with.

A somber mood hung over our training camp. The players became focused and disciplined, with their opener against Nigeria just days away. Jung recovered her health but mostly stayed in her room and avoided me. Ri and the rest of the players did, too, and I wondered if word had spread among the team that I had tried to poison their cook. At least they ate my meals, which I prepared with less joy than before.

To make matters worse, tensions flared even higher between Washington and Pyongyang when the Department of Defense announced it was deploying a battery of Patriot missiles near the Demilitarized Zone, aimed at North Korea. If the women's soccer tournament was producing any goodwill between the people of the two nations, the news hadn't reached our leaders.

I realized I'd been selfishly worried about my own position but hadn't thought of what could happen to Han. If the generals were unhappy with my comments to the *Times*, Han would be held responsible. He could be recalled to Pyongyang and sent away to a labor camp. In the Mafia, people were killed for less. He had already paid a price for his association with me, during his long reeducation period. The thought of something else happening to him because of me was more than I could bear.

On the morning of September 20, we drove the team down to Lincoln Financial Field, home of the Philadelphia Eagles, for the match against Nigeria. More than twenty-four thousand fans packed the lower decks. O'D and I took our seats directly behind the North Koreans' bench. Across the field, Nigerian fans wearing green and white sang and chanted. But they were outnumbered by the sea of red on our side of the stadium. It looked like every South Korean in Greenleaf's district and beyond had shown up to cheer on their supposed enemies from the North. Some waved signs in English and Korean calling for a peace treaty, and one guy stood up and beat a ceremonial *yong-go* drum that went *bung-bung-bung* throughout the afternoon.

A group of visiting North Korean diplomats sat a few rows up from us. Dressed in their usual Chinese-made suits and cheap loafers, they seemed out of place in the colorful crowd. I recognized a few from fishing trips and groups that came to Cubby's. I waved, and two guys waved back. Han wasn't among them. Instead of going up to chat, I ordered a bag of popcorn and shared it with O'D.

The sun broke through the clouds as the referee blew the whistle for kick-off. Ri stood ten paces out from goal, directing her teammates from behind the lines. The crowd around us cheered every time a North Korean woman touched the ball, and O'D and I unabashedly cheered with them. Seventeen minutes into the match, forward Jin Pyol Hui slipped a defender's tackle and right-footed the ball past the Nigerian goalkeeper. The crowd went berserk. All around us, an unforgettable scene unfolded: South Koreans turned toward North Korea's diplomats and shouted *"Pilseung Korea!"* ("Win, Korea!")

Putting decades of fear and mistrust aside, a few charged over and exchanged awkward handshakes and pats on the back with the men from Pyongyang. The North Koreans couldn't help themselves: they smiled and returned the handshakes. For the moment, at least, all thoughts of nuclear weapons, failed talks, and Patriot missiles disappeared.

Han showed up at halftime. I saw him coming down my row toward me, with a troubled look on his face. O'D had the decency to excuse himself. Han's face looked heavy and sad as he stood in front of me, staring at the ground. What if this was the last time I saw him?

"Hey, buddy," I finally muttered, not knowing what else to say. "Did you hear from Pyongyang?"

Han looked up at me and his eyes were squinty and full of tears and I could see that he was starting to lose control. His whole body shook. He could no longer keep a straight face.

"What?" I asked. "What's wrong?"

"They loved it!" he roared.

"What do you mean, they loved it?" I asked, incredulous. "What did they say?"

Han doubled over giggling and then slapped me on the shoulder. "They said it shows strength!"

I put my arm around him and howled with relief. People in the seats turned around and stared at us, but we just kept laughing like a couple of marooned sailors just rescued from a desert island.

I hardly remember the second half of the match. The North Korean women put the ball in the net two more times to take a 3-0 lead. At the final whistle the players ran over and bowed to me and Han. We decided a little celebration was in order—dinner at a Chinese restaurant in Horsham—before training resumed for the next games against Sweden and the United States.

I drove Han back to the Warrington in my Hummer. As we left the Philadelphia metropolitan area, we started to pick up our favorite radio station, 106.7 Lite-FM out of New York, which plays all soft rock, all the time. Both of us were still giddy. When the DJ cued up one of our favorite songs by

Rod Stewart, we leaned back and waited for the familiar words. We glanced at each other as we sang along to make sure we were getting the lyrics right:

I know I keep you amused, but I feel I'm being used
Oh Maggie, I couldn't have tried any more.

It felt good just to drive along the highway with Han, watching the Pennsylvania landscape slip by. We hadn't fished together in a while, and this was the next best thing: a little bit of peace, and some carefree time away from the troubles and politics of the international arena.

15

~~~~~~~~~~~~~~~~

Liberate the *Pueblo*!

THE WOMEN'S SOCCER TEAM lost their second and third games and returned to North Korea with just their memories and as much Walmart merchandise as they could carry. I drove Han and Senator Greenleaf to say good-bye to them, but on the way the senator realized he'd forgotten his wallet at home, so we detoured to his neighborhood to pick it up. As we pulled onto his tree-lined street, the senator motioned for me to park by the curb.

"Two minutes," he said. Han and I sat in the front seats as he strode up his driveway, took the stairs to his porch in one hop, and disappeared through his door.

"Nice place," Han said. He rubbed his forefingers against his thumb, making the international sign for "moolah."

"More than he could afford on seventy grand a year," I said.

"He makes deals on the side? People pay him for favors?" Han knew how Senator Greenleaf could pick up the phone and get humanitarian aid sent to the DPRK or a sports complex loaned to a soccer team.

"The senator's not crooked," I said. "I'm sure he's got family money. He comes from a very respectable background."

"But he *could* do deals," Han said.

"He's not the type. It's illegal," I said. "Even if he wanted to, the IRS watches what he earns and spends. They audit me, too. The taxman knows everything."

Han laughed. "I thought you were a free country! Look at us. We don't get audited."

"That's because you don't have private enterprise. Everything you've got comes from your government, so you don't have extra money to keep track of. We get audited *because* we're free."

Over the years I'd explained to Han how my business worked. I wanted him to get a feeling for capitalism, because good ideas are like the flu—they spread from one person to another and they're hard to stop, and somebody needed to take the idea of free enterprise back to Pyongyang. I broke it down for Han: my yearly receipts versus the wages I paid my cooks and dishwashers and wait staff and, when I was in the black, the quarterly taxes I sent to the state of New Jersey, Bergen County, the city of Hackensack, and the Board of Education. I explained how Washington got its taxes from my payroll, so the more people I employed the more I was contributing to society. I could reward good employees by raising their wages and get rid of others who weren't cutting it, which was the deal with two of my cooks, Bulldog and Efrain.

"You're can't fire Bulldog," Han gasped. He looked at me in horror, as though he suddenly understood that all the schoolbook propaganda he read as a boy was true. Americans *were* wolf-men who stabbed children with bayonets and screwed over the working class any chance they got. In Han's experience, Bulldog and Efrain were fixtures in the kitchen at Cubby's. He always said hi to Efrain in Spanish, and Bulldog liked to high-five him. They'd been with me for years.

I didn't have a choice, I said. Not only was I in debt and unable to pay my taxes on time but, less than a mile from Cubby's, the Riverside Square Mall was expanding, and within months I would have a Cheesecake Factory to contend with. I had to improve my business model. I was adding more sophisticated dishes, like grilled salmon and T-bone steaks, and I needed to get orders out quicker without sacrificing quality. My mediums had to come out medium and a medium rare had to be medium rare, even when we were getting slammed at peak times on Friday and Saturday nights. Bulldog and Efrain weren't able to keep up.

"Why are you competing with cheesecake?" he asked. "You cook barbecue."

I explained that Cheesecake Factory was a full-service restaurant, like TGI Friday's, which had been cutting into my business for years. "The neighborhood is changing," I said. "I have to go more upscale."

"It's not fair," Han said. "You hired them to work according to a standard. They show up every day and do the job you hired them for. It's not their fault that you change the standard."

"That's a typical commie thought," I said. "Here it works both ways. Bulldog and Efrain are free to leave Cubby's if they find better jobs, and I'm free to hire somebody else to keep my business going. If I don't adapt, Cubby's could go under, and then everybody who works for me loses."

"It's immoral."

"I listen to my customers. I notice what's happening in my neighborhood. You should do the same thing. Look at China. Look at Russia. They've changed. You guys need to adapt, too."

"We're not going to start firing our workers—"

"Just send them to prison camps?"

"That's propaganda," he said. We both knew that wasn't true. Han unrolled his window. We stared at the closed door of the senator's house.

"Two minutes," Han huffed. In the window of what looked like the kitchen, Greenleaf and his wife moved back and forth. "He would have invited me inside if you weren't here," Han said. "I would be having a cup of tea."

"Oh, really?" I said. "Which one of us is on the terrorist watch list? Not me, pal. His wife doesn't want any of you Axis of Evil guys near her silverware."

"You're the reason we parked on the street. The senator is afraid she will see the Hummer."

"He's afraid she'll see *you* and call Homeland Security," I said.

"She won't even talk to you! Remember the time you tried to hug her? She told you to get your hands off!" Han shook with laughter. "She said she had tennis shoulder! And you—"

"I said I'd heard of tennis *elbow*, but never tennis shoulder."

"You see? You are a brute!" Han pounded the dashboard. I thought he was going to pee himself.

"She knows we're out here; that's what's taking so long," I giggled. "The senator's hearing it now." I lifted my voice an octave: "'Why do you have to hang around the guy who flips burgers and the one who wants to bomb us—'"

"Here he comes. Be quiet." I looked up and saw Greenleaf loping down the driveway with his long legs. I couldn't stop laughing.

"I'm sure she told him, 'They're not coming over for bridge club, Stewart. Don't even think about it.' He probably won't get laid for a week just for riding around with us. He'll be—"

"Quiet!" Han hissed. The senator was still ten yards from the Hummer, but Han had already dropped his smile, as fast as everybody in Pyongyang does in the presence of authority. When the senator opened the door, Han looked like a schoolkid waiting for the teacher to call his name.

"How's Mrs. Greenleaf?" I asked, as the senator slid into the backseat. Han shot me a warning look, and I pointed the Hummer in the direction of the Warrington Lodge.

We said good-bye to the women's soccer team that night. It made me sad to think that I would probably never see any of them again.

"We've done some good things together," I told Han a few weeks after the team left. We'd been hanging out at the embassy on Second Avenue, and I offered to drive him to his apartment on Roosevelt Island because it was late in the evening. We crossed the Queensboro Bridge onto the depressing strip of land that always reminded me of a prison colony. As we pulled up in front of Han's apartment building, he reached into his coat pocket, pulled out a manila envelope, and handed it to me while nonchalantly looking out the window. The envelope had a thick bulge in it. If it was all twenties, it had to be about four large.

"Just hold it for me," Han said. "You can pay it back."

Just like when he loaned me money after the Olympics, he knew when my back was against the wall. I was deeply, genuinely moved. There's no more sincere expression of love and friendship between two men than an envelope full of cash. Maybe Han thought it would allow me to keep Bulldog and Efrain on staff, and he felt he was making a gesture of solidarity with the workers of the world. I didn't care. I was way behind on my meat bill, not to mention ice skating practice for Andrea, day care for Lori, and utilities.

I looked at Han in the dim lights of the dashboard. "Thanks, buddy," I said. Where I come from you don't ask somebody where they got their cash, and although four grand would never compare to the time and money I'd invested in the North Koreans over the years, I was flattered that when Han got a windfall he let me in on it. He could just as easily have kept it for himself.

"I want to do something for the senator, too," he said. It was a question: what did I think? I figured that, coming from the North Koreans, a manila envelope with cash in it could get the senator in some serious hot water.

"Nothing like you gave me," I said. I thought about it for a few minutes. The only favor Greenleaf would want was something that helped his political career. The senator had let slip to me that he was considering a campaign for governor of Pennsylvania. He'd run for U.S. Congress a few years earlier and lost, and he needed a shot in the arm. The Koreans in his district were already behind him, partly due to his compassion in sending humanitarian aid to North Korea. He needed something that would play to a wider audience.

A real favor to Greenleaf would be to help him grab a national headline, get him on the talk shows for something he'd done. A daring rescue. A bold act that would turn him into a hero.

Han could see I was mentally working out a plan. "Not POWs," he said. "Don't even bring it up. I told you—"

"I know," I said. "You told me."

The headlights of a car swept through the interior of the Hummer as somebody turned around in the street behind us. We watched a sedan drive past. Hard to tell if it was FBI.

"How about something everybody knows you have," I said. "The *Pueblo.* Give it back, unconditionally. And do it through Senator Greenleaf."

The DPRK had captured the USS *Pueblo* back in 1968. Pyongyang alleged it was on a spying mission. The Pentagon claimed it strayed innocently into North Korean waters. It had been docked ever since on the Taedong River, where teachers brought their students to see the "spy ship of the U.S. imperialist aggression forces."

"*Your* government never does something unconditionally," Han said.

"What's the *Pueblo* worth? A little sentimental value. How many tourists do you get a year? Ten?"

"More than that," Han said.

"Think of it as an investment. Give the ship back through Senator Greenleaf, and you're investing in American politics. You're buying influence. You know he's planning to run for governor? Then he'll be like your friend Bill Richardson, but from a much bigger state. And then he's a short step away from the presidency."

"He doesn't have a chance to be president," Han said, sounding unsure of himself.

"Of course he does!" I said. "Remember what George Bush did before he was president. He was governor of Texas. And before that? He ran a baseball team. Senator Greenleaf has years of experience on Bush. And he *looks* like a president. He used to be a basketball player. He's smart, conservative. He's an evangelical. Never done anything wrong in his life. He could be in charge of the free world five years from now. And if you bet on him early, he's your friend."

"He's already our friend."

"No, he's not. He gets things donated to you because it helps him politically. But if you do him a favor that gets him elected, then he owes you. This is how you influence people. You find out what they want, and you provide it to them. You can provide him a political future."

Han shook his head. "Don't you ever have simple ideas?"

Han didn't specifically say no to my *Pueblo* idea, so in late 2003, after I'd made amends with Lilia for spending so much time with the women's soccer team, I drove down to Pennsylvania to talk to the senator about it. On the way, I put together a strategy: I'd let him think there was a proposal on the table from Han, so he would take it seriously. If he liked the idea, I'd go back to Han with it. I'd appeal to the senator's ambition. I figured what he wanted was no different from what I wanted: to rise above his rank; to carve out a piece of history for himself. Personally, I didn't think the senator had the fire or the drive to become president of the United States. He'd gotten pretty comfortable where he was. But I didn't want to tell Han that.

Any idea gets a running start over a meal, so I picked him up and drove him to the Olive Garden near his office in Willow Grove, Pennsylvania. After we ordered bowls of pasta from the big laminated menus, I told him Han and his colleagues were very thankful for all his help during the soccer tournament. Then I said the North Koreans might be willing to give the *Pueblo* back.

"Where's this coming from? You?" The senator tried to gauge whether I was joking.

"It was Han's idea," I said. My advantage was that they rarely spoke, and neither of them knew what the other was saying to me. When you're the middleman, you've got some wiggle room with the truth. I wasn't exactly deceiving anybody. Sometimes you just have to tell people what they want to hear so that truth *becomes* what you said it was. "He's very excited about this," I said. "I put your name forward. I told him, 'You should do it through Senator Greenleaf.'"

The waiter brought the chicken parmigiana and the five-cheese ziti *al forno* for the senator and me.

"The *Pueblo* belongs to the U.S. Navy," he said. "If they really want to give it back, Han should work with the White House or the Pentagon. It doesn't make sense to do it with me."

"You're their only friend in a public office. They trust you." I dipped a piece of bread into the pool of melted cheese on my ziti. "You know how suspicious they are. They're afraid anybody they approach in Washington would try to embarrass them."

"They probably would." He laughed.

"Han and his guys know we're still mad at them for keeping it, but they don't have a lot of options," I said. "The North Koreans aren't going to give the *Pueblo* back to Bobby Egan."

The senator nodded.

I leaned forward so nobody at a nearby table could overhear. "They are also interested in supporting your political career. They know it would be very good for them if you got elected to a higher office, if you know what I mean. They think you're a good horse to bet on." He kept a straight face, but I could tell he was pleased. You can always play to a politician's ego, even a straight-laced, stand-up guy like Greenleaf. "We could get you an ambassadorship. How does Ambassador to North Korea sound?"

"I don't think my wife would like that."

"You'll be able to pick and choose! Whoever brings the *Pueblo* home to America is going to come back a hero," I said. "It'd be a hell of a kickoff for a campaign for governor. What do you think about that?"

Greenleaf twirled a few strands of spaghetti around his fork. "Why would they give it back now, after thirty-five years?"

"Negotiations aren't going anywhere. How else are they going to break the deadlock?"

The senator seemed to think about it as he chewed with precise clicks of his jaw. "The *Pueblo* has a lot of symbolic value for our military," he said.

"We'll make it look like a humanitarian trip," I said. "Nobody will ever know about it unless we succeed."

After the holidays, I ran the idea by McCreary, because I knew Han would respect his opinion. "They'll never give it back—not without strings attached," he said. "And even if they did, you wouldn't be able to sail it out of there. The hull's probably shot by now."

We'd need a barge. I called Wall Street Steve and asked him to look into a shipping company that could carry the *Pueblo*. I called Bill Henry and did the same. Then I talked to a deputy ambassador at the South Korean embassy in New York, who said his government was willing to help in any way to get the *Pueblo* into U.S. hands. The more I filled in details of the plan, the closer it got to becoming reality.

In early 2004, Pyongyang offered to "freeze" its nuclear program if Washington promised not to attack or block the DPRK's economic development. With President Bush already eyeing reelection that year, his administration played hardball, telling Pyongyang to completely dismantle its nuclear program first. With all the mistrust on both sides, the Agreed Framework and KEDO completely fell apart. Nobody was talking about incentives anymore.

Nobody was talking at all. It was like a husband and wife who can only communicate to a marriage counselor. Two more rounds of meetings in Beijing between the six negotiating parties—the United States, the DPRK, China, South Korea, Japan, and Russia—ended with everybody pointing fingers because nobody wanted to be the first to compromise. Pyongyang pulled out of a third round of talks that year, saying the United States was "not interested in making the dialogue fruitful."

In September 2004, the North Koreans claimed they had built nuclear weapons using plutonium from eight thousand spent fuel rods. If they were trying to create an uproar, it didn't work. With six weeks to go in the presidential campaign, and the war in Iraq going badly, Washington hardly noticed. In January of 2005, the North Koreans repeated that they had joined the elite nuclear club that included the United States, Britain, France, Russia, China, India, Pakistan, and Israel. They didn't offer any proof, though, and the Bush Administration basically ignored them.

"What do we have to do to get his attention?" Han asked me one evening at Cubby's.

They needed to put themselves in the spotlight. It wasn't by choice. They liked being an isolated, closed-off society, and if Russia had still been the USSR, they never would have gone out begging. But the DPRK regime was falling apart, a quarter of its people had no food, and many parts of the country went without electricity for most of the day. They could barely feed their military. I thought of the poor rations of rice the soldiers carried on the train to Kumho. Once you can't feed your soldiers, you can kiss your government good-bye.

The North Koreans needed access to the world's monetary system. They needed to be able to trade. Through negotiations they could get concessions. And their only way to get to the negotiating table was to be in the spotlight.

"You give the *Pueblo* back, everybody will notice," I said.

Han grunted. "They will notice we gave up something for nothing."

"Get me and the senator to Pyongyang," I said. "We'll show your generals that the senator is a man of peace. He's a man with a future. Tell your generals he's like your Manchurian Candidate, and this is your chance to manipulate the American political system."

Han laughed, but a few weeks later he came back with an official invitation to Pyongyang. He said he would personally accompany us, and use our trip as an excuse to see his family. It was great news. It meant he was confident in our mission. It looked like Pyongyang was so desperate to improve relations with the United States, they were finally ready to make the first move. And if they gave the *Pueblo* back, it would pave the way to negotiate for American POWs. I was sure of it. I told myself not to get too excited. One step at a time.

I called the senator at home right away. A woman answered.

"Mrs. Greenleaf?" I asked. "How you doin'? It's Bobby Egan. Everything okay with you? How's the family?"

"One minute," she said. She put down the phone and I heard footsteps away from the receiver. Several minutes passed before the senator's voice came on the line.

"She doesn't want me to go," he said in a lowered voice. "She's sure you're going to get me into trouble."

"Lilia isn't happy about it either," I confided. "But this is a higher calling, Senator. We have a chance to bring back our ship."

It took months to convince him, but I knew he was hooked. On one hand, it was a good cause. On the other, he couldn't turn down the chance at a hero's welcome and a ton of free publicity. I didn't care if he took all the credit and got all the glory. The *Pueblo* deal put me back in the game.

The senator finally said he was ready to go, and in late 2005 we booked our trip to Beijing. Han said he'd meet us there for the connecting flight to

Pyongyang. I packed light. In my wallet, I carried a list of the phone numbers of helpful people, such as Wall Street Steve, Bill Henry, and the South Koreans who could help get a barge into North Korean waters. The senator and I spent three days in Beijing getting our visas without any sign of Han. "You think something's wrong?" the senator asked the night before our flight to North Korea. I said I was sure we were in good hands. I didn't want him to know I was nervous, too. I went downstairs and dialed the DPRK mission in New York. One of Han's assistants told me he was out of the country, but didn't know if he was in Beijing or Pyongyang or somewhere else. Why was he avoiding us? The next day the senator and I boarded the flight alone.

We descended through thick, winter clouds toward the empty fields around the Pyongyang airport. It had been seven years since my last trip to North Korea, and I'd almost forgotten how tense it was to enter the totalitarian state. Nobody spoke as we descended the stairs from the plane. Security agents stood guard everywhere we looked. Two handlers in civilian clothes greeted us inside the terminal. They took the senator through customs first. I stood just inside the entrance as they loaded his bags onto the X-ray belt.

"Nice flight?" asked a familiar voice. I spun around. Han smiled. He wore a long coat and a hat. "Sorry I couldn't meet you earlier."

"Were you on our plane?" I asked. "Why didn't you—"

Han cut me off with a look. A few steps behind him, a guy I hadn't seen before stood next to a stack of brown boxes. "You said we're like family, right?" Han asked. "You trust me?"

"Of course," I said.

"Take these through customs." The guy behind Han stepped away from the boxes as though he'd been standing next to them by accident. Ahead of us, the agents were still busy with the senator. The boxes were wrapped in packing tape and string and marked with Chinese characters.

"What are they?" I asked. Instead of telling me what was so sensitive that a high-ranking official like Han couldn't bring it into the country, he and his helper walked ahead through customs without stopping.

I was the last to go through. I put the boxes one at a time on the conveyor belt of the X-ray machine. Two guards peered at the monitor. One of them mumbled something. As I put the other boxes on the belt, four or five more guards came out of a room and joined them. I felt like an idiot. What had Han gotten me into?

"Passport," one of them said. I handed it over and they disappeared into their room, leaving two guys to guard me. From the other side of customs Senator Greenleaf watched with a worried look on his face. Han was nowhere to be seen. The guards came out again with a translator.

"What's in the boxes?" he asked.

I shrugged. "You tell me. You're the ones with the X-ray." The translator spoke, and the guards looked at me like I had just peed all over the floor. The translator repeated the question. "I don't know," I said. "You tell me."

They talked back and forth and then disappeared into their office again. Eventually they brought out some papers for me to sign, which I did without looking at them. If the Koreans wanted to mess with me, they didn't need my signature. Then they let me go.

"What's happening?" the senator asked when I came through. I told him, and he gasped. "You carried a package for somebody else?"

I'd broken the number-one airport rule. In any other country, I'd probably be on my way to jail for not knowing what was in my own luggage.

Han met us at the exit. "Welcome back to the DPRK," he said, shaking the senator's hand, then mine. Han's helper loaded the boxes into a van. Computers, Han told me later. One for him and two for his superiors. He didn't want to leave a paper trail at customs that could be used by his rivals. Han cleared his throat. "I'm sorry I won't be able to join you," he said. "I have important business."

My heart sank. I'd counted on him negotiating with us for the return of the ship. "Are we all set?" I asked.

"You'll get special treatment, don't worry." Han bowed slightly and then followed his helper to the van. I felt better. This was a sign we would be sailing home to America with the USS *Pueblo* in tow. Han would pull strings behind the scenes, while the senator and I fronted the operation. It made sense. He could only stick his neck out so far.

Our handlers escorted us into another minivan and said we wouldn't be staying in a hotel on this visit. They drove us half an hour outside Pyongyang to a mountainside, where a small palace sat a little way up the slope, over-looking a huge reservoir. Our handlers said it was built by Kim Il Sung as a personal retreat, but that now it was used for guests of the military. The senator and I would be the only guests.

We checked in with a uniformed receptionist in the middle of the after-noon and put our bags in our rooms. The bedrooms were luxurious, with high ceilings, tiled floors, and the type of overstuffed sofas and chairs that must have been big with the communist ruling elites in the seventies. They were heated, unlike the rest of the palace, where we had to wear jackets. The gen-erals obviously wanted the senator and me to be comfortable, which I took as a gesture of respect and another sign that our mission was on track to suc-ceed.

Our handlers said we had nothing on our agenda for the rest of the day, so we went exploring. On the ground floor, a big entryway led to a dining room with a few tables and chairs and other rooms with portraits of the Great Leader. We found a bowling alley with wooden floors so cracked it couldn't have been used for many years. A corridor led to an Olympic-sized swimming pool with a high ceiling overhead and not a drop of water in it.

We went outside and walked around the palace. Cut into the steepest part of the slope, a series of heavy steel doors led directly into the mountain. "Bomb shelters," one of the handlers later confirmed.

We walked along a road nearly a mile before we reached a locked gate. A high, barbed-wire fence ran down a bare hill and disappeared into a wooded slope on the next ridge. We turned and saw two handlers about a hundred yards behind us. As we walked back toward the palace, they let us pass with-out acknowledging us. The far bank of the reservoir loomed above the frozen surface of the water. A few fishermen had dropped lines into holes that looked dangerously close to the edge where the white ice darkened and turned to wa-ter. There wasn't another building in sight.

The next morning we got up early, ready for some high-level negotiating. But when our handlers came for us they announced it would be a day of sight-seeing.

"I thought we were supposed to meet some generals," Greenleaf muttered to me.

"Humor them," I said, not wanting the senator to lose heart. "They don't get a lot of visitors. They're afraid that if we negotiate first, we won't stick around to see their attractions."

"We should get *one* meeting today," he said.

I secretly agreed with him. The North Koreans had strange ways of doing things, but they should have at least acknowledged the purpose of our trip. Maybe Han was trying to surprise us.

"They're probably saving us for their big guns," I told the senator.

We toured the same "orphanage" we'd visited eight years earlier and the same depressing hospital that had received medicine donated by the senator's constituents. Senator Greenleaf brought a small video camera with a flip-out screen and shot the children performing a song. He seemed happy. He said a public TV station in Pennsylvania might broadcast his footage. I filmed him shaking hands with the orphanage director and some of the children and striking poses in a governor-like way.

When we returned to the palace in the early afternoon, I plopped myself onto an olive green reclining chair in the foyer, and the senator stretched out on a sofa. "Now what?" he asked after a few minutes.

"Let's go jogging," I said.

We put sweatsuits on and then jogged down the stairs and out of the palace to get a head start on our handlers. Both of us were in pretty good shape, and we started off at a fast pace. After about five minutes, we couldn't see the palace anymore, and there was no sign of anyone behind us. About two-thirds of the way to the gate we came across a double-track path that went up the side of the mountain. "Up here," I said, and ran up it before the senator could protest.

I could hear him behind me, so I stepped up the pace. The cold mountain air stung my chest, and I felt great. We were free from our handlers, even if it was for only a few minutes. The senator sprinted up the hill to catch up with me.

"Look at us, Senator," I said. "The freest men in the DPRK."

"We should go back," he panted. "I don't want to get in trouble."

"We won't," I said. "These are my people."

"No, they're not."

Just then I smelled smoke from a wood-burning fire. We had nearly reached the top of a hill, where the trees thinned and the road leveled off. Up ahead a concrete guard shack stood between us and a narrow valley in which we could see at least fifteen wooden houses. Two guards in olive green uniforms stepped out of the shack and stared as though we were ghosts. We slowed to a walk. I tried to imagine it through their eyes. The senator was probably the tallest person they'd ever seen, silver-haired and regal-looking, wearing a white sweatshirt with the name of his son's college on it. I wore a black sweatshirt with the Cubby's logo and the cartoon pig wearing a chef's hat and holding a big platter of steaming ribs.

"Hey, guys!" I shouted, waving to them as we moved slowly forward. "Everything all right?"

One of the guards yelled something in Korean. They gripped their AK-47s but kept them pointed at the ground.

I bowed deeply. "Friends of Kim Jong Il!" I shouted. I pointed at the senator and myself. "Good friends. Senator from America!"

"Bobby," the senator said. "Let's just go back."

"Very important friend of your leader." I kept bowing and moving forward. Then I pointed at the road to the village and made the walking sign with my fingers. I pumped my arms back and forth. "We get some exercise!" One of the guards ducked into the shack and spoke into an antiquated-looking radio. I took a few steps toward the village.

"Let's go back, Bobby," the senator repeated. But when I turned my head I saw he was following me, so I kept going. The guards didn't stop us, and I walked right past them with the senator behind me. A minute later we entered the village alone. About twenty wood huts stood on either side of the road. Some had fires burning on the outside; in others smoke poured out from a hole in the thatched roof. Inside, the floors were bare dirt. There were no electrical poles or telephone lines or any other sign of the twenty-first century. The villagers wore patched jackets and sweaters and shawls. They were thin, and most of them looked like they could use a bath. Some women carried cooking pots or stacks of kindling and wood. It was late afternoon, and they were probably starting to boil their rice for dinner.

We kept to the middle of the road. If the villagers were as closely watched as everyone else in the DPRK, making contact with them could get them in trouble with the authorities. As we passed the first houses, women and children crowded the doorways to look at us.

"Hi, ladies." I smiled, waved, and bowed. The senator waved, too. A few of the ladies covered their mouths with dirty hands and giggled.

"They probably have no idea where we're from," the senator whispered.

Three men stood around a fire about thirty yards from the road. One of them looked familiar, and I thought I recognized a guy who'd been mopping the floor at the palace the day before. It was winter so there wasn't any work in the fields, and I figured the other village men were either in the military, working jobs in a bigger town, or fishing in the reservoir.

"When you look at these people, what do you see, Senator?" I asked.

We walked a few more paces while he thought about it. "I see poverty. I feel sorry for them."

"What about that guy over there by the fire? I'll bet he snuggles up to his wife at night. He plays with his kids. He doesn't have a TV and a microwave, but he might be happier than you and me."

"He doesn't have freedom."

"Does that mean his life is worse?"

"Are you joking? He's got a guard overlooking his village." The senator lowered his voice further. "His government is corrupt. I feel sorry for everybody in this country."

"I'll bet you there's as much corruption in Philadelphia as in Pyongyang. How many supreme court justices have gone to jail in Pennsylvania? Twelve? And don't get me started about the New Jersey state troopers. You're part of the government, so you don't look at it that way. But where I come from we feel the heavy hand, too. In America Rodney King gets the shit kicked out of him, and the cops hire fancy lawyers and go free. My people see roadblocks,

DWIs, drug tests. We get charged with racketeering while your friends get million-dollar bonuses for skimming billions off the top of the economy. You think we don't resent that? You put cops on the street for one reason: to keep your people safe from my people."

"It's not the same thing," he said under his breath. "This is a dictatorship."

"You're right. We get to vote in elections. But you know what our choices are? Between two guys who were in the same fraternity at college. They look like the same guy to most of us. Maybe their system is more honest. That poor guy over there *knows* he has only one choice."

"Don't point at him, please."

"When you leave the Senate, who's going to take your place? Not somebody like me."

"You could run for office. That's the beauty of America."

"And your rich friends are going to donate to my campaign? Remember, I have a drug history, and I don't go jogging with the name of a fancy college on my sweatshirt. No offense, Senator. But you have about as much in common with everyday Americans as Kim Jong Il does with these people."

"Keep your voice down." The senator glanced around at the villagers gawking at us.

"What are you worried about? These people can't understand us."

"They understand the name of their leader."

My heart still pounded from our run, but that wasn't what had gotten me all riled up. It was the senator's perspective. He was more involved with the Koreans than just about anybody in America. He didn't hate them or call them evil, but he pitied them. He considered them to be lesser people. It was like how our leaders in Washington say they won't negotiate with Pyongyang after they test fire a missile, because that would reward their behavior. I think: reward them? What are they, a pet? I reward my dog when he does something good. We shouldn't think the North Koreans don't understand that kind of language. It's no wonder we can't move forward with them. They know we're talking about them like you talk about dogs, in terms of rewarding and punishing them. It's disrespectful, and the North Koreans are like the Mafia in that the worst thing you can do is show disrespect.

About twenty yards ahead of us, a couple of kids wrestled by the side of the road. Five girls squatted in a semicircle and scratched the dirt with a twig, making pictures or words. Two older boys took turns throwing sticks to see whose went farthest. It was the same stuff you see kids doing in America, but without any toys. As we approached, they stopped playing and stared at us. One of the boys had a goiter under his left ear. The senator sighed heavily, full of pity. We turned to go back.

The poor villagers of North Korea shocked Senator Greenleaf, but he might have been just as surprised if he turned over a few rocks in our own country. People like him don't spend a lot of time in the housing projects of Philadelphia and Newark. If they did, they might not look down their noses at the North Koreans as much.

I waved at the guards as we jogged out of the village and past the concrete shack. Senator Greenleaf ran straight by without looking at them. I wondered if he was consciously telling himself not to wave at the enemy. I couldn't help wondering what benefit we—as the world's only superpower—get from having enemies. There must be some upside, because we keep making them. You could take the cynical view and say that we have to have enemies to create a market for all the weapons we produce. But there has to be something deeper than that. We've got lots of other ways to make money. We make enemies when we compete for resources, like oil or land. Or when the way we see the world clashes with somebody else's ideas, like communism or radical Islam. Sometimes we're enemies with countries we were friends with a few years earlier, like Iraq. We keep some enemies out of habit, like Cuba or North Korea, long after real conflict with them has ended. It's almost like we have an enemy quota to fill. We need "bad guys" so we can see ourselves as good.

At least this is how they seem to see it in Washington. People like Pritchard, or even Senator Greenleaf, tend to see the differences between people. It's like they're afraid of finding too many similarities. They're like the bully in school who makes fun of all the other kids. Everybody's afraid of the bully, but later in life you realize that the bullies were the ones who didn't feel good about themselves. Was that the issue with our leaders? They don't feel good about themselves?

The next morning our handlers greeted us with the news that we were finally going to the *Pueblo*. This was it! My doubts evaporated. The generals must have been too busy before. They probably wanted to give us a personal tour before we negotiated how to release the ship.

The senator and I dressed in suits and neckties to match the decorum of the occasion. On the short drive from the palace to the ship, I tapped my feet against the floor of the minivan with nervous excitement. The senator put his hand through the strap of his video camera and checked his battery levels.

The *Pueblo* sat all by itself, tied to a concrete bank of the Taedong River. Its hull was still the slate gray color of a U.S. Navy ship, and above the water it was in great shape, thanks to the fact that the Koreans had repainted it every year.

"What do those letters mean?" my handler asked. He pointed to "GER 2" painted in large white characters on the prow.

"Beats me," I said. "Don't you guys know?"

He admitted that after having the ship for nearly forty years, they still hadn't figured out what its markings meant. Red McDaniel later told me that GER stands for General Environmental Research, in other words a spy ship.

We were greeted by two military men in their thirties, with only a few medals on their chests. They couldn't have been above the rank of lieutenant. They spoke in Korean to our lead handler.

"Ten dollars each," the handler said.

"You gotta be joking." I laughed. This was obviously a mistake. I told the handler to explain who we were. When the lieutenants said they knew, I pointed out that the *Pueblo* was a commissioned vessel of the U.S. Navy, property of the American taxpayer. In other words: it's our boat, and we're not buying a ticket to set foot on it. The handler translated for the lieutenants, who shook their heads. They wouldn't budge. We went back and forth until we compromised: I pay ten dollars out of graciousness, the senator tours the *Pueblo* for free. I decided I'd complain to higher authorities later. Han would go ballistic when he heard they charged us. But where was he? Where were the generals?

Senator Greenleaf handed me his video camera as we were ushered up the gangplank. I steadied myself against the handrail as I filmed him stepping aboard, in case this turned out to be a historic moment. On deck, a frowning woman in a military cap, jacket, and skirt started a tour in broken English. She and the lieutenants led us to an overhead monitor where we watched a fifteen-minute video about how the brave North Korean sailors captured the *Pueblo* from the American aggressors. They took us to the communications room and showed us encryption machines and radio equipment that the DPRK's technicians had disassembled nearly forty years earlier looking for U.S. military secrets.

By now we could see we were the only people aboard. "We're screwed," I whispered to the senator. "No old men here. No brass."

"Just do the filming," he whispered back. "Let's be patient."

Our guide led us to the back of the ship. They asked the senator if he wanted to have his picture taken at the machine gun. He looked at me and nodded. I raised the camera and tracked him with the flip-out screen as he stepped onto the gunner's turret, gripped the handles with both hands, and pretended to fire the weapon with a fierce look on his face.

I approached the older of the two lieutenants. "When are we going to talk about giving it back?" I asked. He waited for the translation, smiled, and said something in Korean.

"You shouldn't be impolite," our lead handler said. I wondered if he had even translated my question.

Just then I heard the high-pitched babble of children's voices. I lowered the camera and looked back at the riverbank in despair. A group of school kids dressed in uniform followed two teachers onto the ship. Until that moment, I still hoped to have the *Pueblo* loaded onto a barge and headed for South Korean waters within a few days. Why else would Han have organized our visit? The appearance of the schoolchildren killed that hope. The message was clear. We weren't any different than the average visitor.

The senator let go of the machine gun handles. He stepped off the platform and straightened his back so he was standing at least a foot taller than any of the Koreans. "Our understanding is you are prepared to make this an unconditional gift," he said, as though reading from a script. Hadn't he clued in yet? The lieutenants smiled amusedly as the lead handler translated.

"We'll let bygones be bygones," the senator continued, gathering steam. "As you know, this ship is an important part of our military. An American soldier died on board—"

"This is our trophy," the younger lieutenant interrupted in broken English. He tapped a cigarette from a rumpled packet and lit it. "We never give it back to American aggressor."

Now I understood: they'd been planning to dick us around the whole time.

"You guys have some balls," I said to the lead handler. "We came ten thousand miles to negotiate, and you bring us here with some low-ranking, half-wit sailors and a bunch of schoolchildren?"

The handler and the lieutenants started talking in Korean. I turned to the younger officer.

"How about we *take* it back, motherfucker? Or how about this—we'll bomb it right here. Don't think we can't do that—"

"Bobby, please," the senator said.

"You guys are mental midgets!" I shouted. I couldn't believe I'd been defending these people just one day earlier, when the senator and I jogged into the village. I'd been far too kind. They let half their people starve and throw the other half into labor camps. They threaten the world with nuclear weapons. And when somebody finally extends a helping hand, when the senator and I come over here and try to help out of the goodness of our hearts, this is how they repay us. "Senator," I said, "how much humanitarian aid have you shipped here over the years?"

"It doesn't matter," he said.

"It *does* matter." I pointed to him and shouted at the lead handler. "This man found a practice field for your soccer team in Pennsylvania. He hosted your girls!"

"Women," the senator corrected. I felt bad for him. He is a soft-spoken man of diplomacy, and my outburst was making him cringe. But I felt my father's blood boiling up in me, and I was just getting going.

"You call this your trophy, and then you expect us to be your friends and send you free stuff? You can kiss my ass. I ought to have my head examined for dealing with you bloodsuckers." I looked back and forth between the handler and the officers. I got up in the face of the older one. "And another thing," I said. "Fuck you!"

The two lieutenants stood there with smirky expressions on their faces. If it hadn't been for the dignified presence of the senator I would have hauled off and knocked them both upside the head.

As angry as I was with the handlers, I was more angry at Han. Where were the meetings he promised? I couldn't believe he'd have organized the trip without even a chance of seeing the successful return of the *Pueblo*. Had he gotten pushed aside at the last minute? Or was it a sneaky little maneuver—getting me to come ten thousand miles to bring his computers through customs for him and then leaving me high and dry?

The senator and I left the *Pueblo* in frustration. He got over it, but I fumed all the way back to New York. After we got home, I refused to answer Han's calls, even though he left me at least a dozen messages: "Please call me. I know you're there." I blocked his number from my cell phone. I told my staff at Cubby's not to tell me if he called the restaurant, which seemed to please Lilia.

I didn't care whether Han apologized or what explanation he had. As far as I was concerned, we were through. I had extended my hand in friendship, and he betrayed me. Maybe this was all he thought of our time together. It was fine while it was convenient for him, but not when I wanted something. I thought of all the things I'd done for him: the goodie bags for his delegations, the humanitarian aid he took credit for, the Olympics in Atlanta, the fishing trips, the years of chauffeuring him and his buddies around New York, more meals at Cubby's than I could count, tens of thousands of dollars worth of dental work from John the Greek, pheasant hunting, VIP tickets to the Nets and the Giants, and more than a decade of talk: on the phone when he wanted to understand America better, teaching him new words, or cheering him up when he was lonely. What had he ever done for me? An envelope full of cash when I needed it. Maybe that was just to keep me sweet, so the favors would keep rolling his way. I should have listened to my dad. I should have listened to Pritchard. Han was just like any other commie. They were all alike—a one-way street.

16

~~~~~~~~~~~~~~~~~~~~

Helping Hands

A TEENAGE GIRL NUDGED OPEN the front door of Cubby's and crept inside like she was afraid something might attack her. She had a cute, oval-shaped face, with a spray of acne across her cheeks and forehead. She dressed like she was straight off the boat from Pyongyang, in a buttoned-up white shirt and a blue pleated skirt that hung down to the middle of her shins. I squinted at the small badge pinned over her heart. Sure enough, it had the picture of the Great Leader. Who wore a Kim Il Sung pin in Hackensack?

The girl frowned and looked around the nearly empty restaurant.

"Come on in," I said. "Want something to eat? What's your name?"

Before she could answer, the door behind her opened and Han hurried in. He stepped in front of the girl and looked at me uncertainly. "My daughter," he said, half turning to her.

He had a lot of nerve. I'd been back from Pyongyang for a few weeks, and I was trying to forget about him.

Han sent his girl to wait in one of the booths and came up to the counter. "Someone high up changed his mind. That's all I can say."

I pretended to look through a stack of receipts. He could wait a few moments. "Do you know how humiliating that was?" I finally asked. "For me *and* for the senator?"

"I'm sorry," he said. "I'm embarrassed for the way my government behaved."

"I'm not talking about your government. I'm talking about you."

Han grimaced and looked away. A couple of Italian guys from the lumberyard watched us from a corner booth.

"When did you know?" I asked. I'd already figured out the answer: he knew when I saw him at the airport in Pyongyang. He probably knew when he didn't show up in Beijing. "You could have told me we weren't getting the ship. But you asked me to carry your boxes instead."

"I'm sorry," he said. "You were already there."

"You used me."

Han sighed. "I told you it wasn't my decision about the *Pueblo*."

"You're a real piece of work," I said. He and I stared at each other for a few moments. The lumberyard guys went back to their burger plates. On the opposite side of the restaurant, Han's daughter sat quietly in a booth with her hands in her lap. He'd told me a few months earlier that he hoped she could come from Pyongyang for a school year in New York. The regime offered the perk to its longest-serving diplomats. They'd allow one family member to come but would keep the rest behind, as insurance that nobody would defect.

I knew what he was doing—he was appealing to me as a fellow father. It was a cheap ploy. I was still angry at him, but I didn't want to make him look bad in front of his daughter. And he knew that.

"Does she want to eat something?" I asked.

Han brightened. "Chicken sandwich?"

I went into the kitchen to make it myself. I put some fries in. When I brought her plate out, I saw that Han had slid into the booth next to her. He smiled at me, but his expression was full of sadness.

"Here you go, hon," I said. "We usually dab a little ketchup on our fries. You like ketchup?" I slid the bottle from the end of the table and turned it around in front of her so she could see the label. The poor thing was painfully shy. She looked at her father, and he nodded his approval. She twisted the cap off and hesitantly shook it upside down. A big red dollop splashed across her pile of fries and onto the side of her plate. She looked at it in horror and screwed the top back on the bottle. "That's what it's supposed to do," I assured her. They sat in silence. She munched on a fry and stared out the window. As a father of a teenage girl myself, I could tell Han didn't know what to say to her. He'd been living away from home for most of her life, and the distance between them wasn't easy to cross. This was the sacrifice he had made for his country, and I could see it was painful for him.

I realized I couldn't stay mad at Han forever. He'd apologized. That's all it should take between a couple of friends. A simple, "I'm sorry."

Besides, I'd been using him, too. Without Han, I wasn't in the game. I wasn't even near the playing field. I hopped up and put an order in for a rack of ribs with the new cook. He might as well eat something, as long as he'd come all the way to Cubby's.

"Where are you going to send her to school?" I asked when I returned to the table.

Han said he planned to enroll his daughter in a U.N. school for international students. It was the same school that Hamdoun's daughters attended—full of the children of ambassadors and diplomats from other countries.

I worried she wouldn't fit in. I couldn't help thinking of the rich kids at Essex Fells High who drove their Cadillacs and looked down their noses at me and the rest of us from Fairfield. Han's daughter would be at a huge disadvantage alongside the fashionable Italian girls, the cliquey Russian girls, the French-speaking African girls, and the others. I was afraid that even the girls from isolated countries like Yemen and Mongolia would shun her, because nobody could be from a place as uncool and uninformed about the world as North Korea. How would they treat a girl who'd never seen the Internet or a cell phone before?

"You can't let her go to school looking like that," I whispered to Han when she got up to use the ladies' room.

"What do you mean?" he said.

"Her clothes are from fifty years ago. The other kids will eat her alive."

He gave me a helpless look. He hadn't thought about schoolyard politics and the importance of fashion on the playground. He was in for a big surprise. The highly complicated relations between teenage girls can make nuclear talks at the U.N. look like a picnic.

I realized he might not have the cash to take her shopping. "You a little light?" I asked. He wrinkled his nose, meaning yes.

My heart went out to him, father to father. That night I didn't think twice about it. At closing time, I punched the "No Sale" button on the cash register, took out a couple hundred, and said to Lilia and Andrea, "We're taking Uncle Han and his daughter to the mall." I called Han and said we'd pick them up the next afternoon.

"Where are we going?" Han asked. "What are we going to get? Don't we need a list?"

"Don't worry about it," I said. "She's a seventeen-year-old girl. She'll know what to do. They're hard-wired for this stuff. Besides, she'll be with Lilia and Andrea."

Han paused for a second. "I don't want anything too revealing," he said, measuring his words. I knew what he was talking about.

"You mean like my daughter wears?" I asked. I'd seen him look disapprovingly at some of Andrea's shirts that rode high and showed her belly button hanging out.

"Yes," he said, carefully. "Sometimes she wears stuff where you can see a little cleavage. It makes me uncomfortable. You should have her cover up."

My heart beat faster, and my first reaction was I wanted to punch his lights out. You don't talk about another man's daughter that way. If anybody else had said it, he would have been laid out on the floor. But I knew Han had only the best intentions. I appreciated his honesty.

"I'm not happy about it either," I said. "But remember, we're not in Saudi Arabia. You guys are still living in the fifties. Things have changed. Styles have changed."

I drove the five of us to the Garden State Plaza in Paramus, which was the cheaper of the two local malls. While they did their business inside Macy's, I stayed in the Hummer. I put on the radio and reclined my seat for a nap.

The announcer was doing a news report from the Gulf Coast, where Hurricane Katrina had just hit land. It didn't sound good. They were evacuating hundreds of thousands of people from New Orleans. The Superdome had been turned into a refugee center. Entire neighborhoods were flooded. People were dying.

When Han, Lilia, and the girls came out again, they carried four shopping bags overflowing with dungarees, shirts, blouses, and shoes. Han had a proud smile like he'd just reeled in a big sea bass.

"She was so happy," he said when we got on the phone that night. "The only problem is her skin. Do you think we can do something about it?"

"She's beautiful with or without pimples," I assured him.

"It's affecting the way she feels about herself," he said. "Can't you call your cousin?"

"Joe?" I said. "He's a cardiologist."

Han couldn't afford a skin care specialist in New York, so the next day I called my cousin Joe in Fort Lee for a referral. I raided my cash register again, and we drove down to a doctor in the East Village who prescribed Accutane, a powerful drug that had an almost immediate effect on Han's daughter's acne.

That evening, Han left her at home and brought eight North Koreans to Cubby's for an early dinner of steaks and ribs. I sat them at the usual spot—a couple of Formica tables pushed together into a long bench along the eastern wall, underneath the photos of us on some of our early fishing trips. Pak was there. So was Ri Gun. Some of the guys had just come back from Beijing, where a new round of six-party talks on the DPRK's nuclear program had deadlocked over the same old issue—the United States and its allies told Pyongyang to give up its nuclear weapons program; the North Koreans demanded they follow through with building the KEDO project. Washington said the North Koreans gave up the right to peaceful nuclear technology when they pulled out of the Non-Proliferation Treaty two years earlier.

This is what happens when two sides don't trust each other. You can put agreements on paper, you can sign them with expensive pens and duplicate them and distribute the copies to the appropriate embassies and governmental agencies, but if each side doesn't trust the other to live up to it, the whole thing falls apart very quickly. So you need to have trust. But trust doesn't come from a naïve belief in the goodness of the other guy's heart.

Businessmen know this. When the vegetable man delivers tomatoes to me, he does it because he expects to be paid. And he believes I'm going to pay him because he observes people eating at Cubby's. He sees my cooks making salads in the kitchen. He knows I need tomatoes and that *I know* that if I don't pay him, he won't make my next delivery. He trusts I'm going to pay, because he knows my business. That's why I bring him into my kitchen in the first place.

Han and Pak and the others kept flying off to Beijing to meet their American counterparts because the two sides wanted to make a straightforward transaction—nuclear reactors for nuclear weapons—which had been worked out eleven years earlier as part of the Agreed Framework. But they hadn't built any confidence in each other.

I sat next to Han as the North Koreans feasted. After he finished half of his rack of ribs, he stood. He carefully wiped his fingers on his napkin, picked up his glass of Budweiser, and cleared his throat. His colleagues went quiet.

"On behalf of the DPRK Mission to the United Nations, I thank Mr. Bobby for this meal and hospitality," he said. We nodded at each other, and I smiled at everyone at the table. I thought he was going to make one of his typical speeches—starting off in formal-sounding English to compliment me on the meal and then switching to Korean for what I guessed was a flowery tribute to North Korea's bravery for standing up to the evil United States. But then Han continued in English: "We express our solidarity with victims of the Hurricane Katrina. The Korean people understand the effects of storms and flooding. We have sympathy for American people who lose their lives and their homes in this tragedy."

I'd never heard anything like it before: a group of North Koreans expressing sympathy for Americans. Han must have discussed it with his countrymen beforehand, because nobody from Pyongyang makes a public statement without vetting it. I tried to imagine them sitting in front of their TV on

Roosevelt Island and watching the images of poor Gulf Coast residents lining up for relief supplies and desperately searching for loved ones. Were they moved? Did they think about the flooding victims in their own country?

I stood. As the only American at the table, I thanked the North Koreans on behalf of the hurricane victims and their families and my country in general. After the meal, as the Koreans filed into the parking lot to smoke, Han and I hung back in the restaurant. "Why make this speech at Cubby's?" I asked. "Say the same thing to the State Department. It might help change the tone of things."

"Harder to get approval," he said. "You can pass on the message."

It was flattering when Han thought of me as a direct line to Washington, and there was no point in wasting an opportunity like this. Where Han saw the end of something, I saw the beginning. An idea was already forming in my head. Han had thrown me a bone, and I was going to run with it.

"You could do more than express your sympathy," I said.

Han laughed. "What do you expect us to do?"

"Why don't you help out? Send some humanitarian aid. Look at everything we send you. Here you have a chance to return the favor."

Han gave me that look of his, like he thought I might be kidding. "You don't need the amount of help we could give," he said.

"I'm talking about politics," I said as we walked out of the restaurant. "Symbolic gestures. What if you got a couple of your guys to volunteer? Go down to the disaster area and help hand out relief supplies."

Han patted me on the back. He wasn't taking it seriously. I knew him well enough to realize he needed time to process the idea. Just like when we first talked about the *Pueblo* or doing an interview with *The New York Times*. After all our years together, his first reaction was still no-go.

After they left, I called McCreary to see what he thought of my flood-aid plan.

"Never going to happen," he said. "They don't give. They take."

"They loaned me money," I reminded him.

"That wasn't them," he said. "That was Han, and he probably did that on the sly. This is different. It would involve their people traveling around the U.S. He'd have to run it by his superiors in Pyongyang. And they'll say, 'The Americans are trying to destroy us. Why should we help them?'"

I hung up the phone feeling discouraged. McCreary was probably our government's best informed and most open-minded intelligence analyst on Asian affairs. And if he was so cynical, how could I expect anybody else in Washington to deal with the North Koreans in a new way?

But I couldn't let go of the idea. It was too good. Too many pieces lined up perfectly. The United States and the DPRK were at an impasse. A hurricane strikes the United States and floods the Gulf Coast. The North Koreans are experts in floods. It was one of the things they were good at, besides prison camps and missiles.

That evening, I drove to Roosevelt Island, and met Han for a walk along the bank of the East River in the warm, late-summer air. "You could show off your skills," I pressed. "Who knows flooding better than you guys?"

"I don't think so." Han kicked a pebble over the walkway's edge and into the water.

I thought back to how easily we'd agreed to help *his* people. Convincing him to help us was a different ball game. "Tell your generals it's a way to show strength," I said. "The strong always help the weak, right? This is a time when the U.S. is weak and *you* can be the strong one." Han shook his head. "It's cost effective," I said. "A few guys. A few plane tickets. Think how much you spend building missiles to show how great you are—"

"We don't have to prove anything to your government."

I needed to try a different tack. "I'm sure Bill Henry is working on it. You could help him for once." It wasn't like I was asking them to go down and work with some multinational group like Habitat for Humanity or the Red Cross or Doctors Without Borders. America's Heart was a one-man operation, and I figured they could feel comfortable around Henry. This was before he got in trouble with the police for claiming he'd been shot by rival evangelical Christian operatives, and that a Bible in his breast pocket stopped a bullet from piercing his heart. But that's another story.

"You deal with the Syrians and the Iranians and the Pakistanis," I told Han. "What's wrong with doing a deal with some Christians from Florida? They've been helping you for years for free. You got an ambulance. You got X-ray machines. Think of all the boxes of Viagra!"

"Nobody will want to come," he said.

"Sweeten the deal for them," I said. "Tell them Bill Henry will let them pick out some medical supplies and other goodies, and we'll ship them to Pyongyang. Tell them they'll meet him in Florida. They can visit Disney World."

Han laughed. "This is really important to you?"

It *was* important to me. Why? I don't know. Why is anything important to anybody? Some guys fight each other over a football game. Women have been known to pull each other's hair out over a wedding dress. Every year at Christmas, somebody gets trampled at a shopping mall. Politicians ruin their careers for love. A junkie will kill for a fix.

"You can make up for screwing me over on the *Pueblo* deal," I said.

The next day he called and said, "Don't ever tell me I can't deliver." Pyongyang agreed to immediately send four officials from its flood relief department to help the victims of Hurricane Katrina. I could hardly believe it.

I called Bill Henry right away. He said that if Han could get travel permits from the State Department, the North Koreans would fly to Jacksonville, Florida, and drive with him in a convoy of relief supplies to Gulfport, Mississippi, where the hurricane had left thousands of people homeless.

Soon Americans would open their magazines and turn on their TV sets and see images of Han's guys unloading boxes of food to hungry children in the American South. I imagined the headline: *North Koreans Lend a Helping Hand to Katrina's Victims.* I was ready to call *The New York Times*, *Newsweek*, CNN, and *The Record* and tell them about this amazing story.

But then Han called. The State Department had granted permission for the four officials from Pyongyang to travel with Bill Henry to Mississippi. There was just one catch: the North Korean delegation was forbidden from talking to the news media or having their pictures taken.

"Are you sure this isn't coming from Pyongyang?" I asked Han.

"From your State Department," he said, laughing. "Who has the repressive government now?"

I was just getting my head around this when Bill Henry called and said he'd gotten the same instructions from a woman at the State Department. "I'm supposed to keep all media away from the North Koreans," he said. "I'm telling all my people to leave their cameras at home, because we have some dignitaries who can't have their pictures taken."

I'd finally gotten the DPRK—for maybe the first time in their history—to reach out a friendly hand to the United States, and the administration didn't want the public to know about it. It was the most un-American thing I'd ever heard. Even the most repressive dictatorship in the world hadn't taken cameras away from me, Senator Greenleaf, or Mark Sauter when they were guests of the DPRK. When we were in their country, the DPRK government had sent their own TV crews to follow us around. They *wanted* news about us. The difference was that over there the government controlled all the news.

I'm sure some of our politicians in Washington are secretly jealous of the leaders of North Korea, who don't worry about newspapers printing a story that will ruin their chance at reelection. Our leaders can talk all they want about how much they love democracy. But once they're in power, they don't love democracy. They fear it.

Maybe the Bush Administration thought a positive story for North Korea would be a bad thing for them. Or maybe Bush didn't want to be shown up. A few days earlier, he flew over the disaster zone in his helicopter without bothering to stop. He was taking a lot of heat for his administration's slow response to the hurricane. Maybe he didn't want the world to know the North Koreans were getting their hands dirty in Mississippi while he was eating lobster at his parents' house in Maine.

The Saturday of Labor Day weekend, the four DPRK representatives flew to Jacksonville to meet up with Bill Henry. I wanted to go, but I was short-staffed at Cubby's on a holiday weekend. Han didn't go either. He made an excuse about having to catch up on work and spending time with his daughter, but his work didn't stop him from coming into the restaurant for a plate of ribs.

"Aren't you concerned about security?" I asked. He gave me a knowing look, and I realized at least one of the delegation would be a security goon watching to make sure nobody defected.

Bill Henry called every time the DPRK delegation made a move. On Sunday morning they selected some medical supplies for shipment to Pyongyang. That afternoon they had a big lunch with Christian groups that had sent aid to Pyongyang over the years. Henry said the leadership guru John Maxwell, mega-church preacher Rick Warren, and lots of other Christian bigwigs sent their lieutenants to meet the godless men of the Hermit Kingdom.

"Anybody taking pictures?" I asked. I figured I could slip a few photos to the newspapers and get the word out on the sly.

"The only people with cameras are the North Koreans," Henry said. "I don't think they were taking pictures of themselves."

"Can't you sneak a couple?" I asked. "The whole point of this was to get them some positive exposure."

"The point is to let them take part in the Lord's work," he corrected. "And He works in mysterious ways, you know."

Henry had a lot of the Lord's work going on: a thirty-seven-vehicle convoy carrying water, soft drinks, sliced bread, canned food, toilet paper, diapers, candles, and enough volunteers to distribute it.

They set off before dawn on Monday. Bill Henry called in the early afternoon from a rest stop, while Han and I were eating lunch at Cubby's.

"The North Koreans keep asking how much I'm getting paid," Henry said. "It's for the children, I told them."

"How are they doing?" I asked.

"I think they understood, once I explained that I was abandoned at a bus depot when I was six months old. I lived in an orphanage, you know. I told the Koreans how I still remember the cold, hardwood floors. One light bulb per room. Shivering and going to bed with an empty belly, while the kids across the street sat in their bright homes, enjoying Christmas. I dreamed that one day I'd have a plate of warm turkey—"

"Bill, is everything okay, though? No problems?" I looked over at Han, who was sitting at the booth closest to the cash register so he could hear.

"Well, they keep fighting over the radio," he said.

"They what?"

"In the van. Mr. Jong Thae Yang—he's their leader—he wants to listen to NPR. They've got *Prairie Home Companion* on, and he says he likes the way Garrison Keillor sings. Can you imagine that? The younger ones want to listen to a classic rock station."

"I mean with security. Everything is okay?"

"Don't you worry about anything. Our group is full of friendly faces. I weeded out the crazies and the rush-to-judgment types. Do you realize we've prayed before every meal, and each time the North Koreans bowed their heads? I don't know if they are praying. They're atheists, you know, so it's hard to tell what's going on in their minds. But they respect our ways. Today at lunch they joined our prayer circle. They held hands with us as we thanked the Lord for our daily bread. We were sitting around the lunch table, so they were sort of trapped and didn't have much of a choice, but still—"

"What's he saying?" Han asked.

I covered the mouthpiece. "He says your guys don't understand what charity is."

After I hung up with Henry, I sat with Han, who was itching for an argument.

"That's the difference between your system and ours," he said. "We don't need charity. We take care of every worker. Charity is for people who don't have dignity of work."

"You don't have individual responsibility," I countered. "If your neighbor's house was on fire, everybody would sit around and wait for the Party to put it out." I refrained from pointing out that without our charity, more of his people would be starving.

I called Henry back at the end of the day, just before they started the eight-hour drive from Gulfport, Mississippi, back to Jacksonville.

"How'd it go?" I asked.

"It was something to behold," he intoned. "The people here are hurting, and the Koreans saw it all. I drove them straight through downtown Gulfport to the water line. They saw the fury of the Lord, Bob. I believe they were humbled by what He hath wrought. Fishing boats washed up on the shore and under the bridges; the houses with trees stuck into them; hotels with their plate glass blown out; buildings twisted off their foundations. The casino barges are beached like whales—"

"Did they interact with people?"

"Of course! We set up in the parking lot of a shopping mall, where the I-Ten meets Highway Forty-Nine. They saw desperate souls who were hungry and tired. The people wandered in a daze, like the flock of Moses. I think it looked familiar to the Koreans. They know flood victims. We unloaded the trucks in teams of four. It was something to witness, let me tell you: a couple of North Koreans and a couple of rednecks dragging crates of food off a truck together. Getting dirty, getting sweaty. One of the redneck kids was joshing his buddy about how he was so ugly he'd never find a wife. They went on and on. 'You're so ugly a toad wouldn't kiss you,' and things like that. You know, teenage boys. And then one of the Koreans said, 'I have a sister!' And everybody just about died laughing. By the end they were hugging and slapping each other on the back."

"Any news media around?" I asked.

"There was a local TV crew, but they didn't know who the Koreans were."

"Why didn't you tell them?"

"We're not supposed to. The State Department said—"

"Does everybody have to play by the rules? Jesus Christ!" I said. "Sorry. I didn't mean to take the name of the Lord—"

"Speaking of which," Henry said. "They keep asking me if we're going to Orlando. They say they were promised they could stop at Disney World. You know anything about that?"

"Take them," I said. "It might be their only chance to see it."

In Washington and Beijing, our leaders accused each other of being evil and untrustworthy, while in Gulfport, Mississippi, we made progress. Nobody would hear about it because it wasn't going to be on TV. But a few of Bill Henry's volunteers would know, and maybe some of the hurricane victims would find out who unloaded their relief supplies. They'd go home and tell their families about it. And the North Koreans would do the same thing. Maybe they'd get through customs with a pair of mouse ears from Disney World. You have to believe in the power of small actions.

The six-party talks resumed in Beijing on September 13. Han invited me to go with him, just for company, but I didn't want to be a tagalong. What was I going to do, carry his luggage? I wasn't a bellhop. I had a restaurant to run. Han left his daughter in the care of the mission staff and said, "If she needs anything, you're the first number she's going to dial."

He called from Beijing when he felt lonely, during a busy lunchtime when it was the middle of the night in China. He had a few drinks in him. "You don't feel like I'm leaving you out, do you?" he asked. "It's my job. Just like running Cubby's is your job."

"I understand," I said, stepping behind the soda fountain where I could have some privacy. "Don't worry."

Han knew I wanted to experience things beyond my level of access. I appreciated everything he shared with me. I knew, for example, that—when you got past all the tough talk—the leaders in Pyongyang were seriously afraid that Washington would launch a preemptive strike. McCreary told me an attack was unlikely, but that didn't stop the North Koreans from feeling constantly threatened. I don't know how many other Americans understood this. The North Koreans wanted some assurance that they wouldn't be attacked, but they weren't sure what kind of agreement they should trust. They got frustrated when the United States accused them of changing their position, because they felt like Washington kept shifting its position, too.

After five days in Beijing, the Bush Administration announced that Pyongyang had agreed at the last minute to give up its entire nuclear program in exchange for aid and security guarantees. Delegates from six nations left for home congratulating themselves. It took exactly one day for the agreement to fall apart after North Korea insisted it had the right to have light-water nuclear reactors, and the United States hedged on the aid package.

In November, everybody returned to Beijing for another round of six-party negotiations. This time, the talks fell apart. Washington accused North Korea of printing counterfeit U.S. dollars and slapped financial restrictions on banks doing business with them. In January, the North Koreans said they wouldn't return to the negotiating table until the restrictions were lifted.

I asked Han if his government was really interested in normalizing relations with the United States. It was the spring of 2006, and we'd brought our daughters and four counselors from the mission on a half-day fishing charter off the Atlantic Highlands in New Jersey. "Your top guys have a lot to lose if your economy suddenly opens up," I said as he and I unloaded our tackle from the Hummer. "Their absolute power could disappear."

"We'll do it like China, let things open slowly," he said, keeping an eye on the counselors and the girls walking down the dock. "Economic reform before political reform. If we loosen too early we'll end up like Russia, full of corruption."

We boarded a party boat called *The Fisherman*. The boats in this part of Jersey are pretty much divided by demographic. Some have a mostly Korean clientele, but we avoided them because Han and the other embassy guys didn't want strangers recognizing their North Korean accents. *The Fisherman* catered to working-class white guys like me.

We'd arrived late, which meant we had to look for places along the rail between about forty other people. I put us on the leeward side near the stern, which was already packed shoulder-to-shoulder with fishermen aiming for the best drift of water. Han and I found a spot away from the counselors. We baited our hooks with slices of bunker fish and cast them into the Atlantic.

"What happens when you reunite Korea?" I asked, pulling some line from my reel. "Who's in charge—Pyongyang or Seoul?"

Han grinned. "Separate authorities," he said. "At least for ten or fifteen years. Then the Korean people will have to rethink their political agenda. It won't be where one side collapses and the other takes over. Not like Germany."

We watched as the guys at the stern started dropping lines into the good water. "Seoul has all the money," I said. "Their system will be more attractive."

"It's corrupt and weak and a puppet of the U.S.," he said staring out at the waves sparkling in the sun. "We have dignity, and our way is better for Korean people. We won't give up our government."

It always amazed me when Han sounded like a mouthpiece for his government. In reality, there were two Hans—Han the individual, who was my buddy, and Han the North Korean official. The official Han always kicked in when we talked about his regime. "Even if you do," I said, "you don't have to worry. You can come work for me at Cubby's."

Han shook his head. "Not funny." He looked over at his daughter, who stood alone in the shadow of the cabin. "We have to move to the other side of the boat," he said.

"Why?" I said. "What's the problem?"

"You know what the problem is," he said. "Don't make me say it out loud."

I'd forgotten that one of the warnings about Accutane was not to expose yourself to direct sunlight. Han was worried about his daughter's skin. We switched sides, but as soon as we had our lines in the water the boat drifted over them and they got tangled up together.

Han glanced anxiously at his daughter, who stood next to the door of the cabin by herself. I thought about how hard it must be for him to have her in the United States, without his wife to help take care of her, and how isolated she must feel.

I reeled my line in, took Andrea by the elbow, and walked her out of Han's hearing range. "What are you doing?" I said. "Go talk to her."

"I don't want to," she said. "She's boring."

"You do what your daddy says," I said more firmly. "You go talk to that girl and make her feel like you're her friend."

Andrea went over to Han's daughter and the two stood together. Andrea saw that I was watching her, and she struck up a conversation. When Han saw the girls together, he started to relax a little. The morning sun twinkled across the waves.

"We should fish like this all the time," he said.

"Chile. That's where we want to go. Or Costa Rica. You guys have an embassy there?"

"We have one in Peru," Han said.

"I don't know Peru. But we need to go bill-fishing off Chile. Once we get our business going. First we establish Cubby's Pyongyang. Then Cubby's Kumho. We get into real estate. And when you and me are Donald Trumps, we'll take time off and go sport fishing in South America."

"After I buy my big house." Han laughed.

"It's one thing we gotta do together before we die, buddy: hook up a blue marlin and fight him all day. You think you could bring in an eight-hundred-pound marlin?"

"Faster than you." Han felt something on his line, pulled back, and reeled hard. I felt a tug, and we realized our lines had tangled under the boat again. Han sighed. The idea of him and me owning a business together and living in suburban houses in the same neighborhood seemed a long way off. Our kids would probably be all grown up before that day came around.

We got our gear untangled, and Han pulled his empty hook in. It was the worst day of fishing we'd ever had together. We had three inches of water in the bottom of our bucket and no fish. It looked like the back of the boat was catching, though, so I leaned my pole against the gunwale and went to see if I could find a spot for us to squeeze into. I approached three guys, who turned out to be ironworkers from near my old neighborhood in Fairfield. They were big guys, Italian guys. The biggest one was at least fifty pounds heavier than me.

"Come on in, buddy," he said. He pushed the guy next to him and opened up a space at the rail. "Fish with your own people. What are you doing fishing next to those Korean assholes?" Over at the gunwale, Han leaned over the side and peered at the spot where his line disappeared into the water.

The ironworker was right. These were my people. I looked like them. I talked like them. I could have sat down and bullshitted with these guys all day, and you'd never know the difference between us. Like the saying goes, you can choose your friends but not your family. You never escape your childhood or the neighborhood where you grew up. We were northern New Jersey, Irish and Italian, working class. Patriotic Americans. "Best damn people in the world," my dad used to say at the union picnics.

But there were two Bobby Egans, just like there were two Hans. I was Hackensack Bobby and Pyongyang Bobby.

"Maybe later," I said to the ironworker. I walked over to Han, who raised his eyebrows as if to say, "Well?"

"No room," I said. I rebaited my hook with the head of a bunker fish and cast with the wind. Han did the same. Our lines streaked out from the boat in parallel and snaked across the gray-blue water. We reeled in a few clicks as the bait disappeared below the surface. We didn't care how long it took. We were going to catch something. Our daughters watched us from where they sat next to the wheelhouse. It wouldn't look good to come home empty-handed.

17

≈≈≈≈≈≈≈≈≈≈≈≈≈

Write Your Own Ticket

MAYBE I SHOULD HAVE KNOWN that the most ambitious idea Han and I ever came up with would also be our last. At the end of the day, our relationship wasn't sustainable. We were small players in global rivalry, and sooner or later forces stronger than our friendship were bound to pull us apart.

In late June 2006, the United States led Operation Valiant Shield—five days of the biggest military maneuvers in the Pacific region since the Vietnam War. Three aircraft carriers, thirty ships, 280 planes, and twenty-two thousand troops prowled the waters near North Korea, whose neighboring enemies Japan and South Korea also sent their navies to practice maneuvers. For the first time ever, Washington invited the Chinese to observe.

If they were trying to ruffle the feathers of Han's generals, it worked. Pyongyang issued a statement threatening an "annihilating strike and a nuclear war" if anyone tried to attack North Korea. The Bush Administration called the threat "deeply hypothetical." Our governments were back at the level of schoolyard taunts.

Around the same time, the Pentagon announced it was going to station a new group of spy planes in South Korea, which was obviously just another provocation to the North. Who *announces* a spying operation? Pyongyang responded on the Fourth of July by shooting six mid- and long-range missiles over the Sea of Japan.

"Is that your version of fireworks?" I asked Han that afternoon, as we unloaded some fishing tackle from the back of the Hummer. The North Korean diplomats were celebrating our Independence Day with a barbecue on Roosevelt Island. I picked up a box of sliding weights and clip-on leaders, and Han grabbed a few thermal bags filled with BBQ ribs.

"It's our Paris Air Show," he said. When he saw my blank look, he explained: the Paris Air Show was the world's biggest trade show for the aerospace industry, where Boeing and other manufacturers show off their new planes. It's also where militaries shop for the latest fighter jets, spy planes, radar systems, and other high-end defense items. "We're not invited," Han said.

I'd always thought North Korea's missile tests were a way of showing the world they were dangerous. They liked to shoot them off in response to U.N. sanctions or American military moves, like Operation Valiant Shield. Now I realized they were also a sales tool, like the big red Cubby's sign I have on River Street. The message was aimed at potential buyer countries like Iran, Syria, and Myanmar as much as at the United States and its allies.

That Fourth of July the North Koreans test fired their longest-range missile—the Taepodong-2, a three-stage rocket capable of carrying a nuke as far as the coasts of Hawaii or Alaska. "One day, somebody is going to buy it," Han said.

We brought the tackle and ribs to the other North Koreans, who'd spread out a blanket next to the bank of the East River. A few of them were surfcasting for striped bass in the heavy current. I got them set up with the weights and leaders, and then Han and I walked out toward the lighthouse to stretch our legs.

"Do you still have coffee with the FBI?" he asked.

A few cars sat outside a low apartment building about fifty yards away. I couldn't tell, but it was a good bet one of them had two agents sitting in the front seat with a pair of binoculars. "As long as I'm with you, they're with me," I said. "They're not after my barbecue recipe."

"Your friend, Marakovits. He has influence?"

I did a double take. Han never asked about the FBI. I mentioned them once in a while, but I hadn't used Marakovits's name more than once or twice over the years, and I'd never seen Han write it down. He'd been paying closer attention than I thought.

"He has access to the highest levels," I said, making it up, because I wanted to see where Han was going with his questions.

"Maybe it's time to meet your friends," he said.

"You want to *meet* the Feds?"

We walked past the lighthouse to the tip of the island, where the headwaters split around the point. To the north, the East River disappeared around a bend that separated the top of Manhattan from the Bronx. Across the muddy water, apartment towers rose from the bank of Astoria, Queens. We found a couple of rocks to sit on.

Han gazed back toward the parked cars on the street. "You're the biggest arms dealer in the world," he said. "But when we have something to sell, you say it's evil. You have a double standard."

I still couldn't guess where he was going with all this, but I figured he'd come out with it sooner or later. "You sell weapons to our enemies," I said.

"You don't let us have any other market," he said.

"Most countries are afraid to buy weapons from you," I said. "We're more powerful, so they buy from us. It's the law of the jungle. Same thing happens on the street, with drugs. One gang controls the neighborhood. If anybody else wants to sell, they have to work through the dealer who—"

And then it hit me. I almost fell off my rock. "You want to sell your missiles to Washington!"

Han pulled a pebble out of a crevice in the breakwater, felt its weight in his hand, and skimmed it out into the river, where it hopped three times along the surface and disappeared into the current. "Maybe more," he said.

"Missiles and nukes? Anything else?"

Han grinned. "All options on the table," he said. "Everything for sale."

We hadn't talked about this since the soccer tournament in 2003, when I suggested giving the North Koreans cash instead of two light-water reactors. I'd forgotten all about it. But this sounded like something new. The whole banana. I was proud of Han for coming up with a new approach to the old problem. He was finally thinking like a real businessman. Why argue about nuclear weapons? Sell them to the country that's most concerned about them!

The North Koreans had something that everybody wanted, which was the ability to make peace in the region. Naturally, that should come with a price. A lot of underdeveloped countries go about it the wrong way. They get handouts and loans from rich countries until they're in debt so far that they can't even pay back the interest. They don't stand up to the big industrialized countries and say, "You want to have all the weapons? You want us to be under your thumb? That costs something."

I felt like somebody had plugged me into an electrical socket. My body tingled with excitement. I thought of all the things Han and I had tried to do together—nothing compared to this. It was the kind of feeling when you know you've got the biggest fish of your life on the line.

That night, Han and I stayed up half the night on the phone, imagining what a deal could look like if the United States bought North Korea's nuclear and missile programs for cash. We hashed out basic details: the United States and its allies would front a large amount of money; Pyongyang would allow foreign experts to help dismantle their nuclear and bomb-making capabilities; inspectors would stay on the ground to make sure the North Koreans never restarted the programs. The timing was perfect—all other talks between our countries had been dead in the water for nearly eight months. There was a negotiation vacuum, and that was an opportunity for guys on the outside looking for an angle, like me and Han and maybe even Marakovits, if I could get him behind the idea.

Han's asking to meet the FBI could have meant a number of things. Either their nuclear program was such a failure that they wanted to get something for giving it up before anyone found out; they were afraid that going further with it could lead to war; or they were desperate for cash. Or all three. It also showed they had nobody else to turn to. The Russians weren't helping them anymore. The Chinese were getting cozier with the West. Where else was Han going to go? He didn't have access to the CIA or the Pentagon or any other branch of government in Washington. He could have approached somebody like Bill Richardson, but how well did they really know each other? When Han needed a channel to Washington he could trust, all he had was me. And all I had was the FBI.

A few days later, I drove Marakovits to the Pasta Pot in Hackensack, which is owned by a friend of mine named Ronnie and has plenty of mobster atmosphere. I figured the place would impress a farm boy like Marakovits. Like most guys in law enforcement, he romanticized the Mafia life. When he talked about a promotion, he talked about "getting made," like he was straight off the streets.

The Pasta Pot was your typical place, full of a bunch of middle-class Nicky Newarkers—wannabe wise guys and their fake-boob *gumadas*. Real made guys never ate there, so it was okay to bring in somebody wearing a sports shirt tucked into his chinos, whose appearance screamed "Fed" from a mile away.

Ronnie gave us the best table in the house—back corner, where we could have lunch in privacy. Across the room a waiter swirled a white cloth inside of a water glass, held it up to the light, and squinted at it for a few seconds as he turned it in his fingertips.

"You see that guy?" I asked Marakovits. "He polishes each glass like it's a woman he's trying to get into bed. What do you think of that?"

"The glasses are clean," Marakovits said, blushing.

"You Feds could learn a lesson from guys like him," I said. "He takes what other people would see as a routine job and puts a little extra something into it. Suddenly drying dishes isn't boring, it's full of possibilities."

At the bar, a couple of guys in slicked-back hair and pinkie rings hunched over their bowls of pasta.

"I guess I kind of stick out here," Marakovits said. He tried to look nonchalant as he cased the place. He was nervous, and I liked that. I was counting on him being impressionable enough to open up to an idea that an old dog like Kuhlmeier never would have considered.

"Don't worry about it," I said. "You dress like the North Koreans, and *they've* got lots of imagination." We opened our menus and saw that the special was veal scallopini. "You know what I told Han one time?" I asked. "I told him, 'Except for the fact that you dress like squares, you guys are the Italians of Asia.'"

"Did he take it as a compliment?"

"Of course he did! Think about it. The North Koreans have a hot temper. They're very loyal. They're big on honor. And if you want to have a good conversation, you need to sit down to a meal with them first. Remember that."

When the waiter came, I ordered my usual, the linguini combo with red sauce, clams and mussels, and a side of cucumbers. Marakovits ordered a cold seafood salad with minestrone soup. I waited until we'd both had some bread and butter before I came to the point. "They want to meet you," I said.

His knife slipped on a hard piece of butter and clanked loudly against the dish. "Who?" He peeked over his shoulder to see if anyone was looking at us. "The North Koreans?"

"They know you work for the president. I think their guys in New York trust you more than they trust the CIA or the Pentagon. The State Department isn't really talking to them."

Marakovits sat up straighter. Our appetizers arrived. He got some romaine lettuce into his mouth and chewed on it. "Why would they trust us?" he asked. "We've been spying on them for years."

"Maybe that's why. They understand what you do. Domestic spying is the game they're best at."

The possibility dawned on me as I was saying it. The FBI had followed us all those years, and they hadn't interrupted us when we hunted in the woods or fished offshore, and they never swooped in when we drove fifty miles or more beyond the travel limits. They followed at a respectful distance with their cameras and binoculars. To Han and the North Koreans, they might have seemed the least threatening.

I thought of all the arm-twisting I'd done just to get Han to do an interview with Phil Shenon of *The New York Times* or meet Tommy Topousis of *The Record* before the Nets game. The Koreans were probably a lot more comfortable dealing with an intelligence service that kept secrets than a free press whose job it was to give secrets away. If they floated an idea through the Feds, it wouldn't end up on the front page of the newspaper the next day.

"They want to get the message to the White House." I leaned over my salad plate and lowered my voice. "They're willing to put their entire nuclear and civilian weapons program on the table in exchange for cash."

Marakovits poked a crouton with his fork. He looked like he didn't know whether to take me seriously. I explained that Han and I had come up with a figure of sixty billion dollars for the nuclear and missile programs, as a starting point for negotiations. It was enough to get the attention of the highest levels in Pyongyang. And it could be a bargain for Washington, if you looked at all the humanitarian aid, the loans, the light-water reactor projects, and everything else that had been on the table.

"Sixty billion dollars," Marakovits said. I could see him trying to wrap his brain around the figure. It was in the same universe as amounts we spent on wars in Afghanistan and Iraq per year.

"You don't pay it all at once," I said. "You spread it out over twenty or thirty years, like a mortgage. And you share the costs between five or six countries. You see how it starts to make sense? This doesn't even touch the savings that kick in as soon as the DPRK isn't a threat, and we can bring our forces home from South Korea. How much does it cost to keep a combat soldier on the DMZ for a year?" I counted it out on my thumb and fingers, to make it clearer. "At least a hundred thousand dollars, if you add up the costs of the Pentagon planning, logistics, training, equipment, transport, and infrastructure needed to support him. Multiply that by thirty thousand soldiers we have in South Korea, give or take a few thousand. That's three billion a year times twenty years. There's your sixty billion back just by not deploying troops there."

The waiter took our salad plates and brought our main courses. We waited for him to walk away. "This is like the idea to give them cash instead of KEDO," Marakovits said.

"That's right," I said. "Except bigger. The difference is, this time it's coming from them."

"Last time you said it was coming from them."

I put my hands up apologetically. "I might have fudged that a little. But this time it's *really* coming from them. This is the first time they've asked to meet an American intelligence officer." I leaned forward again. "Han mentioned you specifically."

"Me?" Marakovits put his fork down. "How does he know who I am?"

"Just your first name," I lied. "He said, 'What about your friend Tommy from the FBI?' And I said, 'You're right, Mr. Ambassador. Tom's a good guy. Maybe you should bring him to the table.'"

Marakovits watched the waiter, who put down his last water glasses and leaned against the bar with an unlit cigarette between his fingers. "He called me Tommy?"

"Yeah," I said. "They have a lot of respect for you." I wiped my mouth with my napkin. I could see I was getting to him. "They don't know who else to turn to. This is the critical moment. Sanctions aren't working. Something needs to happen, and it needs to happen through the back door, without too many politicians getting in the way."

Marakovits shook his head. "Don't shake your head," I said. "You don't believe me? The United States of America is going to buy this program one way or another. Maybe we'll buy the nukes from the North Koreans and dismantle them, or maybe we'll load up South Korea with Patriot missiles and station troops there for the next hundred years. But either way, we're going to pay. And the more advanced their program gets, the higher the price tag is going to be. The more risk there is that something could go wrong. Do you want that hanging over you for the rest of your life? That you were called to act, and you did nothing?"

"I don't think you can make the case that it's my responsibility."

"They're ready, Tom, and they want to talk to you."

He pronged a chilled shrimp with his fork and dabbed it in some dressing. "Like they were ready to deliver the *Pueblo*?"

I let this go. I expected some resistance. Years earlier, Kuhlmeier said he couldn't talk to the North Koreans, either.

"We don't have to negotiate anything," I said. "It's an intel job. All we do is find out what the North Koreans are proposing and get it to the right ears. It's a supporting role in history. Think about that." I leaned back in my chair and studied Marakovits as he worked a piece of seafood around his mouth. "I'll bet you're already the most interesting guy in your family," I said. "When you're dead and gone, your grandkids and great-grandkids are going to keep a picture of you on their mantle. They'll talk about how Grandpa Tom was an FBI agent. What else will they be able to say? You were an accountant who got a little street time? Or that their granddaddy helped bring peace between two nations? That you were a guy who saw a chance to make your mark, and you took it? If we play our cards right, the historians are going to look back and write that it was an FBI agent—a street-level guy—who went to Pyong-yang and brought home a deal to his president."

Marakovits frowned. "They're not going to send me to North Korea," he said. "I'm domestic. My territory stops at the New Jersey border."

"If you're the guy the Koreans trust, they're going to demand that you have a role. Look at me. Nobody ever appointed me to anything, either. You've got to insert yourself. You write your own ticket to Pyongyang."

Our waiter came and cleared our plates, and we each ordered a cappuccino.

"It must be pretty weird over there."

"It looks normal, at first. The buildings are big, Soviet-style. But there don't seem to be enough people around to fill them. You see shoppers in the stores who never buy anything. They've got these mean-looking traffic women who pivot around in the intersections wearing sexy police skirts and white gloves. But you don't see many cars or even bicycles. Almost everybody is on foot."

"Isn't everybody starving?"

"Not in Pyongyang. You see kids buying ice cream from a guy with a cart. Everybody's well dressed. After you've been there long enough, you start no-ticing the same faces."

The waiter brought our coffees. I dropped a sugar cube into mine. Tiny bubbles floated to the surface. "Then you realize it's just for show," I said. "The people you see are actors, *pretending* to be real people. It's like Disney World, except the workers aren't dressed up like princesses and Donald Duck; they're dressed up like happy citizens."

"Scary," Marakovits said.

"As long as you're my friend, you'll be treated like a king. They know me over there."

"I thought you said they shot you up with drugs," he said.

"Only to find out who I was," I said. "What about you? Would you let them interrogate you?"

"Definitely not," he said. He tore a corner off a packet of brown sugar and stirred it into his cappuccino. I knew a part of him wanted to go overseas and tangle with the enemy. Nobody joins law enforcement unless, somewhere deep inside, they want to be a hero. I felt bad for Marakovits in the way you feel bad for anybody who's not living up to the dream they had for themselves. I wanted to help him.

"You just need to dress different," I ribbed him. "You got to stop going to the FBI barber. And we need to throw a few swear words into your vocabulary. No more 'Excuse me, pardon me' shit. Other than that, you're probably work-able. I could see you on the street. I could see you undercover."

"Yeah?" He looked pleased as he stirred his coffee.

I was starting to think, *This guy's all right. He's got potential.* When the bill came I put my hand out for it, but Marakovits interrupted.

"Separate checks," he said.

The waiter and I raised our eyebrows at each other. "Not in an Italian place, pal," I said to Marakovits. "You want us to look like a couple of jerkoffs?"

"Sorry," he said. "Regulations."

I shook my head and pulled some bills out of my wallet as the waiter brought us two checks. "Don't pull that with the North Koreans," I said. I watched in amazement as he left a three-dollar tip on a twenty-one-dollar meal. "Throw a couple more on there. This is a friend's place." He pulled one more dollar out of his wallet and laid it on top.

I'd almost forgotten I was dealing with the U.S. government—a bunch of by-the-book, cologne-from-Sears-wearing, too-afraid-to-go-fishing-with-the-people-they're-supposed-to-be-spying-on, exactly-fifteen-percent-tipping amateurs. It was like the time years earlier, when Kuhlmeier told me I couldn't give Han's colleague Shun a pair of night-vision goggles to take back to Pyongyang because some piece of paper hadn't been signed by a bureaucrat in Washington. These so-called intelligence agents had no flexibility, no imagination, no *capiche*. This was exactly why North Korea looked like a "black hole" to them. Things were being run by a bunch of tightwads like Marakovits—the goody-goody kids who never got in trouble with their teachers.

What we ought to do is to take our foreign policy with places like North Korea and Syria and Zimbabwe and turn it over to the guys from my neighborhood—people who know how to bend the rules a little. Who have a flair for personal relationships. The waiter who polishes water glasses at the Pasta Pot has a better chance at Third World diplomacy than any of the bean-counting knuckleheads they send. You wouldn't see him leaving a three-dollar tip. That's how it was with me and Han. When I got some extra cash, I took Han out charter-boat fishing or put together bags of vitamins and beef jerky for his buddies. If I was short and he was flush, he threw me a few large. It's cultural.

Send a delegation of roofers from New Jersey to Pyongyang and see what happens. Guys from my neighborhood don't negotiate about principles we read in a book somewhere. We're not going to lecture the North Koreans or the Iraqis about democratic ideals and the greatness of freedom and then wonder why we aren't producing results. We take people out to a nice dinner, find out about each other's families, and then if the time is right and the feeling is good, we talk business. And if that doesn't work, we bust the guy in the mouth.

A couple of weeks later, Marakovits came to Cubby's very excited and insisted on talking to me in the parking lot. When we got outside, he walked me to his car and looked around to make sure nobody was within earshot. He said he'd talked to his station chief in Newark about meeting the North

Koreans. "They're sending it to Washington," he said breathlessly. "Keep your fingers crossed."

He paced around, as nervous as a kid on his first date. We were on the verge of something huge, and he could smell the potential. "Good work, Tommy," I said. I slapped him on the back. Marakovits was going to make an unlikely hero.

Han got excited when I told him that Marakovits was taking our proposal upstairs in Washington. "Remind him one condition is withdrawal of troops from the DMZ," he said. "We want to discuss big changes."

I wanted to test the idea, so I described it to my dad, who called it a hare-brained fantasy. But then I told him Han came forward with it himself.

"And he approached you with it?" Dad asked. I thought I even heard a hint of pride in his voice.

I called Shenon at the *Times*. I reached out to Topousis, who had moved on to the *New York Post,* and the reporter Melinda Liu, who wrote about Asia for *Newsweek* magazine. She took notes for more than an hour, while I laid out our plan.

Marakovits came by the restaurant on a hot afternoon in late July. He asked to see me in the parking lot again. "It's dead in the water," he said as soon as we got to his car. He looked pretty busted up about it. "That comes from Washington." I wondered whether Marakovits's bosses were against the idea, or if they didn't give it credibility because it came from a BBQ cook and a field agent from New Jersey.

"Go back and appeal," I said. "Be a pain in the ass." He shook his head. "Tell them you don't want to have to come back in five or six years and say, 'I told you so.'"

"You don't understand," he said. "This is coming from my boss's boss."

I put a hand on the hood of his car and pushed down to check the shocks. "Tell your guy he needs to reconsider, or else Bobby is going public," I said. "My journalist friends would be very interested to know how you guys wouldn't hear a proposal from some very high-ranking North Koreans. I've been talking to *Newsweek*—"

"That's not necessary," he said.

"You're right. But I'm sure they'd love to hear how you guys are always hiding in the bushes, taking pictures of us while we're fishing, and later on asking me what they said. But when the North Koreans want to talk to you, you run away. I'll tell them the FBI is like the kid who has a crush on a girl but is too scared to talk to her. Would you do that with a criminal case? If you got a call from a *capo* from one of the big crime families, would you say to him, 'I'm sorry, we can't meet you; go talk to your local sheriff?'"

"It's not really the same thing—"

"This is the key to our national security! Don't forget who you work for. The President of the United States is counting on you to be his eyes and ears. You're a field agent, and that's where real intelligence comes from. From street level. You've got to get this idea all the way to the top."

I took heart when Marakovits agreed to go back to his bosses and argue our case. I called Han and told him the FBI was in a second round of discussions over our proposal.

"Tell Marakovits he can bring his supervisor to the embassy," Han said that evening. "Or we can meet him at Cubby's." He said he was getting positive signals from Pyongyang.

Two weeks later, Marakovits came to my restaurant during the slow part of the afternoon and headed straight for the back table. I brought a couple of Diet Cokes over and sat down opposite him. He slowly turned his glass, making a wet ring on the Formica. "I'm getting reassigned," he said without looking up. "Sent out to pasture."

Eight years earlier, Kuhlmeier had used the exact same words. "I guess this means we're not going to Pyongyang together," I said.

Marakovits told me his new assignment would be on a desk in Pennsylvania, doing background checks on white-collar crime suspects. Also Kuhlmeier's fate. Now I really felt bad for him. Even though he was a square, I liked Marakovits.

"What's their problem?" I asked.

"They think you're starting to win me over."

"What's wrong with that? I'm looking out for our country's best interests." I reached across the table and pointed at Marakovits's heart. "And so were you."

He should have been proud. He'd acted with more patriotism than most field agents. At the end of the day, he didn't play it safe. He sacrificed. I walked Marakovits to his car and shook his hand. When I came back into the restaurant, I saw that he had left three dollars for a dollar-fifty soda.

That night I called McCreary and told him I thought my relationship with the FBI was over. "Not as long as you're friends with Han," he said. I took comfort in that. The FBI was my only real link to the power structure in Washington besides McCreary, who was just a friend. Without the FBI behind me, I'd be less valuable to Pyongyang, which in turn made me less of an asset to my country. I could see the downward spiral into insignificance. I was just a few steps from being just an ordinary restaurant owner, like Ronnie from the Pasta Pot.

On a muggy evening in mid-August, I picked Han up at the embassy and we drove around the streets of the Upper East Side. I headed up First Avenue and turned right on 72nd Street, where he worked when we first met. The building that once housed their mission was unrecognizable at first because they'd put a marquee over the front door and redecorated the facade. I parked at the end of the cul-de-sac, where we had spent so many evenings getting to know each other on his first tour.

"How are your discussions with Marakovits?" he asked when we got out of the Hummer.

"It's a slow time," I said. "A lot of people are on vacation." I decided that, for the time being, I wouldn't tell Han that Marakovits was leaving. At least until I got another agent assigned to me. If I stuck with Han, I'd eventually come across a piece of information I could offer to the Bureau, and then we'd be off and running again.

"It's taking too much time," he said. He seemed jittery, like he was under more pressure than usual. We walked across the cobblestone park overlooking the FDR Highway and the East River and leaned against the railing.

Across the water, the apartment buildings of Roosevelt Island created a patch-work of lights. Somewhere out there, Han's colleagues were cleaning their dinner dishes or watching TV.

"Remember one time you said nobody will attack us if we make a nuclear test?" Han asked.

I sucked in a breath of warm summer air. There could be only one reason he'd ask. "Are you ready to test one?"

Han pretended he hadn't heard me. "Was that only your opinion? Or did you get the information from someone else?"

"It was an opinion," I said. "Nobody's going to attack you when you have thousands of missiles ready to hit Seoul from forty miles away. McCreary told me that."

The nightmare scenario was that if Pyongyang tested a nuke and Washington responded with an air strike, the whole situation could spin out of control very quickly. Hundreds of thousands of troops stood on either side of the DMZ, ready to start butchering each other at the blow of a whistle. Once it started it would be hard to stop. If Pyongyang fired artillery and short-range missiles, they'd hit downtown Seoul in a matter of seconds. More than a million South Koreans and thousands of U.S. troops lived within North Korean artillery range. If the shooting started, Washington might take the ultimate step. Some of the nut jobs in the Bush Administration sounded like they were itching to nuke somebody.

I imagined the terror of a nuclear strike on North Korea: a flash of light, and the surprised faces of the little kids in the village where Senator Green-leaf and I jogged; Ri, the soccer goalie I took to Walmart, shouting at her teammates to lie down in the grass; the pleasant doctors who shot me up with truth serum, running for a bomb shelter. I even had a moment of sympathy for Cranky, the guy I'd fought at the War Museum. I thought of Ho Jong leaning out of his apartment window to water the flowers in his window box at the moment of impact. Or Han's daughter walking home from school with her friends when the air raid sirens started wailing.

I wondered if Han had been worrying about a nuclear attack on his homeland—as a father and as the guy responsible for relations with the

United States. "Does this have to do with why you want to sell your program?" I asked.

Han stared out into the darkness. In the middle of the East River, a party boat glowed with light and thudded with dance music. "You ask too many questions," he said.

That night I called McCreary and told him Han asked what the U.S. military reaction would be to a detonation.

"Are they detonating? Did he give a timeframe?"

I realized I might be the first American to know. "He said they were afraid we'll attack them. No details."

There was a pause at the other end of the line. "The most important thing for them is to not surprise people," McCreary said. "The Pakistanis caught us off guard when they did it, and immediately you had people talking about a military response. With North Korea, there's *already* talk of a military strike."

"You think we would bomb them if they test a nuke?"

"I think cooler heads would prevail. But whatever they do, it'll be healthier for everybody if they announce it first."

I called Han from Cubby's the next morning and told him I'd talked to McCreary about their nuclear test. He shouted at me. "I didn't say we were planning a test," he said. "Those are *your* words!"

"I didn't tell him you were. We were talking hypothetically."

Han thought about this for a few seconds. "Hypothetically, what did he say?"

I covered the mouthpiece and called for my manager, Bobby, to come out of the kitchen. We had a line forming at the register for early lunch orders—a couple of businessmen and a few guys from a construction job across the street.

"He thinks they won't attack," I said, stepping away from the counter.

"You got that from McCreary?" Han asked. "What does the FBI say?"

Now I was sure he was fishing for information to report back to Pyongyang. "The FBI isn't saying anything," I said.

I felt for Han. He'd reached out to the Feds in a way that had never been tried before. But Washington wasn't ready to listen. It was as if they weren't even curious, which was strange, considering how much our leaders had talked over the years about wanting to understand the North Koreans. "Find out what makes them tick," Kuhlmeier used to tell me. So I'd spent half of my adult life reporting back on everything Han and his comrades were doing. How they spent their free time. What TV shows they watched. Which candy bars and cowboy boots they bought. What flavor of beef jerky they sent home. Who was arriving from Pyongyang and who was leaving. Who wanted painkillers and who wanted Viagra. I provided diagrams. Lists of names. Tissue samples.

The Feds wrote down my observations that Han liked to sing Rod Stewart and knew all the words to "Pop Goes the Weasel." That he loved baked potatoes, and the American he admired most was Donald Trump. And that he was skillful with a fly rod but basically impatient as a fisherman. They wrote these things down because they were desperate to predict what the North Koreans would do. I could predict what they'd do. You send a few aircraft carriers off their coastline, and they're going to test a rocket or two. It's the law of the street—you threaten me, I threaten you back. Simple.

If we wanted to keep North Korea from going nuclear, the only strategy that made sense was to convince its generals that they didn't need The Bomb. But we were busy doing the opposite—putting missiles on their border, freezing their bank accounts, and trying to turn the Russians and Chinese against them. When we backed the North Koreans against the wall, they saw a nuke as their only hope for survival. Now we were in the most dangerous situation possible. Washington wasn't serious about buying their program and was growing more hostile. Pyongyang had a nuke, but they hadn't gotten the respect that should go with it.

"You should test it," I said. "Put your cards on the table. Take away the uncertainty."

"What makes you so sure?" Han asked.

I *wasn't* sure. But at least it would shake things up between our countries.

"The important thing is to not surprise anybody," I said. "I got that from McCreary. Don't give us an excuse to strike back. Make sure the world knows you're not trying to bomb Tokyo."

On October 3, the Korean Central News Agency issued a one-page statement that because of U.S. military maneuvers and economic sanctions against it, the DPRK stood at a "crossroads of life and death." Parts of it made the newspapers in the United States, but Han read me the whole thing. It ended:

> A people without reliable war deterrents are bound to meet a tragic death and the sovereignty of their country is bound to be wantonly infringed upon. This is a bitter lesson taught by the bloodshed resulting from the law of the jungle in different parts of the world.
>
> The DPRK's nuclear weapons will serve as reliable war deterrent for protecting the supreme interests of the state and the security of the Korean nation from the U.S. threat of aggression and averting a new war and firmly safeguarding peace and stability on the Korean peninsula under any circumstances.

"'Law of the jungle' is good," I said. "You get that from me?"

The Bush Administration took two days to respond. On October 5, Assistant Secretary of State Christopher Hill said that a nuclear test would be a "highly provocative act." He warned North Korea that "it can have a future or it can have these weapons, but it cannot have both."

Han called just as my dinner rush was starting. "Do you think he is making a case for military action?" he asked.

"Hell, no!" I said. "If they were seriously considering attacking you, they'd send out their big guns. You'd get the secretary of state and the president talking about it all over TV, because they'd have to get the American people behind it. Don't worry so much."

"Easy for you to say," he said. "Not your country on the line."

I took an order for a barbecue beef sandwich and a side of breaded zucchini sticks and asked Lilia to take over for me at the register. I'd been thinking about it for the past couple of weeks. "You know what happened to me when I was a kid?" I asked Han. "I got beat up every day. I was a punching bag for Big Mike and Little Mike and their friends. So I started working out. I got muscles. But I didn't get respect from the older kids until I wrestled a guy to the ground and threw a punch or two. Same thing with your nuke. Once you show what you can do, we're less likely to attack you."

"That's your opinion."

"Name one military that's ever been stupid enough to attack a nuclear-armed nation. There isn't one."

"You are always the first country to do anything," he said.

"We *could* try to knock out your facility with a surgical strike," I conceded. A guy refilling his soda a few feet away stopped to listen to my conversation, so I turned the other direction. "But only before you detonate. Not afterwards. Don't give us any more time. You need to blow it up now."

I looked around at my customers, who chowed down on burgers and ribs. Some of them would consider me a traitor if they knew I'd just advised our nation's enemy to go nuclear. I couldn't believe I was doing it, either. It was counterintuitive, but I believed the North Koreans detonating a nuclear bomb might bring us closer to peace. It happens. Look at the Indians and the Pakistanis. They fought three wars in thirty years, until they started testing nuclear weapons. Now they both have the bomb, and how many wars have they fought? Zero. They have to respect each other.

Three days later, a few minutes after ten P.M. on October 8, 2006, President Bush was getting ready for bed when National Security Advisor Stephen Hadley interrupted him with the news: the government of China had just sent an emergency cable warning that the North Koreans were preparing a nuclear test within minutes. By the time the president put his slippers on, seismological stations all over the world had picked up tremors originating at Sangpyong-ri mountain. The U.S. Geological Survey registered the blast at 4.2 on the Richter Scale.

The North Korean detonation made headlines all over the world. *The New York Times* called it a "strategic jolt." CNN aired special reports. *Newsweek* ran an especially detailed story, with a picture of Kim Jong Il wearing big sunglasses on the cover. The writer, Melinda Liu, pointed out that the test could have been avoided. Tipped off by me and confirmed by Han, she wrote that "North Korea reached out to the owner of Cubby's, a New Jersey restaurant, to sell its nuclear programs to the U.S. government," and that Han had wanted to continue negotiations with Washington.

In the days after the test, scientists argued about how big the DPRK's blast had been. The South Koreans said half a kiloton; the French and the Australians estimated its yield at around one kiloton. Either way, it was a lot smaller than expected. India, Pakistan, and other countries' first nuclear tests have all been about twenty kilotons—roughly the size of the bomb dropped on Nagasaki in 1945. Experts speculated that something could have gone wrong with the North Korean detonators or that the plutonium was lower quality than it should have been.

"Is everybody laughing at us?" Han asked when he came to the restaurant the next day. He was responsible for interpreting the American response to the nuclear test, and he didn't want to deliver news that would embarrass the generals in Pyongyang. He worried that North Korea was still vulnerable, because a nuclear explosion in a mountain was different than testing a warhead that can be put on a missile and used as a weapon. They were still years away from that.

"Are you kidding me?" I said. "A nuke is a nuke." I pointed out that the stories in the media weren't about the weakness of the explosion or the fact that the North Koreans couldn't bomb anybody yet. The test might have been a dud militarily, but politically it was a big deal. It was a deterrent.

President Bush made a televised speech the morning after the explosion, condemning North Korea's test as a "provocative act." The Japanese government called it "absolutely unacceptable." Russian President Vladimir Putin said the test had done "tremendous harm" to the world order. The Chinese and the South Koreans also condemned it, but warned that they wouldn't support any military retaliation.

Bush said he was keeping "all options on the table." He called on the U.N. Security Council to find ways to punish North Korea. On Saturday, October 14, the Security Council held a special meeting to sanction Pyongyang. They didn't have a lot of options. It's the problem with isolating another country, year after year. After a while you run out of leverage. The worst the Security Council could come up with was allowing the search of North Korean cargo ships in any port in the world.

Han defiantly skipped the session, on orders from Pyongyang. Pak went just long enough to stand up, accuse the United States of being "gangster-like," and walk out. That left the U.S. ambassador to the U.N., John Bolton, ranting and raving at an empty chair at the end of the horseshoe-shaped table, where a DPRK representative should have been.

Instead of sticking around for an ear-bashing at the U.N., the North Korean diplomats drove across the George Washington Bridge for lunch at Cubby's. I blocked off the whole eastern end of the restaurant for them. Lilia and Andrea were working the counter. I had O'D there for security, and the rest of the place was packed with the regular Saturday afternoon crowd. Han followed me outside to my Hummer on the excuse that he wanted to see my new crossbow. He still looked worried.

"Are they wondering why we only tested one bomb?" Han asked when we got outside. It was obvious why: the North Koreans had enough material for five or six weapons, so they had to conserve, even though it made them look less capable than India or Pakistan, which tested multiple devices when they went nuclear.

"If you're out in the woods and you've got five arrows, you're going to be more careful about how many you use. Every hunter knows that. It doesn't show you're weak; it shows you're thinking strategically."

Han relaxed a little and seemed grateful.

I followed him inside. He and the other North Korean diplomats sat around two long tables underneath the photos of our fishing expeditions and the mural of me at the Vietnam Memorial Wall. A few of the guys were first-timers to Cubby's who I hadn't seen before. One was smaller than the rest and looked like a younger version of Kim Jong Il, right down to the bouffant hairdo. If he was a close relative of the Dear Leader, nobody was saying. A couple of the newcomers kept looking around in wonder at the cartoon pigs, the heaping plates of ribs and wieners, and the Hackensack lunchtime crowd.

Through the window we could see an unmarked sedan parked on the by-road, half hidden by low shrubs. Two FBI agents sat in the front seats wearing sunglasses. The passenger-side agent raised an expensive-looking camera and took a picture whenever one of the Koreans went in or out of the restaurant. O'D posted himself as a sentry inside the front door, by the pinball machine, to ward off any trouble.

Andrea brought out trays of beer in frosted mugs, and Lilia followed with the salads. When everybody had a plate in front of them, I stood and raised my glass of diet soda.

"Gentlemen," I said. The chatter around the table hushed, and my guests turned to me expectantly. I raised my glass a little higher. "Welcome to the Boys' Club!" I beamed at everybody. Some of the North Koreans were slow to raise their glasses. The newcomers exchanged looks with Han and Pak to make sure they understood that an American citizen was toasting their nuclear achievement. Then they all burst out laughing, and there was a great clinking of glasses around the table.

I nodded at Han and went back to the kitchen to make sure nobody's meat got overcooked. On the way, one of my regular customers, a big guy in a Caterpillar baseball cap, came up to me. "Are those North Koreans?" he asked. He must have overheard my toast. I told him proudly that they were, and I was about to show him some of the pictures on my walls, when he interrupted. "I ain't eating with a bunch of commies who want to nuke us. Tell them if they try anything, we're going to send their asses straight to hell."

My first impulse was to take him outside and put a few dents in his skull, but out of respect for Han and the general diplomatic atmosphere among my Korean friends, I let it slide. I said nothing as Caterpillar guy walked out the restaurant past O'D, who looked back and forth between me and the guy and kept one hand on his weapon.

The encounter left me with a bad feeling. I was having second thoughts now that the North Koreans had tested a nuke. I didn't think they'd be stupid enough to attack anybody, but what if they were tempted to sell nuclear material to a terrorist group? I'd feel responsible for encouraging Han to move forward.

I'm not saying the DPRK detonated their nuke because Bobby Egan suggested it. But I'm not saying I had *nothing* to do with their nuclear test, either. Han talked to other people—Bill Richardson in New Mexico and American officials and experts he met over the years. He always felt these guys were giving him canned political arguments. They didn't have daily interaction together. They weren't his friends. I don't know how seriously Han took anything I said, but he knew I'd be straight with him. He considered me his backchannel to the FBI and McCreary, who served the president. Maybe he took me more seriously than anybody else did.

Han never told me what he wrote in his dispatches to Pyongyang, but it wasn't beyond the imagination that they at least heard my opinions. Our own government gets its intelligence from some pretty far-out sources. We went to war in Iraq based on the advice of some exiles, who told us, "Sure, there are weapons of mass destruction in Baghdad. Go ahead. Invade. You'll be treated as liberators and heroes." These guys said what our leaders wanted to hear, and their words became actionable intelligence.

In the end, what matters is that we were right. The United States didn't attack North Korea. Their nuclear test had exactly the effect I told them it would. In the months that followed, the Bush Administration made a few conciliatory moves. It offered more fuel and financial aid and eventually took Pyongyang off the list of state sponsors of terrorism.

After we finished lunch and the other diplomats left, Han stayed behind at the restaurant. A driver and a security guy waited for him in the parking lot. Han motioned to the seat opposite him, like Cubby's was his place and I was the guest. As soon as I sat, he glanced around and pulled out a thin manila envelope and put it on the table between us.

"Put this in a very safe place," he said.

I opened it and looked inside. All it contained was an unlabeled computer disk. "What's this?" I asked.

Han looked out the window. His colleagues stood under a pine tree near their minivan, smoking cigarettes. When he spoke again, his voice was urgent.

"I'm trusting you," he said. "Don't make me explain. Just put it away."

I was afraid of what he'd say next. I folded the manila envelope around the disk and held it under the table. "What's going on?" I asked.

"They've given the order," he said. "I'm going home."

I nodded. "When?"

"Soon."

"We'll get you back. Just like last time." We looked down at our laps. We both knew it wasn't going to happen that way. Han had already spent more time in the United States than any of the other guys from North Korea, and Pyongyang didn't like that. I turned the disk around in my hands. I had the irrational thought that if I threw it away, maybe Han wouldn't have to go.

"With luck, you never have to use it," he said.

What was so important that Han would give me on a disk, when nobody was watching? Computer codes? Bomb designs? Maybe a piece of information he wanted me to pass along to U.S. intelligence or the White House.

When I got home from Cubby's that night, I popped it into Andrea's computer. It contained a single folder with several images—I clicked through the photos one by one. The first two were close-ups of Han's daughters—the shy, oval-faced one and her younger sister, who had a rounder face with wide-set eyes and looked more like Han. The next image showed the girls with their mother, Han's wife. She wore a Kim II Sung pin on her beige dress and a frown that looked fake. The skin around her eyes was creased in a way that told you she smiled a lot. I wondered if Han had told her to look serious for the picture.

The last image showed the three of them with Han in what I guessed was the doorway of their apartment. He wore a blue button-down shirt tucked carelessly into black chinos and his hair uncombed, like he'd just gotten out of bed. I imagined the four of them coming down to the Jersey shore with me and Lilia and our girls, making a fire pit and roasting marshmallows like two normal families.

I figured the photos were copied using one of the computers I'd helped Han smuggle into the DPRK. He'd gone to a lot of effort to get them to me, so I would know what his wife and daughters looked like. If I ever found out that something had happened to my buddy, I would have a way to search for them. It was Han's way of making me the godfather of his children.

I wasn't ready to say good-bye when he came to Cubby's a week later for the last time. He got out of the white minivan dressed in a business suit, and he had an expression on his face like he was going to a funeral. His flight to Pyongyang left the next day. Three guys from the embassy came with him, and I wondered if they were there to make sure Han didn't have any last-minute thoughts about defecting.

I sat them at the usual table in the back. His escorts ordered steak, one medium rare and two medium well-done. Three baked potatoes.

"Anything special tonight, Mr. Ambassador?" I asked.

"Gimme the usual," he said. Rack of ribs. Rare. Baked potato.

I went to the kitchen to grill Han's meat myself. My cooks were busy with orders from regular customers, and I had the big charcoal broiler against the back wall to myself. I'd just gotten the steaks ready to put on the fire when Han showed up at my elbow.

"I don't do this as much as I used to," I said. "Just for special guests." I laid the two medium-well New York strips across the grill. The flames shot up momentarily. Han handed me the basting brush, which I dipped into a deep pan. I stroked orange barbecue sauce across his baby back ribs.

"When I first met you, I didn't believe this is what you did for a living," Han said. "I thought Cubby's was a front."

He'd never told me that, in all these years. Only somebody who'd never run a restaurant would imagine I spent all this time buying meat and vegetables, training and managing staff, dealing with tiny profit margins, to front a spying operation.

"When did you figure out that it wasn't?"

He laughed. "Maybe I'm still not sure!"

"That's because you have no appreciation for hard work," I said. "Wait till you're running a Cubby's franchise in Pyongyang. Then you'll see." I threw the other steak and Han's ribs onto the grill.

Han frowned. "This could be the last time we see each other."

My hand shook as I removed a pair of tongs from their peg. "Don't talk like that," I said. I flipped the first steaks. Fat dripped onto the embers and sizzled.

He was right. Our leaders weren't going to work out their differences overnight. Not much had changed in our thirteen years of friendship, and peace seemed as far away as ever.

I thought about the first time Han left. I didn't hear a word from him for nearly four years. That was our future. It wasn't like he was going someplace where he could pick up the phone. He couldn't write us an e-mail, or even a letter. As soon as Han left, he would disappear from my life.

We were going to miss out on the things other friends get to share. He wouldn't be able to tell me if he got a promotion at the Foreign Ministry or had a good day fishing. I wouldn't see his pictures when his daughters graduated from high school, and he wouldn't see pictures of mine getting married. I wouldn't know if he had a grandchild or if he was happy. We'd have to be content with our memories. His return to North Korea was like dying, I realized. At least for those of us on the outside. It was a reality neither of us wanted to face.

"We're going to buy you that four-bedroom house," I said after a few moments. "I know a great neighborhood in Fort Lee. Good schools for our girls. Not far from the city. But no crime. We'll live next door to each other."

I got a platter, which Han held while I stacked the meat on it. "We have to put a fence between," he said.

"Why? We'll share the lawn!"

"I don't want to wake up in the morning and see you next to the pool without a shirt on."

"You'll have your *own* pool. Think about that." I could see Han fantasizing about it for a second. Then he seemed to push the thought away.

He helped me bring the food out and serve the others, which was a first.

He ate his ribs slowly. Who knew if he'd ever have another plate of meat like this? He was quiet, and I could tell he didn't want to talk about going home, especially with the embassy goons around.

As we ate, my family and the staff came over to wish him farewell, one at a time. He thanked Mike O'D, Lilia, and my girls for being friends to him and the people of the DPRK. He told Lori and Andrea, "When your daddy wasn't around the house, it was because he was serving his country by making our differences smaller." My girls looked at me proudly. It's something they still remember him saying.

I walked Han out to the parking lot. The other Koreans stood by the minivan and watched us, while pretending not to. We stopped halfway across the blacktop.

"Anything happens to you, I'll be there for your wife and girls," I said.

He nodded. "I would take care of *your* kids. If something happened to you, I would find a way."

I took a step forward and tried to put my arms around him. He threw one of his arms around my waist but left the other one dangling. We stepped back and looked at each other. He pulled a pair of sunglasses out of his coat pocket and stole a glance at the other Koreans. "Don't get emotional," he said. "Because I can't."

"I'm not," I said. But it was a lie. I swallowed a couple of times to relieve the tightness in my throat.

"You're my brother," he said.

He put his sunglasses on and made a little wave of his hand. Then he turned and walked to the minivan. He climbed in without looking back at me and slid the door closed. I went out to the edge of the driveway and watched as they drove my best friend down River Street. They made a right toward the on-ramp for the Bergen-Passaic Expressway east, which would take him to Manhattan and his little apartment on Roosevelt Island, where he'd spend his last night in America.

I decided I wouldn't call Han that night, and I figured he wouldn't call me either. Neither of us wanted to say good-bye twice.

I walked back into Cubby's, where the first dinner customers were already lining up. Most of them were just getting off work—a group of regulars from the courthouse and a few construction guys.

"Hey, Bobby!" one of them yelled. "How you doin'?"

I still felt the lump in my throat, so I headed straight to the back of the kitchen where I could be alone. I didn't know what to do with myself, so I brought a tray of tomatoes out of the fridge. I put them on a cutting board and sliced them into salad wedges.

Han's parting gift to me was making me feel proud in front of my daughters. It was hard to measure the worth of what I had done, though. I hadn't accomplished any of the big things I'd set out to do. I hadn't liberated the USS *Pueblo* or helped Senator Greenleaf become governor of Pennsylvania. Han and I hadn't opened a chicken farm. We never caught Osama bin Laden in Pakistan with the help of Korean commandoes. If the United States had prisoners of war stranded in the DPRK, then they were still there, dead or alive. Han and I hadn't organized the sale of the nuclear program. We never made the breakthrough that led to a reconciliation between our countries.

But I had achieved some things. I'd helped get millions of dollars worth of humanitarian aid sent to North Korea. I could feel good about that. I encouraged the North Koreans to reach out to the media and communicate directly to the American public for the first time. Maybe I helped them become more tolerant. Or maybe their friendship with me shows that they were tolerant to begin with. I demonstrated to the FBI that sometimes spying can be done through the front door. It doesn't have to be so secretive, just like diplomacy doesn't have to be so formal. And I showed that an ordinary guy can carve out a place for himself on a major international issue, like war with another country. A lone citizen can be a peacemaker. Or at least he can try, which is a hell of a lot better than sitting on the sidelines and feeling helpless.

I *could* measure what had changed in me. I had journeyed a long way for a guy from North Jersey who flips burgers for a living. And I had learned some things. Han helped me realize that more than one person can live inside you. There's the person you are when you're born—the part of you that comes from your family and your neighborhood and how you grew up. And then there's the unknown. The potential. That unknown part of me was something I'd always wanted to explore, ever since I was a kid and dreamed of fighting in the Vietnam War. That desire led to my friendship with Han. I was Hackensack Bobby, and then I became Pyongyang Bobby, too. I got beyond what my limits were supposed to be.

Han always told me he knew exactly who he was, because he was Korean. One time he said he felt sorry for me, because as an American I was a "lone goose." But he'd lived in my country long enough that he must have some lone goose in him, too. A part of him was North Jersey Han now. A part of him was me. I wondered: how much of me would he carry around in Pyongyang? Would he hold onto that part, or would he try to forget me?

I wondered how long Pyongyang Bobby would survive without Han in my life. Now that he was gone, maybe I had to say good-bye to that part of myself. I didn't want to forget that person, though. I didn't want that part of me to end.

Through the kitchen door, I heard Lilia shout to one of the cooks that she needed extra sauce on a ribs order. I tossed the last tomato wedges into their tray and covered it with plastic wrap. I'd have plenty of time to think about Han's absence in the years to come. For now, I had dinnertime. One of my cooks was out sick with the flu, and my staff needed my help. We had steaks to grill and burgers to flip. I peeked into the restaurant and saw that we were already backed up, with a line of customers waiting at the register. I put the knife down, wiped my hands, and went out to take some orders.

Acknowledgments

⁓⁓⁓⁓⁓⁓⁓

THE AUTHORS WOULD LIKE TO gratefully acknowledge Kimberly J. Levin for her constant support and inspiration, which is evident on every page.

Thanks to St. Martin's editor Kathryn Huck for championing this book from the outset and for her savvy editing throughout; to St. Martin's Press President and Publisher Sally Richardson and Editor in Chief George Witte for believing this was an important story and making the book possible. We truly appreciate the great enthusiasm for this project that John Murphy and Joe Rinaldi have brought to publicity, Tara Cibelli to marketing, Alyse Diamond to editorial support, and Jeff Capshew and the rest of the sales team to getting this story out to the public.

For gracefully shepherding the book from the get-go and many timely insights, thanks to agents Jim Rutman at Sterling Lord Literistic, Alice Martell of The Martell Agency, and Jody Hotchkiss of Hotchkiss & Associates.

Jacklyn Ievoli enriched this book by researching pithy details from primary sources and combing through dozens of hours of tape and thousands of pages of text. Thanks to Charles De Montebello for audio transcription and Arik Roper, Tina Tryforos, and Hermes Marco for artwork and photos.

Thanks to Stewart Greenleaf, Dave Bratton, John Kallis, Mike O'Donovan, Mike Nigro, Steve Miller, Phil Shenon, Mark Sauter, Bill Henry, Joe Jordan, Robert Woodruff, Mark Winkler, and many others featured in this book for their contributions. Many thanks also to early readers of this book, including

Mike, Ron, and Joan Arias, Jenno Topping, Robert Edwards, Ferne Pearl-stein, Paula Pitzer, Pamela Levin, and Ida Rae "Bunny" Levin.

Robert Egan would like to personally thank Lilia and their beautiful daughters, Andrea and Lori, who have always been an inspiration and who sacrificed lots of family time with their daddy so he could pursue a relation-ship with the North Koreans. He deeply appreciates Jon Hanson's knowl-edge and support over the years. He would also like to thank Ambassador Han for his friendship during many years of ups and downs, as well as the Great Leader Kim Il Sung and his son, the Dear Leader Kim Jong Il, for sending Han to the United States for two tours of duty. He would also like to thank Gladys Grullon for supporting him throughout the writing of the book. He would also like to thank the journalists with whom he has worked over the years, especially Michael Bronner, who took an early interest in our story.

Many thanks to Walter and Tina Egan for being gracious hosts to so many commies over the years. Thanks to John McCreary for his intellectual help and guidance. And thanks to the FBI and the National Security Council for absolutely nothing.

For all the prisoners of war who never made it back to the United States, thank you for hanging in there. Sorry we haven't finished the job and brought you home.

Index

~~~~~~~~~~~~~~~~